CW01672836

THE COMPLETE
ILLUSTRATED GUIDE TO

AROMATHERAPY

Rosi

Rose.

io. nature. f. in. i. s. in. 3. melior ex eis. de iunat persia recentes. iuvamentum cerebro calido. nocumentum. efficit quibusdam ineschrie. remotio nocumenti. cum camphora.

THE COMPLETE
ILLUSTRATED GUIDE TO

AROMATHERAPY

A Practical Approach
to the Use of Essential Oils
for Health and Well-being

JULIA LAWLESS

ELEMENT

Shaftesbury, Dorset • Boston, Massachusetts • Melbourne, Victoria

First published in Great Britain 1997 by
ELEMENT BOOKS LIMITED

This edition published in Great Britain
in 1999 by ELEMENT BOOKS LIMITED
Shaftesbury, Dorset, SP7 8BP

Published in the USA in 1997 by
ELEMENT BOOKS INC.
160 North Washington Street,
Boston, MA 02114

Published in Australia in 1997 by
ELEMENT BOOKS LIMITED
and distributed by Penguin Australia Ltd
487 Maroondah Highway, Ringwood, Victoria 3134

NOTE FROM THE PUBLISHER
Any information given in this book is not intended to be taken as a replacement for medical advice. Any person with a condition requiring medical attention should consult a qualified practitioner or therapist.

Designed and created with The Bridgewater Book Company

ELEMENT BOOKS LIMITED
Editorial Director: Julia McCutchen
Managing Editor: Caro Ness
Production Director: Roger Lane
Production: Claire Cutler

THE BRIDGEWATER BOOK COMPANY
Art Director: Kevin Knight
Page layout/make-up: Wendy Thompson
Managing Editor: Anne Townley
Editor: Margaret Crowther
Picture Research: Vanessa Fletcher
Three-dimensional models: Mark Jamieson
Studio photography: Guy Ryecart, Ian Parsons
Illustrators: Ivan Hissey, Mainline Design, Michael Courtney
Printed and bound in Singapore

British Library Cataloguing in Publication
data available.

Book ISBN 1-86204-642-5
Kit ISBN 1-86204-641-7

Acknowledgments

The publishers wish to thank the
following for use of pictures:
A–Z Botanical: pp. 184B, 192B (Sylvia O'Toole), 196T
(W. Broadhurst), 204B
ARDEA: p. 197B (Donald Burgess)
The Bridgeman Art Library: pp. 2 (Bibliothèque Nationale), 14, 30B
(Royal Albert Memorial Hospital, Exeter)
e.t.archive: pp. 43TR, 44T
Fine Art Photographic Library: pp. 9, 15
Holt Studios: p. 186
The Hutchison Library: p. 16B (Felix Greene)
The Image Bank: pp. 20B (L. D. Gordon), 98, 101T
(Paul McCormick), 108T (David de Lossy), 110B, 124B
(Tim P. Kelly), 149 (John Love), 167 (B. Lambert), 170 (Tim Beider)
NHPA: p. 197T (Ted Hutchison)
Oxford Scientific Films: pp. 181B (Deni Bown), 202T (Deni Bown)
The Science Photo Library: pp. 29TR (M. Wurtz/Biozentrum), 89T
(CNRI), 89M (Dr. K. Louantman), 104, 111T (K. H. Kjeldsen), 121
(D. J. F. Burgess), 143M (D. Phillips), 157 (LDC)
Zefa: pp. 19, 20T, 27BL, 29L, 30, 100B, 146B, 152, 171

Special thanks to
Philip Auchnivole, Adam Carne, Rebecca Drury,
Rachel Gould, Wendy Grantley-Oxberry, Julia Holden,
Simon Holden, Carolyn Jikiemi-Roberts, Kay Macmullan,
Chloe McCausland, Jack Martin, Debbie and Max Oliver,
Sunny Pitcher, Bethany Sword
for help with photography

Special thanks to
Peter Coleman (ceramics); Courts plc, Shoreham; The Plinth
Company, Stowmarket, Suffolk; The Wilbury School, Centre
for Natural Therapies, Hove
for help with properties

Author's Acknowledgments

I would like to thank all the following people who have contributed to the completion of this book, especially for their patience and collaboration during the final stages of the project: Caro Ness, Katie Worrall and Allie West at Element Books; Peter Bridgewater, Margaret Crowther, Kevin Knight, Anne Townley and all those at the Bridgewater Book Company; Guy Ryecart and Ian Parsons, the photographers, and the studio models; Rosalind Hadley, beauty therapist at the Retreat; Eileen Lawless for advice on nutrition; and Ann Cooper and all at Aqua Oleum for compiling chemical profiles of all the essential oils.

I would also like to thank all my friends and family who have supported and encouraged me over the last year, especially my husband Alec and daughter Natasha, for their ongoing help and support – without them I would never have completed the task!

PAGE TWO: This early fifteenth-century manuscript shows the cultivation of the rose, already long-established at that time.

Contents

Preface

The last two decades of the 20th century have witnessed a remarkable renaissance of interest in, and practice of, natural healing methods. In recent years, such forms of treatment as medical herbalism, osteopathy, shiatsu, reflexology, acupuncture, and aromatherapy have all attained varying degrees of credibility in the eyes of health professionals, as well as among the general public. Of these, aromatherapy is among the most popular alternative or complementary forms of treatment available in the UK and other Western countries. Yet only half a century ago the therapeutic use of herbs and essential oils was frowned upon or even officially banned. Plant medicines were seen as something archaic and outmoded in comparison to the new pharmaceutical drugs, and in 1941, the British Pharmacy and Medicines Act made the practice of herbal medicine illegal. Fifty years later, the scientific world is reappraising the value of natural remedies: as the limited effectiveness, and unwanted side effects, of aggressively synthesized medications are being recognized, aromatic essences are coming back into their own once again.

ABOVE
The art of herbal distillation has been perfected over the centuries.

But is the current fascination for aromatherapy just another fashion or fad, or is it part of a larger sociological and cultural movement? Firstly, many of the so-called "alternative" therapies, including aromatherapy, are not new or modern techniques. They are based on ancient medical systems that have been built up over thousands of years from accumulated empirical evidence. Medical herbalism, and the use of aromatic remedies in particular, are very much older forms of treatment than Western allopathic, or orthodox, medicine. Unlike many modern drugs, plant remedies have been tried and tested over generations, and any side effects or environmental consequences carefully noted. Herbal medicine and aromatherapy consequently represent a return to nature, being based on principles requiring ecological awareness. This corresponds with many people's interest in "green" issues, and a widespread concern regarding the unknown effects of certain chemicals on the whole ecosystem and the long-term consequences of our exploitation of natural resources.

LEFT
Melissa (lemon balm) is a plant much used by herbalists that also yields a valuable essential oil.

Secondly, alternative forms of therapy embrace a holistic approach to health. They focus on the well-being of the individual as a whole, including that person's emotional or mental disposition. They are thus able to fulfill society's need for some kind of psychological support during an era of instability. An aromatherapy massage, for example, can provide a valuable antidote to the fast pace of 20th-century life and help relieve many of the stress-related problems that are so widespread today.

Thirdly, with regard to aromatherapy massage at least, it is a very comforting yet multi-faceted form of treatment. During a treatment, the pleasingly scented aromatic oils produce both psychological and physiological effects as they are rubbed into the skin and absorbed into the bloodstream. In addition, the essential oils themselves are highly concentrated and easy to use, and require little or no preparation. This means that they can readily be employed by all kinds of people in a variety of ways to enhance their health and the overall quality of their lifestyle, rather than being limited to the hands of health professionals.

This book has been written partly as a companion volume to my previous book, *The Illustrated Encyclopedia of Essential Oils*. Whereas my earlier book focused on the essential oils themselves, including their extraction, chemistry, botanical features, and history, this book concerns itself solely with their therapeutic and cosmetic applications and concentrates on the diversity within the aromatherapy tradition as it is practiced today. It is above all a practical handbook, both for the practicing therapist and for more general use.

Special emphasis is placed in the book on what I call "simple" aromatherapy – a basic, practical approach to self-treatment. It has always struck me as being a great pity that the whole realm of self-help using folk-medicine, which was once a natural part of family life, has been largely lost in Western culture. It is in this middle ground that aromatic remedies have such a lot to offer – playing their part in the home treatment of common everyday conditions such as period pains, headaches, eczema, and other skin complaints. Accepting responsibility for one's own health and condition is also an affirmative statement. It encourages individual responsibility and opens a door to self-knowledge as well as a window into the natural world, for all essential oils are derived directly from plants. In fact the whole field of fragrant plants and natural medicine is a vast area. I have also found that, like gardening, aromatherapy has an addictive quality – once hooked you will find it is hard to let go, for there is always more to learn and discover.

ABOVE
Perhaps the most feminine of all scents, roses have been used to make perfume and healing remedies since ancient times. The ancient Romans used the wild rose as a remedy for the bites of rabid dogs. Roses are still highly valued today and rose essential oil is very expensive.

RIGHT
Massage is one of the main ways in which essential oils are used today. Self-massage is particularly effective on the soles of the feet.

How to use this book

This book is for everyone interested in the art and science of aromatherapy, from the professional practitioner to any newcomers to the subject. The book is divided into four main parts, covering every aspect of aromatherapy as practiced today.

Aspects of Aromatherapy provides a thorough introduction to the many uses of essential oils and describes simple home aromatherapy and perfumery. *Aromatherapy Massage* explains the massage techniques, while *Medical Aromatherapy* focuses on the medical uses of essential oils. The *Index of Essential Oils* is a comprehensive guide to all the aromatherapy oils referred to in the book, with clear, at-a-glance information about the uses and qualities of each oil.

In the appendix, notes on safety data show how to use the oils safely, and the chemical analysis is given for each oil. A nutrition sheet provides a quick source of dietary advice, a glossary explains all the medical and scientific terms used in the book, and there is a list of useful addresses telling the reader where to find the oils and further information about aromatherapy. Finally, there is an extensive list of books for further reference.

The second part of the book describes the approaches to, and techniques of, aromatherapy massage, and gives detailed, step-by-step descriptions with clear illustrations on how to give a full-body massage, therapeutic massage for local areas, and massage for special circumstances, such as sports massage.

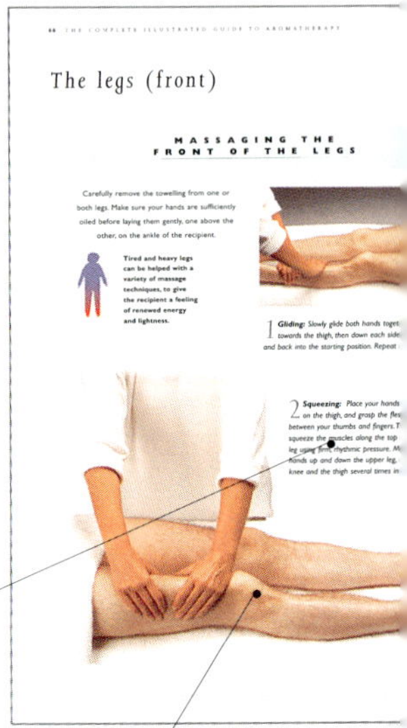

Each stage in the sequence is described with full and detailed instructions

The techniques of aromatherapy are demonstrated using step-by-step photography

Plants and plant materials from which essential oils are derived are shown in full

Clear text details the traditions behind the methods used, and their development

Historical illustrations help explain the background to age-old practices

The first part of the book introduces aromatherapy to the reader. It outlines the various aspects of aromatherapy, and focuses in detail on simple household uses of essential oils, skin and body treatments, and perfumery. Containing simple recipes and step-by-step instructions, Part 1 is designed to help the reader practice aromatherapy at home.

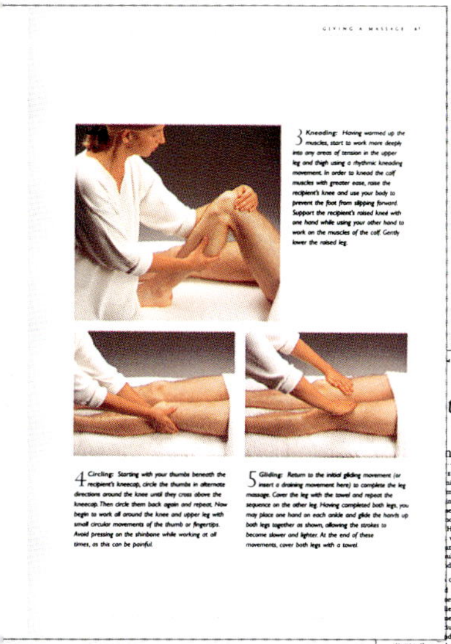

Every section outlines the symptoms of each specific ailment and the dietary factors affecting the condition

The third part of the book describes the ways in which aromatherapy is used in the field of medicine. The science of essential oils and the ways in which the oils are tested in the laboratory are explained, and the links between the chemical constituents of the various oils and their effects on the body are shown. It also shows how essential oils can be used safely and efficiently for medical treatment in the home. Remedies are divided into the different body systems, with clear instructions on the use of oils in treatment.

The aromatherapy oils that can be used for treatment are listed

Clinical notes detail the results of scientific research

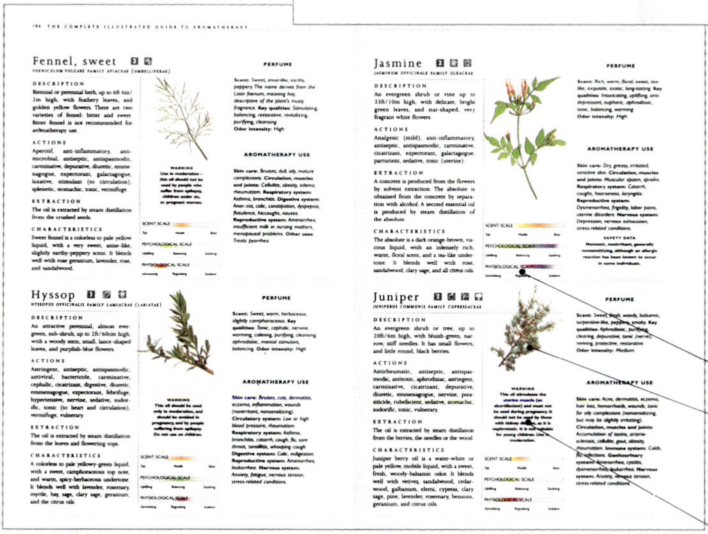

The fourth part of the book is an index of essential oils, listed in botanical name order. Each oil is described in detail, including its characteristics, actions, method of extraction, use in aromatherapy, scent qualities, and physiological, and psychological effects.

Scale bars are used to show the scent quality and the psychological and physiological properties of each oil

Each plant is fully illustrated

Safety data and warning boxes prevent misuse and indicate any possible dangers

PART ONE

Aspects of Aromatherapy

Interest in aromatherapy is growing year by year. As more and more brands of essential oils and aromatherapy products are to be found in the shops there is a steady increase in the home use of aromatic essential oils. Professional aromatherapy treatment is now available in beauty salons, fitness clubs, and hairdressers, while essential oils are used therapeutically in modern hospitals as well as complementary health centers.

Aromatherapy involves using pure essential oils, derived from plants, in a huge range of health and beauty treatments, as well as for pleasure. In offering us a "natural" way of caring for our health, it is just one aspect of the growth of interest in all forms of alternative or complementary medicine and traditional home remedies. Modern (or allopathic) medicine is spectacularly successful in many ways, but increasing numbers of people feel that they would like to know about ways of preventing illness in the first place, and to be able to use simple, safe, and drug-free home remedies for ordinary, everyday ailments. There is also a growing feeling that in modern medicine we are treated as a collection of parts, some of which may have problems, rather than as a whole organism, and least of all as a person. In contrast, complementary medicine, of which aromatherapy forms a part, offers a way of being treated holistically – as a whole being in whom there are many aspects of a disease or illness and for whom individually tailored treatment is required.

In our search for ways of keeping fit and healthy without needing to use synthetic drugs, aromatherapy oils offer the advantage of their complete naturalness and their general safety and simplicity of use. They offer ways of preventing illness and treating ourselves at home, and in the hands of professional practitioners they can be used as part of a multi-faceted holistic treatment.

In fact, of course, things are never quite as simple as they seem. Aromatherapy is complex in many ways. Firstly, it means different things to different people, and secondly the oils used, although simple in that each is the pure, natural product of a single plant, are complex and potent substances that need to be used with care, knowledge and experience.

The oils can be used simply for their fragrance and its effects on mood and emotion, but in professional practice their physiological effect is central. This is generally obtained through the oils being used in massage treatment, but some practitioners (with full medical qualifications) also use essential oils clinically in the tradition of the French pioneer, René-Maurice Gattefossé, in minutely prescribed oral doses and through inhalation.

> **"Volatile essences have healed people since the dawn of time ..."**
>
> RENÉ-MAURICE GATTEFOSSÉ

The word 'aromatherapy' literally means therapy through aroma or scent, without specifying the source of the scent. But aromatherapy in practice uses only essential oils, and no other form of scent. Its richness is that it has so many aspects, which are complementary to each other, and which may also overlap, but which are nevertheless distinct. In professional medical practice, it is the substances or oils themselves and their bio-chemical effects that are central, while in many home uses of essential oils it is the aroma that counts and the pleasure of the scent is the main reason for using the oils. Between these two extremes are cosmetic aromatherapy and massage, where the scent and the beneficial physiological effect of essential oils go hand in hand, and simple medical aromatherapy, which uses the oils' many curative effects. Aromatherapy must be unique in having so many facets, and in offering such a wealth of pleasurable, practical and therapeutic uses.

ABOVE AND LEFT
Aromatherapy offers a range of possibilities from the simple to the sensuous.

Approaches to aromatherapy

The therapeutic use of essential oils covers a very wide spectrum. This is part of their charm and uniqueness. At their simplest, oils can be worn as natural perfumes, made into aromatic bath preparations or used in many ways as home remedies. They can also be combined with both home and professional massage to provide a very effective treatment for stress-relief. At the other end of the scale, specific botanical essences can be used by clinically trained therapists or doctors for the treatment of serious medical conditions.

ABOVE
Potpourri has long been a popular way to preserve aromatic plants and scent a room. Rose petals are a traditional ingredient.

RIGHT
Many of the spicy and more exotic essential oils come from the East.

The ways in which aromatherapy can be practiced can be separated into five areas of specialization. Although it is impossible to draw hard and fast lines between these various aspects, classifications of this kind are helpful, at least in the short term, for the process of clarification and understanding. These different areas are: simple aromatherapy for home use, cosmetic aromatherapy, perfumery and the psychotherapeutic use of oils for the effects of their odors on the mind, massage using essential oils, and medical and clinical aromatherapy, where essential oils are used to treat medical complaints.

SIMPLE AROMATHERAPY

A basic approach uses aromatic oils in a wide range of methods, including vaporization, aromatic bathing, local massage, cosmetic creams, and steam inhalation, for first-aid purposes and in the treatment of common complaints. This approach is in the ancient tradition of herbal "simples" – home remedies or household secrets, originally passed on from generation to generation. It can be adapted by nurses and other professionals and used as an adjunct to medical treatment. As a type of preventive medicine, it can help to ward off infectious illness and promote general health and well-being.

ROSE PETALS

COSMETIC AROMATHERAPY

The use of essential oils for skin and beauty care is an ancient and specialized aspect of aromatherapy. There are records that show that many primitive cultures used natural aromatics as a means of adornment and as a way of enhancing their beauty. Indeed, many indigenous peoples still do so today. However, the earliest and richest associations concerning the cosmetic use of aromatic materials are to be found in the practices of the Ancient Egyptian civilization, some 5000 years ago. Aromatic herbs, gums and oils were incorporated into carefully formulated cosmetic ointments and other beauty preparations, as well as being employed in the embalming process. Seen in his light, the Ancient Egyptians were the original precursors of modern beauty therapists, especially those who use aromatic oils as part of their cosmetic treatments.

ABOVE
"The Roses of Heliogabalus" by Sir Lawrence Alma-Tadema, 1836–1912.

PSYCHO-AROMATHERAPY AND PERFUMERY

The term psycho-aromatherapy is used to describe the use of the pyschotherapeutic benefits of essential oils, effected mainly by inhalation but also by other methods of application. In the practice of psycho-aromatherapy the ways in which botanically derived aromas can influence moods and emotions and help to induce certain states of mind are studied. This can be by bringing about a state of relaxation or through their energizing and stimulating effects. This contrasts with aromachology, in which both natural and artificial scents are studied for their therapeutic value, but principally for purely commercial purposes in the perfume industry. Nevertheless, psycho-aromatherapy does have a great deal in common with the art of perfumery, especially since all perfumes were originally made using natural aromatics, and since they both focus on the psychological effects of scent and require a high degree of olfactory discrimination and knowledge.

AROMATHERAPY MASSAGE

There are many benefits to be derived from combining massage with the use of essential oils. It is the main method adopted by professional aromatherapists working in the field of alternative health care. Aromatherapy massage has been largely influenced by the French pioneer, Marguerite Maury, whose research work was directly aimed at utilizing the healing and revitalizing properties of aromatics, especially through application to the skin. This approach is notably beneficial for the treatment of stress-related disorders and requires a substantial degree of training, both in acquiring massage techniques and in understanding the many and varied properties of the essential oils that may be used.

MEDICAL AROMATHERAPY

Medical aromatherapy includes the systematic use of essential oils in the treatment of clinically diagnosed medical conditions. It adopts a wide range of methods, including oral prescription. It should only be practiced by suitably trained medical doctors or by clinical therapists, who, like qualified medical herbalists, have undergone a training period of at least four years. This is the approach of the 20th-century founder of aromatherapy, René-Maurice Gattefossé, and his scientific and medical successors.

RIGHT
Jasmine is one of the many aromatic plants that have medical properties.

Simple aromatherapy

The practice of aromatherapy benefits from being placed within the context of holistic health care as a whole. Whereas the emphasis in modern allopathic or orthodox medicine is to target a given complaint with a specific remedy, from a holistic point of view, the best form of treatment is always a multifaceted one. The air we breathe, our nutrition, exercise, relaxation, and, above all, our emotional or mental disposition, are all essential factors which need to be taken into account.

> "Consciously or unconsciously, every being is capable of healing himself or others ..."
>
> INAYAT KHAN

Holistic health care is more concerned with cultivating an understanding of healthy living and of preventive techniques than with providing symptomatic relief. In any case of "dis-ease," it is vital to assess the overall health of the person, both physically and mentally, and then to try and ease the problem at its source, while at the same time building up the body's natural immunity. It is preferable to prevent the problem from occurring in the first place.

Preventive medicine is not given enough value or emphasis in Western society today. It is all too easy to let health slide, then reach for a bottle of pills when something goes wrong. Yet most people are prepared to service their car regularly, rather than wait for the inevitable breakdown to occur. Why do we not seem to take the same precautions to nuture both our bodies and minds as in the East? There, many patients traditionally receive acupuncture treatment at each change of season to ensure that the body and mind remain in optimum health for the following quarter. It is also still traditional for Chinese people of all ages to gather outside in the mornings to practice tai chi, an ancient martial art form which combines gentle exercise with moving meditation to promote good health and longevity.

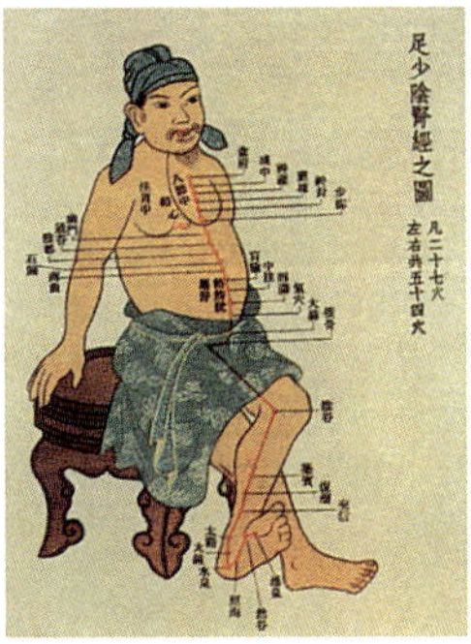

ABOVE
In Chinese medicine acupuncture has always been a form of preventive medicine.

ABOVE
Tai chi exercises provide a way of keeping fit both mentally and physically.

From the perspective of holistic health care, a wholesome diet, fresh air and sufficient exercise, together with a sense of emotional security, intellectual satisfaction, and some form of daily spiritual or psychological nourishment are all factors that can help to preserve a sense of well-being. Herbal tonics and natural aromatics have also held a traditional place in the preventive medicinal practices of many cultures, both ancient and modern. It is certainly true that people who are exposed to the beneficial effects of essential oils on a daily basis tend to have a greater resistance to disease in general.

"People who use essential oils all the time, as part of their daily bathing, skincare and household routines ... have a high level of resistance to illness, 'catching' fewer colds ... than average and recovering quickly if they do."[1]

Essential oils exert a psychological lift (called their "cephalic effects") and help to promote a positive mental state, while, on a more physiological level, they stimulate the immune system and exhibit all types of preventive and curative properties. In the words of the French medical aromatherapist, Dr. Daniel Penoël:

"Aromatic medicine is a preventive healing focusing on the evolutionary side of all living beings in the Biosphere, be it in the animal or the vegetable kingdom."[2]

The pressures of Western society place many stresses and strains upon the individual. If these are not recognized, they can lead to more serious health problems. Aromatherapy, with its holistic approach to health and well-being, can be used to intervene and prevent long-term problems occurring.

A holistic approach

Apart from aromatherapy and medical herbalism, there are many other types of alternative treatment that can be used in holistic medicine to complement and enhance one another. A condition such as osteoarthritis, for example, benefits from a multifaceted approach that would include specific herbal remedies, dietary changes, gentle exercise, aromatic baths, and massage treatments, as well as osteopathy, and possibly even pyschotherapeutic advice. On the other hand, it is possible to treat a condition such as a boil or bruise more simply at home with a combination of dietary nutrients and local aromatic applications. This book refers to the related treatments wherever possible.

In the section on aromatic remedies (pp. 96–175), each complaint is defined and a number of different methods of treating the problem are suggested, both with the use of essential oils in a variety of ways and with supportive techniques. "We are what we eat" is perhaps overused as a slogan, yet its truth remains. In holistic health care, and in the field of preventive medicine in particular, diet, together with a positive mental attitude is very influential in maintaining well-being. Details of the specific vitamins that are required by the body, and their dietary sources, are given at the end of the book in the Appendix, Vitamins and dietary sources (p. 215).

Other types of treatment that are raised and given emphasis in the discussion of treatment in this book are the use of Bach flower remedies, allergy testing, osteopathy, psychotherapy, counseling, yoga and relaxation, and meditation and prayer. Despite this emphasis upon alternative medicine as prevention and treatment, orthodox and alternative approaches should not be seen as necessarily working in opposition. Each has its own value: what is required today is an integration of modern scientific techniques and traditional knowledge. In India and China, for example, traditional forms of medicine are being used alongside the newly adopted surgical skills and other modern innovations, while in the West there has been a surge of interest in the medicinal potential of aromatic materials and herbal medicine.

ABOVE
Borage is used to make a base oil and is very beneficial to the skin.

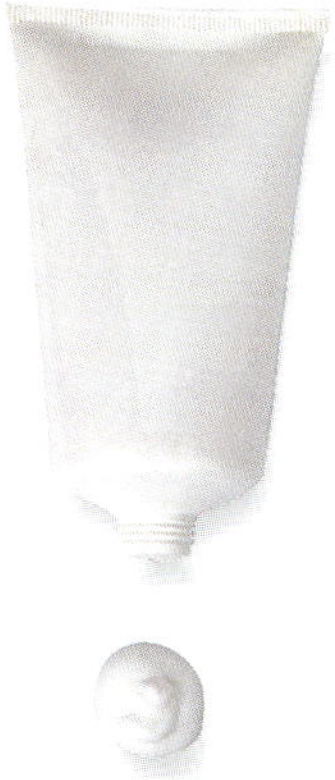

ABOVE
Herbal ointments are prescribed by medical herbalists as part of the treatment for a range of conditions.

ORANGE

APPLE

ABOVE
A wholesome and balanced diet, with plenty of fresh fruit, plays an important part in maintaining health.

RIGHT
Yoga quickly makes the body more supple and helps to maintain mind–body awareness.

BODY AND MIND

Aromatherapy treats mind and body together. The scent of the essential oils used can have a powerful effect on the emotions while the oils' chemistry affects the body.

The aromatic medicine chest

Like traditional herbal remedies, essential oils are very valuable self-help tools because they are effective in the prevention and treatment of many common conditions, yet are simple and easy to use. It is wise to build up a collection of the most useful essential oils, together with a small selection of vegetable base or carrier oils and creams for use in the home medicine chest. The most important of these are arnica ointment, calendula cream or oil, grapeseed oil, sweet almond oil, jojoba oil, and wheat germ oil (*see pp. 84–5 for a full list of base oils*).

Many essential oils, apart from being used for first aid or for the treatment of common complaints, are also ideal as bath oils, perfumes, or room fresheners. Even when they are used purely for esthetic purposes, they are still fulfilling a positive preventive and therapeutic role. A small, essential aromatic oil kit can prove to be an extremely valuable asset at home, in the workplace, or while on vacation, and when traveling. There is a group of five invaluable oils to keep in the home medicine cabinet, or to take with you when traveling: *lavender, tea tree, rosemary, Roman chamomile,* and *peppermint*.

There is a second group of 30 other oils that can also prove very useful, although they are not always the most popular or pleasantly scented (*see below*). In the section on specific remedies (p. 96), several essential oils are usually mentioned for each illness, including some from an additional group of 30 (*see below*). It is not, however, necessary to buy all the oils listed, as it is possible to treat many common illnesses by using up to five oils, especially when the oils are mixed or blended together in various combinations. The recommended blends which are highlighted in the section on the treatment of specific problems are always made up from a selection of the essential oils listed below.

ABOVE
A simple home medicine cabinet is ideal for storing essential oils.

ESSENTIAL OILS FOR THE MEDICINE CHEST

GROUP 1

Lavender is extremely versatile, especially for stress-related disorders and for skin complaints.

Tea tree is invaluable for its antiviral, antiseptic, fungicidal and immune-stimulant properties.

Rosemary has stimulant properties, and is an expectorant as well as being a tonic to the entire system.

Roman Chamomile is a mild relaxant and anti-inflammatory agent, especially as a children's remedy.

Peppermint is good for digestive complaints such as nausea or indigestion, and for respiratory problems, and for treating fever.

GROUP 2

Atlas cedarwood · Bergamot · Black Pepper · Carrot seed · Clary Sage · Clove bud · Cypress · Eucalyptus blue gum · Frankincense · German (blue) chamomile · Ginger · Grapefruit · Jasmine · Juniper · Lemon Eucalyptus · Myrrh · Myrtle · Neroli · Patchouli · Rose geranium (geranium) · Rose (Rose maroc) · Sandalwood · Scotch pine needle · Spanish sage · Sweet basil (basil) · Sweet fennel (fennel) · Sweet marjoram (marjoram) · White thyme (thyme) · Valerian · Ylang Ylang

GROUP 3

Angelica · Aniseed · Benzoin · Cajeput · Camphor · Cardamom · Celery seed · Cinnamon leaf · Citronella · Coriander · Dill · Elemi · Galbanum · Hyssop · Lemon · Lemongrass · Lime · Mandarin · Melissa · Nutmeg · Palmarosa · Parsley seed · Petitgrain · Rosewood · Sweet orange · Tagetes · Virginian cedarwood · Vetivert · West Indian bay · Yarrow

Aromatic bathing

One of the simplest and most pleasant ways to use essential oils is in the bathtub, where the oils enhance the relaxing effect of a warm slow bath, or the stimulating effect of a brisk hot bath or cold dip. The therapeutic effects of bathing have been recognized for centuries. The sophistication of many of the Ancient Roman spa bath houses can still be seen, with their hot and cold compartments, steam rooms, and aromatic massage quarters. Very hot baths stimulate perspiration, which is valuable in cases of infectious illness and for encouraging elimination of wastes and detoxification. However, they can also be draining and, in the long run, can cause the skin to lose its elasticity. A medium-hot or warm bath has a soothing and relaxing effect on both the mind and body, while cool or cold water has a more invigorating and stimulating effect. Lukewarm baths are good for lowering the temperature in cases of fever.

ABOVE
A scented bag will release its fragrance under running water.

MARJORAM

PURE ESSENCES

This is the easiest and most popular way of using essential oils for bathing. Simply add from 5 to 10 drops of your chosen essential oil (or a blend of oils) to the bathtub when it is full, and relax in the aromatic vapors. Use lavender oil for promoting relaxation, rosemary as an invigorating tonic, or marjoram for soothing tired muscles.

LEFT
Soaking in a bathtub of Epsom salt is a traditional remedy for stiffness.

WARNING

Always check with specific safety data before using a new oil in the bathtub, to avoid possible irritation. Details are given for each oil in the information on *pp. 176–210.* Increase the dilution during pregnancy and for babies or infants to at least half the recommended amount. For babies, avoid the possibly toxic or irritant oils altogether.

ROSEMARY

ABOVE AND CENTER
Rosemary invigorates and marjoram relieves aching muscles.

BATH BAGS

Gather a selection of fresh herbs or aromatic flowers together, such as lavender sprigs, rose petals, lemon balm leaves, and chamomile flowers, and tie them loosely in a muslin bag with a piece of string or ribbon. Choose specific herbs both for their therapeutic properties and for their scent. If you wish, add a few drops of a chosen essential oil to the bundle to enhance the fragrance. Then tie the bag to the faucets and let it hang in the stream of hot water while the bathtub is filling.

BATH SALTS

Epsom salt (magnesium sulphate) or Dead Sea salts are healing substances in themselves, and make an excellent medium for combining with essential oils. Salt contains precious minerals, has an alkalizing effect on the body, promotes the elimination of acidic wastes from the muscles and joints, and induces copious perspiration – good for infectious illness, rheumatism, arthritis, and for promoting relaxation. Dissolve one or two handfuls of Epsom salt in boiling water, add a few drops of essential oil, and pour into the bathtub. Alternatively, simply add 5 drops of essential oil to every handful of Epsom salt or Dead Sea salts, pour directly into the bathtub and agitate the water before getting in.

BELOW
Relaxing in a scented bathtub is one of life's pleasures.

MOISTURIZING BATH OILS

A few drops of an essential oil can also be mixed in a teaspoonful of vegetable oil, such as sweet almond oil, before being added to the bathtub. This helps to moisturize the skin and ensures an even distribution of the essential oil, which is especially important in the case of babies and young children.

To make a larger quantity, mix 200 drops of an essential oil (or blend) with 3½fl oz/100ml jojoba oil or another base or carrier oil (*see* pp.84–5) containing five percent wheat germ oil and store in a tinted glass bottle. Add a teaspoonful of this mixture to the bath water when required.

LEFT
Two or three drops of soothing oil can be used in a baby's bedtime bath and this may lead to a more restful night for everyone.

FOOT AND HAND BATHS

Valuable for warding off chills, for easing arthritic or rheumatic pain, and for the treatment of specific foot complaints, a hot aromatic foot bath can also be very effective for relieving stress and over-exhaustion (use lavender and sweet marjoram) and is a quick aid to combating excessive perspiration (use tea tree and rosemary). Simply sprinkle 5 or 6 drops of essential oil into a bowl or basin of warm or hot water and soak feet or hands for about ten minutes. Alternatively, dilute the essential oils in a teaspoonful of cider vinegar, honey, or a moisturizing vegetable oil beforehand.

LEFT
Valerian produces an oil used to relieve nervous tension and insomnia.

THERAPEUTIC HIP BATH OR DOUCHE

This method can be helpful in the treatment of urinary or genital conditions, such as pruritus (itching), thrush, or cystitis. The area can be bathed in a hip or sitz bath or a bowl of warm water to which 3 to 5 drops of a suitable essential oil have been added – a mixture of cypress and lavender, for example, can help to heal the perineum after childbirth. Alternatively, an enema pot or plastic douche can be bought from some pharmacies. Mix 3 to 5 drops of a suitable essential oil with warm water before inserting – bergamot and tea tree mixture is effective for the treatment of thrush.

THE SAUNA

In Scandinavia, the sauna is the traditional method of cleansing and toning the whole system. Dry heat and steam are used to open the pores and promote the elimination of waste products. This is followed by a plunge into very cold water that closes the pores, and tones and refreshes the skin. In Finland, where the tradition of the sauna originates, bundles of fresh birch twigs are slapped on the skin, stimulating the circulation and imparting a delicious fragrance. Essential oils that are most suitable for use in the traditional sauna include fresh-scented oils such as pine, juniper, myrtle, eucalyptus, and cedarwood. (Very rich or floral oils such as lavender, ylang ylang, or patchouli are too heady and should not be used.) Add 2 or 3 drops to 17fl oz/500ml of warm water and throw on the heat source for an aromatic and refreshing steam bath.

ABOVE
The traditional Scandinavian sauna is followed by a stimulating swish of birch twigs over the skin. Pine and other fresh-smelling oils are best for sauna use.

Therapeutic massage and body oils

L DROPPER

Therapeutic aromatic massage is the main method used by professional aromatherapists, but it can also be practiced at home – either on oneself, or on a friend or partner. Body oils are best applied after a warm bath, when the pores of the skin are still open to encourage rapid absorption.

For the purpose of massage or general application to the skin, a few drops of essential oil are always mixed with a larger measure of base or carrier oil, usually a light vegetable oil such as sweet almond oil or grapeseed oil. When preparing a body oil or massage oil, the dilution should be in the region of 5 to 30 drops of essential oil in a bottle of 2fl oz/50ml of base oil, depending upon the type of essential oil used and its specific purpose. For general massage purposes, a dilution of 2.5 percent (see below) is suitable for adult use. To calculate how much essential oil to add to a base oil, assess the amount of base oil in fluid ounces/milliliters and add half the number of drops of essential oil.

Complaints of a physical nature, such as aching muscles or rheumatism, require a stronger concentration (around 3 percent) than disorders related to the emotions, such as depression, insomnia, and stress (1.5–2 percent). Body oils for those with sensitive skin, and facial lotions should be even more dilute (0.5–1 percent). Babies, children and pregnant women also require *very diluted* blends (0.5 percent) – *see also Safety Data, p. 211.* To calculate how many drops of essential oil to add to the base oil in each of these cases, see the charts below.

A body or massage oil blended in this way will keep for a few weeks if stored in a well-stoppered container in a cool, dark place. If you blend from 5 to 15 percent wheat germ oil into the main carrier oil used, the mixture can be kept for up to three months. Alternatively, use jojoba oil as the base or carrier oil, as this is in fact a liquid wax that does not go rancid. For more information on the properties of various base or carrier oils, *see pp.* 84–5.

STANDARD DILUTION (2.5%)

Base oil amount	*Essential oil in drops*
1 tsp/5ml	2–3
1 tbs/15ml	6–7
1fl oz/25ml	12–13
2fl oz/50ml	25
3.5fl oz/100ml	50

SPECIAL DILUTIONS

For 2fl oz/50ml of base oil:

Blend percentage	*Essential oil in drops*
0.5%	5
1%	10
1.5%	15
2%	20
2.5%	25
3%	30

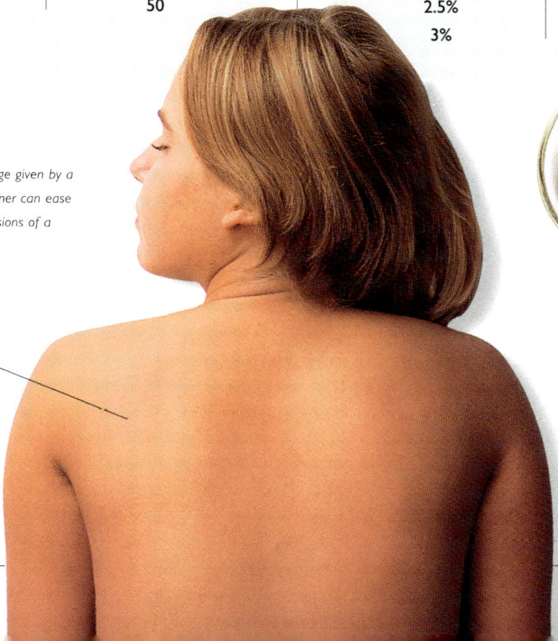

RIGHT
Home massage given by a friend or partner can ease away the tensions of a stressful day.

Tension builds up in shoulders

ABOVE
Oils for massage can be mixed up in advance and kept in dark glass bottles for about twelve weeks.

Vaporized oils and steam inhalation

All essential oils are highly volatile, and evaporate or vaporize on exposure to air, giving off their aroma. In inhaling these aromas we absorb the essence in two ways: while the scent itself directly affects receptors in the brain, molecules of substances from the oils are absorbed into the bloodstream and circulated around the body. Many oils have a medicinal effect in the air itself as well as on the person breathing them, as they are powerful antiseptics that can kill airborne bacteria. Heating the oils speeds up their evaporation rate.

LEFT
This traditional vaporizer uses a night light.

Vaporized essential oils can be used for various purposes: a penetrating oil such as sweet basil to scent a room and dispel unwanted odors; an antiseptic oil such as eucalyptus to rid a room of germs in cases of infectious illness; insecticides such as citronella to repel mosquitoes and other insects; steam inhalation, using an oil such as rosemary, for respiratory disorders. The five main methods of assisting the vaporization of essential oils are described in detail below.

VAPORIZER

Purpose-made ceramic or metal vaporizers are now readily available in specialty shops and some health stores. A few drops of essential oil are put in the bowl of the burner and a night-light is then placed underneath, causing the oil to heat up and evaporate. A little water can be mixed with the oil in the bowl to slow down the evaporation rate if required. Because they have a naked flame, vaporizers of this type should be kept well out of reach of children or pets.

ELECTRIC DIFFUSER

BASIL

An electric diffuser is more expensive to buy than a ceramic or metal vaporizer, but has the advantage of not needing a naked flame to generate the heat. This makes it more suitable for night use, especially in children's bedrooms. In addition, many electric diffusers have a variety of settings to adjust the rate of evaporation. Such diffusers are readily available through specialist aromatherapy suppliers.

LIGHT BULB RING

LIGHT BULB RING

A very easy and cheap way of vaporizing essential oils is to use a ceramic or metal light bulb ring. Simply put a few drops of essential oil into the ring, place on top of a light bulb, then switch the light on.

WARNING

Do not apply essential oils directly to a light bulb, as this can cause the bulb to explode.

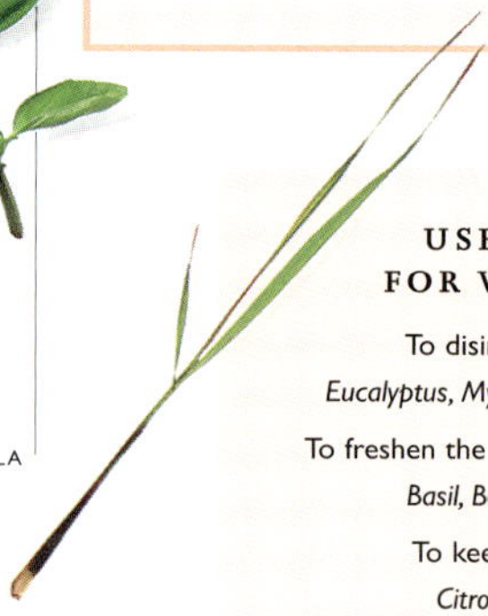

CITRONELLA

USEFUL OILS FOR VAPORIZERS

To disinfect a sickroom:
Eucalyptus, Myrrh, Thyme, Pine, Tea tree

To freshen the air and cheer the spirits:
Basil, Bergamot, Lavender

To keep insects at bay:
Citronella, Geranium

For sensual perfume:
Black pepper, Clary sage

To clear the head and mind:
Hyssop, Marjoram, Peppermint

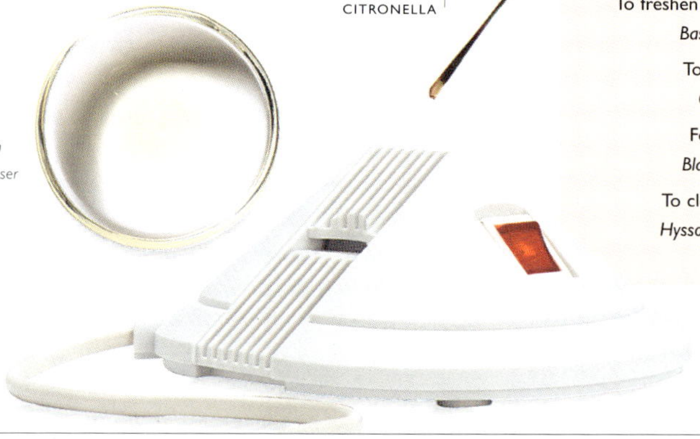

RIGHT
Antiseptic oils can be used in a diffuser to help fumigate a sickroom.

LEFT
A sophisticated electric diffuser is safe to operate and can control the speed at which evaporation takes place.

ABOVE
A few drops of an appropriate oil on strips of ribbon or fabric can deter insects, kill germs, or give a lovely fragrance to a room.

STEAM INHALATION

Vaporizing an essential oil using hot water as a medium is especially valuable for respiratory conditions, such as whooping cough. It can also be used to help to keep up the humidity levels in centrally heated rooms. For environmental purposes, simply add a few drops of essential oil to a bowl of hot water placed on a radiator or any other source of heat.

Direct steam inhalation is especially suited to congested sinus, throat, and chest infections. Soaking in a steaming hot bath to which have been added 5 or 6 drops of expectorant oils such as myrtle or rosemary, which are both non-irritating to the skin, helps to clear congestion. This method also acts as a kind of facial steam or sauna: the use of cleansing, antiseptic oils such as tea tree can help unblock the pores and clear the complexion of minor blemishes.

SCENTED FABRICS

A simple technique to help combat coughs and colds is to apply a few drops of an expectorant essential oil such as myrtle to the pillow, pajamas, night clothes, or handkerchief. If you wish to keep insects at bay, applying a few drops of an essential oil such as geranium to hanging ribbons or sprinkling the oil onto your clothing can be a very effective way of doing this. Because essential oils are volatile, unlike vegetable oils, they will not leave a stain on linen or clothing.

INHALATION FOR A COLD

Add about 5 drops of a decongestant essential oil such as peppermint to a bowl of steaming water, cover the head with a towel, and breathe deeply for three minutes, keeping the eyes closed

PEPPERMINT

RIGHT
Inhaling vaporized essential oils from a bowl of steaming-hot water is a simple way to treat respiratory infections.

ABOVE
Oils sprinkled onto a handkerchief can be inhaled throughout the day.

Simple medicinal and household uses

There are many other beneficial and pleasurable ways in which to use essential oils in the home, many of them closely allied to uses of herbs in medicine, or linked to well-established, long-standing household traditions of using flowers and herbs. The five quintessential oils for the medicine chest (*see* p.18) are all good standbys for simple first aid treatments and straightforward medical care for common complaints, while for perfumery and fragrance the choice is largely a question of personal preference.

WARNING

Essential oils should never be used neat or taken internally except as specified in this book or on the advice of a trained physician. Always follow the instructions carefully.

HOT AND COLD COMPRESSES

This method is suited to a variety of first-aid cases – use a hot compress for abscesses, muscular aches, pains, and severe tension; a cold compress for bumps and bruises, headaches, migraine, and sprains.

PREPARING A COMPRESS

Prepare a hot compress by dipping a clean facecloth or piece of absorbent cotton in a small bowl containing about 17fl oz/500ml of steaming water to which have been added 5 or 6 drops of an essential oil such as lavender. Squeeze out any excess water, and then apply to the affected area. Apply a bandage if required and repeat as necessary.

Make a cold compress by dipping a clean facecloth or cotton pad in a bowl of cold water to which have been added 5 or 6 drops of a cooling oil such as peppermint, squeezing out any excess water. Alternatively, wrap the cloth round an ice cube before applying to the affected area. Refresh the compress regularly and apply until the swelling or pain subsides.

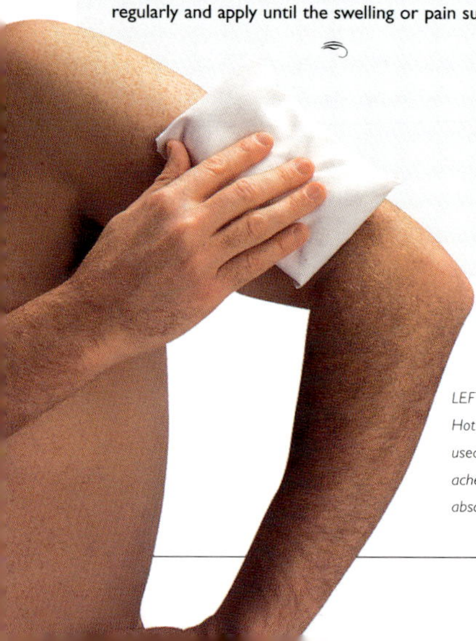

LEFT
Hot and cold compresses can be used with appropriate oils for injuries, aches and pains, headaches, abscesses, and indigestion.

GARGLES AND MOUTHWASHES

For the treatment of mouth ulcers, sore throat, bad breath, or other mouth or gum infections, simply add 3 to 5 drops of an essential oil such as fennel or thyme to a glass of warm boiled water and mix well. Then swill the mouth out well and/or gargle.

NEAT APPLICATION

In general, essential oils should not be applied neat to the skin as they are highly concentrated. Some oils can cause irritation or a burning or tingling sensation when they are applied in an undiluted form. However, there are exceptions to this rule. (*See First aid, p. 25; Perfumes and household fragrance, p. 25.*)

THYME

RIGHT
Gargling with water and a few drops of thyme oil soothes a sore throat and is a useful treatment for a range of mouth infections.

FIRST AID

ABOVE
Bee stings can be soothed with a cold compress.

Lavender oil is very soothing and rapidly helps the skin to heal, usually without even leaving a scar. It can be applied directly to burns, insect bites, cuts and spots as first-aid treatment. Tea tree is another oil which can be used neat for first aid purposes. However, before applying any oil neat to the skin, always do a patch test as described on p. 211.

DISINFECTANTS

Such oils as tea tree or lavender can be used for disinfecting clothes and diapers. For washing by hand, add up to 50 drops of essential oil to a bowl of warm water; otherwise add the same quantity to a liquid detergent and use in the washing machine. For washing floors and kitchen and bathroom surfaces, add up to 50 drops of essential oil to a bucket or bowl of water.

PERFUMES AND HOUSEHOLD FRAGRANCE

Some essential oils can be applied undiluted to the skin in minute amounts as perfume. Several essential oils are ideal natural perfumes – either on their own or combined with others. Ylang ylang is renowned as a well-balanced fragrance in its own right; others, such as rose, jasmine, neroli, and sandalwood, are well-known traditional perfume ingredients. Such oils can be dabbed on the wrists or behind the ears, either neat or diluted to 5 percent in jojoba or a bland base oil. Always carry out a patch test on the skin before using a new oil as a perfume (*see* p. 211).

Aromatic oils can be used to scent the hair, linen or clothes, paper, ink, potpourris or other items, directly from the bottle. Pure essential oils have a totally different quality to synthetic perfumes, since they are derived from natural sources. Artificially made perfumes do not have the subtle balance of constituents and the therapeutic qualities of real essential oils.

LEFT
Jasmine is used to scent soaps, toiletries, and perfumes.

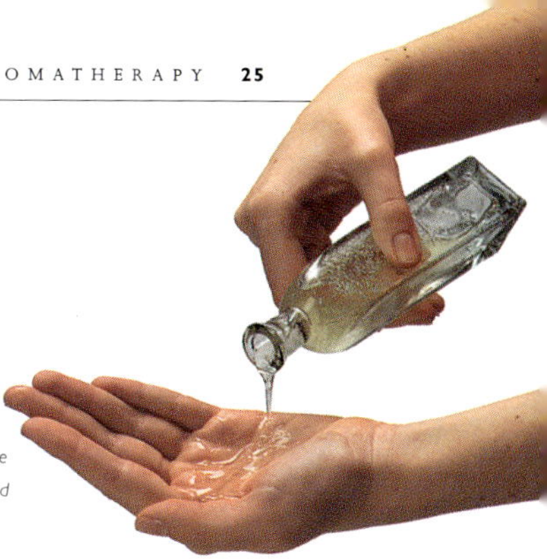

RIGHT
Dilute essential oils in a carrier oil before using them to oil and perfume large household items.

OILS FOR FURNITURE AND WOOD

A few drops of an essential oil such as cedarwood or rosemary can be used to perfume wooden items such as beads or boxes, or added to furniture polishes. Freshly scented oils such as these can also be sprinkled on logs before they are burned on an open fire.

LAVENDER

AROMATIC SACHETS AND PILLOWS

As well as having a pleasing fragrance, lavender oil makes an excellent insect repellent. Lavender has been used for centuries to protect clothes and linen from moths. It imparts a lovely scent when used in aromatic sachets kept in the linen closet or in drawers. Use dried herbs impregnated with a few drops of oil as the stuffing and seal them in small linen or lace sachets, which can be tied at the top with ribbon. Scented pillows can be made for the bedroom in similar fashion.

SCENTED PAPER AND INK

An easy way to scent writing paper is to put a few drops of a chosen essential oil onto a ball of absorbent cotton and store this in a sealed box together with the sheets of paper. After about ten days, the paper will have absorbed a good deal of the fragrance. A few drops of aromatic oil can also be dropped into writing ink. Many household items can be scented in a similar manner.

POTPOURRIS

Essential oils can be used in making potpourris or used to revive them. Making dry potpourris is quick and straightforward. The principles and basic method for making dry potpourris are given on p. 26, together with a sample recipe for a traditional floral potpourri.

RIGHT
Any oil you choose can be used to scent writing paper and ink for special correspondence.

Making a potpourri

Many traditional dry potpourri mixes displayed in open ceramic bowls in the bedroom or living room are based on rose petals, often with the addition of lavender flowers. However, a great deal of flexibility and individual creativity can be used in choosing plant material and other ingredients. A fresh-citrus blend based on herbs such as lemon balm and lemon-scented geraniums together with dried lemon peel and marigold petals can make a refreshing bathroom blend. Spicy mixtures, which are suitable for the kitchen or for festive occasions, may include ingredients such as lemon or orange peel, cinnamon sticks, vanilla beans, whole cloves and other spices, bay leaves, and sprigs of dried rosemary.

DRIED INGREDIENTS

TRADITIONAL POTPOURRI RECIPE

Ingredients

- *2 cups (25g) dried rose petals*
- *1/2 cup (6g) dried lavender flowers*
- *1/2 cup (6g) dried mint leaves*
- *1/2tbs/7.5ml orris root powder*
- *half a nutmeg, grated*
- *20 to 30 drops rose oil*
- *20 to 30 drops lavender oil*
- *decorative rosebuds*
- *small glass mixing bottle*
- *mortar and pestle*
- *small spoon for mixing*
- *glass or ceramic storage jar*
- *decorative bowl*

1 Measure out the essential oils and blend them together in a glass bottle. Put on the lid securely and set aside.

2 Grind the grated nutmeg and orris root powder together, using the mortar and pestle. Add half the total quantity of essential oils and mix with a spoon.

3 Place the main ingredients in the storage container and add the remaining essential oils, mixing well.

4 Add the powdered material from the mortar and mix gently, so as not to damage the plant materials. Seal the container and leave to mature for two to six weeks in a dark place.

5 Transfer the potpourri mixture into a decorative bowl or jar and arrange a few tiny rosebuds on top. Later, as the aroma starts to fade, more essential oils can be added to revive the mixture and prolong its life.

BELOW
Display your potpourri in a decorative open bowl. The orris root powder in the blend ensures that the scent will last.

Cosmetic aromatherapy

PARACELSUS 1493–1541

Cosmetic aromatherapy aims to rejuvenate and beautify the body through the use of aromatic oils, and generally to improve our outward appearance. Much of this section focuses on the different methods by which essential oils can be used to improve the complexion or to treat specific skin conditions. Beauty, however, is not just skin-deep. The condition of the skin expresses the overall health of an individual. A relaxed attitude, together with a well-balanced diet, enough exercise, and a daily intake of plenty of spring water or herbal teas, all help to keep the system in top condition.

Our outward appearance is certainly kept high on the cultural agenda today, with health and beauty issues attracting a wide audience among the general public. New weight control programs, fitness plans, and nutritional regimes are emerging all the time. But the emphasis that our culture places on the body and the importance of beauty, like all things, has both a positive and a negative side. On the positive side, it can encourage a sense of well-being, self-confidence, self-awareness, and self-motivation. On the negative side, it can foster addictions, narcissism, or a lack of self-worth by holding up a concept of perfection or beauty that is ultimately unattainable. Taken to the extreme, an over-materialistic attachment to the beauty of the body can lead to a youth-oriented society in which people have an exaggerated fear of growing old.

Essential oils have themselves been linked to the old alchemical tradition of the search for physical immortality – but, as the medieval alchemists discovered for themselves, ultimately it is not possible to transmute base matter into gold. What they did discover through their laborious experimentation was how to perceive an "inner map" for the transformation of the psyche or nature of the soul. In the end, as Paracelsus realized, the material body is only a receptacle or instrument for the transcendental soul.

> **"Why not take care of this body, which is the receptacle of our soul, so that it may remain as healthy, strong, and perfect as possible ..."**
>
> PARACELSUS

However, before considering the contribution or limits of an aromatherapeutic approach to rejuvenation, and the value of essential oils in beauty and cosmetic preparations, it may be helpful to take a look at the structure of skin itself and the types of physical problems to which it is exposed.

RIGHT
Essential oils are especially good for beauty treatments; they are pure, simple, and easy to use.

BELOW
Women wearing perfume cones on their heads depicted in an Ancient Egyptian wall painting.

The skin and its health

The skin is the largest organ of the human body, consisting of over three million cells. Like the heart or liver, the skin is a very active organ and is responsible for all kinds of bodily processes, including temperature regulation, elimination of metabolic waste, and the manufacture of vitamin D, as well as protecting the body from external invasion. The skin is divided into three main layers:

* The subcutaneous or bottom layer – this contains muscles and fatty tissue that help to keep the skin toned and firm.
* The dermis or middle layer – this contains sensory nerve endings, blood and lymph vessels, hair follicles, and the sebaceous and sweat glands. This is also the place where new living skin cells are manufactured before emerging on the surface.
* The epidermis or top layer, known as the "stratum corneum" – this is the visible surface of the skin, which is composed of flat, essentially dead cells.

The more rapidly the dead surface cells are replaced by new ones from beneath, the softer and smoother the skin looks. A mass of lifeless cells clinging to the surface of the skin creates a tired and dull-looking complexion. On the other hand, an excessive turnover of epidermal cells, due to a dysfunction of skin enzymes, gives rise to psoriasis. Since the natural process of renewal slows down as we age, rejuvenating aromatherapeutic skin products are largely aimed at stimulating rapid cell regeneration in the dermal layer, thus protecting the health of the skin from within.

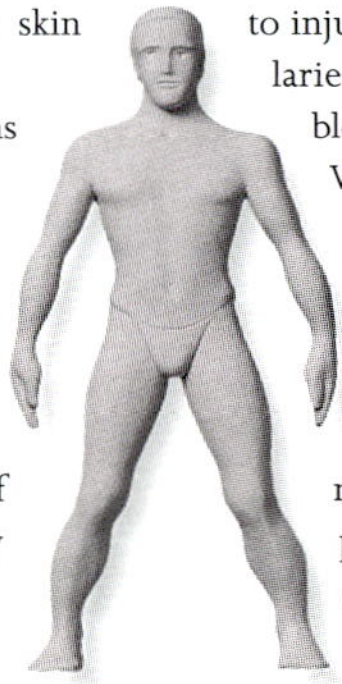

ABOVE
The state of our general health often manifests itself in the condition of our skin.

ALLERGIC REACTIONS

As the body's first line of defense from external invasion, the skin is prone to attack from pathological organisms such as bacteria or viruses, as well as from other external dangers through injury or potential allergens. Many common skin complaints are due to an allergic reaction, or hypersensitivity to certain conditions or substances. Allergies are associated with the level of histamine, a protein that is released in response to injury or tissue damage. Histamine causes the capillaries to dilate in the affected area, bringing extra blood to the damaged cells to help in their repair. When fluids seep out of the dilated blood vessels this can also cause local redness, swelling, and irritation. Other actions of histamine include contraction of the bronchi (this is the cause of asthma attacks).

The release of histamine is a normal defense mechanism, but in allergic reaction the level produced becomes excessive. For example, an excess of histamine can quickly build up after insect bites or plant stings, since histamine is also present in their poisons. Excessive amounts of histamine may also be released in response to inhaling pollen, animal hair or other irritants, as is the case with hay fever.

Why such reactions arise is not known, but there is often a hereditary pattern involved in such conditions, with a tendency for one allergy to lead on to another. Alternatively, there may be a sudden breakdown in the body's resistance to potential irritants which were previously tolerated. Stress, and psychological or emotional factors, often trigger an attack.

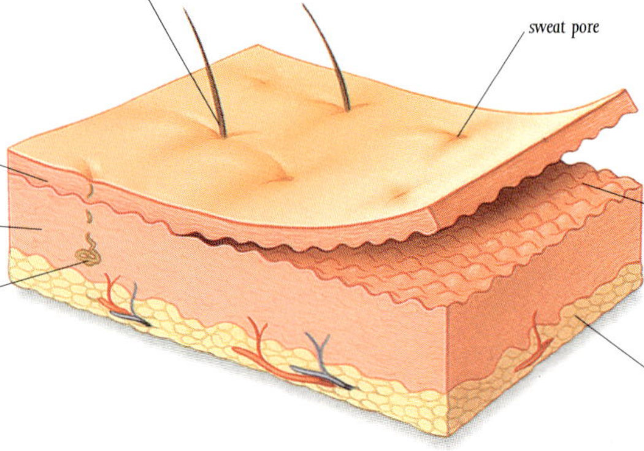

LEFT
This diagram shows the three layers of the skin.

ABOVE
Cinnamon leaf. The oil is used to treat fungicidal and bacterial infections, but must be used with extreme caution.

Allergies are said to be on the increase, due to higher stress levels and the general over-exposure to food additives, insecticides, and other synthetic chemicals to which we are subjected on a daily basis. Essential oils such as chamomile, melissa, tea tree, or lavender can be very helpful for many types of allergic skin conditions, although it is vital to carry out a patch test beforehand to check for individual sensitization levels, as described on p. 211.

Antihistamines are used in the treatment of allergic reactions, Vitamin C being a good natural example. Pantothenic acid (Vitamin B5) is also valuable in treating allergies, as it builds up the adrenal glands, which produce cortisone, a substance known to have protective qualities against allergies. Infantile eczema usually responds to treatment with gamma linoleic acid (GLA) in the form of evening primrose oil capsules. Allergic skin conditions most commonly affect those with dry or sensitive skins.

FUNGAL INFECTIONS

Fungal or viral organisms are another common cause of skin irritation. Tinea, for example, which manifests in several forms, all characterized by red, flaky skin and itching, is caused by a microscopic fungal mold. Forms of tinea are athlete's foot (tinea pedis), ringworm (tinea capitis), dhobi itch (tinea cruris), which affects the groin, especially in hot climates, and tinea barbae, sometimes known as barber's rash, which affects the face and neck. Candida is another fungus that causes infection, and it thrives in moist, warm conditions. It is often found in the vagina, where it can cause thrush, with irritation, itching, and sometimes severe redness and discomfort. However, thrush also occurs in the mouth, where it erupts in a white speckled rash, and is also seen in some forms of the irritating childhood complaint known as "diaper (nappy) rash." Like viral infections such as herpes, which in its various forms can cause cold sores, shingles, genital herpes, and chicken pox, fungal infections tend to attack the body when it is run down.

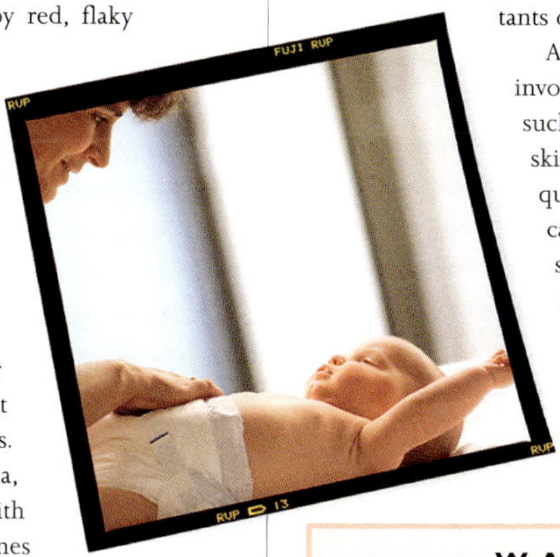

ABOVE
Fungal infections can cause a form of "diaper rash" in babies.

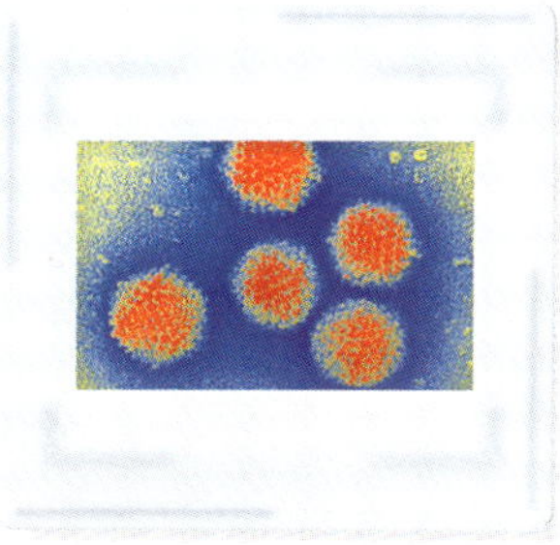

LEFT
Irritation caused by viruses can be combated with oils such as tea tree and lemon eucalyptus.

Essential oils that have a powerful fungicidal and antiviral action include tea tree oil, lemon-scented eucalyptus, and cinnamon leaf (see Warning box, below).

BACTERIAL INFECTIONS

Other forms of skin infection are bacterial, and may be caused by a wide range of invading organisms such as types of Streptococci or Staphylococci. Tea tree, cinnamon leaf, clove, rosemary, marjoram, thyme, lemon, oregano, and savory are all effective bactericidal agents – but some of the most powerful antibacterial oils also have high toxicity levels or are skin irritants or skin sensitizers.

A condition such as acne often involves bacterial infection – so an oil such as tea tree, which is mild on the skin yet has powerful antiseptic qualities, is very valuable in such cases. Congested skin conditions such as acne, boils, and blemished skin tend to affect those with oily or greasy complexions, since the pores of the skin are already blocked by sebum, a greasy substance formed around the base of hairs.

WARNING

Cinnamon leaf oil is an irritant to the skin and thus can only be used in low dilutions, whether used singly or in combination with other oils.

Beauty and rejuvenation

Apart from their role in preventive medicine, and in the treatment of common disorders and skin complaints, essential oils have been utilized for thousands of years purely for their cosmetic potential. The Ancient Egyptians were renowned for their expertise in this field, successfully using aromatic essences and herbs in the embalming process for their preservative qualities. Recent research has confirmed that certain essential oils, such as rose, neroli, lavender, frankincense, and myrrh, can indeed stimulate cellular granulation, which is the first stage of healing after an injury, and keep the skin looking youthful. Many traditional preservative herbs, such as rosemary and sage (but not their essential oils), have also been found to have potent antioxidant properties which prevent the decomposition of organic material.

The pioneering French aromatherapist Marguerite Maury spent many years researching the specific ways in which essential oils could be used to preserve the youth of the skin, and the best ways in which oils could be utilized for their rejuvenating properties on the body and spirit as a whole. She summed up her findings as follows:

"Passionately interested by works dealing with the essential oils, perfumes and aromatics we have discovered their vast possibilities – particularly with regard to the problem of regeneration."[3]

According to Mme. Maury, certain essential oils can rejuvenate the skin by regulating the activity of the capillaries and restoring vitality to the tissues – in her own words "they make the flesh more succulent". She used individually formulated aromatic treatments or prescriptions (IPs) which were specifically adapted to the physical and emotional disposition of her clients in order to bring about a transformation in both their physical health and mental attitude. This aromatic mixture complemented exactly the needs of the patient, and was compared to the negative of a film, with its reversed shadows and light. It was made up using essential oils of different densities. She also found that in the course of a treatment, it was often necessary to modify the mixture as the client's condition changed.

ABOVE
The Ancient Egyptians used plants for their cosmetics value, and also knew about their powers as preservatives.

Mme. Maury did not use an alcoholic base for her prescription, as would a perfumer, but mixed the essences with a vegetable oil carrier for direct application to the skin. She noted that essential oils were rapidly absorbed in this way, but that different essences passed through the skin at different rates according to their viscosity. Although the heavy, resin-bearing essences often had the greatest influence on the quality of the tissues on a deep cellular level, they were the slowest to be assimilated, while the very light and fluid essences penetrated easily into the extra-cellular fluids that play a key role in maintaining the body's state of balance. When preparing aromatic remedies for rejuvenation, it is therefore valuable to incorporate several essences of various densities so as to create a synergy, or, to use the language of perfumery, a perfect accord of top, middle, and base notes.

Further information on the blending of oils, and the principles of perfumery can be found on pp. 42–49.

BELOW
Many products containing essential oils can help to keep the skin looking fresh and youthful.

Essential oils for the skin and hair

ABOVE
Essential oils have a long history of use as cosmetic aids.

There are many essential oils that are useful skin care agents: oils such as sandalwood, geranium, palmarosa, bergamot (which should be bergapten-free), myrrh, and frankincense. These are all very valuable additions to the beauty therapist's list of ingredients, or an aromatherapist's collection of massage oils. There are also many essential oils which make excellent conditioning treatments for the hair and scalp due to their pleasing scent, gentle action, and powerful antiseptic properties. These include rosemary, West Indian bay, and sage, which can help to regulate the activity of the sebaceous glands, cleanse the scalp of bacterial infection, and disperse dead skin cells. Lavender oil is also said to smooth knots and tangles and encourage hair growth.

However, there are five essential oils (*see* p.32) that stand out as being especially valuable for general skin and hair care because of their skin compatibility. They are all mild on the skin (nonirritant, nonphoto-toxic and generally nonsensitizing), yet they possess powerful medicinal properties, being bactericidal, antiseptic, cytophylactic (healing), or anti-inflammatory, and all have a long history of use as cosmetic aids. These five oils are indispensable for all who wish to take an interest in the overall health and beauty of their skin.

SKIN CARE OILS

For a guide to the properties of essential oils *see pp. 178–210* and for details of base oils used in skin care *see pp. 84–5*.

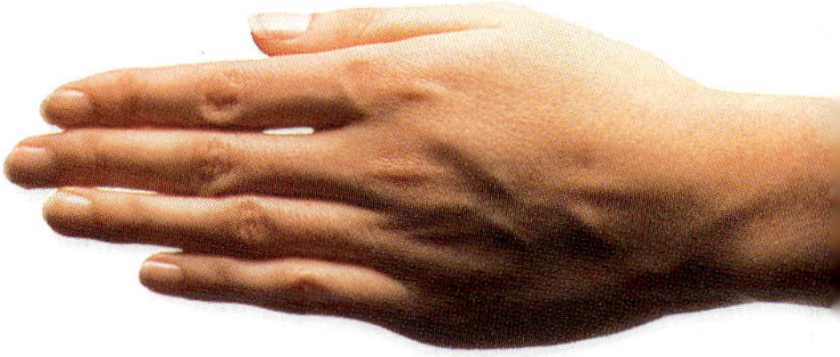

ABOVE
Many aromatherapists find that handling carrier oils and essential oils improves the condition of their hands and nails.

PALMAROSA

ROSEMARY

GERANIUM

LAVENDER

ABOVE AND RIGHT
Sources for some of the best oils for the skin and hair.

LEFT
Essential oils can be used for hair, scalp, and face in many ways.

VALUABLE OILS FOR THE SKIN

ROSE

* Rose

Rose has long been used as a favorite perfume ingredient and cosmetic oil. It is one of the most useful skin-care oils because, apart from its rich, feminine scent, it has good wound-healing properties which help in the daily process of skin repair. Rose oil and rose water have been used as ingredients in cosmetics for centuries, and their effects have been well tried and tested. Rose oil can help to keep the skin healthy, lubricated, and elastic, making it less prone to wrinkles. For general skin care, it is suited to all types of complexion, particularly dry, sensitive, and aging or mature skin.

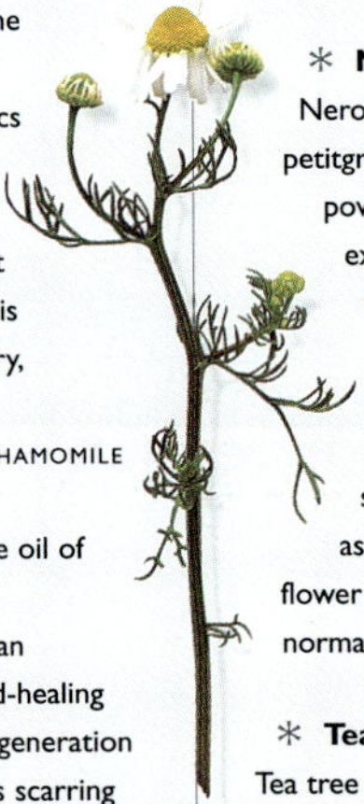

CHAMOMILE

* Lavender

Lavender is perhaps the most versatile skin-care oil of all because, although it has excellent antiseptic properties, it is very mild on the skin. It is also an excellent cicatrizant or wound-healing oil, which promotes tissue regeneration in everyday use and prevents scarring when used to treat damaged or injured skin. It is a valuable oil for all types of skin injury, but also for the treatment of a wide range of specific skin conditions. It is suited to all types of complexion, particularly oily and blemished skin. This gentle oil can safely be used neat if required.

LAVENDER

* Chamomile

Chamomile oil is a well-known soothing remedy, and particularly well suited to children. Because of its sedative and relaxant properties it is especially good for all types of skin complaints that have a nervous or stress-related element, such as the many types of dermatitis or eczema. It is also the best anti-inflammatory herb. Like rose oil it is good for sensitive skin, but it is especially indicated for all types of swelling, irritation, rashes, red or sore skin, including allergic skin conditions. Both Roman and German chamomile can be used in skin care.

* Neroli

Neroli (derived from orange blossom) and the similar petitgrain (from the leaves of the bitter orange tree) are powerful bactericidal and antiseptic agents with excellent cytophylactic properties (encouraging the formation of new skin cells). Like rose and lavender, they have a most beautiful, classic scent, which is uplifting, fresh, and citrus-like. Orange flower water is traditionally used to soften the skin and it also has a gentle toning and astringent action. Neroli, petitgrain, and orange flower water are beneficial for all skin types, including normal or combination skin.

* Tea tree

Tea tree is a valuable skin-care agent because it has excellent antiseptic, fungicidal, and antiviral properties, yet is very mild on the skin. It can be used for a wide range of specific skin conditions and for more general disinfectant purposes. In a theoretical comparison between tea tree and other antiseptics used for skin care, tea tree oil came closest to having all the properties of an ideal skin disinfectant.[4] Although this oil is generally used medicinally, it is a useful addition to a collection of oils for cosmetic use.

LEFT
Roses have been cultivated for use in beauty and therapeutic products for centuries.

TEA TREE OIL AND ITS USES

Tea tree oil is particularly indicated for infected skin conditions, including injuries (especially where there is pus or dirt), and for combating fungal diseases such as tinea or candida. It is also excellent for treating problems of viral origin such as cold sores, genital herpes, warts, and veruccas. It is especially recommended for use by those with blemished skin, acne, and greasy complexions.

- It acts swiftly and effectively against a wide range of bacterial and fungal organisms, has good persistence, and the added benefit of excellent absorption into the skin.
- It possesses powerful cleansing properties noted repeatedly in the clinical literature.
- It does not irritate the skin, is not poisonous, does not harm tissue cells, and has no significant side effects.
- It is not easily contaminated.
- It is cosmetically very suitable, being colorless and having a pleasant, clean odor.
- It is nearly neutral in pH.
- It is notably effective where there is organic detritus (pus).
- It can be used to treat viral complaints with success.

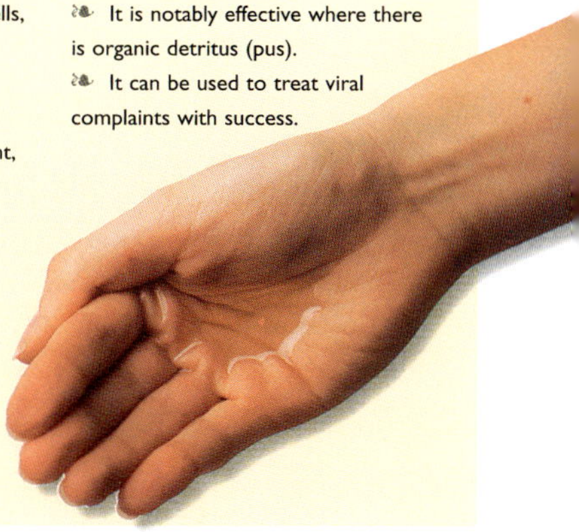

ABOVE AND RIGHT
In massage tea tree is diluted, and usually combined with other oils.

BASIC SKIN CARE

In skin care, most essential oils are used diluted. In the simplest treatments an essential oil is mixed with a suitable base oil *(see pp. 84–5* for a list of base oils) or with spring water. Basic creams and moisturizers for both cosmetic and medical use can also be made very simply. When making healing ointments, choose the oils you use for their therapeutic value, following the guide to aromatherapy use in the index of essential oils *(pp. 176–210)* and specific remedies on *pp. 96–175*. For cosmetic use, choose oils by reference to skin type, or by their scent.

Simple healing ointments

Ointments for treating specific skin complaints can be made by blending essential oils with a ready-made nonallergenic cream base, a herbal cream such as calendula cream, or homemade cold cream *(see p. 37)*. Dilute to between 0.5 and 2.5 percent depending on the type of disorder and the area of the body *(see p. 21)*. For a small quantity mix 2 to 3 drops of essential oil to a teaspoonful of cream base in a small container.

Simple Moisturizer

To make an aromatic facial moisturizer mix 8 to 10 drops of an essential oil (according to skin type) with a ready-made hypoallergenic, unscented cream or lotion (3½fl oz/100ml tube or 3½ oz/100g jar). In a glass or ceramic container, mix the essential oils into the cream, using a spoon. This blend can be used therapeutically and cosmetically for the face, neck and hands, but also for body massage. Store in a sealed container away from light and heat.

Skin-care routine

Maintaining a healthy, youthful-looking skin depends on everyday skin care as well as on general health. Products containing mineral oil are not absorbed into the lower dermal layers where the newly emerging cells require optimum nourishment. Mineral oil is also known to leach fat-soluble vitamins, especially A, D, and E, from the body. Most commercial toners contain alcohol, which has a drying effect on the skin and can cause irritation, as can many other synthetic ingredients found in creams and lotions. Even lanolin, though natural, is heavy, animal-derived and rather unpleasantly scented, and can cause allergic reactions. In contrast, natural vegetable oils, waxes, and creams, with selected essential oils, are ideal cosmetic aids because they are highly penetrative and can reach the small blood capillaries in the deeper dermal layers, thus rejuvenating the skin from within, while gentle flower waters tone without dehydrating the skin, and have a mild bactericidal action.

Many beauticians and body therapists now regularly use essential oils as part of their cosmetic treatments. It is also possible to carry out many effective beauty treatments at home, as part of a regular skin-care routine. Simply by using a selection of vegetable oils and essential oils together with other natural ingredients such as yogurt, clay, honey, oatmeal, and distilled water, it is possible to achieve and preserve a youthful-looking skin.

EVERY NIGHT

- Remove grime and make-up with a light vegetable oil (such as coconut, sweet almond, or apricot kernel oil) or a mild cleansing cream (such as the cold cream made as described on *p. 37*) with a cotton pad.
- Wipe away any excess using a cloth or pad dipped in warm water.

- Refresh the face and neck by applying flower water or a toner or cleanser *(see p. 38)* suited to your skin type.
- Apply a moisturizing oil or night cream suited to skin type.
- Sparingly apply a moisturizing eye oil, cream, or gel (as shown, right). Wheat germ or rosehip seed oil is ideal.

A BASIC SKIN-CARE ROUTINE

Different skin types require individual treatment but a good basic skin-care routine, which takes very little time, involves cleaning, toning, and moisturizing every morning and evening, and giving the skin extra-special nourishing, cleansing, and revitalizing treatments once a week. Recipes for basic oils, gels, and creams are given on *pp. 36–7*, recipes for masks and moisturizers are on *p. 37*, and recipes for simple fresheners and toner/cleansers on *p. 38*.

SOURCES OF INGREDIENTS

Oils derived from fruits are nourishing and beneficial to the skin in many ways. Research has shown that they encourage the formation of fresh cells.

EVERY MORNING

- Cleanse with a light cream or oil, then remove any excess with a cloth or pad and warm water.
- Refresh the face and neck with a flower water or toner/cleanser suited to your skin type.
- Apply a light moisturizing oil or cream (with sun protection if wished). Let it be absorbed by the skin before applying make-up, if worn.

ONCE A WEEK

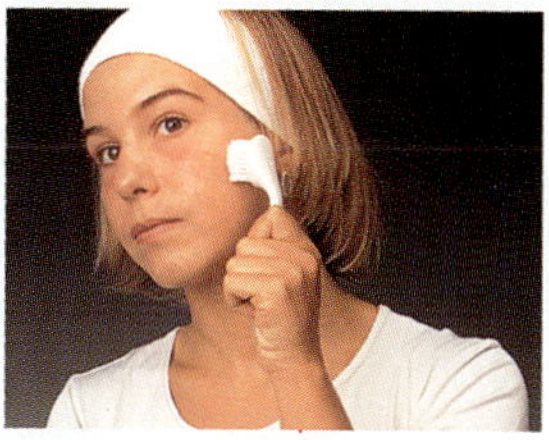

- To remove dead cells and debris from the skin surface, use dry skin brushing, a skin scrub, or an exfoliant.
- Give the face a nourishing massage (or receive a professional facial treatment) using rich oils, such as evening primrose, avocado, or borage. Massage with upward strokes.
- Give your face a steam treatment or facial sauna as described on *p. 39*. This opens the pores and deep-cleans the skin, to get rid of accumulated grime or dirt as well as detoxifying and bringing fresh blood to the surface.
- Apply a mask made from natural ingredients, as shown right. The ingredients of the mask should be chosen according to skin type. For instructions on making a mask and choosing ingredients *see p. 37.*

Oils and creams

Beauty, especially skin- and hair-care, is central to the practice of aromatherapy. But while receiving a full body massage from a professional aromatherapist or having an aromatic facial in a beauty clinic is certainly a treat, it is not essential for maintaining a clear and healthy complexion. Many aromatic recipes are simple to make, and regular treatment can easily be carried out at home.

AVOCADO

FACIAL OILS

Facial oils are made up in the same way as general massage or body oils (*see* p. 21), except that the base or carrier oil, as well as the essential oils, can be adapted to the type of skin which is to be treated. Suitable carrier oils include avocado, olive, wheat germ, hazelnut, apricot kernel, peach kernel, borage seed, carrot, and evening primrose, as well as the more basic carrier oils such as sweet almond, grapeseed, jojoba, or sunflower oil. Apart from nourishing and toning the skin, facial oils can also be used for facial massage and local self-massage.

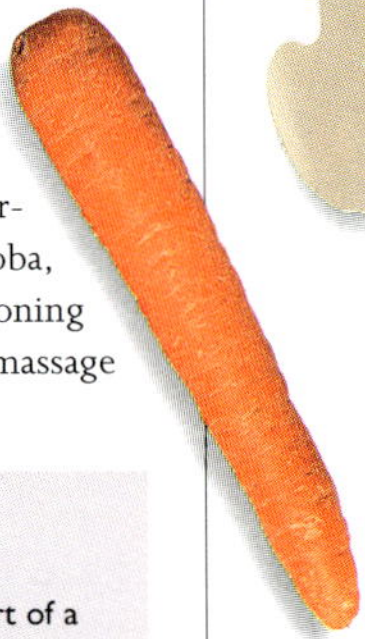

CARROT

FACIAL OIL RECIPE

Mix two parts of a basic carrier oil and one part of a specific carrier oil suited to the skin type, with 0.5 to 1 percent of an essential oil (or a blend of oils).

Base oil	Percentage	Drops
1tsp/5ml	0.5–1%	1
1tbs/15ml	0.5–1%	1–3
1fl oz/25ml	0.5–1%	3–5
2fl oz/50ml	0.5–1%	5–10
3½fl oz/100ml	0.5–1%	10–20

TAPIOCA GEL RECIPE

Use 3½fl oz /100ml water to 1½tsp/7.5ml tapioca. Mix and simmer until the tapioca is dissolved. Strain off the liquid and let it cool to form a transparent gel. Stir in a few drops of essential oil just before it sets.

GRAPES

BELOW AND LEFT

Making your own beauty treatment oils and creams enables you to choose ingredients best suited to your skin, and a fragrance to your liking.

HAZELNUTS

FACIAL CREAMS

An aromatic facial cream should moisturize, heal, and nourish the skin, trapping the moisture in, but also letting the skin breathe. To make up a basic cream at home, use the instructions on p. 37, based on what is traditionally known as Galen's cold cream recipe.

GELS

Water-based gels provide a useful, nonoily medium for the application of essential oils, as an alternative to oils and creams when required. A gel can be used to dilute any essential oils for irritating skin conditions such as eczema or athlete's foot, particularly if the skin is broken or sensitive. Gels are also suitable as a substitute for base or carrier oils for general skin care, especially if the skin is apt to be greasy. The percentage of essential oil to add to the gel base depends on where it will be used and for what purpose. Healing gels may include up to 2.5 percent of an essential oil when applied to the feet, whereas 0.5 percent is enough for application to the face or for general skin-care purposes. A natural soothing and cooling gel can be made with tapioca and water.

MASKS

Face masks or packs have many benefits – they can nourish, rejuvenate, stimulate, cleanse, or soothe the skin, and generally improve its texture and quality. Masks can be made from a wide range of natural ingredients, including fruit pulp, oatmeal (for allergic and irritated skin conditions), egg yolk (for all skin types), yogurt, honey, and clay. Fruits such as avocado (for dry skin) or strawberry (for oily skin) are extremely nutritious. Powdered oatmeal is also very nourishing and gives the skin a smooth, silken appearance, and brewer's yeast is good for all types of skin. Egg yolks are rich in lecithin, an invaluable skin aid. Natural yogurt contains lactic acid, which is good for large-pored, oily, and blemished skin and to balance combination skin. Honey is moisturizing and slightly antiseptic and can be incorporated into masks to soothe, soften, and nourish the skin – especially dry, sensitive, and mature complexions.

Clay is a useful ingredient for making masks, and is suitable for all but very dry skins. An aromatic clay mask is excellent for the treatment of acne and congested skin conditions, and can nourish dry or mature complexions and help to balance combination skin. However, those with dry, sensitive, or mature complexions should not use a clay-based mask more than once a week because they do have an overall drying effect. Masks are best applied after a bath or shower, when the pores are open and the skin is still warm and slightly damp.

BEESWAX

Clay cleanses and draws out toxins. It also aids skin regeneration, stimulates the circulation, and soothes inflammation. There are many different kinds of clay available, but green clay is the most versatile, being rich in minerals and a good antiseptic. Fuller's earth is also a good neutral clay base, which is more readily available.

SIMPLE CLAY MASK

To make a simple mask just add 2 to 3 drops of an essential oil to 2 tbs/30ml of wet clay paste, and apply to the skin. Leave in place for 10 to 30 minutes while you relax. Rinse off with warm water.

COLD CREAM RECIPE

Ingredients

4fl oz/120ml almond oil · ½ oz/15g beeswax beads or grated wax · 2fl oz/50ml rose water · 6–10 drops rose essential oil or other essential oil according to skin type

1 Put the beeswax beads into a toughened glass bowl and pour in the almond oil.

2 Place the bowl in a pan of water over a gentle heat, and mix until the ingredients are melted together.

3 Warm the rose water in a second bowl or jar, and then add to the wax and oil mixture bit by bit, beating all the time.

4 Finally, stir in the essential oil, transfer the mixture to a pot, and put into the refrigerator to set.

ALTERNATIVE CLAY MASK

To make a more elaborate mask first mix 2oz/50g green clay powder with 2 tsp/10ml collodial oatmeal and keep in a jar. To make the mask, mix 1tbs/15ml of the basic mixture with 1 tbs/15ml runny honey or plain live yogurt, one egg yolk, 2 to 3 drops of an essential oil suited to your skin type and enough water to give a smooth consistency. Apply to the skin and leave for 10 to 30 minutes – less for dry skin and longer for greasy/blemished skin. Rinse off with warm water. Finish by patting on a floral water.

Flower waters and steams

It is easy to make flower (or floral) waters at home, and they are beneficial for all types of skin. Simply add 10 to 30 drops of essential oil (or a blend) to a 3½fl oz/100ml bottle of spring or distilled water, leave it to stand for up to a month, and then filter the liquid using a coffee filter paper. (A more basic preparation can be made without filtering, but this must be shaken before each use.) Even a few drops of essential oil will impart their scent to this amount of water, making it very lightly fragranced. These delicately scented waters can be used to freshen and hydrate the skin, either dabbed on with absorbent cotton or sprayed from a small plant spray. This can be helpful during pregnancy, when traveling by air, in hot, dry climates, or simply to help counter the drying effects of central heating.

LEFT
A few drops of essential oil can be added to spring water for the simplest toilet water.

REFRESHING TOILET WATERS

LEMON PEEL

A variety of essential oils can be diluted in a minute proportion with alcohol, cider vinegar, or witch hazel to make toilet waters, eau-de-Cologne, or after-shave lotions. For example, a traditional toilet water called eau-de-Portugal can be made as follows:

Ingredients

20 drops sweet orange ❦ 5 drops bergamot
2 drops lemon ❦ 2 drops benzoin
1 drop geranium ❦ 1 tbs/15ml of vodka
3½fl oz/100ml spring water

Method

Dissolve the oils in the vodka, then add to the water, shaking well. Leave the mixture to mature for a month at least, then filter and bottle.

LEMON LEAF

RIGHT
Lemon oil is a lightly astringent, fresh-scented ingredient of eau-de-Cologne and eau-de-Portugal.

TONER/CLEANSERS

Using a flower water as the base, add a little witch hazel, which increases the overall astringency for a greater toning action. For additional moisturizing and cleansing properties, add up to 25 percent of natural glycerine to the mixture. Flower waters that contain a proportion of witch hazel and glycerine will remove oily residues from the skin as well as acting as an astringent and antiseptic. If no make-up (or very light make-up) is worn, they can be used for simple one-step cleansing and toning.

LEFT
Chamomile water soothes the skin.

FACIAL TREATMENT

Used once a week, steaming can help to hydrate the skin, cleanse the pores, and eliminate deep-seated grime and toxins. It is possible to buy a special facial sauna or steamer, but the same result can be achieved by simply filling a basin with boiling water, covering your head with a towel, and letting the steam work for five minutes on your face.

To make the steam treatment even more effective, add to the water 6 to 10 drops of an essential oil (or a blend) suited to your skin type. Soaking in a steaming hot bathtub containing a few drops of aromatic oil can also help clear skin congestion.

After steaming, the skin should be cooled and balanced with a flower water to close the pores. This should be allowed to dry naturally. When the skin is completely dry, a light moisturizer should be applied.

ABOVE
Spray the face with fragrant flower waters to hydrate and freshen the skin.

RIGHT
Eau-de-Cologne and toilet waters should be decanted into decorative glass bottles and kept well stoppered.

BELOW
Rose oil is one of the best skin treatments.

WARNING

Avoid steam treatments if your skin is prone to thread veins. This type of skin reacts adversely to extremes of heat and cold and should be treated gently at all times.

JASMINE

LEFT
Jasmine oil is good for all skin types

Toiletries and treatments

OATMEAL

FACE SCRUB OR EXFOLIANT

To remove dead cells from the surface of the skin and stimulate the circulation, moisten a little medium-ground oatmeal (or colloidal oatmeal – available from pharmacists) in the palm of your hand using a suitable aromatic flower water (*see* p. 38), and rub gently all over the face. For dry or sensitive skins, use ground almonds.

DRY AND WET BODY-BRUSHING

Rub one or two drops of a chosen essential oil into a dry loofah or a natural-bristle brush to make it smell fragrant. Start by rubbing the feet firmly with the brush, then gradually work your way up the body, concentrating on any congested or fatty areas, such as the hips or thighs. Work up the arms, paying special attention to the backs of the upper arms, up the back from the waist, up over the abdomen, and down the front from the shoulders.

Popular in Scandinavia, this technique stimulates the circulation, helps break down fatty deposits, and brings a glow to the skin. Used in combination with other approaches, it is helpful for removing cellulite. For a milder effect, the same technique can also be used in the shower or bath, using a few drops of essential oil on a wet brush, loofah, or sponge.

ABOVE
A loofah or sponge can be used as a body brush, to give an invigorating tingle.

AROMATIC SCALP OIL PREPARATIONS

Local massage is very effective for conditions such as hair loss and brittle or dry hair, if it is carried out on a regular basis. Massage also stimulates scalp circulation and nourishes the deeper layers of the skin, bringing more nutrients to the follicles and improving the hair. To make a scalp massage oil, mix 8 tsp/40ml coconut oil and 2 tsp/10ml wheat germ oil with between 10 and 25 drops of essential oil depending on hair and skin type.

BODY BRUSH

HAIR CONDITIONER

To make a good hair conditioner to encourage hair growth and improve the quality of the hair structure, mix 10 drops of essential oil with 5 tsp/25ml of slightly warmed jojoba oil, castor oil, or extra virgin olive oil, and rub this thoroughly into the scalp. Cover the hair with a layer of waxed paper, wrap in warm towels, and leave for an hour. Wash out, applying shampoo before the water; otherwise the hair will remain oily. Repeat weekly.

ABOVE AND LEFT
Body-brushing or an oatmeal scrub improves the circulation and acts as an exfoliant to remove dull-looking dead cells.

ABOVE
Fuller's earth is used for scalp treatment.

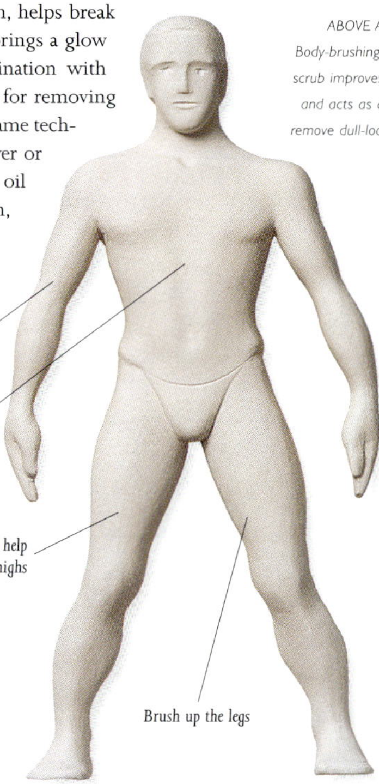

ABOVE
Powdered orris root can be used as the basis of an effective dry shampoo.

BODY POWDERS

Aromatic body powders can be made by mixing about 4 tbs/30g unperfumed talc or cornstarch with 5 to 6 drops essential oils. Seal the mixture in a closed container and let the base absorb the oils for at least 24 hours before use.

HAIR TONIC

LIME

Aromatic hair tonics are especially recommended for oily or thinning hair, because they can help to balance sebum levels (the oil produced at the base of the hair) and promote hair growth. Dissolve about 10 drops of essential oils suited to your hair type in one tablespoon of cider vinegar and add to $3^1/_2$fl oz/100ml of lavender water. Shake well and massage into the scalp.

QUICK SCALP RUB

A quick method to use for treating the scalp between washes if required, is to rub about 10 drops of pure tea tree or lavender oil into the scalp using the fingertips. This is beneficial for the treatment of dandruff and as a general conditioner.

DRY SHAMPOO

It is not beneficial to wash the hair too often, as this can strip the hair of its protective acid mantle. When short of time, or between shampoos, simply add a drop of rosemary essential oil, or an oil chosen for its fragrance, to one tablespoon of orris root powder or fuller's earth. Part the hair in sections and sprinkle the mixture on. Leave for five minutes, then brush out thoroughly.

LEMON

ABOVE
Citrus oils are unstable.

AROMATIC SHAMPOO

Buy a neutral pH shampoo (this is marked on the label) and add your own choice of essential oils to it. Add one or two drops of essential oil to a capful of shampoo at each wash, or add 30 to 50 drops of your chosen essential oil (or a blend) to a $3^1/_2$fl oz/100ml bottle of shampoo, and shake well before using.

AROMATIC RINSE

Add a few drops of a suitable aromatherapy oil, such as chamomile, lavender, or rosemary, to the final rinse water together with one tablespoon of cider vinegar. This very effective, yet simple, procedure gives the hair a wonderful shine and maintains the acid mantle of the scalp. It also imparts a delicious fragrance and new vitality to the hair.

RIGHT
Store homemade hair preparations in attractive, well-sealed bottles.

WARNING

Some oils, including ylang ylang, cedarwood, cypress, lemon, lime, juniper, mandarin, and pine, are not stable in shampoo or detergent and should therefore not be used.

RIGHT
An essential oil scalp rub refreshes and cleanses the scalp between shampoos and helps to keep the scalp and hair in good condition.

ROSEMARY OIL

Aromatherapy and perfumery

FRANKINCENSE

The psychological effects of fragrance have long been recognized, while herbs have probably been used for their specific effects by so-called "primitive" peoples since the dawn of time. It is certain that in the past natural aromatic substances were often employed successfully for their hallucinogenic, sedative, stimulating, sexually arousing, or anesthetizing effects on the mind, but a proper study of the action of scents, and specifically of essential oils, on the mind and behaviour has never been completed.

PSYCHO-AROMATHERAPY

Psycho-aromatherapy, which focuses primarily on the psychological potential of essential oils, consists of two separate but interrelated fields – aromatic medicine and perfumery. In psycho-aromatherapy, the physiological effect of specific essential oils on the systems of the body is combined with the individual's emotional or psychological reaction to their fragrance – with both aspects working together in a psychosomatic unity. It could be said that there are three different dimensions involved:

- the physiochemical dimension: the chemical structure of the odor, its quality and concentration or intensity
- the physiological dimension: the primary and secondary biological processes that are initiated upon contact with the oil
- the psychological dimension: the subjective individual response to an odor – how the individual describes and is affected by it.

Some fragrances are generally experienced as pleasing, while others are widely perceived as repugnant, yet it is difficult to make hard and fast rules about how any individual will react to a particular smell. This is because the physiological effect of a given odor can be overridden by an individual's specific emotional associations and psychological preferences. Sometimes even an unpleasant smell can have beneficial results if the associations are positive.

The close connection between the sense of smell and the experience of emotion has often been noted. It is suggested that, physiologically, molecules of odor in some way stimulate the same brain centers that signal the drives toward or away, which underlie almost all human emotion.[5]

> "He saw that there was no mood of the mind that had not its counterpart in the sensuous life ..."
>
> OSCAR WILDE

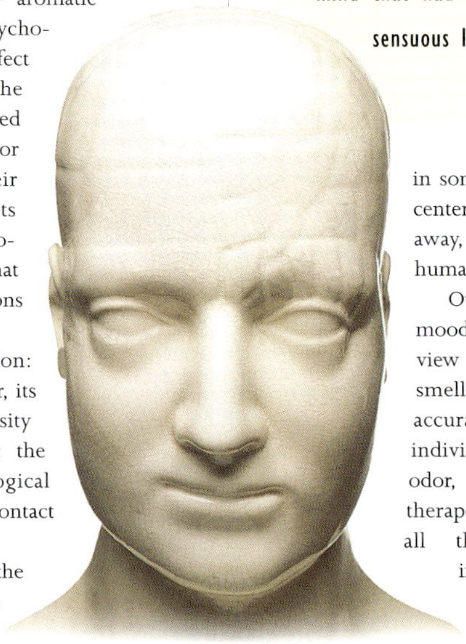

ABOVE
Strong odors such as frankincense are thought to affect mood and emotion through a physiological effect on the brain.

Our sense of smell influences our moods, emotions, and memories. In view of the idiosyncratic quality of smell, it is virtually impossible accurately to assess in advance an individual's reaction to a particular odor, or to prescribe a fragrance for therapeutic purposes without taking all the following considerations into account:

- biological: the effect the odor is likely to have physiologically on the systems of the body – whether it is stimulating or sedating
- archetypal associations: any universal associations the odor may have – the scent of the rose, for example, suggests femininity, love, divinity, and sweetness in all cultures
- cultural connotations: certain scents take on a specific meaning according to the environmental, social, and cultural factors involved – the odor of frankincense, for example, will be especially significant in a culture that is Roman Catholic
- individual responses: personal associations and preferences due to first-hand experience, which may be either positive or negative.

RIGHT
Responses to scents vary, but the rose has a perfume that is universally appreciated.

ABOVE
Masked Venetian ladies buying perfume in "The Perfume Seller" by Pietro Longhi, 1702–1785.

Since our response to scent is so individualistic, to what extent is it possible to use odors to bring about a predictable response? The writer Michael Stoddard asserts that although there is no odor capable of systematically inducing a given reaction in human beings, it is nevertheless possible that we are still subconsciously manipulated by odors. Since the sexual and social instincts of human beings are no longer controlled by scent-signals as they are in other mammals, odors do not bring about overt changes in human sexual or emotional behavior; rather, they create changes in mood or feeling states, often at a subliminal level. Such changed states, as studies have shown, can subtly color and redirect our thoughts, often without our noticing.[6]

Scents largely influence us unwittingly. This is what endows them with such great psychological potential, for better or for worse. At present, there is a great deal of scientific interest in the potential psychological effects of aromas, and the Fragrance Research Foundation in New York has in recent years coined the term "aromachology" to describe the study and use of natural or synthetic odors in this field. The current commercial trend is also moving toward a rapid increase in the utilization of fragrance as a marketing agent. For example, in a trial test using fragranced shoes, it was shown that customers were attracted to the scented items in preference to nonscented items – even if they did not know why.

ABOVE
Simply inhaling a favorite calming perfume induces relaxation.

For exactly the same reasons that scent can sell shoes, fragrance can also be used as a very powerful therapeutic tool, especially for psychological or psychosomatic complaints. Fragrance has been found to be an ideal candidate for use in relaxation work, because it directly targets the inner mind, and bypasses any critical interference by the verbal, conscious mind. The word "osmotherapy" has been suggested specifically to describe the utilization of scents, both natural and artificial, for therapeutic purposes.[7]

This approach, however, is quite distinct from psycho-aromatherapy, in that the latter employs only natural fragrances derived from botanical sources, and also combines inhalation with other methods of treatment. In aromatherapy therapeutic massage forms a large part of the individual's treatment. Aromatherapy massage is particularly beneficial because it combines inhalation with the healing effects of touch. Aromatic bathing also harmonizes scent with relaxation, as well as promoting absorption of the essential oils through the skin.

Thus, the practice of psycho-aromatherapy, while concentrating on the power of smell, actually embraces a variety of methods and techniques. In this respect it is a truly psychosomatic type of treatment for it operates on the body, mind, and emotions.

SCENT AND STRESS

The sense of smell is intimately connected with, and influences the functioning of, the central nervous system. Moreover, many illnesses could be said to be rooted in the mind – in a person's negative outlook or underlying fears. It is well known that mental states such as anxiety, irritation, or anger cause physical changes in the body, including an increase in heart rate, and change in breathing pattern and muscle tone. Stress and mental unrest, which are thought to be at the root of so much of our 20th-century "dis-ease," eventually produce a degenerative effect on the entire organism.

ABOVE
The effect of the scent of incense is reinforced by ritualistic association.

There is also a reciprocal relationship between stress and scent, in that certain smells, especially those with pheromonal potential (the potential to influence others of their species), can cause stress reactions and vice versa. Animals are particularly sensitive to this phenomenon, but the smell of fear or the smell of disease can sometimes be picked up by humans with a trained nose. Happiness and good health have their characteristic scents too.

A person's subconscious attitudes are related to the limbic system, the most primitive part of the brain concerned with basic emotions and mood. Since the body and mind are intrinsically related, a change in the mental or psychological disposition of an individual can have dramatic results on the person's physical health. And, since the limbic system is especially susceptible to the effects of fragrance, it is possible to heighten or influence a person's underlying dispositions and attitudes by subjecting him or her to certain scents.

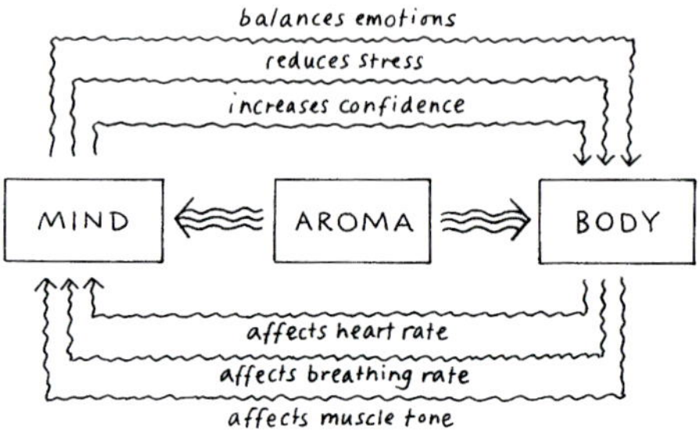

ABOVE
Scents function at the psychobiological level.

While scents have a chemical effect as they are absorbed by the bloodstream via the nose, they also work at a psychobiological level: for example, when we savor a pleasant fragrance, we take perceptibly deeper and slower breaths, relaxing our respiratory pattern much as we do in meditation. A scent can also serve to distract us, by becoming the focus for our attention, or by inducing positive memories and emotions.[8]

RIGHT
Scents rapidly affect our mood and emotions via the brain.

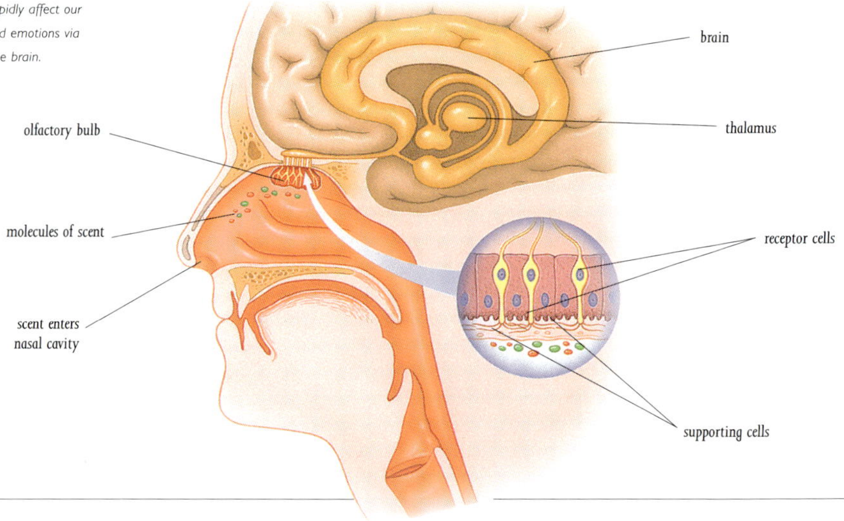

Aromatherapy massage treatment can take advantage of the fact that the benefits of the massage are reinforced by the scent of the oils used, and that the scent comes to be associated quickly with the beneficial, pleasure-giving and relaxing effects of the treatment. The odors of the oils used thus carry a positive association that makes the recipient more receptive and reinforces the effect of subsequent treatments, by causing positive anticipation. The subtle choice of oils to match a person's emotional make-up can open the door to helping that person to re-experience pleasure or joy.

This is similar to the use of incense in ritual and religious practices, where the familiar scent of the incense helps to bring about, through repetition as well as in its own right, a receptive and uplifting state of mind.

In a recent research trial, J. R. King found that some fragrances were normally very effective in promoting relaxation through association, despite individual variations. He has utilized a seaside fragrance in his relaxation work, because of its widespread positive associations, although he points out that if it is then used to counteract negative moods in stressful situations, such a fragrance would be best used sparingly and for brief periods, to preserve its value as a conditioned stimulus. Judiciously chosen and employed, however, essential oils, used in conjunction with massage in aromatherapy, can form a counter-vibration to that of the negative mood, and help to restore harmony.

Different attempts have been made to structure the relation between mood and scent. In *Essential Oils as Psychotherapeutic Agents*, Robert Tisserand proposes eight mood categories, in which essential oil can be used to help counteract or balance extremes of emotion (as illustrated above). The essential oils are highlighted in terms of the mood which they generally evoke. Ylang ylang generally inspires passion and also helps combat anger, and can be used to help frigidity and introversion. Jasmine may be used as a valuable oil for a person who is uninspired, dull, and in need of new ideas.

There can be a danger in linking particular essential oils too closely with specific emotions, because of the idiosyncratic nature of smell. When using natural aromatics for psychotherapeutic purposes, it is important to assess the personality or temperament of each person and to take his or her odor associations and preferences into account. In choosing fragrances which may correspond to the needs of an individual, personal preferences can often be of value as a therapeutic guide. Much as at times we crave certain foods that can supply nutritional elements which our body is lacking, so we may be emotionally drawn toward particular fragrances that have a balancing effect on our psychic disposition as a whole. Even a disagreeable reaction to a particular scent may give the aromatherapist an indication of a hidden or repressed area of psyche that needs attention.

Aromatherapists will frequently observe that their clients are instinctively drawn toward the essential oil that is right for their needs, and that as the client's emotional state alters, so, often, does an aroma preference.

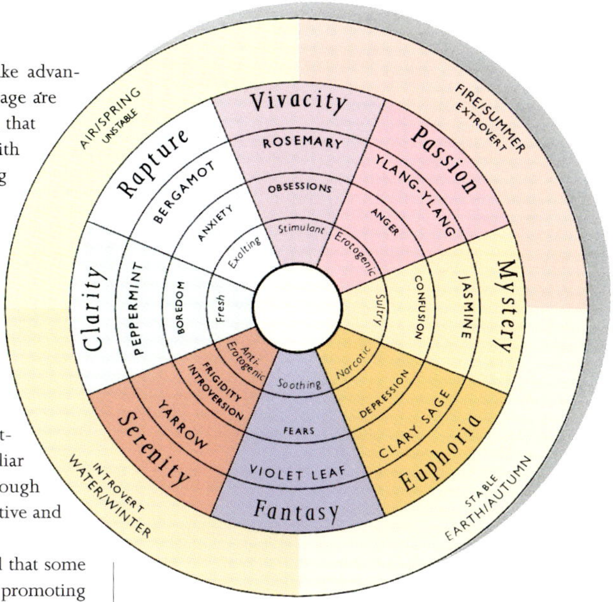

ABOVE
The Tisserand wheel illustrates the links between some common emotional states and specific oils. Personality type is shown in the outer wheel, then the "emotional" quality of the perfume and name of the oil, next the emotional state the oil can act on, and finally the type of action that the oil has.

MOOD AND FRAGRANCE

Some negative emotional states that can be altered by fragrance are:

Passive

Depression • Apathy • Melancholy • Indecision • Despair

Active

Anxiety • Nervous tension
Anger • Impatience • Panic

Perfume and personality

Choosing a perfume to suit their mood and personality is one way in which most women – and, increasingly, many men – practice a form of aromatherapy on themselves. We can all observe that choice of perfume, just like color preference, is highly individual, despite prevailing fashions, and moreover that there is a distinct link between personality types and the type of perfume worn.

Why does a person like or dislike a particular scent or choose one perfume rather than another? The relationship between perfume and personality, between the "essence" of a person and the "essence" of a perfume, is an area which has intrigued the perfumery industry for centuries. The correlation between personality and fragrance was initially a supposition based on observation, but research into the psychophysiological factors involved in this field now supports the truth of the theory. Whatever the scientific explanation, the perfume chosen can highlight the personality of the wearer, and a personalized perfume, made as a unique blend for the person alone, can do this even more perfectly. An English physician of the 19th century stated that, in his opinion, a perfume should correspond to the personality, physical, emotional, and mental characteristics of its wearer, and should be as specific to each woman as the sound of her voice.[9]

PERSONALITY TYPES AND COLOR AND PERFUME PREFERENCE

A specific correlation of different scent types with personality types was made by the scientist and perfume expert R.W. Moncrieff. He noted that extroverts were less finely tuned in their odor preferences than introverts, and that they preferred lighter fragrances while introverts tended to be drawn to heavier, oriental scents.

The researchers Mensing and Beck have developed these notions further, showing a link between color and perfume preferences. They produced a series of eight circles, each with eight different overlapping color segments. The colors within each circle were chosen to match the preferences of the eight most common personality types, as shown below.

Orange/yellow/red/green:
"extroverted mood tendency" – readiness to take risks, sociable, like stimulation. Fragrance has fresh (green) notes.

Purple/violet/white:
"introverted mood tendency" – need inner tranquility, less need for stimulation, individual/alternative lifestyle, younger age group. Fragrance has oriental notes.

Black and white:
"emotionally ambivalent mood tendency" – highly sensitive, moody, romantic, fashion-oriented. Fragrance has floral, powdery notes.

Bright pastels:
"emotionally ambivalent with extroverted mood tendency" – idealistic, cheerful, impulsive, satisfied, and content. Fragrance has floral fruity notes.

Dark violet/warm colors:
"emotionally ambivalent with introverted mood tendency" – materialistic, need security, avoid conflicts, like stability. Fragrance has oriental floral notes.

Dark red/green/orange:
"emotionally stable with extroverted mood tendency" – conservative, socially active, family-oriented, radiate warmth and strength, appreciate quality. Fragrance has chypre (sandalwood) notes.

Bright blue/yellow:
"emotionally stable with introverted mood tendency" – well-mannered, self-controlled, do not overstep others' boundaries. Fragrance has aldehydic (almost overpowering) floral notes.

Brown/green/yellow:
"indefinable" – straightforward, uncomplicated people with very stable moods. These people do not have a typical preferred fragrance.

Formulating an individual blend

A more elaborate version of Mensing and Beck's color chart is still used widely in the perfume industry to create new scents and to help target specific markets. It has also been adapted for psycho-aromatherapeutic purposes, where it can be employed to help aromatherapists select an essence from the range of natural aromatics. An introverted individual, for example, is likely to be attracted to oriental oils and incense materials, such as frankincense, patchouli, sandalwood, or galbanum – while an extroverted type will prefer fresh, fruity oils such as bergamot, lemon, or grapefruit.

When we move into the therapeutic use of essences, there are other factors to be considered apart from the esthetic appeal. While in perfumery the esthetic consideration is paramount, in therapeutic work the efficacy of the remedy is of prime importance. When dealing with the therapeutic application of essences, there are two separate dynamics to consider:

- a fragrance that corresponds to the physical, emotional, and mental characteristics of the wearer
- ingredients that are needed to balance what is absent in the health or personality of the wearer.

The need to choose a fragrance specifically tailored to the requirements of each individual client was the conclusion reached by the aromatherapist Marguerite Maury in her therapeutic work. She found that, of all the aspects of plant oils and their fragrances, "the greatest interest lies in the effect of fragrance on the psychic and mental state of the individual. Powers of perception become clearer and [events] are seen more objectively, and therefore in truer perspective."[10]

In devising her individual prescriptions, Mme. Maury assessed the physical, mental, and emotional disposition of each patient so that the remedy perfectly mirrored the patient. There is, for example, the case of the sad and anxious elderly man suffering from stress and insomnia, with a heart and kidney weakness. The individual mixture for this client was made up from rose, sandalwood, lavender, geranium, and benzoin. Benzoin dispels anxiety and interposes "a padded zone between us and events. Rose and sandalwood oil compensate for renal and cardiac deficiencies; lavender and geranium normalize..."[11]

Since remedies are so allied to the patient's state, blends evolve and change during the course of treatment in a subtle interaction between oils, blender, and patient.

LEFT
Select ingredients to include top, middle and base notes.

MAKING A PERSONAL PERFUME

You will need:

A selection of essential oils with dropper tops
Jojoba oil or fractionated coconut oil *(see p.84)*
A small, clean glass bottle with a tight stopper or lid
A note pad and pen · Blotting paper strips

Before beginning, lay out all the ingredients and materials needed on a clean surface in an odor-free environment. Using the blotting strips to assess the scent is described in detail on *p.49*.

1 Select the oils that you think will be required to constitute the dominant notes in the blend *(see p. 48)*, including base note, middle note, and top note oils. Measure out the base oils in drops into a small glass bottle containing 1 tsp/5ml jojoba or fractionated coconut oil, following your intuition as to proportions. Record the name and exact quantity of each oil used.

2 Shake the bottle and assess the scent with a blotting paper strip. Add the middle note oils, measuring and recording carefully. Shake the bottle again and assess the effect as before.

3 Add the top notes, measuring and recording as before. Shake well and test.

4 Fine-tune, either by adding more drops of some ingredients, or by incorporating a new element. Add these oils a drop at a time, as one drop can radically affect the overall balance. Test the revised mixture on a new blotter strip

5 When satisfied, seal the mixing bottle. Store it in a dark place for several weeks to mature. Check again to ensure the scent is rounded and well balanced.

The art of perfume blending

FAR LEFT
The art of perfumery is as old as civilization.

LEFT
A fine perfume is worthy of a fine container.

Perfumery is both a science and an art – it requires precision and sensitivity, but above all the ability to translate an intangible emotional experience or idea into a tangible composition.

In blending a perfume, the "rules of composition" have to be obeyed, as in music or painting, but the blender's creative skills transcend these rules to produce an indefinable blend that stirs the emotions and echoes a mood. A professional perfumer has to have a thorough knowledge of the properties of a huge range of ingredients, and how they interact, but it is nevertheless possible to make successful perfumes for one's own use, and as gifts for other people, using essential oils.

People generally prefer a many-layered fragrance, since a combination of different aromas tends to be more interesting and intriguing. When natural aromatic oils are combined, the effect is a chemical reaction that breaks up their original molecular structure and they recombine to form entirely new molecules. The final quality of the blend is always an unknown factor. The aim is to make a "bouquet" or a "seamless scent," where the whole adds up to more than just a sum of its parts. The famous French perfumer Pierre Dhumez declared that the ideal perfume consisted of a basic harmonious blend of just three or four dominant "bodies." When combined in "inspired" proportions they form a whole in which it is impossible to distinguish one odor from the other. The scent is a perfectly balanced mixture which smells as a separate entity. This basic harmony, once it has been achieved, is enhanced by the addition of tiny amounts of other fragrances.[14]

In the art of blending, balance is everything. In his book *The Art of Perfumery*, Charles Piesse was the first to draw an analogy between odors and sounds. To create a perfect "bouquet" of odors, he chose scents that combined to create a harmonious chord and added other scents to act as half-notes.

Modern perfumery still uses Piesse's terms to describe the art of blending, although in a simplified form. The perfume should be a perfect balance between the top, middle and base notes. The top notes are immediately apparent – the ones that are light and fresh – and are the most volatile ingredients. Typical top notes include lime, lemon and bergamot. The middle note lies at the heart of the fragrance, and usually forms the bulk of the blend – typical middle notes are florals such as lavender, rose, or geranium. The base note gives depth to the fragrance and acts as a fixative for the more volatile components – typical base notes include oakmoss, benzoin, or patchouli.

Another simple way of blending oils is to put them into families. Fragrances from the same family tend to mix together well, as well as with those from neighboring families. A small proportion of a scent from an opposed or diverse family can add interest or piquancy to an otherwise dull blend.

BELOW
A good perfume has a range of top, middle and base notes.

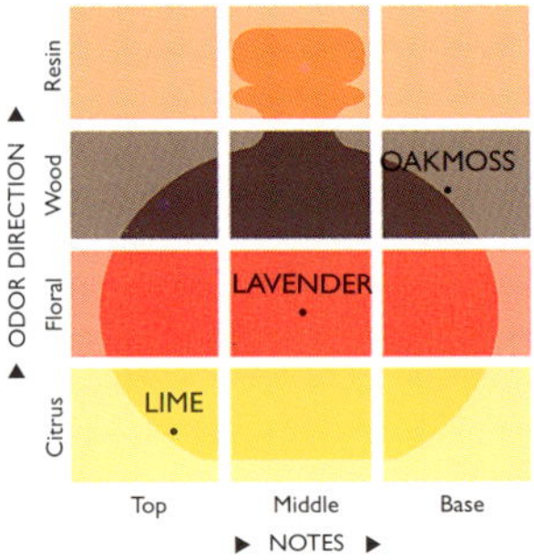

Fragrance families

The birth of modern Western perfumery as we know it today occurred during the 14th century with the discovery of alcoholic extraction techniques. Before that time, perfumes had been based on fatty or oily materials which did not allow the finesse afforded by alcohol or synthetics. Many modern perfumers consider that it is impossible to make a good perfume without the use of synthetics or alcohol. This is because these ingredients can impart lift, radiance, and diffusion to an accord. In their view, only eau-de-Colognes can be made wholly from simple, natural ingredients (known as naturals).

On the other hand, synthetics can have a flat and two-dimensional quality, whereas natural essences are more full-bodied and complex. In addition, many people are sensitive to certain chemicals used in modern perfumes and toiletries, which can cause skin allergies, headaches, or other side effects in sensitive individuals. Some modern perfumes contain well over 100 different ingredients or compounds, but for the purpose of aromatherapy, it is enough to blend as few as three oils to produce an interesting result. This is because pure essential oils, unlike synthetic chemical fragrances used in modern perfumery, already contain many different components, each being made up, in some cases, of hundreds of different constituents, including trace elements. Rose oil, for example, contains over 300 constituents, which is why it is so difficult to imitate it or to construct a "nature identical" rose scent.

To gain familiarity with the different essences and to develop your sense of discrimination, test oils individually. Do not smell essential oils directly from the bottle. Always use a strip of blotting paper. Ideally, dilute the oil to 50 percent, using a bland base. Dip the paper into the essence, then study the odor immediately. After a few minutes smell it again, then periodically over several hours. You will see that the most volatile components will rise quickly up the blotting paper and disperse, while the more viscous elements will remain at the tip. Mark the strip clearly at the other end and record your results on the perfumery dial shown below, starting at the top with the floral notes and then moving round the face. For example, if floral notes are absent, put a dot in the center; if predominant, put a dot in the outer circle. Continue around the circle, trying to detect each note in turn, to complete the profile.

Trying to identify or verbalize a particular scent is difficult, yet odor classification is most important for developing scent discrimination and perfecting the art of blending. In modern perfumery work, this discrimination includes knowledge of all the synthetic fragrances now available. Indol, for example, is a natural component of jasmine absolute, now produced chemically. In concentration, it smells strongly camphoraceous, but in minute proportions it adds sweetness and volume to heavy, floral-based accords. In psycho-aromatherapy, however, the groups of aromas are wholly natural in origin, as in original perfumery classifications.

FRAGRANCE FAMILIES AND THEIR EFFECTS

The following table is based on the Austrian perfumer, Jellinek's concept of relating perfumes to skin and hair type.

Fresh (blond)
Green ❧ Reviving (e.g. thyme)
Herbaceous ❧ Stimulating (e.g. basil)
Medicinal ❧ Clearing (e.g. eucalyptus)

Soothing (brunette)
Spicy ❧ Warming (e.g. nutmeg)
Woody ❧ Appeasing (e.g. sandalwood)
Earthy ❧ Grounding (e.g. vetivert)

Sultry (black)
Musky ❧ Aphrodisiac (e.g. patchouli)
Oriental ❧ Comforting (e.g. benzoin)
Honey ❧ Heady (e.g. ylang ylang)

Exalting (red)
Floral ❧ Uplifting (e.g. geranium)
Fruity ❧ Enlivening (e.g. petitgrain)
Citrus ❧ Refreshing (e.g. lemon)

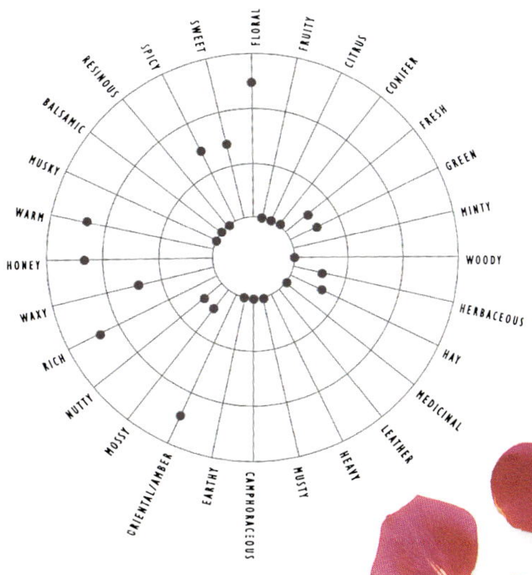

RIGHT
Many essential oils are a complex blend of fragrances in their own right. Using this perfumery dial helps in analyzing the individual elements and building up a fragrance profile for a particular oil. The dial is shown marked up for rose oil.

FUJI RVP

PART TWO

Aromatherapy massage

Massage is one of the most fundamental forms of therapy, and has been utilized by many diverse cultures for thousands of years. The need to be touched is itself an essential and primitive human instinct, for without physical contact, the overall health of the individual suffers. Recent research has shown that a lack of tactile contact is associated with immune depression, and positive touch with immune stimulation.

Over the course of time, many different massage techniques have been developed, each having its own individual therapeutic approach. The oriental art of shiatsu massage, for example, works primarily with specific pressure points along the lines of the meridians or channels of energy in the body, to influence the overall balance of energy within the body, much like acupuncture. In contrast, the Western style of Swedish massage concentrates more on releasing areas of tension trapped within the muscles, joints, and connective tissues of the body. Even performing the same stroke in different ways can produce different effects. A single movement performed vigorously can stimulate the body, while a similar movement performed slowly can promote relaxation.

Massage not only improves circulation and relaxes muscles, but also has psychological benefits, making the recipient feel comforted and cared for, and produces a unique sense of well-being.[12] However, when the general benefits of massage are combined with the effect of specific essential oils being rubbed into the skin, the healing dynamics already at work can take on a completely new dimension.

The actual techniques of aromatherapy massage are adapted mainly from the Swedish massage style, combined with a more individualistic approach to body work, adopted from the intuitive massage style initiated in the early 1960s. The theory behind the preparation of the essential oils themselves is based largely on the ideas of the French dermatologist, Marguerite Maury. Her concept of the individual prescription is still utilized by most professional aromatherapists working today, and they always prepare an individually chosen blend of essential oils for each client and for each massage session, depending on the needs of the client on each separate occasion.

There are three distinct but overlapping aspects of an aromatherapy massage treatment and this form of therapy can therefore be seen as being beneficial in three quite distinct but interrelated ways:

> "The way to health is to have an aromatic bath and scented massage every day."
>
> HIPPOCRATES

* the massage itself and its effects on the body
* the interraction between therapist and recipient
* the effect of the essential oils.

Each aspect supports the others in such a way as to provide a multidimensional therapeutic action. During a treatment, the essential oils themselves also interact with the body in two ways:

* through inhalation (primarily psychological effects)
* through absorption into the bloodstream via the skin (primarily physiological effects).

BELOW
Essential oils increase the benefits of massage.

Touch and smell: a healing synergy

The synergy of essential oils and massage has been shown to be a very effective combination in the treatment of stress-related disorders, due to the powerful interaction of touch and smell. During the course of a massage, a certain amount of the essential oils will be absorbed through the skin and into the bloodstream to affect the nervous system, as well as other parts of the body directly, by toning, sedating, or stimulating. When this is backed up by a comforting and supportive relationship between patient and therapist, it can provide a vital key to breaking the stress cycle of anxiety, insomnia, and nervous fatigue which underlies so many common physical complaints.

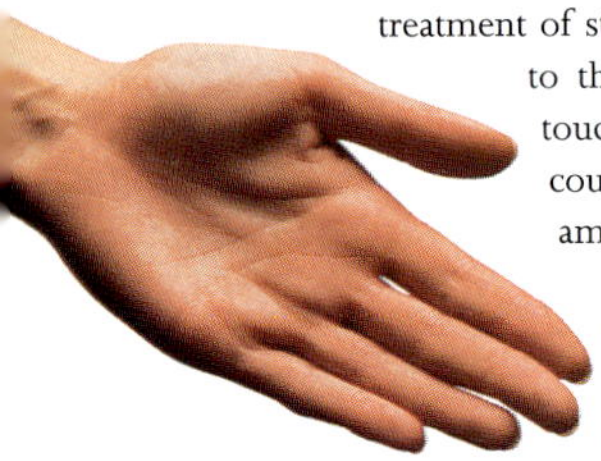

ABOVE
Oils and massage work hand in hand.

There is increasing evidence to show that stress affects not just the mind, but also the nervous, immune, and endocrine systems, and that it constitutes a factor in physical, as well as mental health.[13]

It is not surprising that stress-related problems are an area in which aromatherapy massage enjoys a great deal of success, because it simultaneously operates on both a physical and psychological level. An aromatic massage, for example, is especially valuable for those who suffer from a number of different responses to stress at the same time. Stress-related illness often presents a wide range of contradictory symptoms. Aromatherapy, rather than dealing separately with individual symptoms such as high blood pressure, indigestion, and back pain, deals with the stress itself. In the words of Dr. Ann Coxon:

"Obviously, the approach of holistic treatment is to help enable people to manage their primary life situation, and the ability of aromatherapy to get at the knot, at the stress reaction itself within the body without using yet more pharmacological treatment is terribly important."[14]

Evidence of the widespread sense of "disease" experienced today in the West is shown in the high consumption of tranquilizers and stimulants, although it is well known that addiction, toxicosis and other side effects can be caused by these products if taken regularly. Any treatment that can help to revitalize and de-stress the organism, without producing detrimental side effects, is therefore of great value. Essential oils, used in the appropriate doses, are safe and harmless, and it is widely agreed that, while they can be highly effective, they "do not cause troubles like those produced by the ordinary psychological drugs."[15]

LEFT
Aromatherapy may be an alternative to pills.

ESSENTIAL OILS TO RELIEVE STRESS

There are many essential oils that are particularly suited to the treatment of stress-related conditions, both on a physical and psychological level. Lavender is possibly the most useful oil employed in this context, because of its regulating effect on the nervous functions, and due to its versatile nature. Other oils which are especially valuable for stress-relief include chamomile, rose, jasmine, neroli, bergamot, geranium, frankincense, and ylang ylang.

JASMINE

CHAMOMILE

LAVENDER

Massage techniques

The following massage techniques should be carried out with a steady, repetitive, rhythm. Throughout the massage, try to link the different techniques together into a seamless sequence. If possible, keep at least one hand in contact with the person being massaged at all times, even when moving from one part of the body to another. Before working on the deeper muscles, it is important to warm and relax the superficial ones. While working on a specific part of the body, therefore, the techniques progress from gentle stroking movements to more active rubbing or kneading movements, and eventually to vigorous percussion-type strokes. In general, the more slowly a stroke is performed, the more relaxing it will be. Conversely, the more briskly and rapidly a movement is performed, the more stimulating its effects will be.

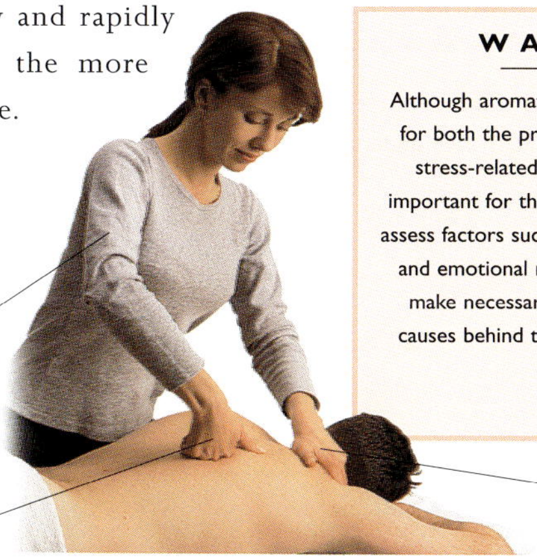

RIGHT
A relaxing massage is ideal treatment for the body and mind.

Use your whole body to massage the person

A steady, repetitive rhythm helps the recipient to feel at ease

Keep at least one hand in contact with the recipient's body at all times

WARNING

Although aromatherapy massage is effective for both the prevention and treatment of stress-related disorders, it is also very important for the individual to be helped to assess factors such as lifestyle, work patterns, and emotional relationships, and to try to make necessary changes to combat the causes behind the stress reaction directly.

SOURCES OF BASE OILS USED IN MASSAGE

Essential oils used in massage are nearly always diluted in a base or carrier oil. Use good quality, preferably cold-pressed oils, as they are absorbed more effectively into the skin. Some good carrier oils for general use include sweet almond, sunflower, grapeseed, and coconut oil (see *pp. 84–85* for further details on base oils).

Effleurage~stroking movements

This is the basic stroking movement, and the first technique to be used on any part of the body. Using slow and gentle strokes to cover the surface of the skin ensures that the aromatic oils will be readily absorbed. Effleurage promotes relaxation and draws blood to the area, improving both the assimilation of nutrients and the flow of lymphatic fluids, and aiding the elimination of toxins. It is a soothing and comforting type of movement that can also be used to link other techniques throughout the course of the massage.

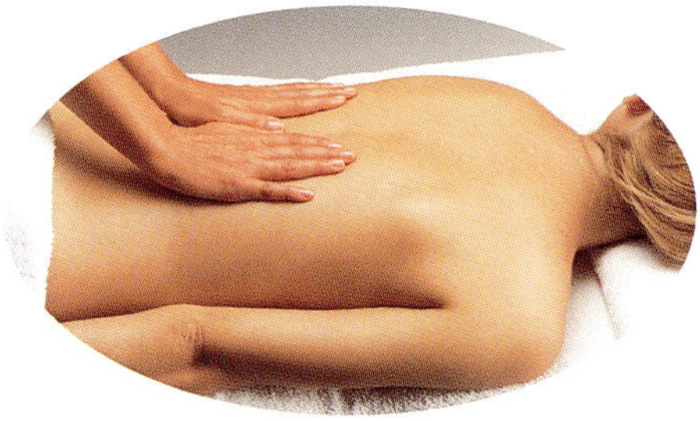

STEP 1

STROKING

Using the whole flat area of both palms (not just the fingertips), gently lay your hands side by side on the skin (step 1). Slide your hands together rhythmically along the skin, to cover a large or small area (step 2). At the end of each stroke always return to your starting position by skimming lightly over the surface (step 3). This movement is best employed on the back.

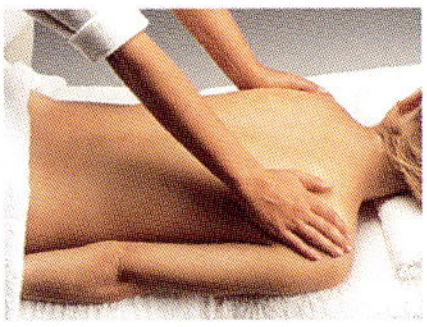

STEP 2

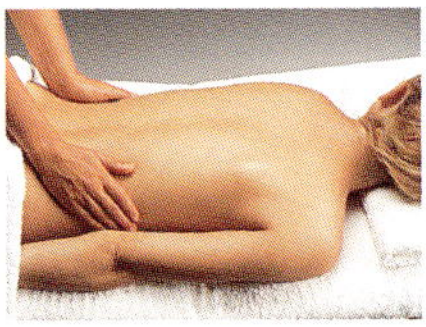

STEP 3

GLIDING

This is a variation of the basic stroking movement, performed with the hands gliding together, side by side and pointing in opposite directions, as shown in steps 1 and 2. The hands may also be placed one on top of the other when extra pressure is needed. As with stroking movements, at the end of each stroke you should always return to your starting position by skimming lightly back over the surface of the skin (as shown in step 3). This movement is a particularly useful stroke for massaging the recipient's arms and legs.

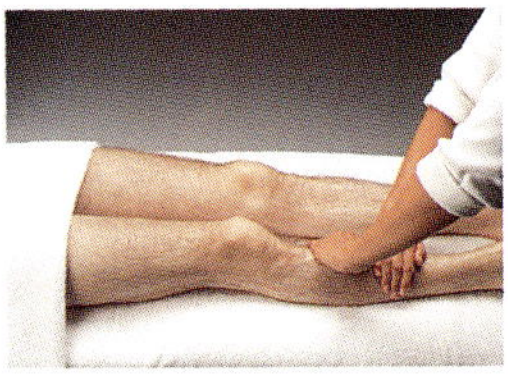

STEP 1

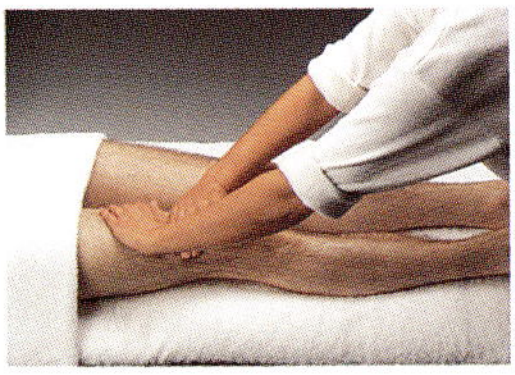

STEP 2

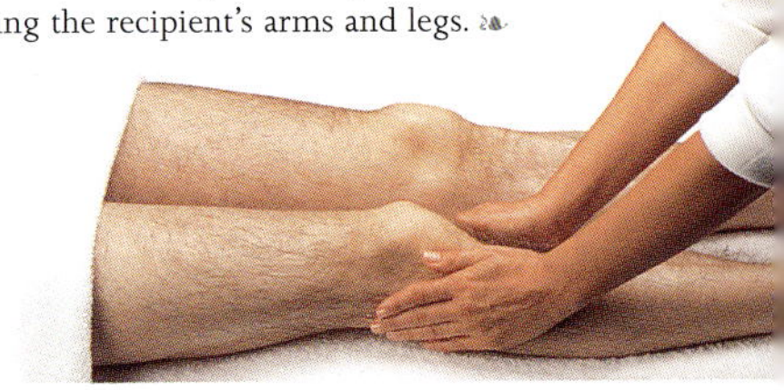

STEP 3

PULLING

Like stroking, this is a firm, but gentle, rhythmic movement, but here the emphasis is on pulling rather than pushing. Using alternate hands, methodically work your way along a specific area and back again, with a slight lifting and pulling stroke. This is especially useful for the sides of the torso or the limbs.

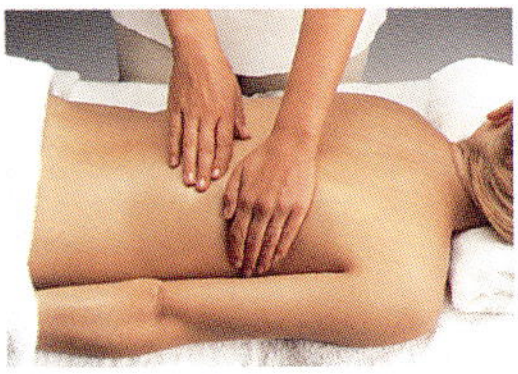

STEP 1

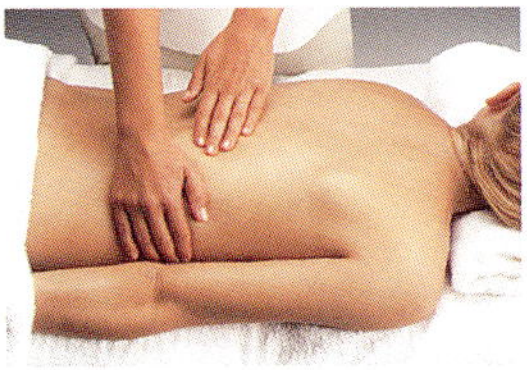

STEP 2

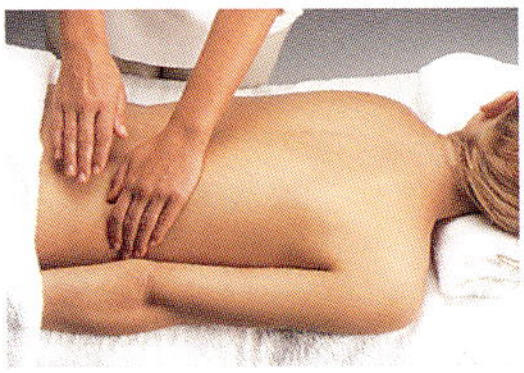

STEP 3

Petrissage~kneading movements

These techniques involve picking up and slightly squeezing or twisting the muscles and are used on all muscular and fatty regions of the body. Using the whole hand, or just the fingertips, the muscle is first squeezed and then released in a rhythmic fashion. As it is released, the muscle relaxes. The overall effect is to pump the vessels of the muscles, so that circulation is improved and lymphatic activity increased. It is an effective technique for easing muscular tension and bringing warmth to an area. Always relax a muscle with effleurage (step 1) before attempting petrissage.

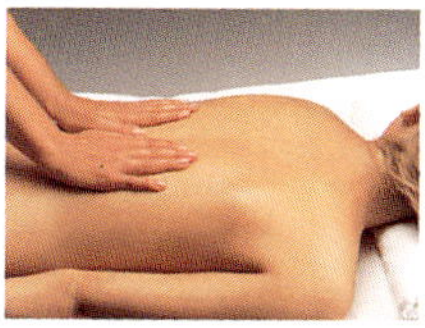

STEP 1

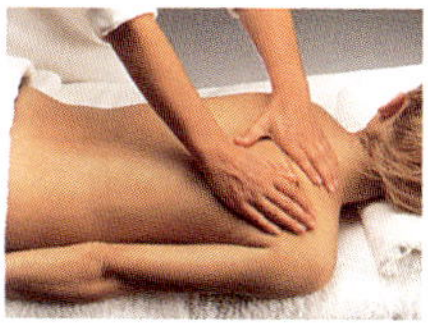

STEP 2

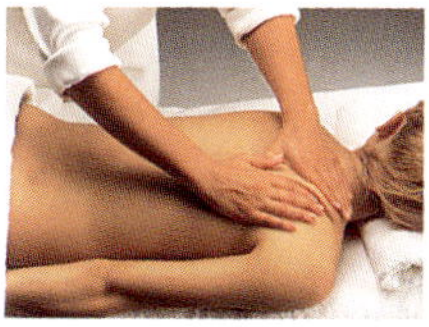

STEP 3

KNEADING

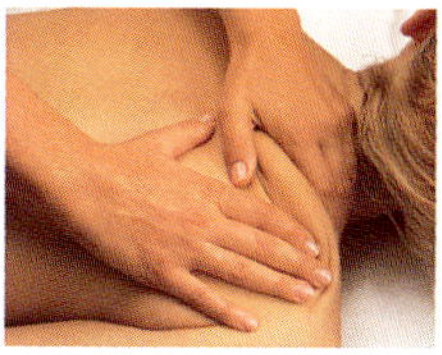

KNEADING TECHNIQUE

The hands are placed on either side of a muscle, with the palms slightly facing each other. The movement is an alternate downward pressure, then a picking up, rolling and squeezing of the muscle. The basic kneading technique is a bit like kneading dough (*see* illustration above). It is applied on muscular areas, such as the shoulders, back, and limbs. Picking up, which involves lifting up the muscle and stretching it as far as possible from the bone, and rolling, which involves lifting up a section of muscle and rolling it transversely in both directions, can also be practiced as individual movements.

WRINGING

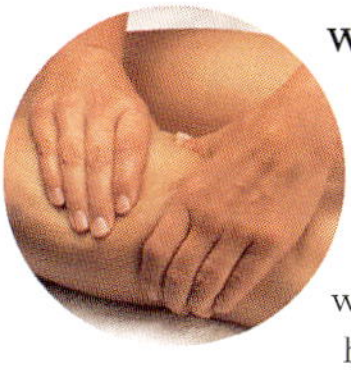

WRINGING TECHNIQUE

Like kneading, this movement involves squeezing the muscles and the soft underlying tissue adhesions connected to the muscle, in this case with an additional twist. Place the hands side by side on a limb (step 1), and grasping firmly with the fingers, start to work the hands in opposite directions as if wringing out a cloth (step 2). Work your way up the limb and down again methodically, squeezing the flesh between the hands a little at each stroke (step 3). This technique is extremely warming and stimulating, but it is only applicable to the limbs.

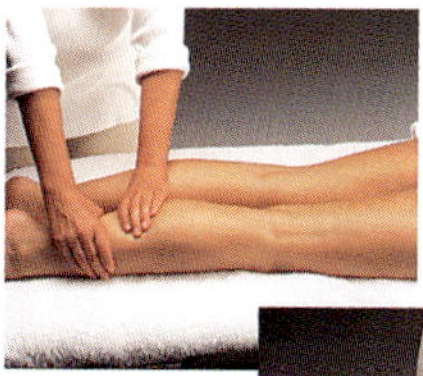

STEP 1

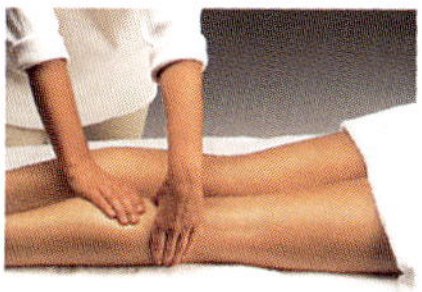

STEP 2

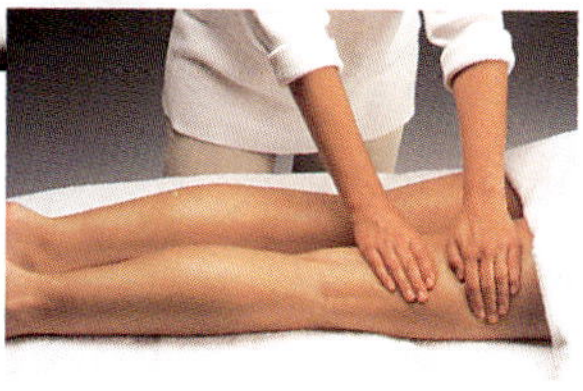

STEP 3

SQUEEZING

Grasping a portion of flesh, squeezing, and then releasing, is a simple technique which can be applied either to large muscular or fatty areas, or to a small area such as the ear lobes or the pads between the fingers or toes. In the former case, all the fingers and both thumbs are used to exert firm pressure; in the latter, simply the forefinger and thumb are employed (as illustrated).

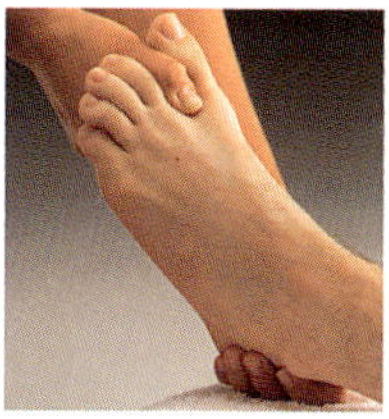

STEP 1

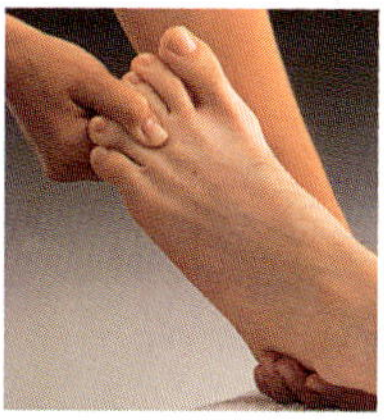

STEP 2

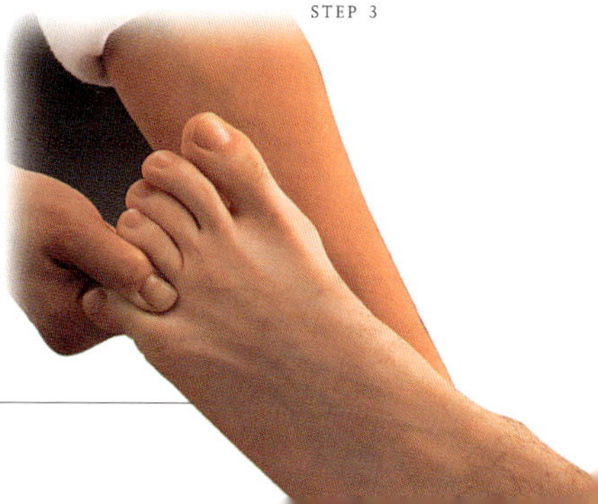

STEP 3

Friction ~ rubbing movements

Friction techniques are carried out using the palms or heels of the hands, the finger pads, the ball of the thumb, the knuckles of a loosely clenched fist, or even the elbow. The movement is usually made in small circles, often stretching the tissue and muscles away from the bone. It helps to increase blood and lymphatic flow, and to break down congestion in the tissues and toxic deposits. Friction can be used to penetrate deeply into the tissues but do not tackle tight or knotted areas without adequate preparation through effleurage and petrissage, or the body will resist and tighten further.

RUBBING

Rubbing is the lightest form of friction, using the fingers, palm, or heel of the hand in firm, brisk circular movements. Some pressure is involved, but it is not specifically localized as is the case with circling and pressing. To exert greater pressure, place one hand over the other (step 3). This movement is stimulating yet comforting, bringing a warm glow to the whole area. It is usually used on the back.

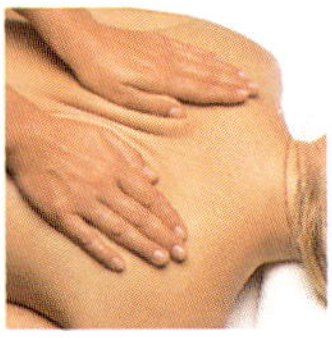

FRICTION TECHNIQUE

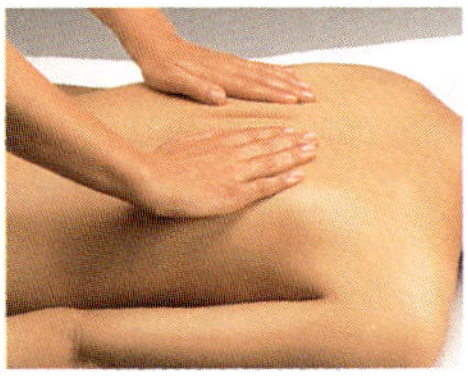

STEP 1

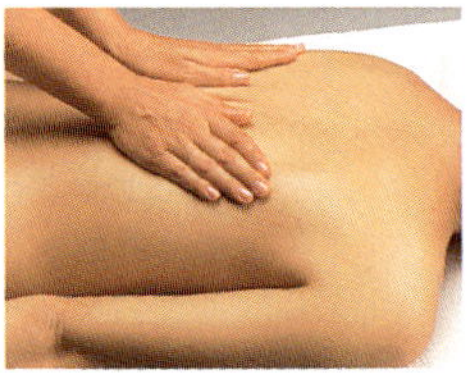

STEP 2

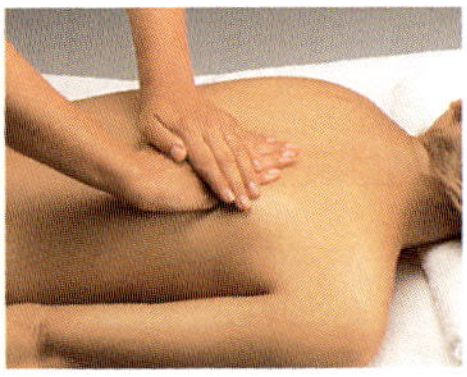

STEP 3

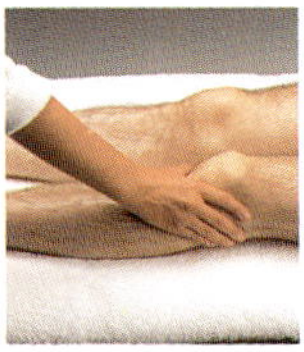

STEP 1

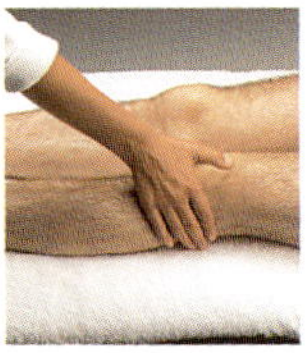

STEP 2

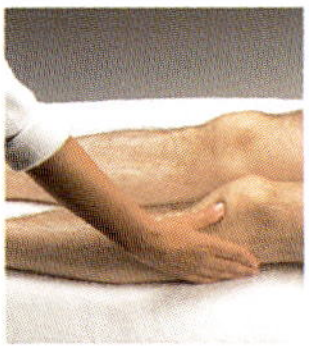

STEP 3

CIRCLING

Circling is a deeper technique, done with the ball of the thumb, finger pads, or knuckles, in small, circular movements. It works on especially tight areas, and helps eliminate uric acid deposits and other toxins. It can be used around the knee or elbow joint, down each side of the spine, or indeed on any area demanding attention, such as the soles of the feet or the palms of the hands.

PRESSING

Pressing is a very penetrating technique, which is employed to its greatest effect in shiatsu or pressure point massage. By pressing or stimulating certain points on the skin, it is possible to influence the health of the internal organs and the flow of energy along the meridians of the body. Similar principles also apply in reflexology. To use the pressing technique with confidence, it is necessary to know the main pressure points of the body, how to locate them, and what they may be used for (*see* shiatsu chart, p. 59, and reflexology chart, p. 59). The point between the eyebrows (step 3) is good for relieving headaches and sinus congestion. Pressing can be carried out with the thumb, the forefingers, or sometimes the elbow.

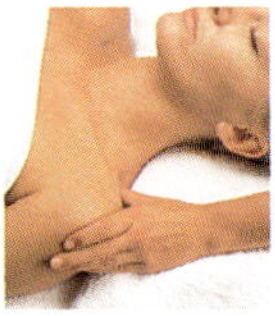

PRESSING TECHNIQUE

WARNING
Pressure should not be applied directly to any area causing pain, and should penetrate only as deeply as the body is willing to receive it.

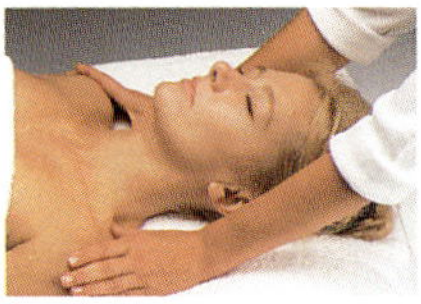

STEP 1

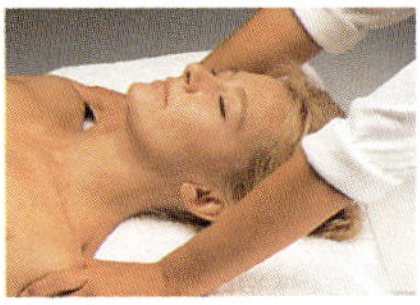

STEP 2

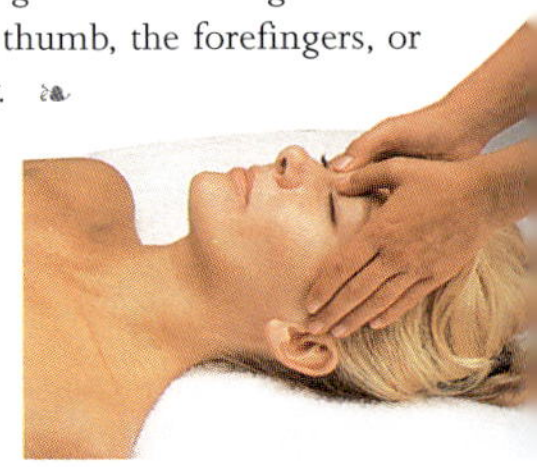

STEP 3

Tapotement ~ percussion-like movements

These are all vigorous, brisk movements, which can be incorporated into an aromatherapy massage to give the sequence a more stimulating and toning effect. Tapotement consists of a series of light blows made in quick succession, with the movement springing from loosely held wrists. It is a good movement for breaking down fat, eliminating toxins, toning the muscles, and generally stimulating the circulation.

PUMMELING

Using loose fists, and keeping the wrists close together, gently pummel the skin with the padded side of the fists. This technique can be used on fleshy parts of the body (as illustrated) and also over muscular areas, such as the shoulders.

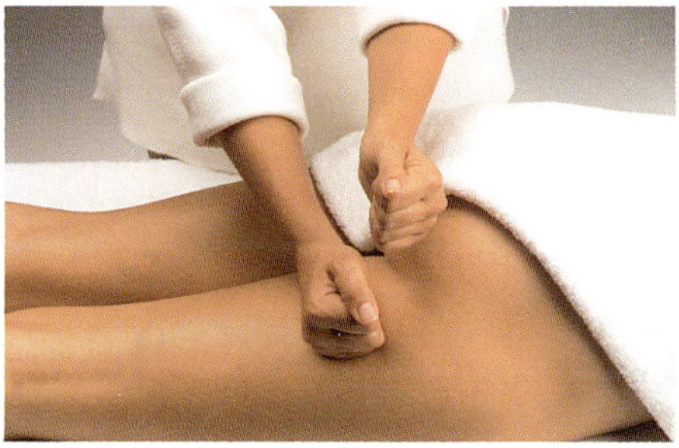

STEP 1

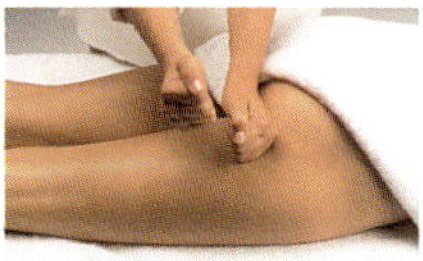

STEP 2

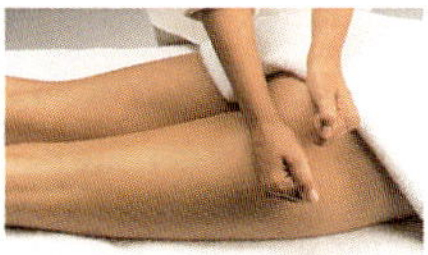

STEP 3

HACKING

This is performed with the outer sides of the hands, keeping the wrists close together. Use brisk alternate chopping strokes with the hands, but do not let them rise too high above the body. This movement feels very good when it is carried out on fleshy parts of the body, such as the buttocks.

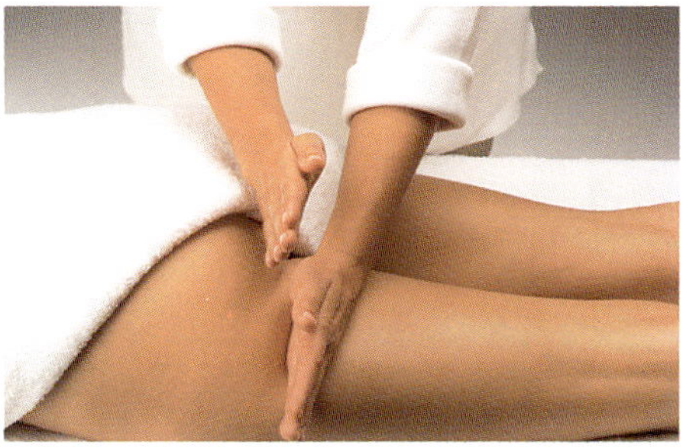

STEP 1

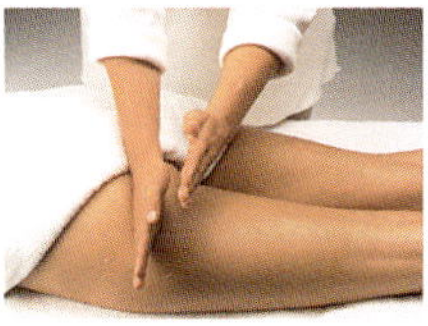

STEP 2

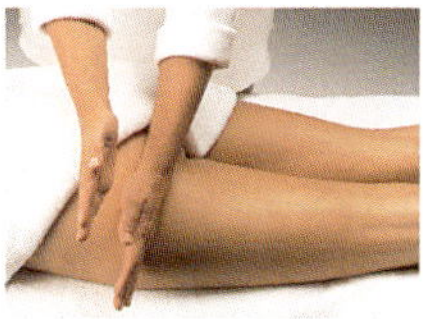

STEP 3

WARNING
Tapotement should never be used on paralysed muscles, on pregnant women, or on delicate areas of the body, such as the neck or abdomen.

WARNING
Hacking should never be performed on or over bones.

CUPPING

This movement should be performed with the fingers slightly extended and the palms cupped to form a hollow. It should not sound like a slap. Cupping is a very effective technique for use on the areas of the thighs and buttocks, but it can also be used on the upper back, where it offers surface and capillary stimulation. It is generally used on fleshy areas. Cupping is a bouncy, brisk massage movement.

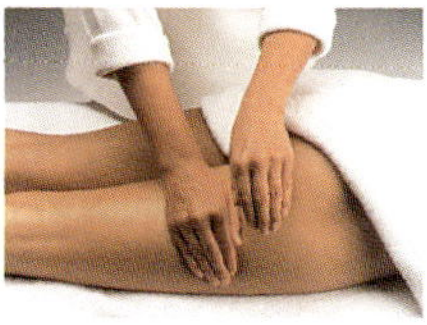

STEP 1

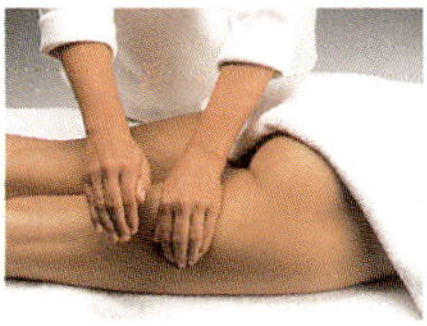

STEP 2

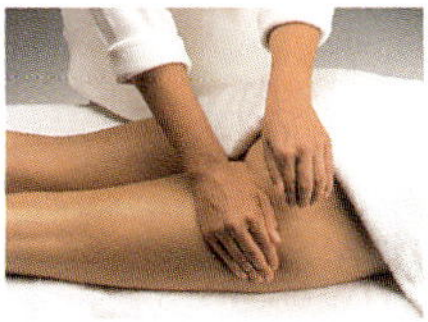

STEP 3

Other useful techniques

Although these additional techniques are not specific to aromatherapy massage, they can all be useful movements to incorporate into a full aromatherapy body massage when required for particular problems. ❧

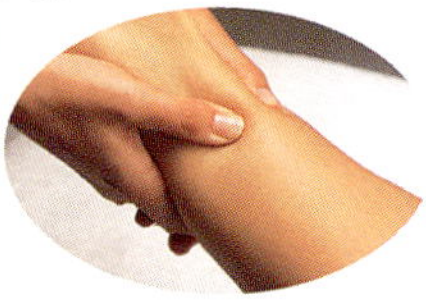

DRAINAGE TECHNIQUE

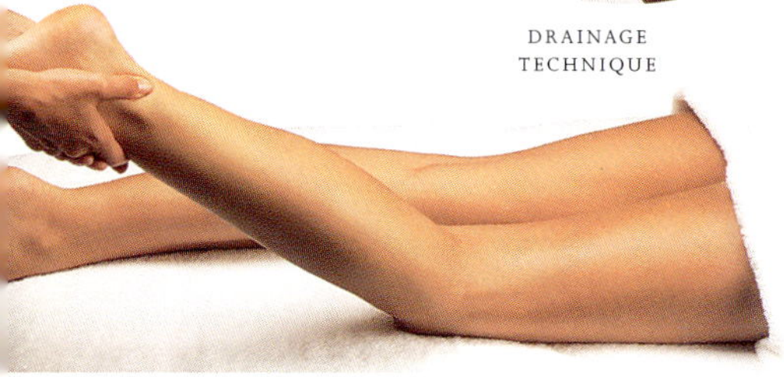

STEP 1

DRAINING

This technique is used specifically when performing a manual lymphatic drainage massage (MLD). Draining improves the circulation of lymphatic fluids, aiding the elimination of toxins via some of the main lymph nodes of the body, especially those on each side of the groin and beneath the armpits (others are in the neck). The direction of the stroke is always toward these nodes, using a firm sliding pressure. Making a V-shape between the fingers and thumbs (steps 1 and 2) is a good way of draining the limbs. ❧

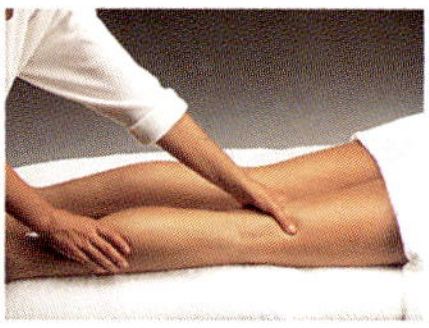

STEP 2

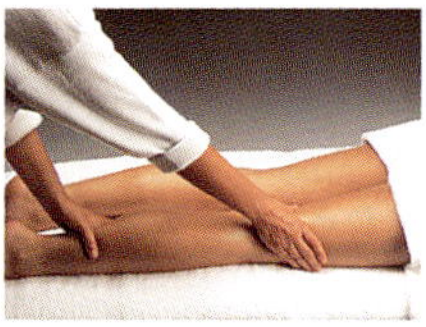

STEP 3

STRETCHING

Like pressing (p. 56), stretching has more in common with shiatsu than with the usual aromatherapy massage routine. However, it is a useful technique for easing muscular tension – especially beneficial as part of an aromatic sports massage or as a pre-exercise warm-up. Stretches should always be gentle and firm, with a brief pause at the end – never jerky. Always ask permission and check for contraindications such as a stiff neck or slipped disk, which require gentle treatment only, before performing any stretch. ❧

WARNING
Check with your medical practitioner before undergoing drainage massage if you suffer from a serious illness or inflamed lymph glands, or if receiving medication.

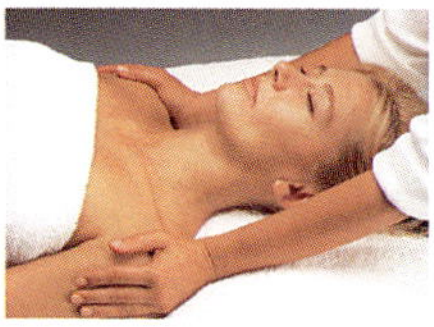

STEP 1

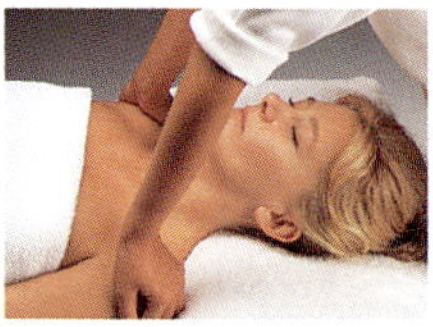

STEP 2

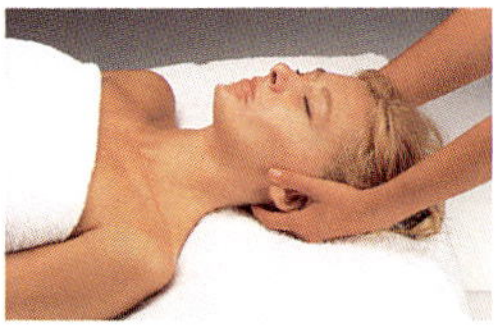

STEP 3

FEATHERING

This term refers to touching the skin very lightly and gently – or even moving the hands just above the surface of the skin in a stroking fashion. Feathering may be performed either at the beginning, or, more commonly, right at the end of a whole sequence or series of strokes, to give a feeling of completion. Used right at the end of the massage sequence, feathering allows the contact between the masseur and the recipient to be gradually diminished, and ensures that the massage does not end too abruptly. It can also be employed (as shown, left) as a kind of "auric" massage to cleanse the subtle envelope surrounding the body, and remove any residues of tension from the recipient on this level. ❧

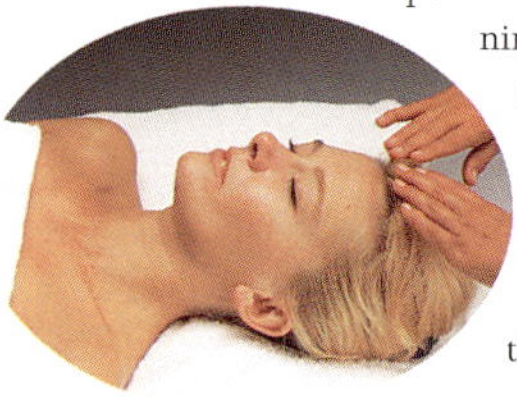

STEP 1

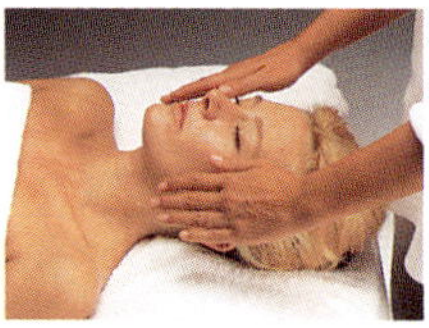

STEP 2

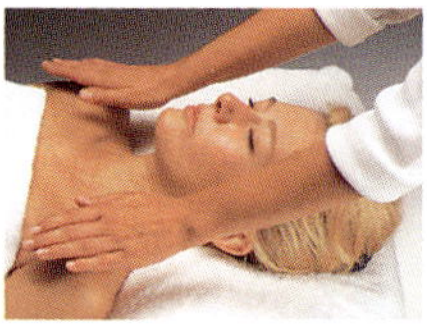

STEP 3

REFLEXOLOGY POINTS

Reflexology is a specialized form of massage based on the theory that the body is divided into zones that run the length of the body. The soles of the feet reflect these zones and can enable the experienced reflexologist to detect "imbalances" in the body. The application of pressure on the correct "reflex points" can help to correct these.

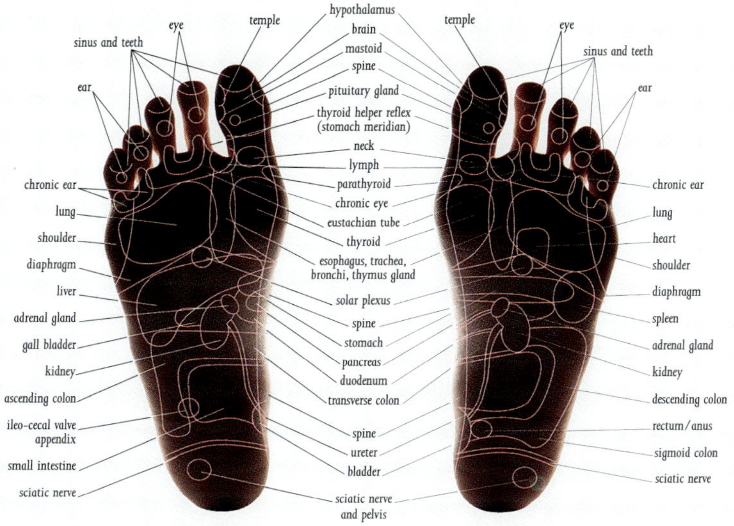

SHIATSU POINTS AND MERIDIANS

The Japanese massage technique of shiatsu or "finger pressure" is based on the same principles as acupuncture. Combining acupressure, massage, elements of physiotherapy, and osteopathy, it aims to restore a balanced flow of energy within the meridians, enhancing well-being and vitality, through the application of pressure on specific points along the meridians.

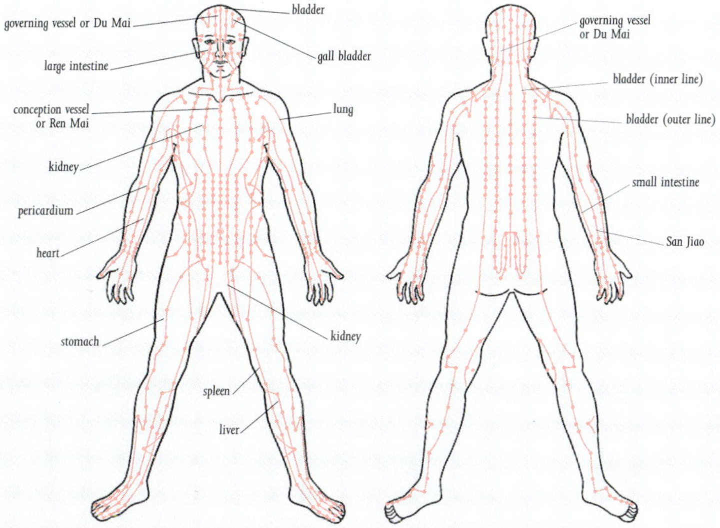

Giving a massage

Before giving a massage, it is important to ensure that both you and the recipient are comfortable with the atmosphere in which it is to take place. Massage is best undertaken in a quiet room, and the only language needed is the language of touch.

Massage should be a nonverbal type of therapy. Silence and touch are two of the most important elements or principles at work during a massage and become a language of their own. In general, keep words to a minimum during a massage, and if you need to speak, do so in a quiet tone. If the recipient wants to speak, remain receptive and responsive to what he or she has to say without engaging in or encouraging conversation.

During the course of the massage, it is not unusual for the recipient to experience a release of emotion, such as laughing or crying. Again do not block or suppress this expression, but just let it come and go naturally without passing judgment.

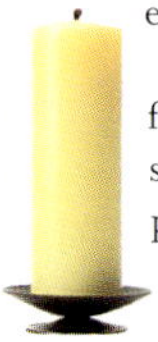

LIGHTED CANDLE

BENEFITS OF MASSAGE

- Provides a soothing and comforting alternative to verbal therapeutic techniques, such as counseling.
- Eases muscular aches and pains and promotes muscle relaxation and tone.
- Improves the circulation and lymphatic drainage, and helps to eliminate toxins from the body.
- Lowers blood pressure, reduces stress levels, and will help combat insomnia.
- Generates confidence and a feeling of well-being by releasing endorphins, the brain's natural opiates.
- Stimulates the immune system and strengthens resistance to disease.
- Aids digestion, eases constipation, and relieves abdominal spasm.
- Imparts a warmth and glow to the skin, and is revitalizing and rejuvenating to the whole body.
- Can alleviate tension headaches, and help the recipient to deal with difficult emotions, such as anxiety, depression, grief, or a sense of being unloved.

MASSAGE CONTRAINDICATIONS

Do not massage in the following cases or conditions:

- If you are feeling unwell or drained of energy.
- Immediately after a meal.
- In cases of infectious disease and/or if you have, or the recipient has, a high temperature.
- In cases of serious injury such as torn ligaments or broken bones.
- If it causes pain.
- Over any areas of skin infection, rashes, cuts, sores, burns, or varicose veins.
- Over a recent wound or an operation site that is forming scar tissue.
- In cases of acute inflammatory conditions, such as sprains, and some forms of arthritis/rheumatism.
- If the recipient has, or has had, thrombosis.
- If the recipient has cancer: give hand, foot, or facial treatments only.
- If the recipient has, or has had, a serious heart condition or any other serious medical condition.
- During the week following a vaccination.

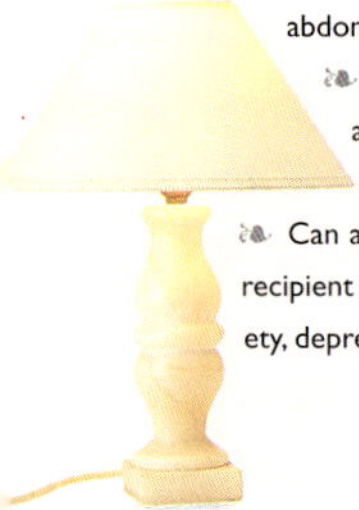

SOFT LIGHTING

ESSENTIAL OILS

MASSAGE COUCH

POTTED PLANT

LEFT AND ABOVE
Organize the environment to make the massage a pleasant and relaxing experience and keep towels and oils within easy reach.

THE ENVIRONMENT

The easiest place to do a massage is on a massage table or a massage couch. This needs to be adjusted to the right height so that you can get enough leverage for deeper tissue work but do not need to stoop, or bend your back too much. Alternatively, a futon or a piece of foam padding 1–2 inches (2.5–5cm) thick, placed on the floor, also works well. This can be covered with a clean cotton sheet and/or a towel. The most important thing is to feel comfortable while you are performing the massage and to be able to move freely around the person, and to change your position with ease. Make sure you are not strained or uncomfortable during the massage

The room in which you give the massage (or the environment) should be warm enough – a person with massage oil on their skin becomes easily chilled. Always cover areas of the body which are not being worked on with a towel. The place should be secluded and quiet enough for there to be a minimum of disturbance – interruptions or loud noises can be disconcerting. Quiet background music is optional depending on the situation and preferences of the recipient. Do not use direct overhead lighting: the light source should be as natural as possible and slightly dimmed.

* Ask the recipient to remove jewelry or contact lenses.
* While you withdraw, ask the recipient to take off all his or her clothing apart from underpants and to wrap him or herself in a large towel. (If he or she feels uncomfortable about removing items of clothing, adapt your routine to suit these particular requirements.)
* Ask the recipient to lie down comfortably, face down, arms by his or her sides, on the couch or futon.
* Adjust one towel to cover the recipient's back and buttocks, and cover the legs and feet with another large towel.
* Ask the recipient to relax and let the body go as limp as possible, and to let you move or lift his or her limbs as required.
* Ask if he or she needs a pillow for support, and for him or her to move the head from one side to another if the neck is getting stiff – unless the massage table has a special "face hole."
* Quietly take a few deep breaths to center yourself, and to tune in to the needs of the person you are about to massage.

LEFT
Allow plenty of time for the massage.

BEFORE BEGINNING

Before beginning a massage, it is important to ask the recipient about his or her personal health record and check for any contraindications, such as a skin infection, inflammation, or illness (*see Contraindications panel, p.* 60). For a guide to preparing massage oils, *see p.* 21, and for base oils for blending, *see pp.* 84–5.

Allow at least an hour for a full-body massage, and plan to give extra time for a prior consultation.

* Check your nails are short enough beforehand.
* Wash your hands and remove any rings.
* If you have long hair, make sure that it is tied back.
* Wear loose clothes, and check that your clothing will not impede the massage.
* Prepare the massage oil in a bowl, and keep it warm and accessible.

WARNING

For people with high blood pressure or epilepsy, or who are pregnant, or receiving medication or medical treatment, or if you intend to massage a baby or young child, see Safety Data, *p. 211*.

BELOW
Make sure your nails are kept well trimmed.

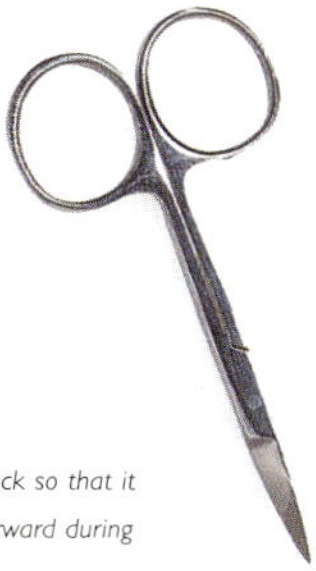

LEFT
Tie long hair back so that it does not fall forward during the massage.

The complete massage sequence

Having ensured that the environment is suitable and that there are no specific contraindications, you can start the full-body massage sequence. First of all, check that the recipient of the massage is lying comfortably, positioned face down, and that he or she is warmly covered with one or two towels. The arms should be lying alongside the body and the head resting to one side – a cushion may be required. Before beginning the massage or removing any portion of the covering, gently lay both your hands on the recipient's back, one at the base and one at the top of the spine. Breathe deeply a few times while allowing your hands to remain in place. This helps to attune the recipient of the massage to your touch.

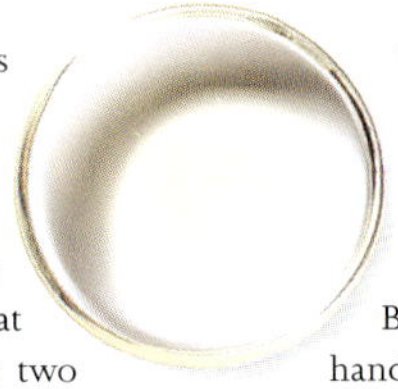

MASSAGE OIL

The back

MASSAGING THE BACK

Gently peel back the towel to expose the whole of the recipient's back. Make sure that your hands are warm by rubbing them briskly together if necessary, before pouring a little of the prepared massage oil into the palm of just one hand.

A full back massage does much to alleviate the effects of stress felt throughout the whole body, and brings relief to aching and knotted muscles.

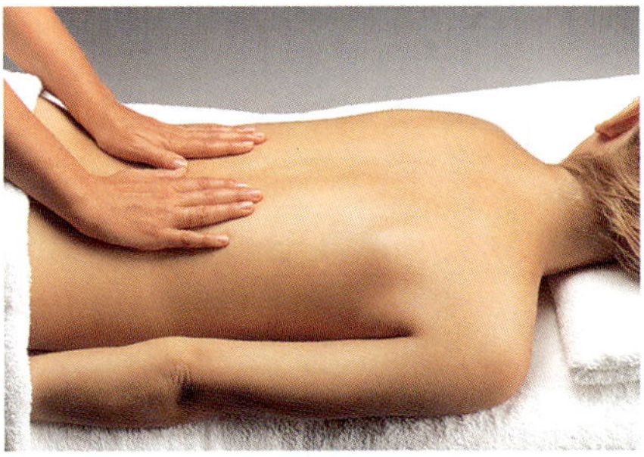

1 **Stroking:** *Rub your hands together, then place both hands at the base of the recipient's spine, with your fingers pointing toward his or her head. Slowly slide your hands up the back, one on each side of the spine, until you reach the neck. Fan your hands out over the shoulders and slide them down the sides of the torso and back into the starting position. Repeat several times, using smooth, rhythmic strokes so that the whole of the back is coated with a thin layer of oil.*

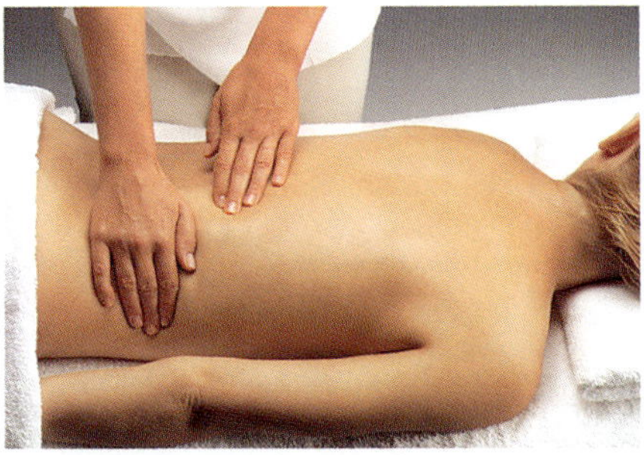

2 **Pulling:** *Without losing contact with the recipient's skin, move both your hands to one side of his or her torso, just above the hips. Then, using alternate hands with a firm and rhythmic pulling motion, work your way slowly up the side of the body to beneath the arm and back down again. Repeat a few times before performing the same movement on the other side.*

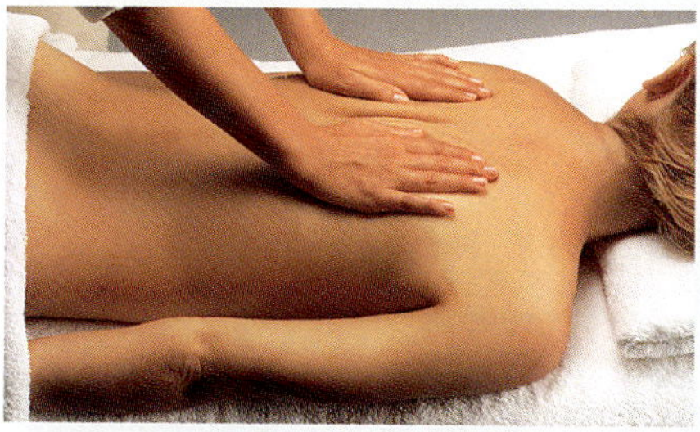

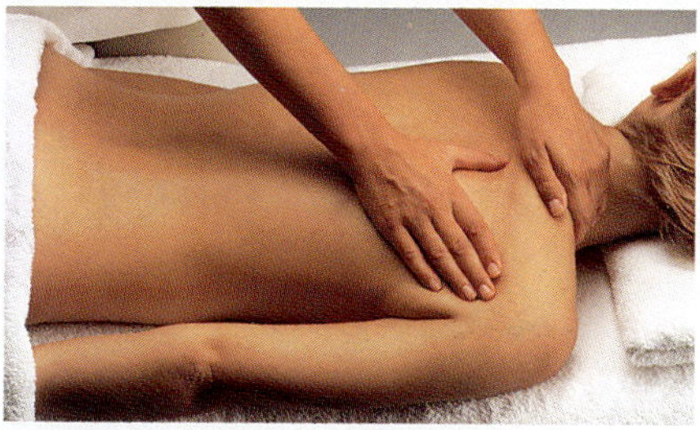

3 **Rubbing:** *Before working on the back's muscular areas with deeper pressure, loosen the whole area around the neck and shoulders with a brisk, circular rubbing movement, using the flat of your hands. One hand can be placed on top of the other to make the movement more vigorous and bring greater warmth.*

4 **Kneading:** *Using a firm but gentle kneading movement, gradually start to work your way around all the fleshy, muscular parts of the back, paying particular attention to any possible areas of tension around the neck, shoulders, and upper buttocks.*

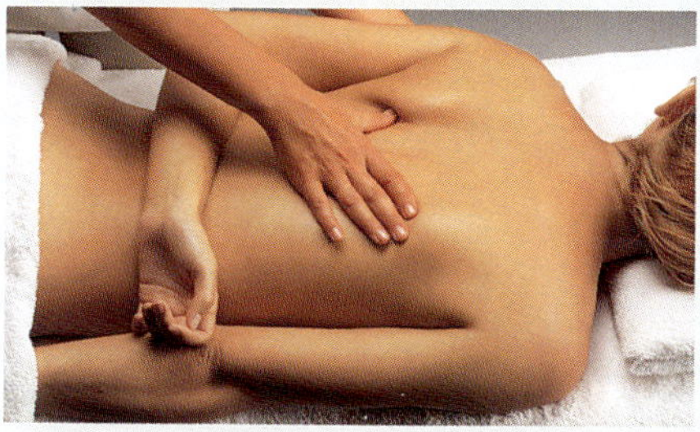

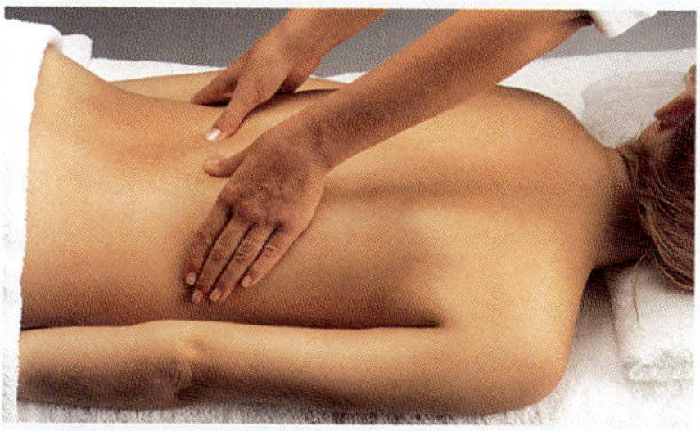

5 **Circling:** *Having released some of the muscular tension in the back, it is now possible to work more deeply on any particularly tight or knotted areas, using small, circular movements with the thumbs or fingertips. It may be helpful to lift the recipient's arm across his/her back (as illustrated) in order to penetrate more deeply into the area beneath the shoulder blades. Support the shoulder with one hand, and lift it slightly while working with the other hand. Then repeat on the other side.*

6 **Pressing:** *Positioning yourself at the recipient's head, run your thumbs firmly down the channels on either side of the spine with a smooth, slow, pressing movement. Glide the hands up each side of the torso and repeat this movement several times.*

7 **Stroking / Feathering:** *To complete the sequence use slow, stroking movements over the entire area. Standing at the recipient's head, start with your hands at the top of the back, fanning the hands out over the buttocks and up the sides of the torso. Gradually make the strokes slower and lighter, until your hands barely touch the skin. Cover the back with a towel before moving on to the legs.*

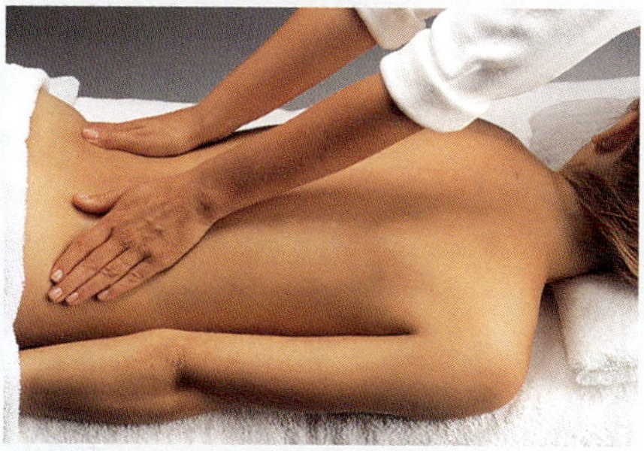

The legs (back)

MASSAGING THE BACK OF THE LEGS

Peel back the towel to expose one or both legs, depending on the warmth in the room. Apply more oil to your hands if necessary.

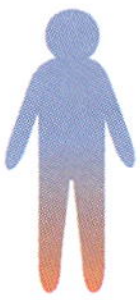

A good massage on the back of the legs can stimulate the lymphatic system and improve circulation.

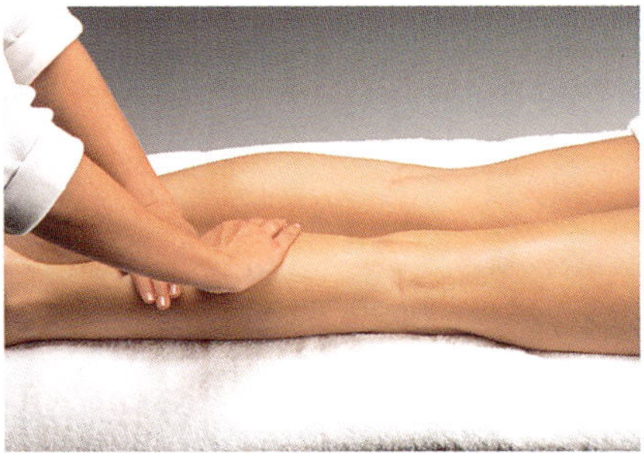

1 ***Gliding:*** *Place the hands, one above the other, on the ankle of the recipient. Slowly glide your hands together to the top of the leg, then run them down each side of the limb until they are back to their original position. Repeat several times, ensuring that the whole of the back of the leg is oiled.*

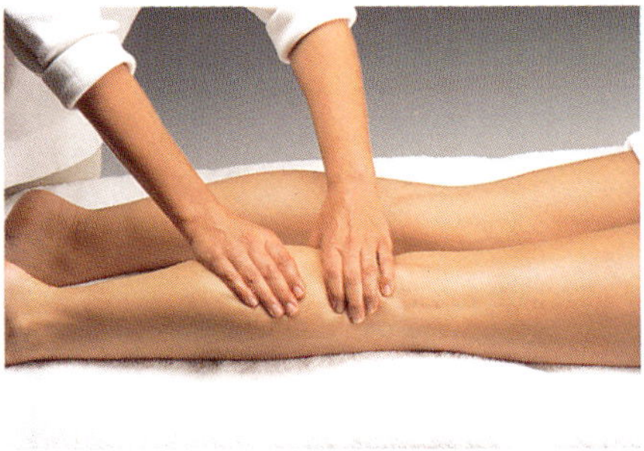

2 ***Wringing:*** *Start with the hands next to each other, grasping the ankle lightly. Then using a firm wringing movement, start to work your way rhythmically up the leg and down again, squeezing the flesh between your hands with each change of position. Avoid the delicate area behind the knee, focusing rather on the muscles of the calf and upper thigh.*

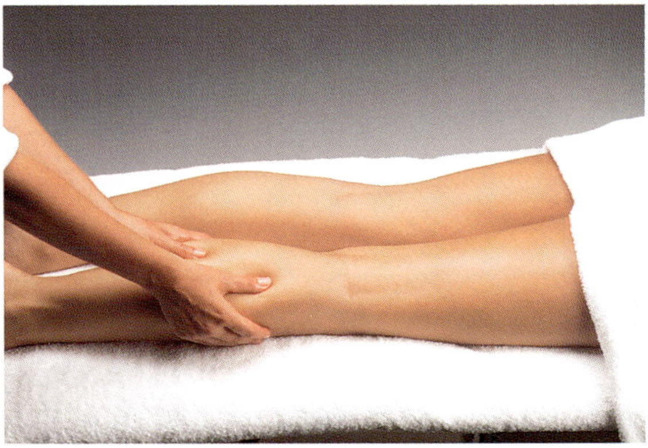

3 ***Kneading:*** *Knead the calf muscles and then the thigh and buttocks, with rhythmic strokes. Pay special attention to any especially tight or knotted areas, and again avoid the delicate area at the back of the knee.*

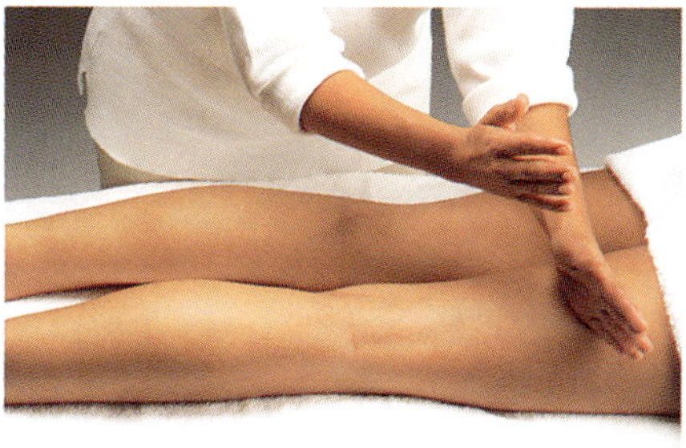

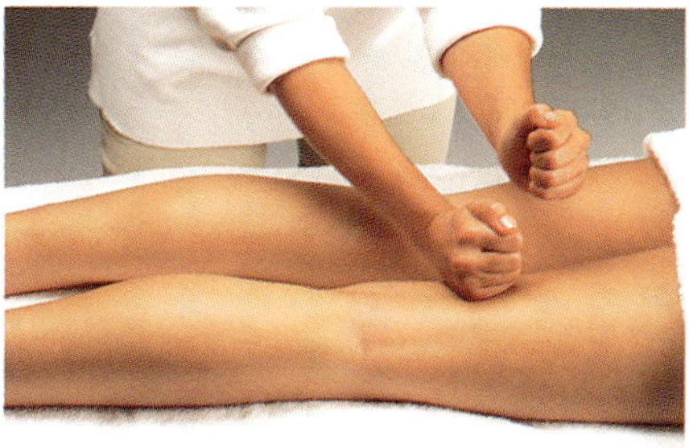

4 ***Hacking:*** *Use a rhythmic hacking motion on the fleshy parts of the upper thigh and buttocks – and, more gently, on the calf if it is sufficiently developed. This movement, like the following one, is quite a vigorous technique which may not apply if you are performing a very soothing or relaxing type of massage. It is, however, extremely beneficial for releasing deep-seated muscular tension, and helping to break down fatty deposits.*

5 ***Pummeling:*** *To further stimulate the circulation and release tension in the fleshy area of the thighs and buttocks, use a rhythmic pummeling motion with gently clenched fists. (Cupping, using lightly cupped hands, is also best employed in this area.)*

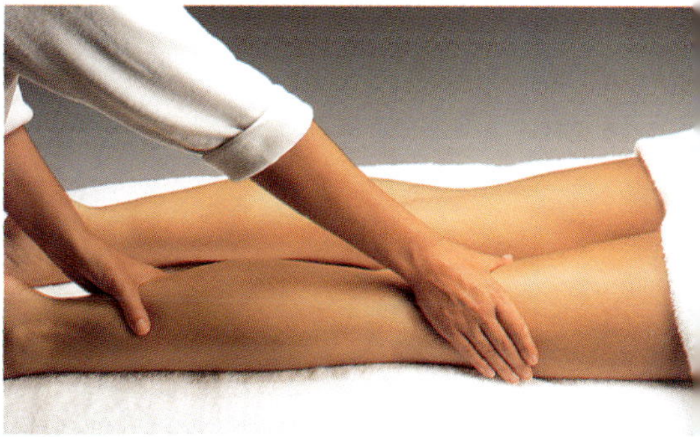

6 ***Draining:*** *To encourage lymphatic drainage, make a V-shape between the thumb and forefinger of each hand and lay one hand above the other on the recipient's ankle. Using the V-shape to press in an upward motion, start to run your hands alternately up the back of the leg in a firm, rhythmic movement. Continue up to the thigh, then lift and replace each hand in turn at the ankle, before repeating.*

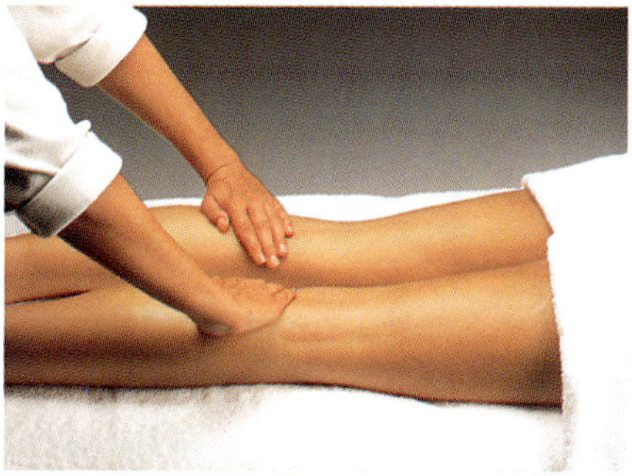

7 ***Gliding:*** *Finish the sequence of movements on the leg by repeating the initial gliding movement, allowing the strokes to get gradually lighter. Cover the leg with a towel and go on to the other leg. Finally, when both legs have been massaged, you may place one hand on each leg and glide them up both legs together, before covering the legs with a towel.*

To proceed to the front of the legs, quietly ask the recipient to turn over, help him or her to reposition the towels, and ensure that he or she is comfortable.

The legs (front)

MASSAGING THE FRONT OF THE LEGS

Carefully remove the towelling from one or both legs. Make sure your hands are sufficiently oiled before laying them gently, one above the other, on the ankle of the recipient.

Tired and heavy legs can be helped with a variety of massage techniques, to give the recipient a feeling of renewed energy and lightness.

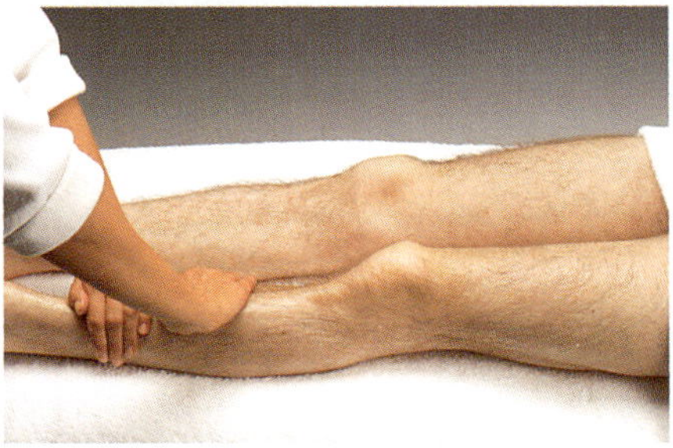

1 ***Gliding:*** *Slowly glide both hands together up towards the thigh, then down each side of the leg and back into the starting position. Repeat several times.*

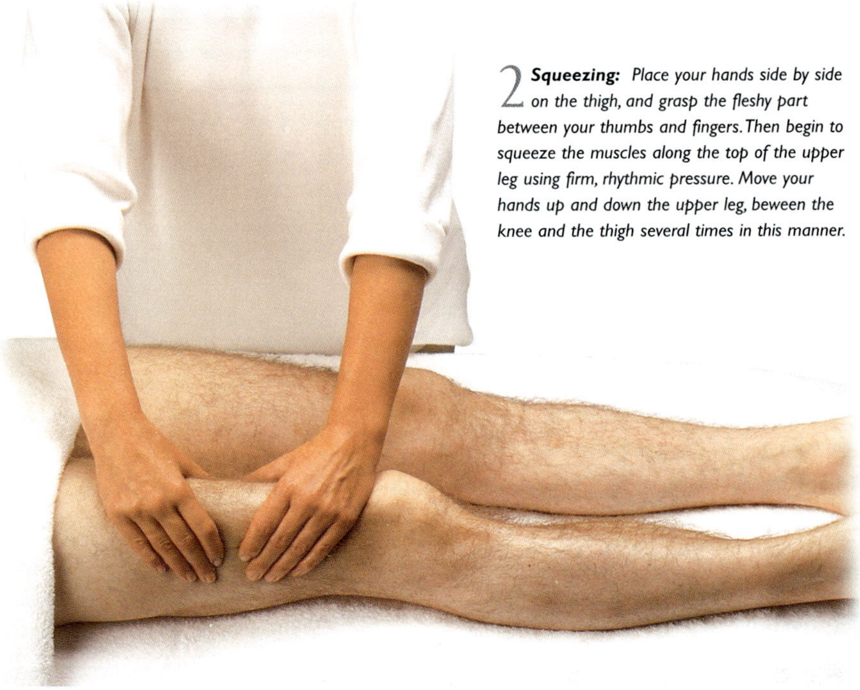

2 ***Squeezing:*** *Place your hands side by side on the thigh, and grasp the fleshy part between your thumbs and fingers. Then begin to squeeze the muscles along the top of the upper leg using firm, rhythmic pressure. Move your hands up and down the upper leg, beween the knee and the thigh several times in this manner.*

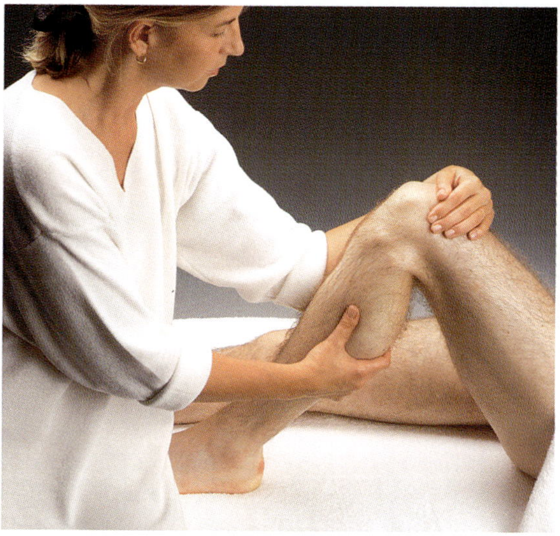

3 Kneading: *Having warmed up the muscles, start to work more deeply into any areas of tension in the upper leg and thigh using a rhythmic kneading movement. In order to knead the calf muscles with greater ease, raise the recipient's knee and use your body to prevent the foot from slipping forward. Support the recipient's raised knee with one hand while using your other hand to work on the muscles of the calf. Gently lower the raised leg.*

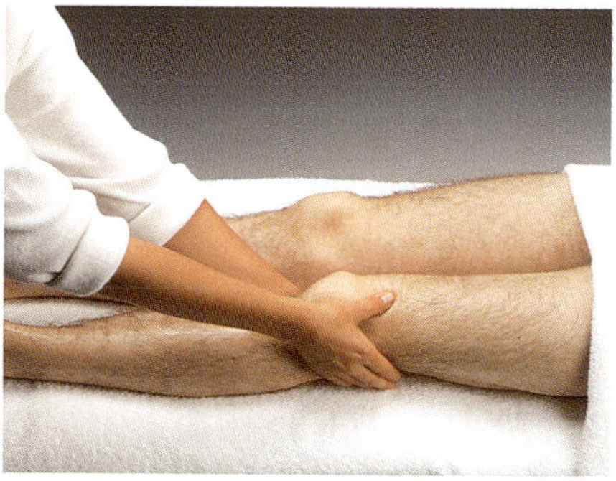

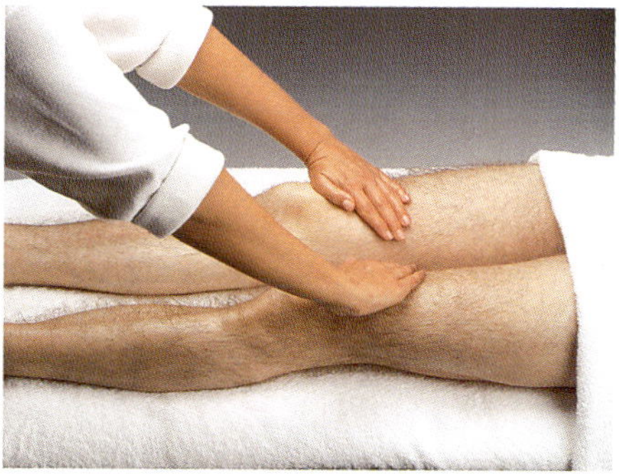

4 Circling: *Starting with your thumbs beneath the recipient's kneecap, circle the thumbs in alternate directions around the knee until they cross above the kneecap. Then circle them back again and repeat. Now begin to work all around the knee and upper leg with small circular movements of the thumb or fingertips. Avoid pressing on the shinbone while working at all times, as this can be painful.*

5 Gliding: *Return to the initial gliding movement (or insert a draining movement here) to complete the leg massage. Cover the leg with the towel and repeat the sequence on the other leg. Having completed both legs, you may place one hand on each ankle and glide the hands up both legs together as shown, allowing the strokes to become slower and lighter. At the end of these movements, cover both legs with a towel.*

The feet

MASSAGING THE FEET

There are thousands of nerve endings in the foot, and a relaxing massage to the feet will help alleviate nervous tension and restore vitality.

Uncover one, or both feet. Check that your hands are only lightly oiled, and that you are comfortably positioned.

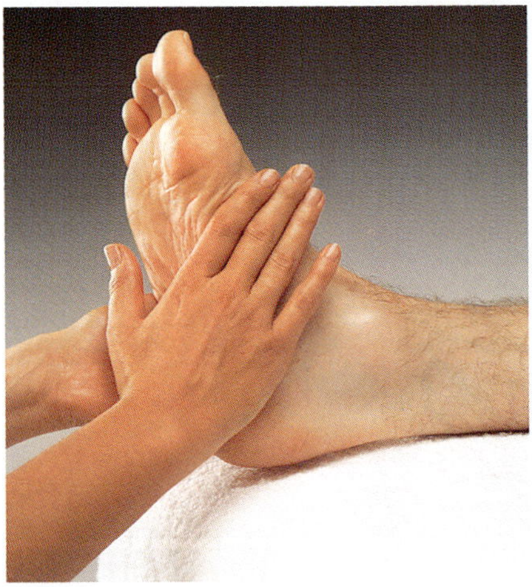

1 ***Stroking:*** *Using both hands, gently stroke the recipient's foot, from the toes toward the ankles. Repeat several times in a rhythmic manner.*

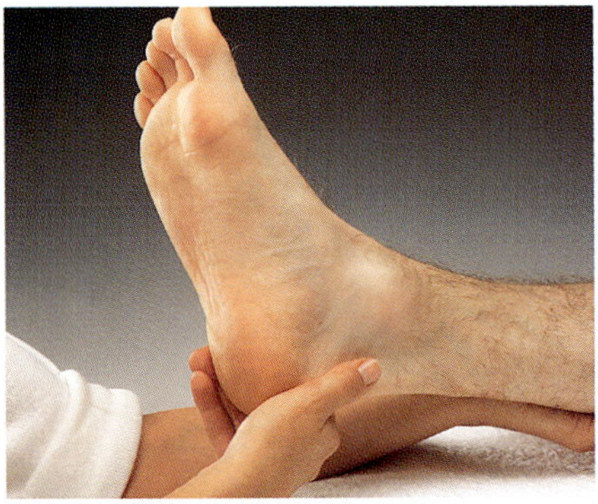

2 ***Rubbing:*** *Carefully supporting the foot with one hand, gently cup the fingers of your other hand around the heel of the foot. Using a firm, circular rubbing movement, massage the whole of this area. This position can also be used to flex and loosen the ankle.*

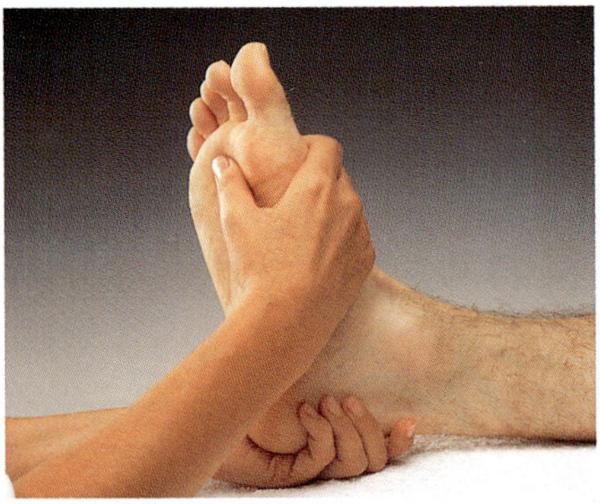

3 ***Circling:*** *While continuing to support the foot firmly with one hand, use the thumb (or knuckles) of your other hand to make small circular movements all over the sole of the foot. Be aware of the sensitivity of this area, and the fact that some spots may be particularly tender or congested. (A reflexology chart may be used to identify the significance of these different areas, see p. 59.)*

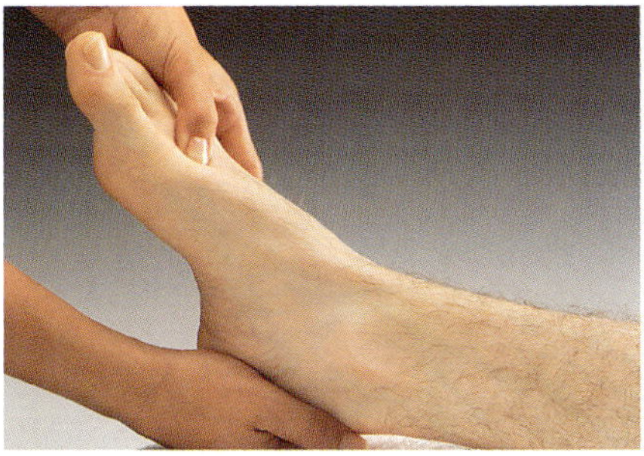

4 ***Pressing:*** *Having covered the entire sole, continue to support the foot with one hand while working on the top of the foot with your other hand. Using the thumb or fingertips, press gently but firmly down the channels running between the bones of the foot. Starting with the channel between the big toe and the next toe, slowly work your way down each channel at a time, until you reach the little toe.*

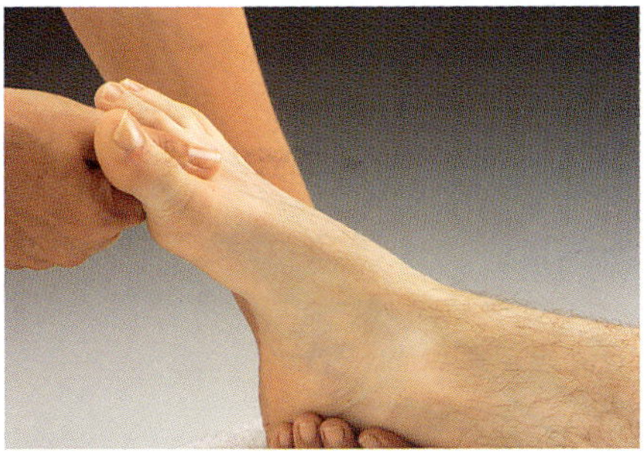

5 ***Squeezing:*** *Still supporting the foot, grasp the fleshy pads between the big toe and the next toe, using the thumb and forefinger of one hand. Squeeze gently, then slowly pull your hand away. Repeat between each of the toes in turn.*

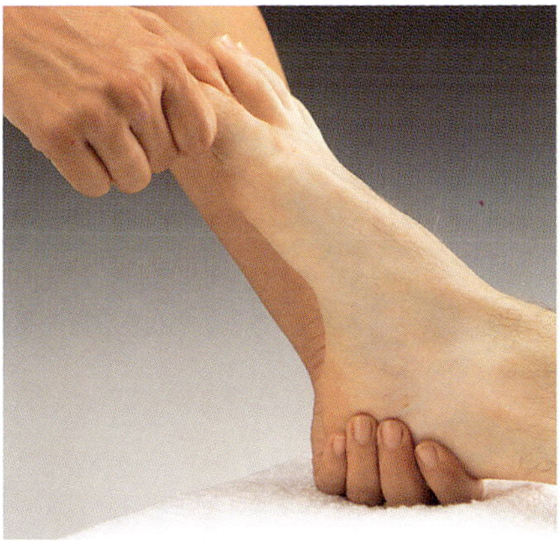

6 ***Stretching:*** *While still supporting the foot with one hand, grasp the sides of the big toe between the thumb and forefinger of your other hand. Squeeze and pull the toe, with a stretching movement, until your fingers slide off at the end. Repeat with each of the toes in turn.*

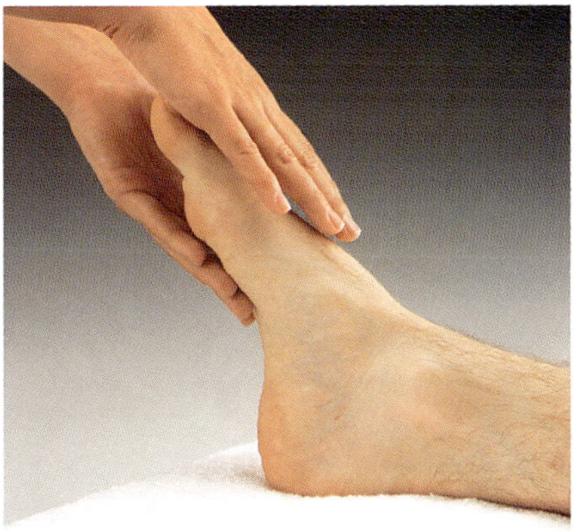

7 ***Stroking/Feathering:*** *Complete the sequence on the foot by stroking it all over, moving the hands rhythmically from the heel toward the toes. Finally, using a light feathering movement, stroke the foot in the direction of the toes, until your hands are hardly touching the skin. Cover the foot with a towel before repeating the sequence on the other foot. You may finish by stroking/feathering both feet together, before covering them both.*

The hands and arms

MASSAGING THE HANDS AND ARMS

Uncover one arm from beneath the towelling. Check that your hands are sufficiently oiled, then place them, one above the other, on the wrist of the recipient.

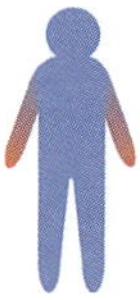

Tension often creeps into the hands and arms; massaging them helps release pent-up anxieties and promotes a sense of well-being.

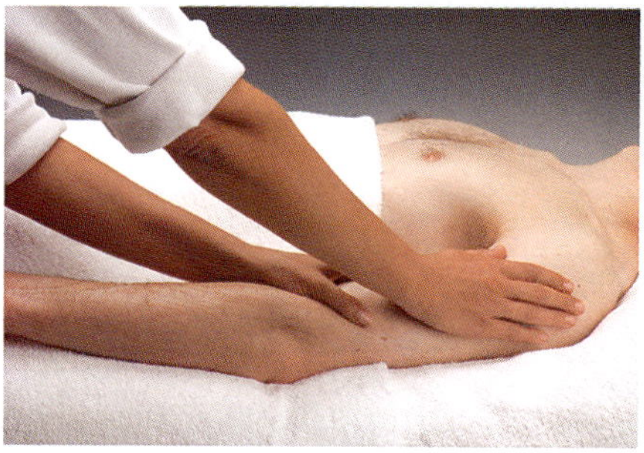

1 ***Gliding:*** *Keeping the hands together, glide them firmly up the arm to the shoulder, returning down the sides of the arm and back to the wrist. Repeat this movement several times.*

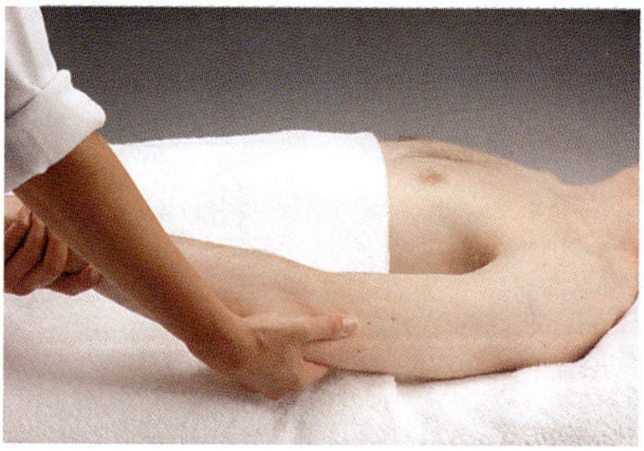

2 ***Rubbing:*** *Supporting and lifting the arm a little with one of your hands, use the fingers of the other hand to cup the elbow. Rub the area gently, using slow circular movements. Replace the arm gently beside the body.*

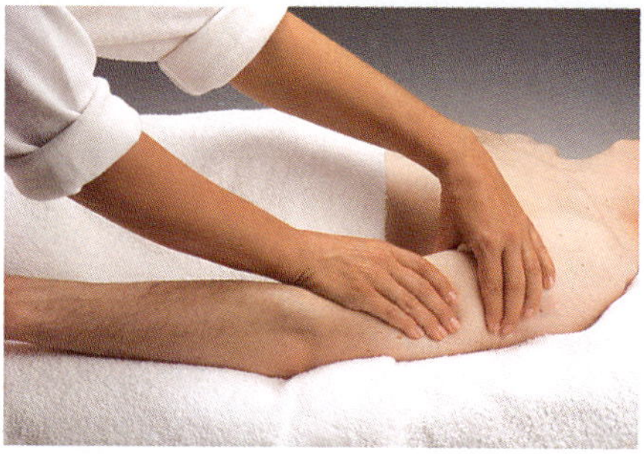

3 ***Kneading:*** *Using both hands together, start to knead the muscles of the forearm and upper arm in a rhythmic motion. Pay special attention to any tight or knotted areas, before moving on to the hand.*

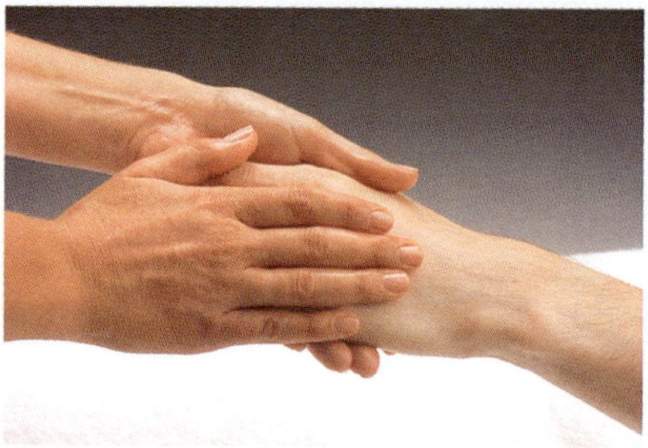

4 ***Stroking:*** *Check that your hands are lightly oiled before beginning on the hands – although the hands (like the feet) require very little oil for general massage purposes. Using both hands, cover the entire surface of the recipient's hand with smooth stroking movements.*

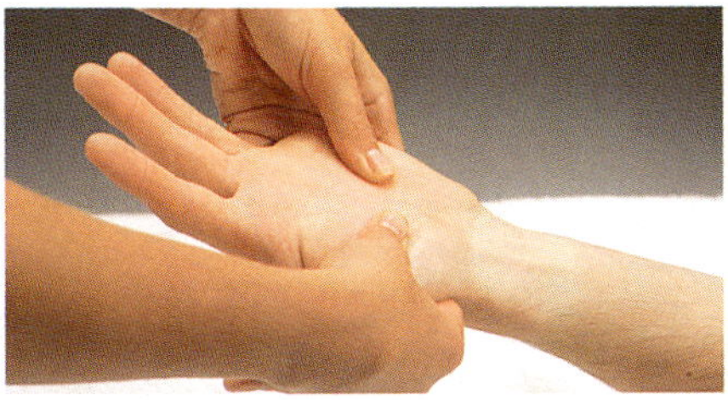

5 **Circling:** *With the recipient's palm facing upward, use small, gentle circular movements with your thumbs (or knuckles) to massage all over his/her palm. Hold the back of the hand with your fingers while pressing firmly with the thumbs. For a more elaborate, but very effective, technique, use the following hold:*

Place the little finger of your left hand between the recipient's (right) forefinger and middle finger, with the fourth and middle finger of your left hand between his or her forefinger and thumb. At the same time, place the little finger of your right hand between his or her middle and fourth fingers, the fourth finger of your right hand between his or her fourth and little finger, and the middle finger and forefinger of your right hand on the other side of his or her little finger. Push all your fingers back hard against the back of his or her hand so that the palm is stretched and taut. Using small circular movements with your thumbs, work over the whole surface of the palm.

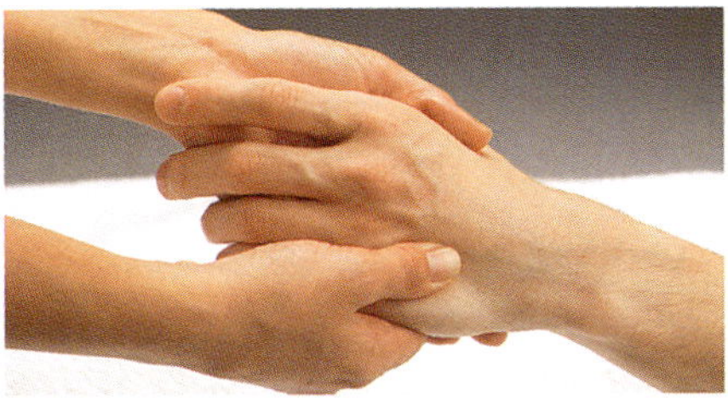

6 **Pressing:** *With the recipient's palm facing down, and using one of your hands as a support, use the other hand to press firmly down the channels between the bones on the top of the hand. Press and slide your thumb evenly down the hand to between the thumb and forefinger, then take each channel in turn until you reach the little finger.*

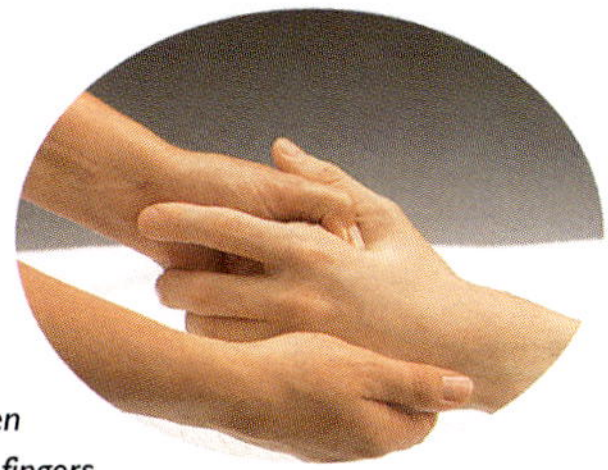

7 **Squeezing:** *Gently squeeze the fleshy pads between each of the recipient's fingers, using your thumb and forefinger. Pay particular attention to the muscular area between the thumb and forefinger.*

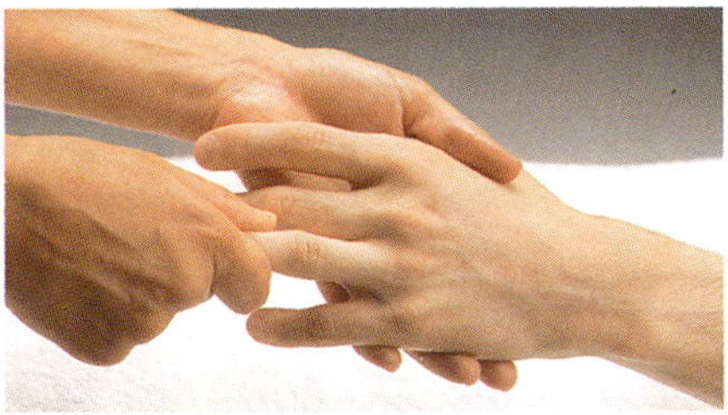

8 **Stretching:** *Supporting the recipient's hand with the palm down, use your other hand to massage the joints of each finger in turn. Then squeeze the outer edge of each finger and give it a firm pull or stretch, until your fingers slide off at the end. To give an additional stretch, while still supporting the wrist with one hand use the other hand to push all the recipient's fingers back together in an arc.*

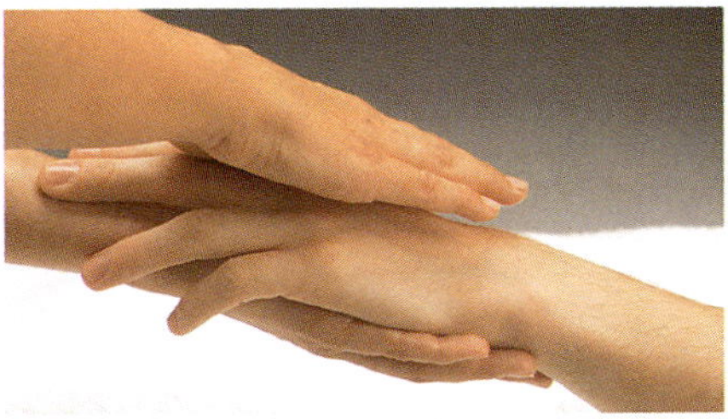

9 **Stroking/Feathering:** *Finish this sequence by stroking the hand from the wrist toward the fingers several times. Hold the hand firmly in yours for a few seconds, before sliding your hands lightly off at the fingertips. Repeat this last movement several times, allowing your touch to become progressively lighter. Cover the hand and arm with a towel, then repeat the same sequence on the other side.*

The abdomen and chest

MASSAGING THE ABDOMEN AND CHEST

Fold the towel carefully back from the abdomen and chest. Make sure your hands are warm and well oiled before placing them on each side of the recipient's navel with your fingers toward his or her head.

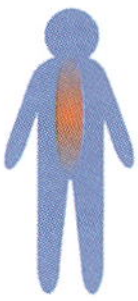

Massaging the abdomen stimulates the digestive system and improves the elimination of waste products. A chest massage helps prevent stiffness and inflexibility in the neck and shoulders.

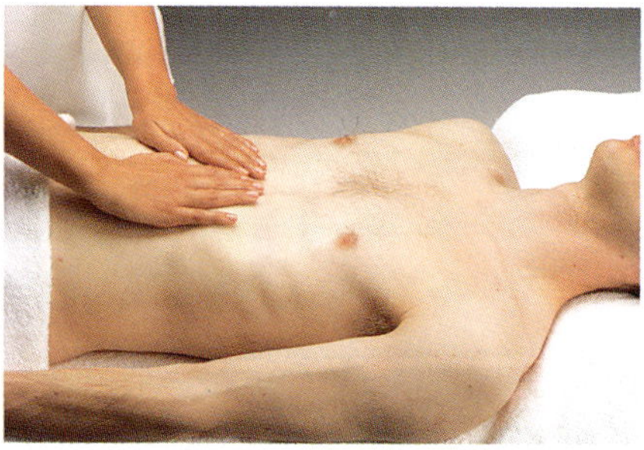

1 ***Stroking**: Gently stroke your hands up the center of the recipient's chest, over the shoulders, and down each side of the torso. Repeat several times. If the recipient is a woman and is uncertain about having her chest massaged, this area can remain covered and the movement restricted to her abdominal region only.*

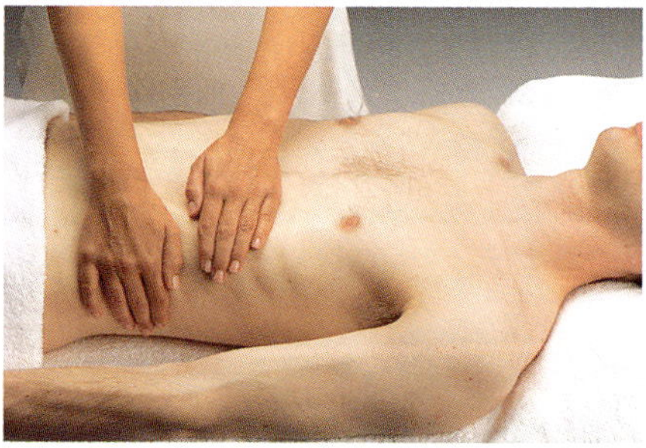

2 ***Pulling:** Place your hands together on the side of the torso, next to the hips, then, using a firm, rhythmic pulling motion with alternate hands, work your way up toward the armpits and down again. Repeat on the other side.*

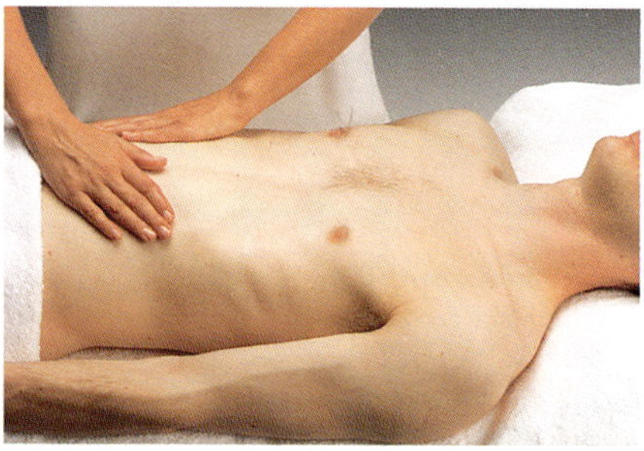

3 ***Circling:** Rest your hands lightly on the abdomen, then slowly begin to move the hands one after the other, in a large, gentle circular motion, always moving in a clockwise direction. As one hand completes the circle, you will have to lift off the other hand repeatedly to let the first hand pass, then replace it again and continue with the circling movement.*

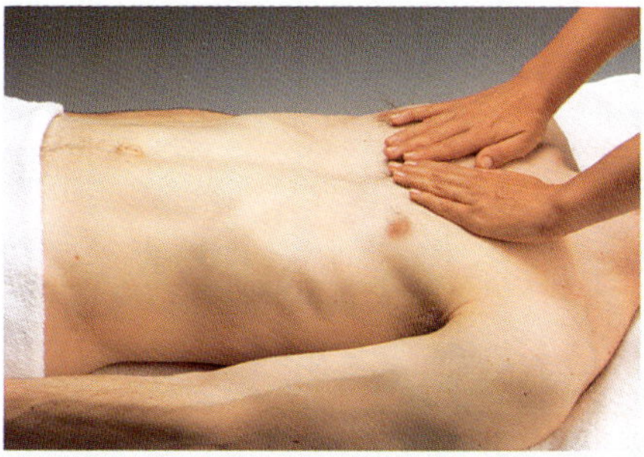

4 Stroking: *Standing at the head of the recipient, place both your hands gently on his or her upper chest. With a smooth stroking movement, fan your hands out over the top of the chest, continue toward the shoulders, back along the shoulder blades and up to the base of the neck. Without losing skin contact, resume the starting position and repeat several times.*

5 Rubbing: *Start by cupping your hands over the recipient's shoulders, then, with a gentle circular movement, use your palms to rub his or her upper arms, chest and shoulders all the way up to the base of the neck. Cover the chest and abdominal region with a towel. Alternatively, this sequence can be completed with stroking movements to the whole of the upper torso before covering it over.*

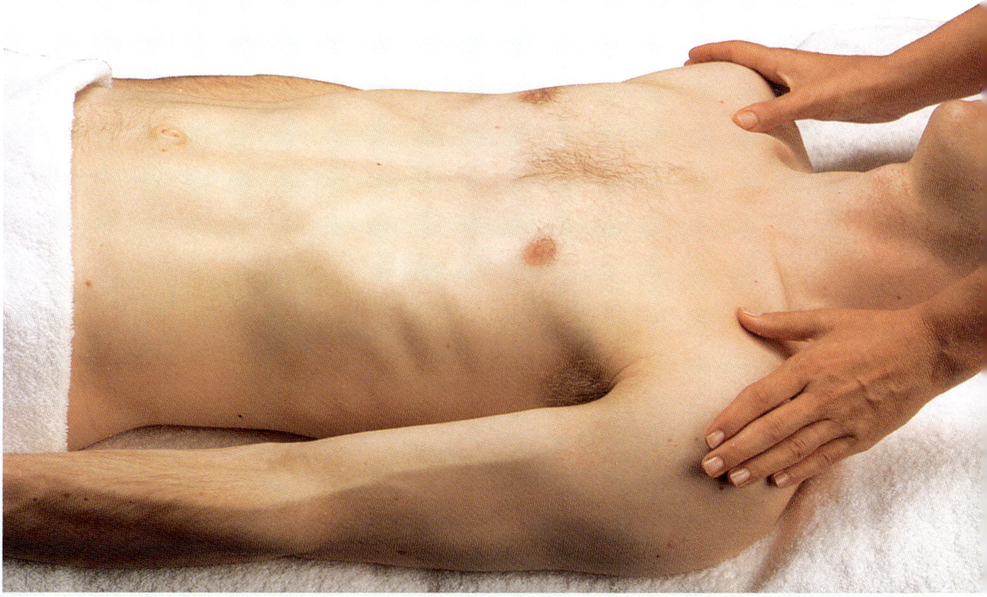

The neck

MASSAGING THE NECK

Stand behind the recipient's head. Oil your hands and place them side by side on each side of the neck.

Many of the tensions that we feel manifest themselves in the neck. A good neck massage helps get rid of stiffness.

1 **Pressing:** *Start by pressing your thumbs firmly into the hollow between the base of the neck and the shoulder blades, on each side. Use your weight to increase the pressure, hold for a few seconds, then release. Move your thumbs along the shoulders a fraction and press. Repeat until you have covered the whole length of the top of the shoulders.*

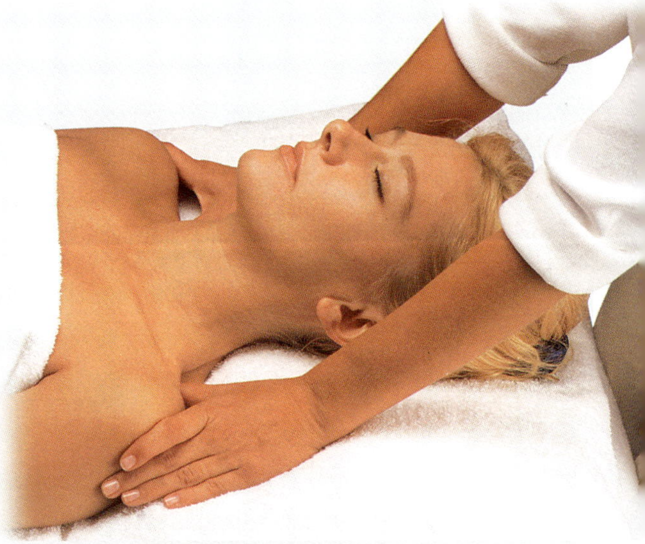

2 **Pulling:** *Ask the recipient of the massage to lift his or her shoulders and back up a little, to let you slide your hands beneath the upper back, with the palms up. Place one hand on each side of the spine, with your fingers curved slightly upward. Ask the recipient to relax back as you slowly pull your hands toward you, giving the muscles on either side of the spine a good stretch. Remove your hands from beneath his or her neck, and repeat twice more.*

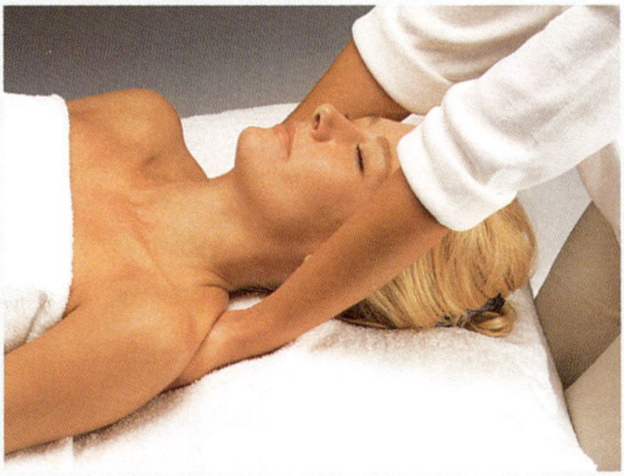

3 **Stretching:** *Place both your hands firmly beneath the neck at the base of the skull, clasping your fingers together at the back of the recipient's head. Very gently, lift and stretch his or her neck toward you, keeping the movement even and straight. Hold for a few seconds, then release.*

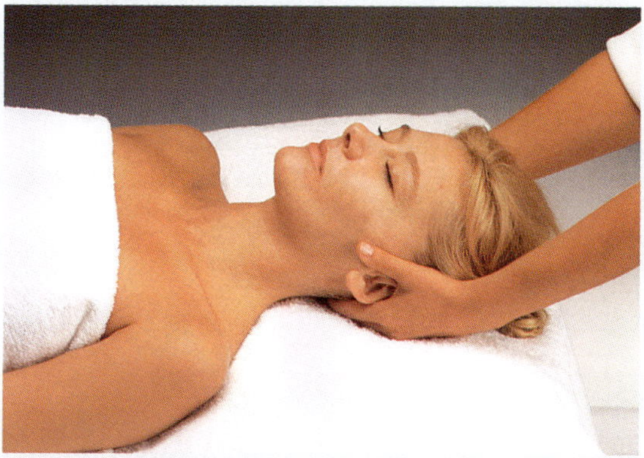

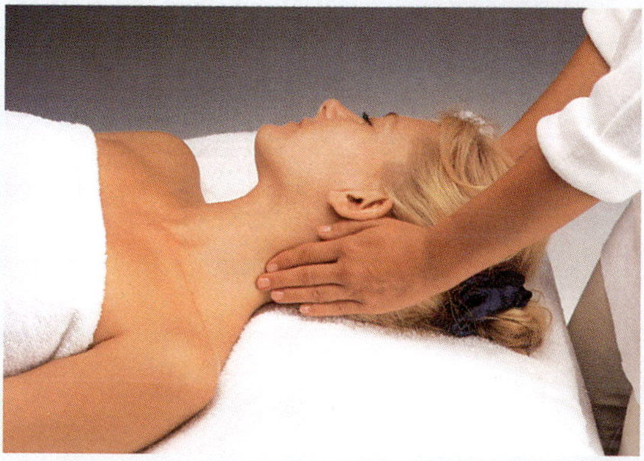

4 **Stroking:** *Gently move the head to the right, supporting it with your right hand, then place your left hand on the recipient's shoulder. With a slow and gentle stroking movement, slide your left hand along the shoulder and up the neck, to just behind the ear. Repeat the movement several times. Then gently massage the area at the base of the skull with the fingers to release any tension.*

5 **Circling:** *With the recipient's head still to one side, place your fingers at the base of the neck. Using the tips of the fingers, make small circling movements all the way up the neck, then along the base of the skull toward the ears. A great deal of tension can become trapped in this particular area, so repeat this sequence several times very slowly. Slowly move the head to the left and repeat the last two movements, then return the head to an upright position.*

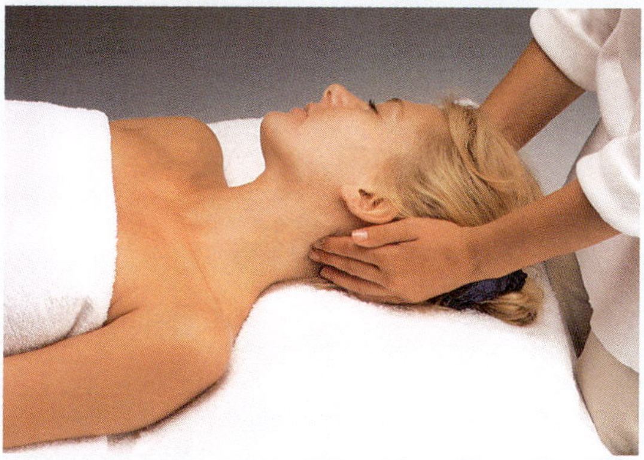

The face and scalp

MASSAGING THE FACE AND SCALP

Stand at the end of the table behind the recipient's head. Make sure that your hands are sufficiently oiled, then begin with step 1.

A facial massage improves circulation and brings a healthy glow to the skin. Headaches and tension disappear, and the recipient experiences a deep serenity.

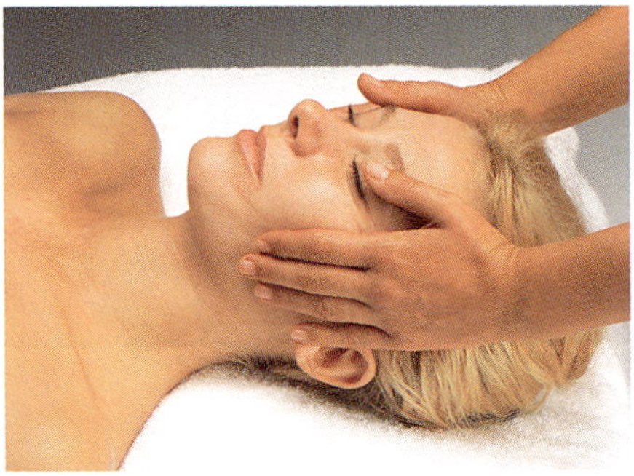

1 ***Stroking:*** *Start by placing your hands very gently on the recipient's forehead at the hairline in order to establish contact, perhaps stroking his or her hair a little. Then oil your hands lightly, and positioning yourself behind his or her head, place the palms of your hands on either side of the chin. With a gentle sweeping movement, slide your hands from the throat, across the cheeks, and up to the forehead, avoiding the delicate area immediately around the eyes. Let the strokes get gradually firmer, until you are pressing slightly upward against the jawbone. Repeat several times, slowly, until the face is lightly lubricated all over.*

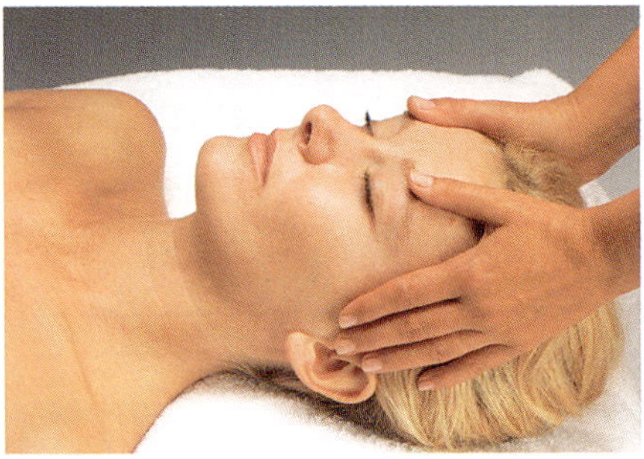

2 ***Stroking:*** *Now place your thumbs together in the center of the recipient's forehead. Slowly start to stroke his or her forehead from the center down toward the temples, using your thumbs. Begin with the panel next to the hairline and progress gradually in strips, moving toward the eyebrows, until the whole of the forehead has been covered.*

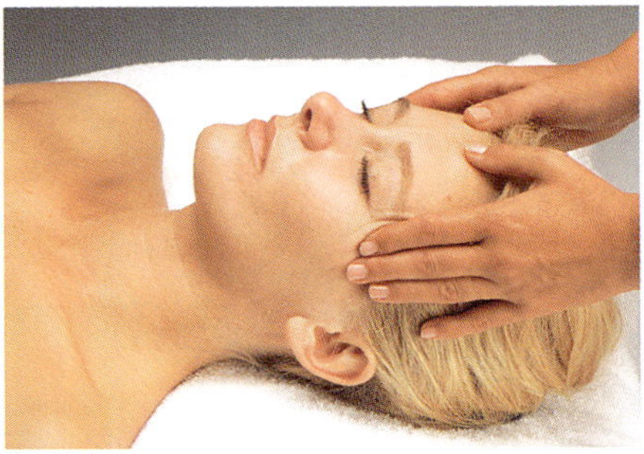

3 ***Circling:*** *Using small movements, circle the temples lightly with the fingers. This is extremely soothing and can help to calm mental tension and provide relief from headaches or anxiety.*

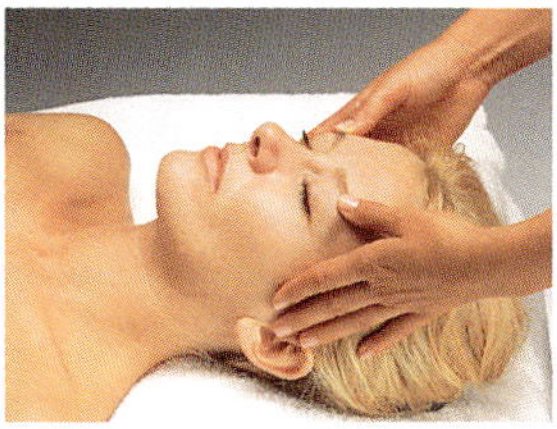

4 Pressing: *Place both your thumbs on the bony ridge above the eyes, in the center, next to the nose. Press down quite firmly, hold for an instant, then release. Move each of your thumbs out a few inches/centimeters and repeat the pressure. Repeat this movement until you reach the outer corners of the eye. Then continue, using slightly less pressure, along the bony ridge beneath the eye, again starting on the inner side of the socket.*

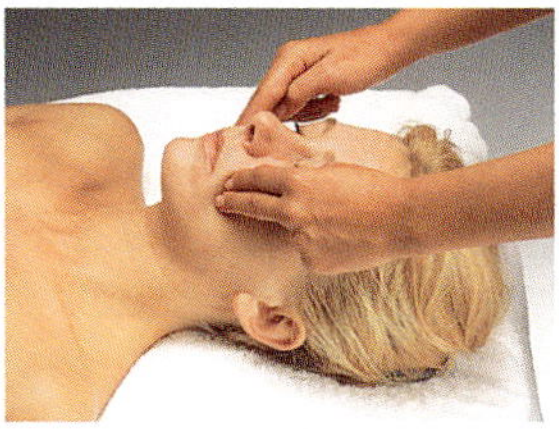

5 Circling: *Again using small circular movements, this time with the forefingers, begin to massage the area on each side of the nose, starting near the bridge and working downward. Repeat on the cheeks on either side of the nostrils, across the upper lip area, and over the chin.*

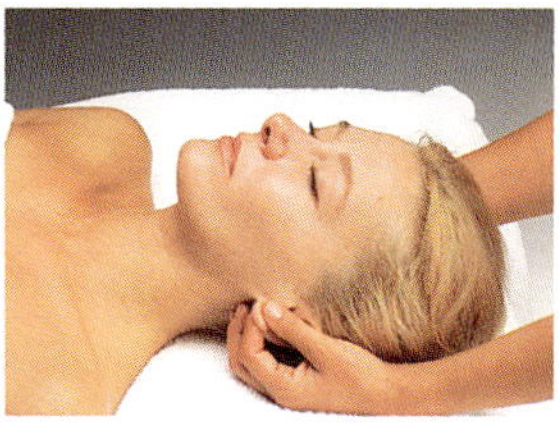

6 Squeezing: *Now gently grasp the recipient's ear lobes between your thumbs and forefingers and give them a squeeze. Pinch the edges of the ear all the way around from bottom to top and then back again. Finally, pull the ear lobe downward two or three times – this is good for headaches.*

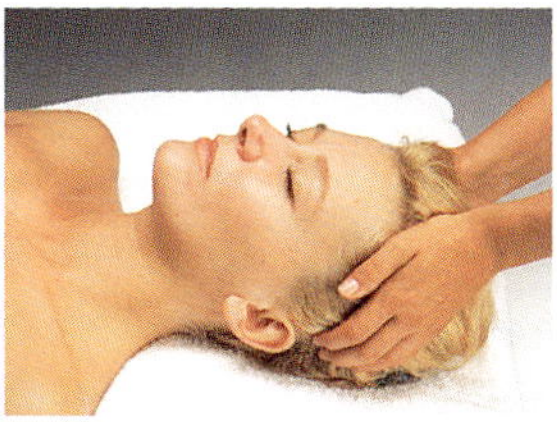

7 Circling: *Slide your hands around to the back of the neck. Starting behind the ears, begin to work your fingers all along the underside of the ridge at the base of the skull. Without letting the hair get too oily, continue to massage all over the recipient's scalp, using your fingers and thumbs.*

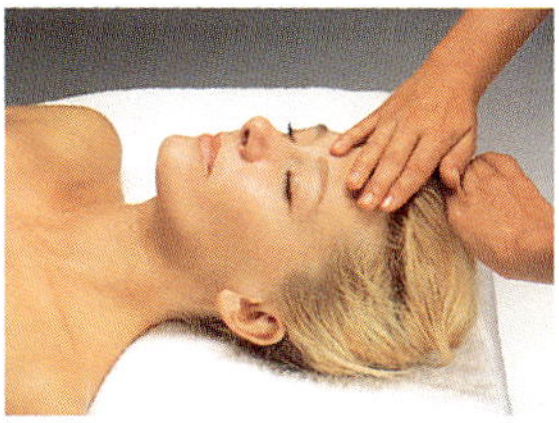

8 Stroking: *Finish by stroking the recipient's forehead and brushing the hair gently back from the forehead (as you began), using progressively lighter and lighter strokes.*

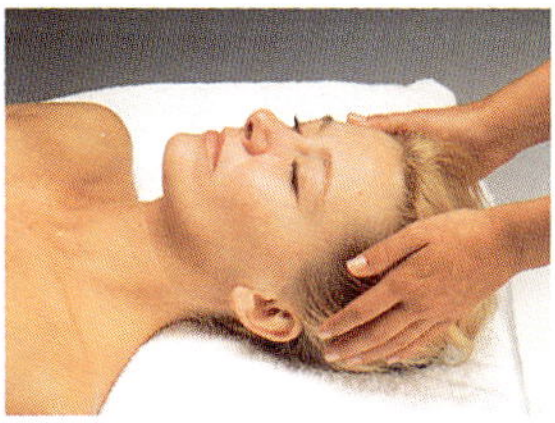

9 Feathering: *To complete the entire massage sequence, move the hands over the recipient's face (and the rest of the body if you wish), using a light sweeping movement and without touching the skin's surface at all. On a subtle level, this helps to disperse any residue of physical or psychological tension that may have been released during the massage.*

When the massage is over, encourage the recipient to relax peacefully for a few minutes at least, in order that the full benefits of the massage can be assimilated. Any surplus oil can be removed using paper tissues or, if the situation allows, with a warm, moist towel. Withdraw discreetly to wash your hands, while the recipient "comes round" and gets dressed.

Massage for specific areas

Apart from performing the full-body massage detailed on pp. 62–77, it is also possible to concentrate on one part of the body, such as the back, feet, hands, or face, or to use massage for purposes other than relaxation or stress-relief. For example, massage can be used specifically to stimulate the body, and may be enjoyed as a sensual experience between lovers or developed as a bonding link between parent and child. Curative and diagnostic massage techniques, such as shiatsu and reflexology, focus on specific parts of the body – the meridian lines in the body, and the feet, and various forms of massage are used in the treatment of illnesses.

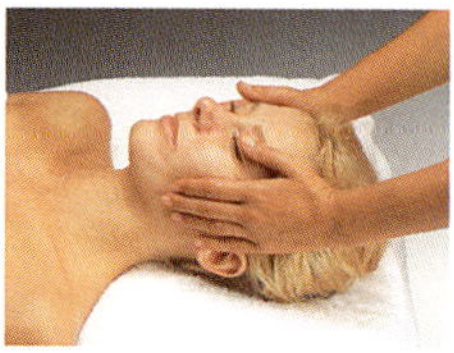

FACIAL MASSAGE

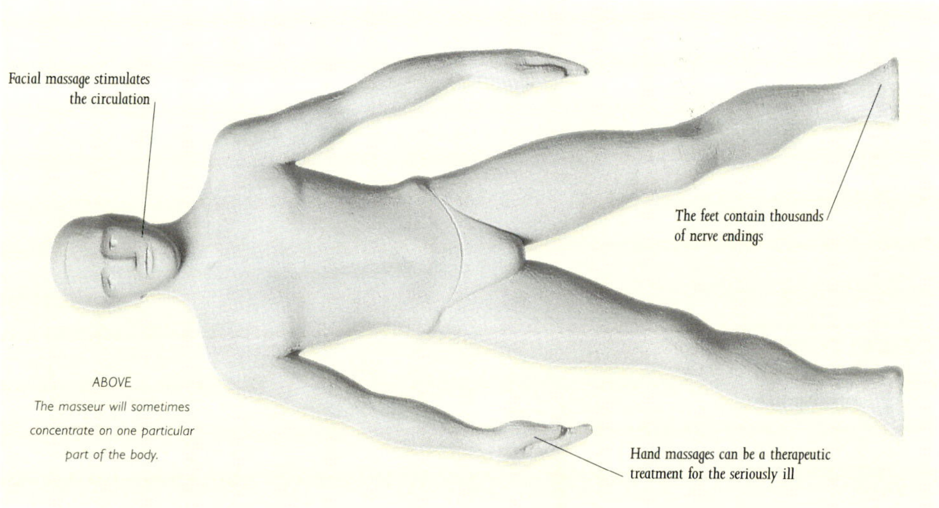

Facial massage stimulates the circulation

The feet contain thousands of nerve endings

Hand massages can be a therapeutic treatment for the seriously ill

ABOVE
The masseur will sometimes concentrate on one particular part of the body.

BACK

A back massage can be an extremely relaxing experience in itself, if time is too limited to carry out a complete body sequence. A great deal of tension is often trapped in the muscles of the back, neck, and shoulders – the back is also the part of the body which allows for the greatest absorption of aromatic oils. Simply refer to the section on the back in the full-body sequence (see pp. 62–3), but allow more time for each set of strokes, and adapt your technique specifically to the needs of the recipient.

HANDS AND FEET

Massaging the feet and hands can be a valuable form of treatment, especially in situations where the recipient is ill, or feels uncertain about receiving a more intimate type of contact. It is also useful in hospitals, for example, where it may not be possible to move the patient, or as a complementary form of therapy alongside other types of medication or treatment. The soles of the feet contain nerve endings that connect to all the organs, glands, and systems of the body. This is the principle behind reflexology (see p. 59). It is therefore possible to treat the whole body simply by massaging the feet – refer to the relevant section in the full-body massage sequence (pp. 68–69) as a guide.

FACE

Performing a facial massage requires the most refined and sensitive type of touch. The facial massage sequence, detailed in the complete massage (see pp. 76–77), clearly lends itself to application as part of a beauty treatment or as a general boost to the complexion. It stimulates the circulation, nourishes the deep dermal tissues, and imparts a healthy glow to the surface of the skin. However, a face and scalp massage should not be regarded solely as a cosmetic aid, since it is also very effective in relieving stress-related complaints, especially the more psychological conditions such as insomnia, headaches, or depression. Always make sure the face is cleansed of any make-up before commencing.

Self-massage treatments

Although self-massage may never be as relaxing as receiving a massage, it still has many benefits. One of the main advantages is that it can be done where and when it is required, without another person's assistance.

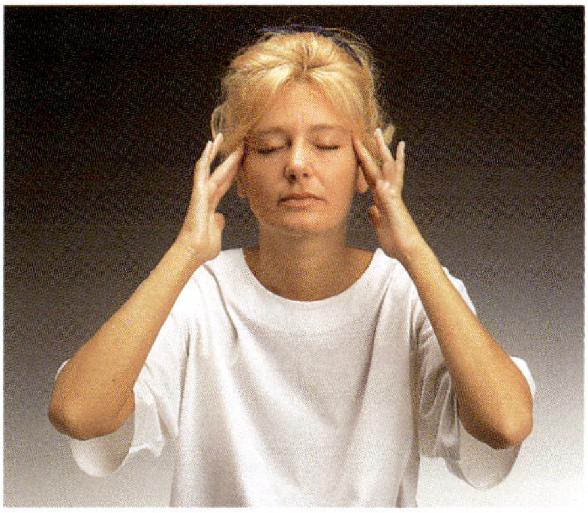

RELIEVING HEADACHES

EASING TENSION

Self-massage can be performed in the bathtub, in a car, on the bed, or while sitting at a desk – whenever you most need it. The areas most easily worked on are neck, shoulders, arms, hands and feet.

HEADACHES AND EYE STRAIN

To relieve headaches or the strain of VDU work, cup your hands over the eyes and look into the darkness. Then circle the temples with the middle fingers, and sweep the fingers from the center of the forehead out toward the sides (as illustrated left).

LEFT
Self-massage to the feet can benefit the whole body.

THE SHOULDERS AND NECK

Ease the shoulders up and down a few times, using a circular movement, and gently move the head from side to side. Then rub the neck, shoulders, and scalp firmly with both hands, using the fingertips to massage the whole area with small circling movements (illustrated above). Tilt the head to one side and stroke the opposite shoulder, and down the arm to the elbow. Repeat on the opposite side. This can be done while sitting in a traffic jam, or at a desk.

PROMOTE WELL-BEING

This can be carried out in the bathtub, on a bed, or on the floor. The best part of the body to massage in this case is the soles of the feet – this way we can give ourselves a complete self-treatment (*see reflexology diagram, p. 59*).

Massage during pregnancy

Massage during pregnancy can be extremely helpful, especially in the last few months, when the body can begin to feel strained, and very heavy. Since a pregnant woman is unable to lie on her stomach, some types of massage need to be performed while she is lying on her side or seated in a chair. A good alternative position for performing a massage treatment to the back during pregnancy is for the woman to sit astride a chair, with the front of her body supported by a cushion. Massage to the neck and shoulders can help to alleviate muscular tension and anxiety.

Lower back pain is a common problem, as are feelings of physical tiredness and nervous exhaustion, especially toward the end of pregnancy. Massage to the back can help to ease aches and pains, and help revitalize the whole body.

Local massage to the hands, feet, neck, and face are also very beneficial. For example, gentle massage to the feet and ankles can help to overcome edema (swelling) when performed regularly. A massage to the neck and face can give a boost to self-confidence and promote a sense of well-being.

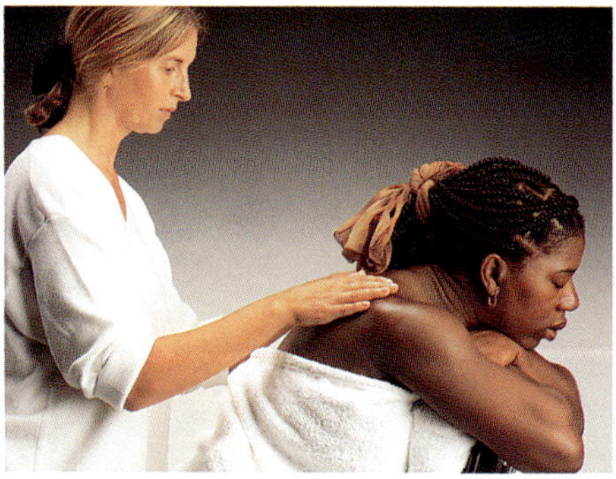

NECK MASSAGE

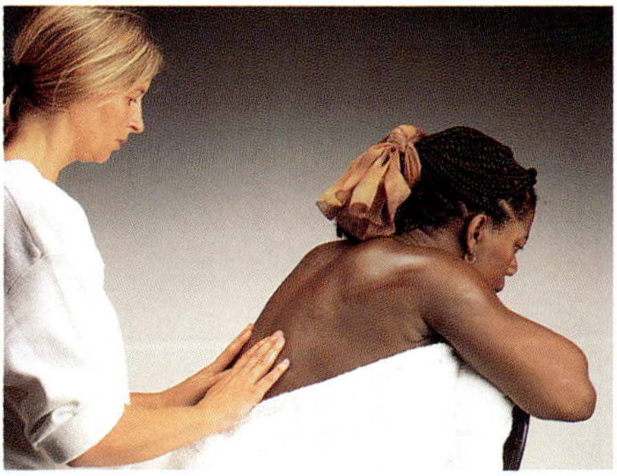

BACK MASSAGE

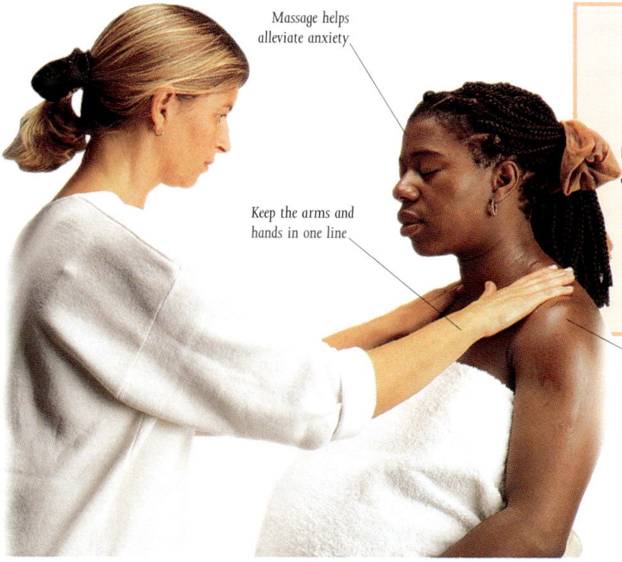

LEFT
Toward the end of pregnancy neck and shoulder massage can release tension.

WARNING

Special care and precautions should always be taken when performing any kind of massage during pregnancy because of the sensitivity of the growing child. All essential oils should be used in a very diluted form. For specific contraindications during pregnancy see Safety Data, *p. 211*.

Baby massage

Many doctors now accept the power of massage to ease anxiety in sick babies and children. New studies indicate its ability to help healthy infants, too. Research has shown that babies who are massaged are more alert, gain weight faster, sleep more soundly, and suffer less anxiety than nonmassaged infants. Massage can also reduce stress levels in parents, help them to be more responsive to their child's needs, and aid in the natural bonding process. Conditions such as hyperactivity, insomnia, colic, and stomachache respond well to massage. With a few exceptions, babies over the age of six weeks, and young children, can safely be massaged on the legs, arms, back and stomach. This can be done three or four times a week, or even every day. A pre-bath massage lasting for 20 minutes will often make a restless child to straight to sleep at bed-time.

1 *General massage to the feet, legs, arms, and torso is very soothing and relaxing and is good for insomnia and restlessness.*

WARNING

Babies should not be massaged during the six-week period after their birth, for at least a week after a vaccination, or if they have joint problems. Essential oils should be used in the correct dilution according to age. See *Safety Data*, p. 211.

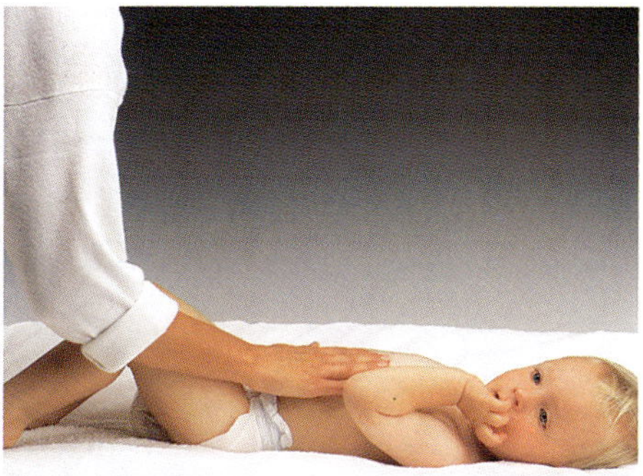

2 *Rubbing the back or stomach gently, using a diluted aromatic oil, with a circular clockwise movement can ease colic, stomach ache, or other complaints.*

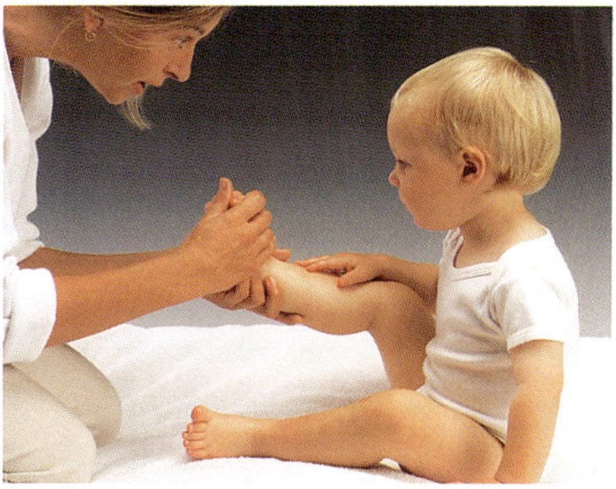

3 *Performing a simple local massage, to the hands or feet, for example, helps to establish a caring contact. This can be a very valuable aid to establishing trust, intimacy, and a loving bond between parent and child.*

Sports and detoxifying massage

Massage can be beneficial both before and after exercise, and also as an aid to the body's natural process of eliminating toxins, as an anti-cellulite treatment and for people recovering from illness.

SPORTS MASSAGE

A stimulating or sports massage tends to use deeper pressure and more vigorous movements than a massage aimed primarily at relaxation. Deep-tissue massage employs techniques such as kneading, rubbing, hacking, and pummeling traditionally associated with masseurs in Turkish baths. Exercise is the most important way of stimulating the circulation and increasing vitality.

WARNING

Some forms of exercise, such as jogging or aerobics, can have negative side effects in the long term. Studies show that yoga, fast walking, and swimming are more gentle, but effective, ways of staying fit.

RIGHT
Warming up before sport prevents injury. Pre-and post-sports massage can prevent and treat problems.

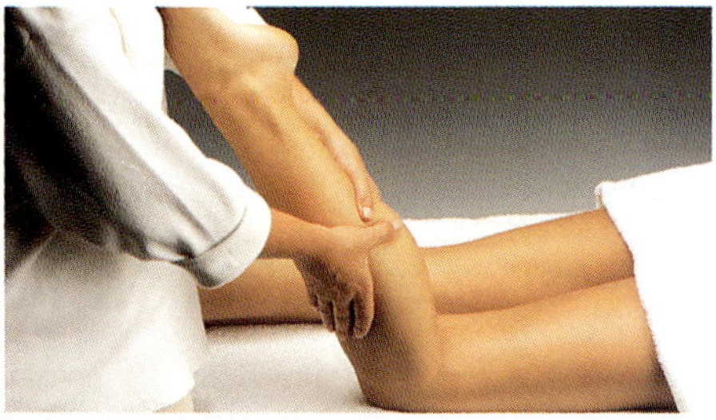

WORKING ON THE CALF

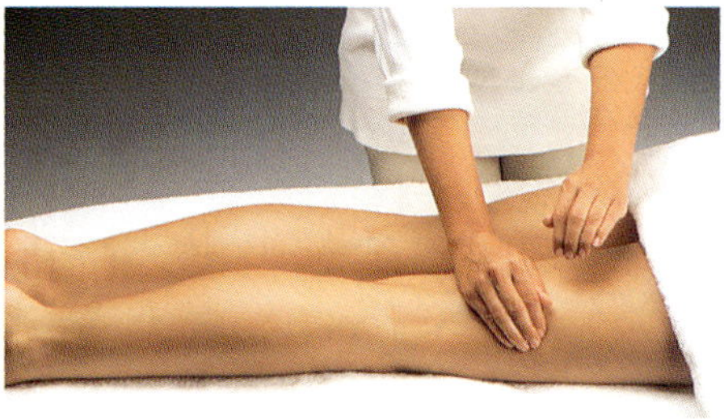

MASSAGING THE THIGH MUSCLES

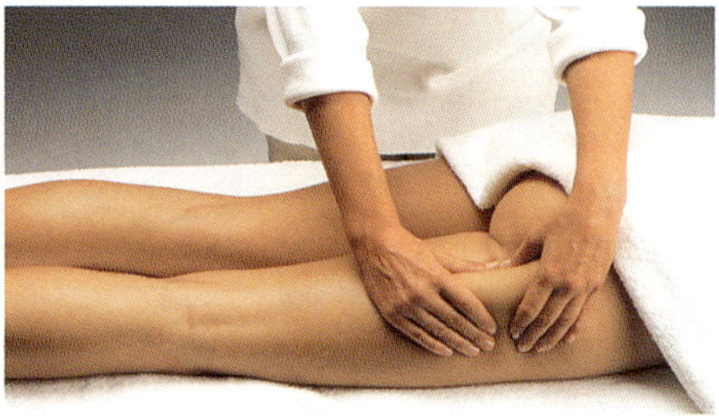

SQUEEZING THE MUSCLES

DETOXIFYING MASSAGE

A detoxifying or manual lymph drainage (MLD) massage gently pumps toxins and foreign material such as bacteria, and lymph fluids through the body's network of lymph canals. It can help clear acne and eczema, and can be used to treat edema (swelling due to water retention). In one London hospital, it is used to help reduce painful swellings following breast cancer treatment. A detoxifying massage may also help to shift cellulite and break down fatty deposits. Cupping, squeezing, and draining (*see pp.* 55–58) are especially valuable in this context. In MLD massage, the stroke should always be in the direction of the nearest lymph node.

Sensual massage

Massage can also be a very sensual experience, and massage between partners can help to bring a new depth to the relationship, as well as to enhance sexual enjoyment. Make sure the room is warm and comfortable beforehand, and select the aromatic oils you wish to use. Some oils have a reputation for having aphrodisiac qualities (*see* p. 94) but it is best to choose oils with scents that appeal to both partners.

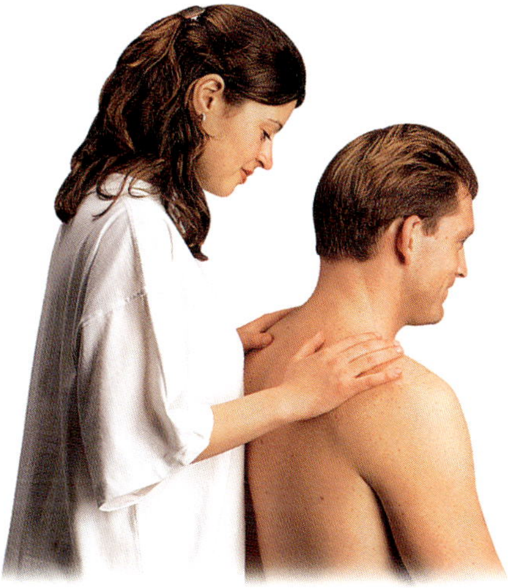

1 An aromatic massage is a relaxing and enjoyable experience in itself, promoting new levels of intimacy. It also provides an opportunity to explore different experiences and sensations.

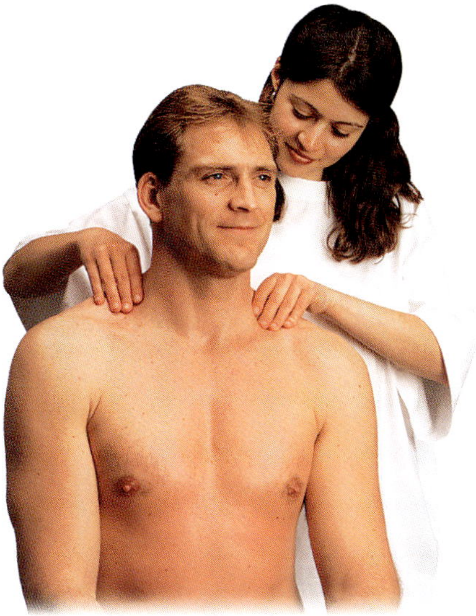

2 A sensual or sexual massage need not focus entirely on the erotic regions of the body, but on the sensitivity of the body as a whole.

3 Like love-making, sensual massage between partners should be a two-way communication in which each person has the opportunity to touch and be touched.

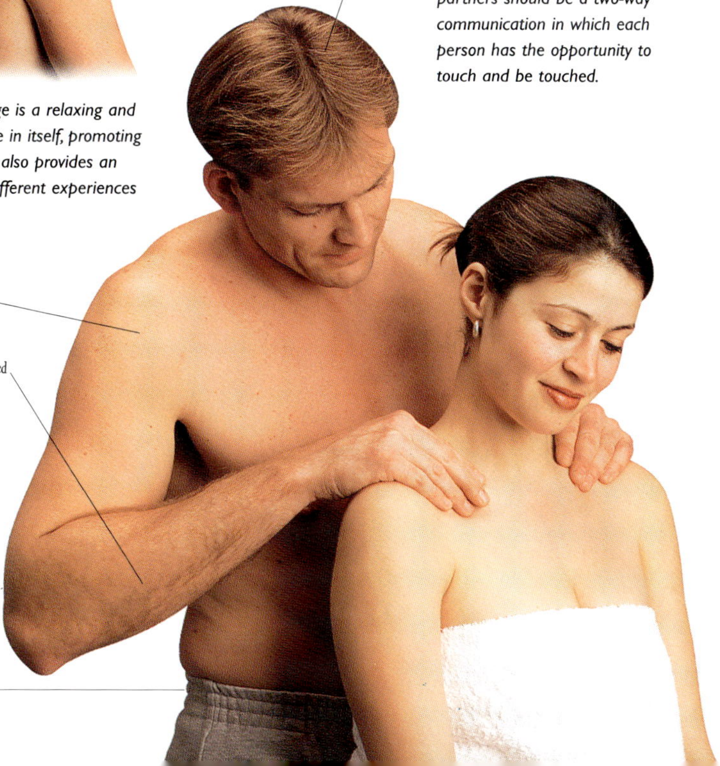

LEFT
Candlelight helps provide a sensual atmosphere.

Base oils to use as carrier oils

VEGETABLE-BASED OILS AND OTHER CARRIERS

* **Sweet Almond Oil:** A very pale yellow oil with a slight nutty odor containing olein, glyceride, and linoleic acid. Rich in minerals, vitamins, and protein.
MAIN USES: It is an excellent lubricant and is softening, revitalizing and nourishing to the skin, and especially good for dry, sensitive, and irritated skin conditions. This is one of the most useful medium-light, versatile multipurpose massage or facial oils.

* **Apricot Kernel Oil:** A pale yellow, light-textured oil, rich in minerals and vitamins and easily absorbed. Unrefined versions contain small amounts of vitamin E.
MAIN USES: Mainly used in beauty treatments, especially for prematurely aged, dry, sensitive, and inflamed conditions. It may also be used as a light massage oil.

* **Avocado Oil:** The unrefined oil is a dark green, viscous and rich, yet highly penetrating substance, containing essential fatty acids, proteins, minerals, beta carotene, and vitamin E. The refined oil is pale yellow with little odor and few nutrients.
MAIN USES: Unrefined avocado oil aids dermal regeneration and is highly nutritious. It is recommended for dry, dull, dehydrated, aging skin and eczema. Best used in combination with a lighter-textured carrier oil, such as sweet almond oil.

* **Borage Seed Oil:** A pale yellow oil, rich in essential fatty acids, especially gammalinolenic acid (GLA), and in vitamins and minerals.
MAIN USES: A skin rejuvenator, it is excellent for all skin types, especially dry, aging or scarred skin. Also indicated for psoriasis, eczema, PMS and menopausal problems. Best used in combination with a lighter-textured carrier oil, such as sweet almond oil.

* **Calendula Oil:** An oily infusion containing the lipid soluble active principles of the marigold flowers Calendula officinale in a light-textured carrier oil, such as sunflower seed oil.
MAIN USES: A very valuable oil for promoting the healing of wounds, scars, burns, swellings, and other injuries. It aids tissue regeneration and is helpful for all types of complexions. It is best used in combination with other carrier oils for general skin care.

* **Carrot Oil:** A bright orange oil, rich in beta carotene, plus minerals and vitamins, especially vitamin A. It should be kept cool and protected from light.
MAIN USES: Rejuvenating and nourishing, this oil is indicated for premature aging, dry, or itchy skin conditions and nail infections. Use in low dilutions only, in combination with other carrier oils/creams.

* **Castor Oil:** A thick, slightly sticky oil with a strong odor. It has good lubricating and waterproofing qualities and is best known as a laxative.
MAIN USES: Mainly used in aromatherapy in hair care, especially as a conditioning treatment for brittle, damaged, or dry hair, and for treating hair loss.

* **Coconut Oil:** Coconut oil is available in two forms: natural and fractionated. While the natural oil solidifies at cool temperatures, the fractionated coconut oil remains mobile. The fractionated oil is an extremely light, clear and odorless oil that does not go rancid with age, making it a very versatile carrier.
MAIN USES: The fractionated oil can be used as a light and easily absorbed massage oil base or as a general lubricant. However, it is especially recommended for perfumery use as a general purpose carrier or starting material.

* **Evening Primrose Oil:** This golden yellow, fine-textured oil is derived from the seeds of the plant *Oenothera biennis*. Rich in vitamins and minerals, the oil is best known for its high gammalinolenic acid (GLA) content. It is often used as a nutritional supplement. Store evening primrose oil away from light and heat.
MAIN USES: Due to its high GLA content, the oil is valuable

for a wide variety of conditions, including eczema, psoriasis, PMS, and menopausal problems. It is also an excellent moisturizer, indicated for dry, aging or chapped skin.

* **Grapeseed Oil:** Available only in refined form, this has an exceptionally fine texture, low odor, and a faint greenish hue. It contains some vitamins, minerals and proteins.
MAIN USES: A popular massage oil base, due to its fine texture and low odor. Best blended with more nutritious carrier oils for beauty or skin treatments.

* **Hypericum (Saint-John's Wort) Oil:** Like calendula oil, this product is an oily infusion extract of a plant, in this case *Hypericum perforatum*, in a light carrier oil, such as sunflower seed oil. A rich reddish color, it contains an essential oil and hypericins as its active principals.
MAIN USES: Having anti-inflammatory and nervine properties, the oil is especially indicated for neuralgia, sciatica, and nervous disorders. It can cause sensitization.

* **Hazelnut Oil:** This pale yellow, fine-textured oil has a strong, nutty aroma. It contains vitamins, minerals, proteins, and essential fatty acids, including linoleic acid.
MAIN USES: Easily absorbed and slightly astringent, this oil is valuable for all skin types, especially inflamed conditions. Usually used in dilution with other carriers.

* **Jojoba Oil:** This yellow "oil" is actually a liquid wax which has a light-textured, highly penetrative quality. The chemical structure of jojoba resembles sebum, the skin's own oily secretions, giving it excellent moisturizing and emulsifying properties. It also contains protein, minerals, and myristic acid, an anti-inflammatory agent.
MAIN USES: Jojoba is one of the most versatile carrier oils, both for massage and beauty care. It is suitable for all skin types, including blemished and oily skin, as it helps to unclog the pores. It is also indicated for inflamed and irritated conditions. May also be used as a hair conditioner and as a natural mild sunscreen.

* **Olive Oil:** Several qualities are available, but the extra-virgin cold-pressed olive oil is best. A viscous oil of dark greenish colour, it is rich in proteins, minerals, and vitamins, plus essential fatty acids – mainly alpha linolenic acid.
MAIN USES: Good for dehydrated or irritated skin; the prevention and treatment of stretch marks or scars; as a natural sun-screen agent; and for conditioning the hair. Often used in combination with lighter-textured base oils.

* **Peach Kernel Oil:** A fine-textured, pale golden oil with a delicate, sweet aroma. It contains minerals and vitamins, especially vitamin E.
MAIN USES: It is mainly used in beauty treatments as it is easily absorbed by the skin. Especially recommended for aging, dry or sensitive skin and thread veins.

* **Rose Hip Seed Oil:** A very pale yellow, light-textured oil with low odor. Rich in vitamins, it contains up to 35% linoleic acid and 44% gammalinolenic acid (GLA).
MAIN USES: An excellent cosmetic oil for promoting tissue regeneration and for the treatment of eczema, psoriasis, PMS, and menopausal problems.

* **Sunflower Seed Oil:** The unrefined oil is a light-textured, golden yellow oil with a slightly nutty aroma. Although it is less readily available than the refined version, the former is higher in nutrients, containing minerals, essential fatty acids, and vitamins, notably vitamin E.
MAIN USES: A useful multipurpose massage and beauty and skin-care carrier oil, suitable for all skin types.

* **Wheat Germ Oil:** A heavy, dark reddish-orange, slightly sticky oil with a strong, earthy odor. Rich in proteins, minerals, and vitamins, especially vitamin E.
MAIN USES: Stimulates tissue regeneration and is excellent for aging skin, wrinkles, scars, and stretch marks. Added to other less stable vegetable carrier oils (up to 15%), it can prolong their shelf-life due to its antioxidant properties.
May cause sensitization in some individuals.

LEFT and RIGHT Generally speaking, essential oils should be diluted in carrier oils to avoid causing skin irritation.

PART THREE

Medical aromatherapy

EUCALYPTUS LEAF

Essential oils have been used by specialist French doctors and surgeons for many years to treat a wide range of complaints. Depending on the practitioner and on the particular case, aromatherapy may be used exclusively, in conjunction with conventional treatment, or with other forms of alternative medicine. Professional practitioners may also prescribe essential oils for internal use as well as using them in the ways described so far in this book.

The treatment of serious medical complaints, and internal use, are the sphere of qualified medical practitioners, but many forms of aromatherapy can safely be used at home to treat minor illnesses or to act as a back-up to conventional medical treatment. A large section of this part of the book (*pp.*97–175) covers the home use of essential oils for specific complaints. Ailments are grouped into body systems, and as a quick way of finding a particular ailment and aromatherapeutic treatment they are listed below in alphabetical order.

> "Whilst being the oldest of all systems, phytotherapy and aromatherapy are also those which have most effectively proved themselves ..."
>
> DR. JEAN VALNET

AN INDEX OF AILMENTS AND TREATMENT

GARLIC CAPSULES

Clinical aromatherapy

In France today, many medical doctors and hospitals prescribe essential oils as an alternative to antibiotic treatment, whereas in most other countries the idea of using natural aromatics as a form of medical treatment is still very radical.

Until recently the very concept of clinical aromatherapy has been ignored or treated sceptically by scientists, and by many in orthodox medical circles. However, such attitudes are beginning to change and plant medicines are being revaluated using modern research techniques. It is now accepted that many modern medications can have harmful side effects and that growing numbers of bacteria are becoming resistant to once successful synthetic medications.

The use of essential oils to fight infectious disease by oral prescription does however, require great care and a high degree of medical expertise. In France, doctors have the opportunity to incorporate a more naturopathic approach (using herbs and essential oils) into their treatment program only after they have undertaken the full orthodox medical training. In sharp contrast, qualified aromatherapy masseurs and those working in the field of beauty therapy in the UK are only permitted to use the oils externally, and professional bodies such as the International Federation of Aromatherapists clearly indicate that employing aromatic oils for internal use is outside their jurisdiction.

Essential oils can indeed be extremely dangerous if they are taken by mouth without qualified supervision. This is because, although natural products, they are highly concentrated, and, in an undiluted form, can damage the delicate mucous membranes of the digestive system. Some essential oils, for example pennyroyal, can also be highly toxic when ingested, even in small amounts, and can even cause death.[17] The safety aspects of using essential oils for aromatherapy purposes have therefore been justly highlighted by the media over the last 20 years, with the result that such potentially dangerous oils as pennyroyal have been withdrawn from sale. Regulations covering usage, contraindications and general safety data have also made the purchase of essential oils by the general public much more strictly controlled and have ensured a much higher degree of safety. Legally, all essential oils should now carry precise safety data on the label, including the warning "Do not take internally" and "Keep out of reach of children." Considering the potential dangers of misusing oils, it is indisputable that the practice of clinical aromatherapy should be the preserve of highly qualified professionals. It is beyond the scope of the majority of people, including most aromatherapists working in the field of alternative health care.

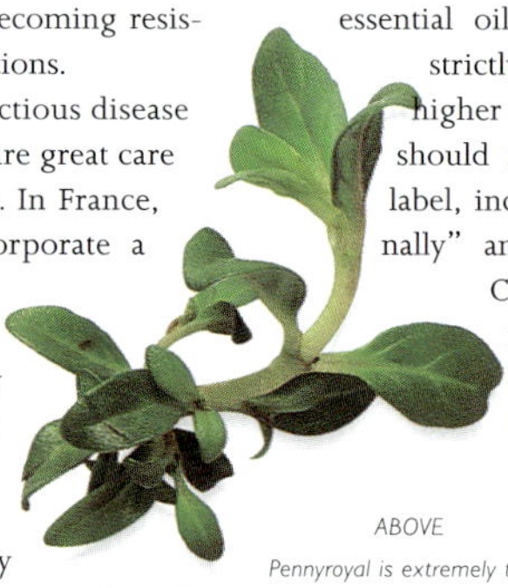

ABOVE
Pennyroyal is extremely toxic when ingested and should never be taken internally.

WARNING

Taking essential oils internally can cause adverse reactions, and, in extreme cases, may even be fatal.

LEFT
No essential oil should be taken internally unless recommended by a highly qualified practitioner.

SCIENTIFIC STUDIES

The device known as the aromatogram promises to open the way for the use of natural aromatic medicine in the clinical field, and to help make the therapeutic use of essential oils accepted within the established medical arena. As a surgeon during World War II, Dr. Jean Valnet used essential oils for the treatment of both physical and psychiatric disorders, sometimes administering them by oral means, with outstanding success. His method, which involved testing specific oils on cultured bacteria taken from the site of the infection, was

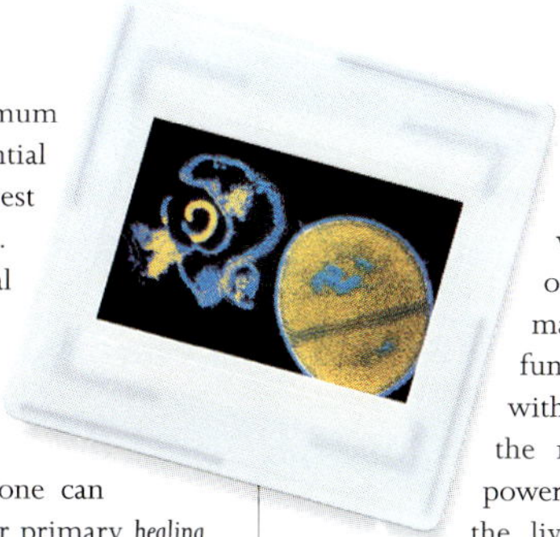

used not only to ascertain the minimum dosage levels required for various essential oils, but also to find which oils were best suited to treating a particular infection.

The results often showed that several oils had similar effects on the same infection. This is thought to be because they help to create a healthy environment in which pathogens are unable to survive. According to Valnet: "... one can select them [the oils] according to their primary *healing powers*, such as those oils which act in the region of the lungs: niaouli, eucalyptus and pine, or on the urinary system: juniper and sandalwood ... determined by the aromatogram."[18] Most importantly Valnet also discovered that bacteria treated with essential oils do not develop resistance as they do with antibiotics.

ABOVE AND ABOVE RIGHT
The bacterium Staphylococcus aureus *(above) can be successfully treated with essential oils (as shown, top).*

A demonstration of the aromatogram at a meeting of the Royal Society of Medicine in London in 1995 caused widespread interest. Of particular value to many who were present was the ability of certain essential oils to clear up infections caused by MRSA (methicillin-resistant *Staphylococcus aureus*). Essential oils could prove to be very useful allies in the fight against these new strains of "superbug".

This is thought to be true because antibiotics are, chemically, relatively simple substances; "they may only involve a single molecule, and that is why bacteria are constantly able to develop resistance to them. Aromatic oils, on the other hand, are very complex, containing an array of molecules in different proportions which reinforce each other."[19] It has been found that if the most active anti-infection ingredient in an essential oil is extracted and used on its own, it is less effective.

One enthusiastic British physician has initiated the use of essential oils in his general practice. He does not advocate abandoning modern antibiotics, but believes that they should be used, by those trained in both systems, in harmony with essential oils. "For instance an inner ear infection (caused by pseudomonas) needs to be brought under control very quickly with antibiotics or there is a danger of the eardrum bursting... But it makes far more sense to treat [a fungal infection of the toenail] locally with an oil which can actually penetrate the nail, rather than handing out a powerful drug that has known effects on the liver and will probably knock out some of the bacteria in your guts as well."[20]

The delicate balance of benign bacteria naturally found in the gut and the vagina is upset not only by antibiotics but also by other common medications such as the contraceptive pill, anti-inflammatory drugs, and antacids. Rosalind Blackwell, a medical herbalist who trained in France, regularly prescribes aromatic oils internally for specific conditions, especially to rebalance intestinal flora and clear up all sorts of chronic infections, such as thrush or cystitis. Fully aware of the dangers of using essential oils internally, she carefully monitors dosage levels and systematically checks her patients for any signs of adverse effects. Although many common conventional drugs are far more toxic than natural aromatic materials, Blackwell stresses the fact that aromatic oils should only be used internally by specifically trained practitioners.

Other fully qualified medical herbalists have also started to use essential oils as part of their treatment program. One British medical herbalist, Colin Nicholls, uses the aromatogram regularly to diagnose and treat his patients using essential oil and herbs. In one case history, a woman came to him suffering from chronic cystitis. Clary sage, an essential oil with an estrogen-like quality, was indicated by the aromatogram, even though it does not have outstanding bactericidal properties. Yet, when the woman took the oil in the form of a vaginal pessary, clary sage got rid of the infection. Putting the estrogen balance right meant that the body could take care of the infection itself. This shows the high degree of accuracy and unique value of individually tailored aromatic remedies when the aromatogram is used as a diagnostic technique.

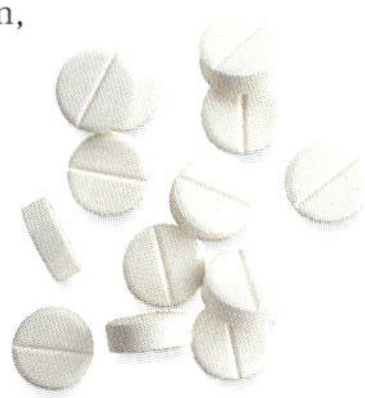

ABOVE
Many bacterial infections have developed a resistance to antibiotics. Alternative methods of treatment may provide the key to dealing with such illnesses.

Diagnosis and prescription

The aromatogram is clearly a very sensitive and highly refined diagnostic tool when applied to the field of clinical aromatherapy. However, Jean Valnet, like other doctors, also made use of other more traditional diagnostic measures, including examining the presenting symptoms of the patient and making an assessment of their overall disposition.

When faced with any kind of illness it is always beneficial to build up an overall picture of the individual concerned and to highlight any contraindications that may be relevant. In the context of clinical aromatherapy, for example, a person who is using high levels of paracetamol should not be given oils containing certain phenols, because both these chemicals have similar elimination pathways and this can lead to an overdose. Before performing an aromatic massage, it is important to make an overall assessment to ensure that there are no contraindications, as in the case of thrombosis, where massage itself is inadvisable. Certain essential oils are also contraindicated in conditions such as epilepsy, high blood pressure, and pregnancy.

OTHER DIAGNOSTIC TECHNIQUES

Other diagnostic techniques which are of particular value for the practice of aromatherapy, apart from the conventional examination tests, are those associated with reflexology. This is used as a form of treatment in its own right, but it is also a useful diagnostic tool. It consists of an examination of the feet by a trained practitioner. Problematic areas show up as points of congestion or pain in particular points on the soles of the feet, which are linked to specific areas of the body. Iridology may also sometimes be used. Here, areas of discoloration within the iris of the eyes are interpreted as an indication of areas of the body in which there may be problems. Even within the context of clinical aromatherapy, it is valuable to assess the overall temperament and disposition of the individual concerned rather than simply focus on the presenting symptoms.

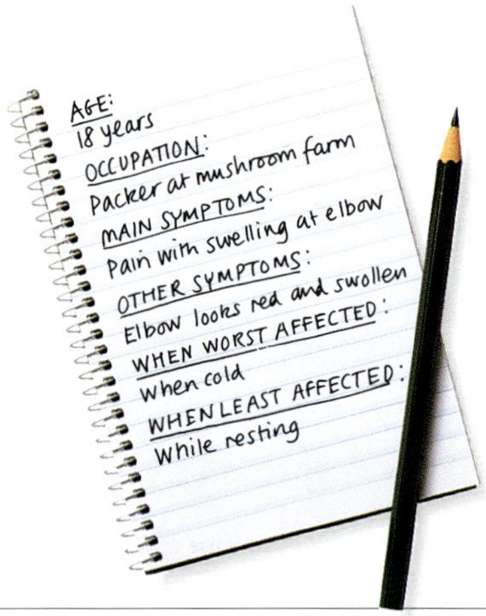

LEFT
It is important to build a complete picture of the patient when assessing him or her for clinical aromatherapy.

PRESCRIBING SPECIFIC BLENDS

In medical herbalism, when preparing a prescription, it is common to mix a number of herbs together to make an individual remedy – usually given in the form of a tincture (an alcohol-based preparation) or an infusion/decoction (a tea made by infusing the herbs in boiling/cold water). The reason for combining herbs in this way is that they can have a synergistic effect upon one another. This means that the therapeutic potential of a single herb is enhanced by the chemical combination with other plant materials; in other words, the end product is greater than the sum of its parts. In medical herbalism, it is also valuable to mix herbs together in order to target different aspects of a particular complaint.

ABOVE
Remedies are individually prepared by mixing together a number of essential oils.

In aromatherapy, likewise, essential oils are usually mixed together to create a synergistic blend or personalized remedy. In this way, each blend develops a unique chemical structure and therapeutic action determined by the combined constituents of all the essential oils used. Unlike herbs, however, essential oils cannot be prepared as aqua-based (water-based) solutions, because they do not mix with water. They are too concentrated to be taken or used on the skin in any way in an undiluted form, but they do mix readily with alcohol and with vegetable oils and fats. When essential oils are prescribed for internal use, they are therefore mixed with an alcoholic base beforehand (much like a tincture) or made into pessaries using a fatty base (e.g. cocoa butter), for insertion into the anus or vagina. This method of medication is not generally used in Britain or the US except as a form of local treatment, but in Europe as a whole it is widely used as a way of introducing therapeutic substances into the system through absorption.

CASE STUDY: TREATING A CHILD WITH COUGH

The subtlety of the way in which aromatherapy treatment can be tailored by a clinical practitioner to suit an individual case is illustrated in the following case study of a child who is suffering from a chesty cough. In this case there is also insomnia (due to coughing at night) and it is thought that there may be an underlying nervous component in the disposition of the child. In such a case, it is vital to use remedies that will simultaneously combat and support the different aspects of the overall condition, on both a physical and emotional level. Here, the following types of action are required: expectorant (to expel mucus or phlegm); bactericide (to fight infection); balsamic (to soothe irritation); sedative (to induce sleep); nervine (to strengthen and calm the nerves).

A herbal tea or syrup using a combination of remedies including chamomile (relaxant), coltsfoot (expectorant), echinacea (antimicrobial), and peppermint (decongestant) would be indicated in this case. For each aspect of the illness there is a choice of oils to be used. In this example, myrtle would be a good oil to include in the prescription as a general aid for the child suffering from a chesty cough and insomnia. This is because although myrtle shares many of the properties of eucalyptus oil (widely used in the treatment of coughs and colds), it is much milder (thus it is more suitable for children), and is not so stimulating (thus it would not interfere with sleep patterns).

For a detailed consideration of the way in which aromatherapeutic oils could be selected for use in this particular case, *see p. 92.*

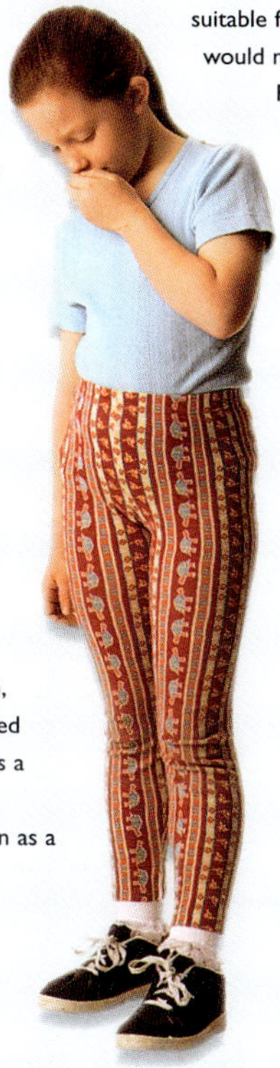

MYRTLE

LEFT
The treatment of a child's cough depends on the way in which the symptoms manifest themselves.

ABOVE
Some oils, such as myrtle, are particularly useful for treating children, as they are mild and not too stimulating.

PRESCRIBING FORMS OF TREATMENT

Research has shown that oral prescription is not always the most effective form of aromatherapeutic treatment. Even within the context of clinical aromatherapy, both Gattefossé and Valnet advocated a wide range of treatment methods, to be used simultaneously. These included steam inhalations and aromatic bathing, as well as application to the skin using a suitable oil or cream base. This method of treatment means that a multiplicity of substances – specifically combined to treat the illness as it manifests in the particular patient – is absorbed into the body in a variety of ways. Gattefossé found, for example, that the inhalation method brought about an almost immediate effect on the nervous system, in contrast to the slow absorption rate via the digestive system when essential oils were administered orally.

The experienced practitioner can take advantage of all these nuances in the behavior of essential oils to formulate a unique prescription and form of treatment that is tailored to the patient, and make optimum use of the oils' qualities.

LEFT
Steam inhalation, using a few drops of oil in a bowl of steaming hot water and covering the head with a towel, causes rapid absorption of the volatile oil.

EUCALYPTUS BARK

LEFT
An experienced practitioner will know the character and therapeutic value of an individual oil, such as eucalyptus, before mixing it with others.

LEMON EUCALYPTUS

For most practitioners, perhaps the most important ingredients in preparing any kind of aromatic remedy, are knowledge and experience. Initially, it is imperative to get to know the character and therapeutic potential of each essential oil in its own right before mixing it with others. In considering a blend of oils to treat coughs and congestion, take eucalyptus blue gum (*E. globulus*), for example: it has a camphoraceous, sharp, slightly herbaceous scent; its principal areas of action are as an expectorant, bactericidal, antiseptic, and febrifuge agent; its main chemical constituent is cineole; it is specifically indicated for infectious disease and respiratory illness – especially congested coughs and bronchitis; it is contraindicated for very young children (due to toxicity levels) and will cause the skin to tingle if more than about 3 to 5 drops are added to the bath water.

Having got to know an individual oil, with all its strengths and weaknesses, it is possible to move onto its immediate family. There are various other types of eucalyptus oil, apart from E.globulus, but only a few are used therapeutically – notably *E. citriodora* and *E. radiata*. Related family members, in this case of the Myrtaceae family, include tea tree, cajeput, niaouli, West Indian bay, allspice, clove, and myrtle.

Other oils to combine in the case described on *p.* 91 might include lavender (*L. officinalis*), an effective sedative and tonic to the nerves; and benzoin (well known as an ingredient of friar's balsam, used for chesty conditions), with a mild warming, drying, and soothing effect on the whole respiratory system. The synergistic combination of myrtle, lavender, and benzoin also represents a balance of top, middle and base notes or an accord – as described in the section on perfume blending (*see p.* 48). Mixed in equal proportions, these blended essences could then be used for vaporization, in baths or for local massage. If the infection persisted, a little tea tree oil could be included for its powerful antimicrobial properties, but it has to be admitted that many children dislike its strong medicinal smell.

There are no magic rules for creating a good aromatic blend or "synergy": it is just a matter of using a combination of common sense, knowledge, and intuition. Whether preparing a blend for massage or for other simple aromatherapy uses, try to match the remedy to the person being treated as precisely as possible, and avoid discordant or unpleasant combinations of aromas. Always consult the safety data for each individual oil (*see pp.* 177–210) and check for any contraindications before using an aromatic remedy.

The chemistry of essential oils

An important aspect to consider when combining essential oils for therapeutic effect is their chemistry. Essential oils are very complex chemical compounds – a single oil can be composed of hundreds of chemical constituents. The majority of these constituents, however, can be grouped into eleven main chemical families, as shown in the panel below.

A knowledge of the chemical components of essential oils is important for several reasons. Essential oils which share a high proportion of common constituents generally blend well together. For example, clary sage and bergamot combine well because they both contain a high proportion of linalyl acetate (an ester), although they belong to different botanical families and odor groups. The chemical make-up of an individual oil, or a blend of oils, can also provide a very useful key to its potential properties and bioactivities, on both a physiological and psychological level.

The book *L'Aromathérapie Exactement*, shows an analysis of the eleven basic chemical families, each of which has an overall stimulating, sedating or balancing effect. To make the analysis, a grid or scale was produced by spraying essential oils between two electric plates, then noting down their properties. It was found that chemical components with a negative charge, which were attracted to the positive pole, exhibited stimulating, tonic, and warming properties, whereas those components attracted to the negative pole exhibited relaxing, cooling, and anti-inflammatory properties. The effect of individual essential oils and their blends could therefore theoretically be predicted according to their major constituents and their polarity. The different chemical families are graded and coded in detail, and placed in order of their stimulating and relaxing properties.

Esters are generally the most relaxing of the chemical families whereas phenols are the most stimulating. Certain other activities or properties have also been found to be generally associated with particular chemical groups. For example, esters are generally considered to have good anti-inflammatory, fungicidal, and cicatrizant (wound-healing) properties. Phenols, on the other hand, display excellent antiseptic and bactericidal properties, although they can also cause skin irritation. For details of the main chemical families found in the oils referred to in this book, *see* pp.212–214.

GLASS BOTTLE

CONSTITUENTS

The main families of chemical constituents are:

esters: relaxing
aldehydes (aliphatic): relaxing
keytones: relaxing
sesquiterpenes: balancing
lactones and coumarins: balancing
oxides: mildly stimulating
acids: mildly stimulating
aldehydes (aromatic): mildly stimulating
monoterpenes: stimulating
alcohols: stimulating
phenols: stimulating

BELOW
Oils, which should be stored in dark bottles, as above, are largely stimulating, balancing, or relaxing (sedating) in their effects, as determined by their major ingredients. Red is used to represent oils that are stimulating, purple is used to show that an oil is balancing, and blue is used to show that it has sedating effects.

RED – STIMULATING

PURPLE – BALANCING

BLUE – SEDATING

Nevertheless, as Dr. Lis-Balchin points out in her book *Aromascience: The Chemistry and Bioactivity of Essential Oils*, it would be wrong to group together essential oil components of similar chemistry, and assume that certain biological properties can be allocated to these groups with complete predictability. She points out that similar components can influence the action of different essential oils in different ways.[21]

Therefore, although it is interesting to keep the chemical constituents and related potential biological effects in mind, and to use this as a guide to the expected action of individual essential oils, it remains, at best, an estimation. Of greater value in this field are the clinical research studies that have been carried out on the specific effects of botanically classified essential oils. Many such studies have been published, providing precise information on the bioactivity and pharmacology of individual essences.

Among such studies is the systematic research into the possible stimulating or sedating effects of specific essential oils on the nervous system undertaken by Gattefossé, Valnet and Rovesti earlier this century. Using the inhalation method, they found that certain essential oils stimulated the nervous functions on a purely physiological level, while others helped induce relaxation.

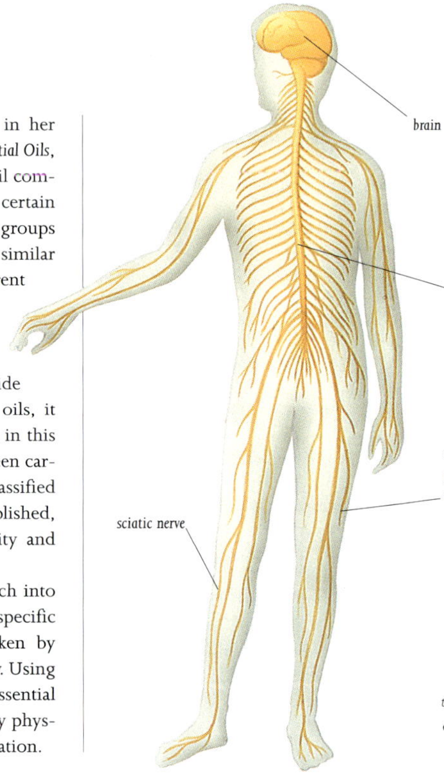

LEFT
Scientific studies have been carried out to determine the effect of specific essential oils on the nervous system.

THE EFFECTS OF INHALED ESSENTIAL OILS ON THE NERVOUS SYSTEM

The sedative or stimulating effects of some of the essential oils tested by Gattefossé, Valnet and Rovesti are shown below. Geranium proved to be an adaptogen, able to be both sedative and stimulating, depending on the circumstances.

LEFT
The oil obtained from fennel is generally stimulating to the nervous system.

Sedative	Stimulating	Aphrodisiac
aniseed	angelica	borneol (camphor)
bergamot	basil	cinnamon
carrot seed	borneol (camphor)	clove
chamomile	cardamon	myrtle
clary sage	cinnamon	rose
cypress	clove	sage
geranium	fennel	ylang ylang
lavender	geranium	
lemongrass	jasmine	**Anaphrodisiac**
marjoram	lemon	camphor
melissa	sweet orange	
neroli	pine	
	rosemary	
	sandalwood	
	sage	
	ylang ylang	

Further research aimed at distinguishing between those oils which have a sedative effect and those which have a stimulating effect was then taken up in Japan by recording brain wave patterns. During each experiment, the subjects had electrodes attached to their scalp which showed their normal electroencephalogram (EEG) trace, while the measuring device used was the contingent negative variation (CNV) curve, an electrical brain wave pattern created by anticipation. True to expectation, initial studies showed that lavender suppressed the CNV trace, while jasmine increased it – in other words lavender had a sedative effect and jasmine a stimulating one.

However, some of the CNV traces on individual oils were contrary to expectation. Notably, neroli and rose, which had previously been classified as sedative oils, were shown to have a stimulating effect on brain wave activity, while lemon and sandalwood, which were thought to be stimulating, both showed a marked sedative effect. Subsequent research has shown that some oils can simultaneously stimulate brain activity and sedate other parts of the nervous system, or vice versa. While neroli and rose essence do indeed stimulate the brain and uplift the spirits, at the same time they reduce the heartbeat and blood pressure, and soothe the nerves. Many oils, such as bergamot and geranium, also have this dual-action capacity, and have been found to have special value in stress-related disorders through helping to establish a state of calm vitality. Certain oils, such as lavender, can also produce a stimulating or sedative effect depending on the state of the individual concerned – such oils are known as "adaptogens." Using the polarity test (*see p.* 93), lavender shows an almost equal balance of stimulating and sedative components, which may help to account for its regulating effect. On the other hand, clove oil, well known to be a stimulant in treatment and containing approximately 70 percent phenols, shows an overall stimulating quality in polarity tests and the well-known relaxing and calming oil of Roman chamomile, with over 70 percent esters, was proved to be an overall relaxant.

On a purely psychological level, results show that the response can also vary or change according to concentration levels. Gattefossé had noted earlier that some essences were stimulating in small doses, but sedative in larger amounts – much like wine. For example, "angelica essence at low doses stimulates the brain, but at high doses it becomes a narcotic."[22]

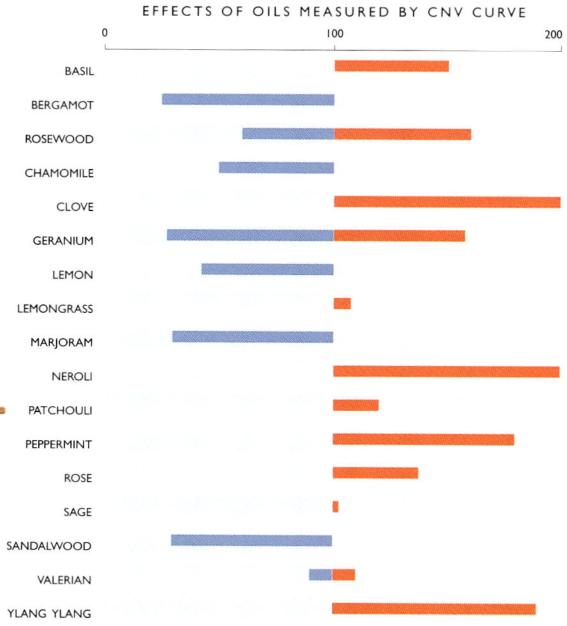

RIGHT
Brain wave patterns recorded in the contingent negative variation (CNV) curve, reveal whether a particular essential oil is sedative (left) or stimulating (right).

Aromatic remedies

Medical aromatherapy has many useful home applications. The simple treatments, such as aromatic bathing and steam inhalation, described in the first part of the book (pp. 16–41) can all be varied and used for medicinal remedies, and the massage and facial oils, moisturizers, toner-cleansers, and simple creams and gels described throughout the book can be used in treating medical complaints or common skin problems. From the facing page to page 175, a range of frequently occurring medical problems and suitable aromatherapeutic remedies is described.

ABOVE
Bee stings can be treated with essential oils.

This section begins with advice on home first aid remedies, and then covers common medical problems and methods of treatment and prevention. Aromatherapy oils that may be useful are highlighted in each case, and methods of using them described, but advice on dietary and other factors, and on complementary methods of treatment, is also given. Instead of being listed alphabetically, the complaints covered on these pages are divided into the following body systems: the skin, first aid (p. 97); skin disorders (p. 102); the skin, beauty care (p. 113); hair and scalp care (p. 118); bones, muscles, and joints (p. 122); circulatory system and heart (p. 128); respiratory system (p. 134); mouth, teeth, and gums (p. 142); digestive system (p. 145); genitourinary/endocrine systems (p. 150); immune system, infectious diseases (p. 161); nervous system (p. 167). For a complete list of entries see p. 87.

ABOVE
Home-mixed oils can be stored in glass bottles.

Always note any Warning boxes or notes on Safety data for remedies described, and consult the profiles of the oils used in treatments on pp. 178–210 for further information on each particular oil. See also the notes on using oils safely on p. 211. Do not treat serious or long-term medical problems without the advice of a fully qualified physician.

KEY TO THE SYMBOLS

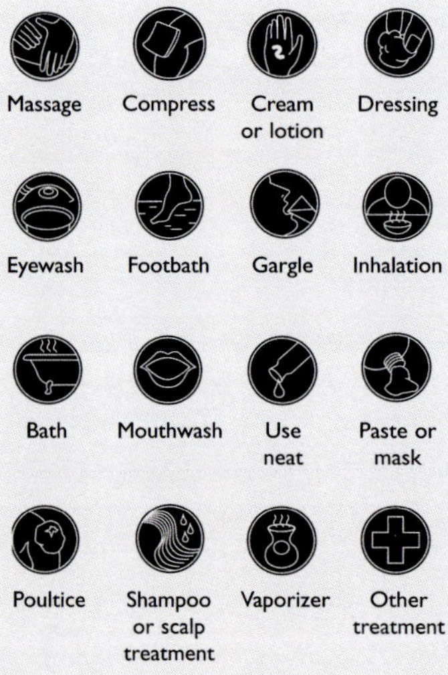

CHAMOMILE

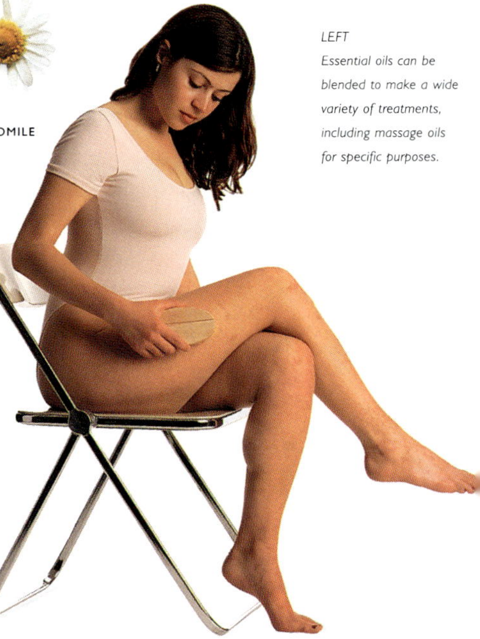

LEFT
Essential oils can be blended to make a wide variety of treatments, including massage oils for specific purposes.

THE SKIN

First Aid

Bruises

INITIAL PAIN and swelling are followed by blue, purple, or blackish discoloration of the skin, fading to yellow or brown. This indicates that the underlying tissue is damaged as a result of a knock or pressure. The skin becomes especially prone to bruising when the diet is lacking in vitamin C. Obese and anemic people are most susceptible to bruising. Frequent bruising of the skin may also indicate a kidney complaint.

WARNING
Severe bruising can cause considerable internal bleeding – if worried, seek medical help.

DIETARY FACTORS

Eat foods high in vitamin C or take a course of vitamin C tablets – recommended daily intake is 60mg.

OTHER MEASURES

The Bach Flower Rescue Remedy is recommended if there is shock. Raise and support the injured part if necessary.

BELOW
A high intake of vitamin C may help prevent frequent bruising. Oranges are a good source.

THE HUMAN SKIN

REFERENCES

BITES *see* STINGS
page 101

GRAZES
see CUTS AND WOUNDS
page 99

SCRATCHES
see CUTS AND WOUNDS
page 99

SWELLING *see* BRUISES
page 97

CLINICAL NOTES

Case study notes show tea tree to be an effective bruise remedy: "Suppurating bruise checked in 24 hours using solution diluted 1:40 as a compress. Condition cured in one week by continuing this treatment."
SEE J. LAWLESS, TEA TREE OIL, P.48

METHODS OF USE

For minor bruises, an application of neat lavender or tea tree oil reduces inflammation, and speeds up the healing process.

If the swelling is severe, apply an ice compress to ease inflammation. Then gently apply witch hazel lotion to which have been added a few drops of chamomile (Roman or German) or lavender oil. Apply this treatment two to three times a day until the condition clears.

Arnica ointment is one of the most effective bruise remedies.

WARNING
Arnica must not be applied to broken skin.

AROMATHERAPY OILS

Lavender, tea tree, chamomile (Roman and German), fennel, hyssop, geranium, cypress, yarrow.

BELOW
Arnica ointment is an excellent herbal remedy.

RIGHT
Yarrow oil can be used in dilution to treat bruises

Burns

BURNS ARE classified into three degrees of severity: superficial (redness and swelling); intermediate (swelling and blistering); and deep (numbness and charring). They can be caused by dry heat, or moist heat (scalds), and are among the most common household injuries. Burns can also be caused by contact with chemicals, radiation, or electricity.

ABOVE
Burns are frequently the result of accidents in the kitchen.

DIETARY FACTORS

Eat plenty of garlic to help build up the immune system and combat any infection. Alternatively, take a course of garlic capsules.

OTHER MEASURES

The Bach Flower Rescue Remedy is recommended if there is shock. *See also* Sunburn.

WARNING
Severe burns, especially if accompanied by shock, require immediate medical attention.

CLINICAL NOTES

Minor burns respond extremely well to treatment with essential oils, which reduces pain, prevents blistering or infection, and promotes healing without scarring. Both lavender and tea tree oil are being increasingly employed for treating burns in hospitals. (See Lawless, *Tea Tree Oil*, p.49, *Lavender*, p.55). Natural bisabolol, found in German chamomile, has been shown to be: "More effective than synthetic racemic bisabolol in healing burns."

POTTER'S NEW CYCLOPAEDIA OF BOTANICAL DRUGS AND PREPARATIONS

METHODS OF USE

Immediately hold the affected area under the cold tap for ten minutes, then apply neat lavender or tea tree oil to the burn. Reapply at least three times a day until the skin has healed.

For larger areas, especially if there is inflammation, apply an ice compress. Then gently apply a lotion made from 8 to 10 drops each of lavender and German chamomile oil in a 2fl oz/50ml bottle of distilled water, lavender water, or rose water, shaken well. Shake the bottle before each application.

Cover with a sterile gauze treated with a few drops of lavender, tea tree, or German chamomile. Replace the dressing every few hours. Do not use adhesive plasters.

Calendula cream or oil helps the skin to heal in the latter stages and prevents scarring.

AROMATHERAPY OILS

Lavender, tea tree, German chamomile, eucalyptus blue gum, geranium, yarrow.

WARNING
Avoid fatty oils or ointments when treating burns during the initial stages, as they can cause the skin to "fry."

BELOW
A gauze dressing with a few drops of essential oil is placed on the burn.

Cuts/wounds

SMALL CUTS, grazes, and scratches are some of the most common injuries. Where glass, rust, splinters, or dirt are concerned, special care should be taken to avoid secondary infection.

DIETARY FACTORS

Slow healing may be due to lack of vitamin C, which also leaves the body more open to infection, especially when the skin is broken. Eat foods rich in vitamin C or take vitamin C tablets. Garlic is indicated for infection.

OTHER MEASURES

The Bach Flower Rescue Remedy is recommended if there is shock.

RIGHT
Garlic capsules may be taken to guard against infection.

WARNING
Seek immediate medical help in cases of severe bleeding or very deep wounds, which may require stitching.

AROMATHERAPY OILS

Tea tree, lavender, chamomile (both Roman and German), yarrow, myrrh, patchouli, benzoin, palmarosa, eucalyptus blue gum, clove.

WARNING
Do not apply fatty oils or ointments to broken skin during the initial stages of healing, as these can delay the formation of scar tissue.

RIGHT
Cuts and grazes are a normal part of childhood. Aromatherapy treatment can help the body's natural healing processes.

BELOW
Lavender has excellent healing properties and is often used to treat cuts and wounds.

CLINICAL NOTES

Tea tree and lavender are excellent first aid remedies for all skin abrasions and wounds, due to their excellent antiseptic and wound-healing properties. They do not sting the exposed raw skin, even applied neat, while encouraging a rich flow of blood to the damaged area. They also prevent scarring. Clinical research has shown tea tree to be especially effective for septic conditions, pus-filled infections, and dirty wounds: "... it dissolved pus and left the surfaces of infected wounds clean, so that its germicidal action became more effective without any apparent damage to the tissues ... most effective germicides destroy tissue as well as bacteria."

SEE J. LAWLESS, TEA TREE OIL, P.9

METHODS OF USE

Cleanse with water, to which a few drops of any of the above essential oils have been added, removing any dirt or fragments.

Apply a few drops of neat lavender or tea tree oil. Cover with a plaster if required – but let the skin breathe whenever possible. Reapply several times a day until the skin has healed.

For splinters, clean the area gently, then apply neat lavender or tea tree oil. Cover with a warm clay poultice and leave for two hours. Remove the splinter with tweezers, then apply a few drops of lavender or tea tree oil and cover with a plaster.

For swelling, apply a cold compress of witch hazel lotion to which have been added a few drops of chamomile or lavender oil. Apply two or three times a day.

Cover larger injuries with a sterile gauze semi-saturated with lavender or tea tree oil. If the wound is weepy or slow to heal, include a few drops of myrrh or yarrow. Myrrh can also be applied neat to weepy wounds.

Calendula cream or oil helps the skin to heal in the latter stages, and prevents scarring.

SUN

Sunburn

THE SKIN is red, itching, and tender, eventually becoming hot and swollen. In severe cases it can turn lobster red, with acute pain, blistering, and peeling. Sunburn is a type of radiation burn due to overexposure to the sun. Radiation burns can also be caused by direct ultraviolet light (e.g. sunbeds) or reflected light (e.g. mountain snow). People with fair skin (and children) are more susceptible to burning than people with dark skin, until their pigmentation increases.

DIETARY FACTORS

Drink plenty of water, or other liquids, to avoid dehydration. People who are especially prone to sunburn can increase their tolerance levels by taking para amino benzoic acid (PABA), a member of the B vitamin family.

OTHER MEASURES

Sunbathe for short periods only, using effective sunscreens (jojoba oil is equivalent to a factor 6 sunscreen) and avoid the midday sun (12–3pm). Keep vulnerable areas covered by wearing loose clothes and a hat. *See also* Burns, Heat rash.

ABOVE
It is essential to use a good protective cream or lotion before being exposed to the sun.

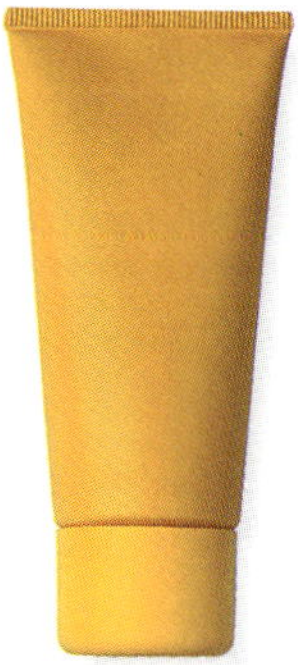

SUNSCREEN

CLINICAL NOTES

Clinical evidence has shown that lavender and tea tree can provide great relief from the effects of burns.

SEE J. LAWLESS, TEA TREE OIL, P.49 AND LAVENDER OIL, PP.50, 55

Chamomile (Roman and German), and rose oil have also both been used clinically in the treatment of radiodermatitis (burned, red, and sore skin caused by radiotherapy).

SEE J. LAWLESS, ROSE OIL, P.20, DATA BASE, VOL. I. P.7

METHODS OF USE

For patches of sunburn, apply lavender or tea tree oil neat.

For large areas, make up a lotion using 3 to 4 drops of lavender, chamomile (Roman or German) or tea tree oil (or a blend) in 1 tbs/15ml of distilled water (or chamomile or rose or lavender water) and dab the area gently.

Soak in a lukewarm bath containing 8 to 10 drops of chamomile (Roman or German), lavender or tea tree oil; afterwards gently apply a light moisturizing lotion to the skin.

Calendula cream or (infused) oil containing a few drops of rose, chamomile (Roman or German), or neroli oil, helps the skin to heal in the later stages, and prevents scarring.

AROMATHERAPY OILS

Lavender, tea tree, rose, chamomile (Roman and German), yarrow, geranium, neroli.

LEFT
Beware of reflected light when skiing or sailing, and remember that the nose is always particularly vulnerable.

WARNING
Overexposure to the sun can cause skin cancer. Excessive sunbathing also causes the skin to wrinkle and turn leathery.

WARNING
Avoid fatty oils or ointments when treating sunburn during the initial stages as they can cause the skin to "fry."

Stings/bites

STINGS AND BITES vary from minor to severe, and there may be swelling or a gash. Poisoning or an allergic reaction can cause further inflammation and pain, fever, or headaches. Among the more common bites and stings are those of jellyfish, dogs, bees, wasps, ticks, bedbugs, fleas, horseflies, gnats, sandflies, hornets, and mosquitoes. It is important to try to identify the exact cause, since the different types require individual antidotes.

HONEY BEE

DIETARY FACTORS

Vitamin C helps the skin to heal more quickly. Garlic is indicated for infection.

OTHER MEASURES

The Bach Flower Rescue Remedy is recommended if there is shock. Prevention is always better than cure in the case of all bites or stings.

CANE SPIDER

CLINICAL NOTES

Tea tree oil is traditionally used in Australia for bites and stings, including those of mosquitoes, sandflies, fleas, horseflies, wasps, and bees, and some types of spider and jellyfish.

SEE J. LAWLESS, TEA TREE OIL, P.79

In France, lavender oil has been traditionally used. Lavender has also successfully treated adder bites.

SEE J. VALNET, PRACTICE OF AROMATHERAPY, P.81

AROMATHERAPY OILS

Lavender, tea tree, chamomile (Roman and German), melissa, basil, bergamot.

ABOVE AND BELOW Insect bites may be treated with melissa oil. It is a particularly effective remedy for wasp and bee stings.

MELISSA (LEMON BALM)

WARNING
Bee stings can cause an allergic reaction, with severe swelling – seek medical help immediately if this happens.

WARNING
Snake bites can be extremely dangerous, especially in tropical countries. Get help immediately.

WARNING
Bites from rabies-infected animals or poisonous snakes, and severe insect stings inside the mouth or throat, require immediate medical attention.

WARNING
Treat bites from the black widow spider with lavender until medical help arrives.

METHODS OF USE

Bee stings Remove the sting with tweezers (avoid squeezing the venom sac). Apply an ice-cold compress saturated in a solution containing 1tsp/5ml bicarbonate of soda, and 1 tbs/15ml chamomile or lavender water (or distilled water mixed with a few drops of chamomile or lavender oil). Reapply frequently until the swelling subsides.

Ant bites and hornet stings Treat with a compress as described for bee stings (above).

Jellyfish/Sea urchin stings Remove any spikes or tentacles carefully, then apply neat tea tree or lavender oil. Repeat at intervals.

Mosquito and other insect bites Apply neat lavender or tea tree oil (or a blend of the two). Repeat every hour, or as required. If there is inflammation, apply an ice-cold compress with a few drops of chamomile, lavender, or melissa oil. To soothe irritation and prevent infection, add 8 to 10 drops of the above oils to the bathwater daily.

Ticks and leeches Apply neat tea tree oil to the live tick or leech and surrounding skin and leave. After 20 minutes, remove by hand those ticks or leeches which have not already fallen off. Apply the neat oil to the bite three times a day for a week to soothe any irritation and prevent possible infection.

Snake bites Call medical help. Do not move the bitten area, and tie a bandage around the limb to slow down the circulation. For adder bites, apply copious lavender oil.

Spider bites Mix 2 to 3 drops each of tea tree and lavender oil in 1 tsp/5ml alcohol or cider vinegar and apply three times a day.

Wasp stings Apply a cold compress saturated with cider vinegar and 2 drops of lavender or tea tree oil. Reapply fresh compresses frequently until the swelling subsides.

THE SKIN

Skin Disorders

Eczema

ECZEMA AND dermatitis are terms for a variety of inflamed or irritated skin conditions with redness, flaky skin, rashes and itching, leading to blisters, weepy sores, and scabs. In hives there is burning and itching, and white bumps, red blotches, or small boils. Sometimes large red weals may appear. Cradle cap affects very young babies. A thick, yellowish crust develops on the scalp, and there is often scaling behind the ears.

Atopic (chronic) eczema is associated with inherited allergic tendencies, especially to dairy or wheat products. Contact dermatitis is the result of hypersensitivity to an irritant such as detergents or cosmetics, dust or wool. The reaction may appear some time after the initial contact, or the skin may suddenly react to a familiar substance.

DIETARY FACTORS

Lack of fatty acids in the diet has been associated with atopic eczema, and too little pantothenic acid (vitamin B5) has been connected with allergic tendencies. Vitamin C and the B vitamins are indicated. Evening primrose oil is also beneficial. It may be necessary to consult an allergy specialist.

OTHER MEASURES

In contact dermatitis, try to isolate the allergen by a process of elimination. In both atopic eczema and contact dermatitis aim to reduce stress levels and emotional anxiety.

RIGHT Cradle cap is a form of dermatitis common in young babies. As their hair grows the condition usually disappears.

THE HUMAN SKIN

REFERENCES

BOILS *see* ABSCESSES *page 104*

CRADLE CAP *see* ECZEMA *page 102*

ONYXIS *see* NAIL INFECTIONS *page 107*

PARONYCHIA *see* NAIL INFECTIONS *page 107*

WHITLOWS *see* NAIL INFECTIONS *page 107*

WARNING

Even mild essential oils, such as chamomile, can cause an allergic reaction in some individuals, especially children. Always carry out a patch test (*see p.211*) before applying any oil for treatment. It may be necessary to experiment with different essential oils and types of treatment, due to the individual nature of the problem.

AROMATHERAPY OILS

Chamomile, tea tree, yarrow, rose, melissa, lavender, myrrh, patchouli, benzoin, carrot seed, cedarwood, Virginian juniper berry, neroli, bergamot, geranium.

METHODS OF USE

Although pure lavender or tea tree oil can be effective, very low dilutions (1 percent or less) are better suited to conditions involving allergies.

Apply a soothing cold compress, dipped in rose or chamomile or lavender water to which 1 to 2 drops of the following oils have been added: weepy eczema – patchouli or myrrh; scaly eczema – rose or melissa; inflamed eczema – chamomile or yarrow; infected eczema – tea tree or lavender. Repeat as required.

If the skin will tolerate light creams or oils, make up the following mild blend: 5 tsp/25ml calendula cream or oil or evening primrose oil with 5 to 6 drops of blended chamomile, lavender, and rose (or melissa). Apply to the affected area twice daily.

Add a few drops of a recommended oil to the bathwater as a general measure. A handful of baking soda in the water can reduce itching.

Treat eczema of the scalp, and cradle cap with 2 to 6 drops (according to age) of lavender or tea tree oil blended with 1 tbs/15ml of slightly warmed olive oil. Rub gently into the scalp, leave for 5–10 minutes, then wash out. Avoid the eyes while rinsing. Repeat daily initially, then use lavender or tea tree shampoo regularly to prevent recurrence.

CLINICAL NOTES

Clinical studies and case histories have shown tea tree oil, chamomile oil, and rose oil to be effective in various forms of dermatitis and eczema.

Barber's rash

BARBER'S RASH, tinea barbae, or shaving rash, is characterized by a mass of small red pimples on the face and neck – the skin is also often flaky and sore. The rash is a fungal infection. The condition is aggravated by shaving, and can be compounded by acne.

AROMATHERAPY OILS

Tea tree, lavender, myrrh, lemongrass, patchouli, peppermint, lemon eucalyptus, geranium.

DIETARY FACTORS

Eat plenty of garlic, or take a course of garlic capsules, to help build up the immune system and combat infection.

OTHER MEASURES

Avoid using after-shaves containing alcohol, and harsh chemical products, including scented soaps, which aggravate the skin. *See also* Acne.

RIGHT
Use mild, unscented soap for shaving.

CLINICAL NOTES

Clinical studies in California (1991) showed tea tree oil to be effective against various types of tinea, including tinea barbae.

SEE J. LAWLESS, TEA TREE OIL, P.16

METHODS OF USE

Add 10 to 12 drops of tea tree oil to a 2fl oz/50ml bottle of lavender water and shake well. Apply to the affected area using absorbent cotton. Shake the bottle well before each application.

Make up a soothing, nourishing cream or oil using 3 to 4 drops each of tea tree, lavender, and myrrh in 5 tsp/25ml of calendula cream or (infused) oil. Apply sparingly, morning and night.

Put a few drops of tea tree oil (or any of the above oils) in a basin of warm water for washing.

BELOW
Tea tree oil can be applied neat or diluted.

Athlete's foot

THIS IS CHARACTERIZED by red, soggy, or flaky skin, and itching between the toes. The soles and heels may become white and scaly. Fingers or nails may also be affected. The skin may become cracked and painful. Athlete's foot is a highly contagious fungal infection. Excessive perspiration and poorly ventilated footwear are often contributory factors to the condition.

DIETARY FACTORS

Eat garlic or take garlic capsules to help build up the immune system and combat infection. Vitamin A is necessary for the health of the skin. If you are very run down, take a course of multivitamin and mineral supplements.

OTHER MEASURES

Do not wear hosiery or footwear made from synthetic materials, and go barefoot to air the feet when possible. Meticulous hygiene is vital.

METHODS OF USE

Wash and dry the feet thoroughly, then apply neat tea tree oil – repeat two or three times daily. If the skin is soggy, dissolve the tea tree oil in a little alcohol for the first few days.

Soak the feet for 5–10 minutes daily in a tea tree oil foot bath. Use 5 to 10 drops in a bowl of warm water; a little added cider vinegar is also helpful.

Make a foot powder for daily use by mixing 3 tbs/45ml unperfumed talc or cornflour with 5 to 6 drops each of tea tree, lemon eucalyptus (or lemongrass), and lavender. Allow the base to absorb the oils for 24 hours before applying.

If the skin is cracked and painful, apply 3 to 4 drops each of tea tree, lavender, and myrrh in 5 tsp/25ml of calendula (infused) oil or cream.

AROMATHERAPY OILS

Tea tree, lavender, myrrh, lemongrass, peppermint, patchouli, lemon eucalyptus, geranium.

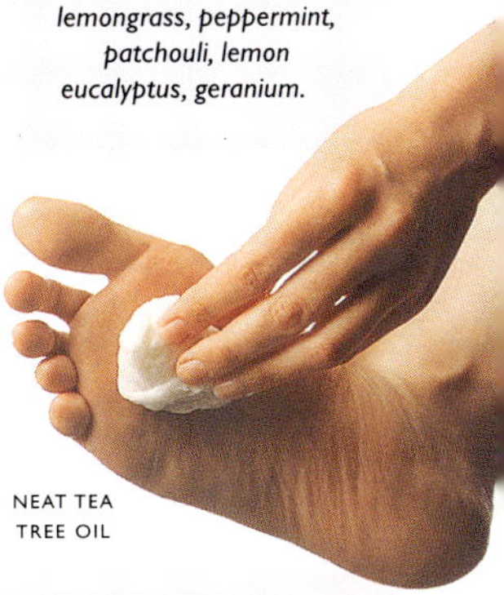

NEAT TEA TREE OIL

CLINICAL NOTES

Pure tea tree oil was used successfully to treat athlete's foot in research trials carried out by Dr. M. Walker in 1972.

Abscesses/boils

An abscess or boil is a localized painful swelling containing pus and/or serum (tissue fluid), which can occur on any part of the body. The cause appears to be an invasion by bacteria such as staphylococci or streptococci, usually occurring when the body is run down or stressed, at times of hormonal upheaval, or due to a blood disorder. Poor diet and acne are often found to be contributory factors.

DIETARY FACTORS

To purify the system, avoid stimulants, eat lots of fresh fruit and vegetables, and drink plenty of water or herb teas. Include garlic in the diet, or take a course of garlic capsules, to stimulate the immune system.

OTHER MEASURES

Never burst a boil or abscess. Immaculate hygiene is vital to stop the infection spreading. *See also* Acne vulgaris, Toothache/Tooth abscess, Stress.

BELOW
Any of the essential oils listed can be applied to the skin, diluted in a carrier oil.

ABOVE
Cleanliness is a traditional aid in treating this skin condition.

CLINICAL NOTES

Medical research has confirmed that tea tree oil is especially effective against boils and abscesses because it penetrates the skin to combat the infection and disperses the pus without making it necessary to break the skin. In a series of clinical trials, it was also shown that tea tree oil: "encouraged more rapid healing without scarring than conservative treatment."

SEE J. LAWLESS, TEA TREE OIL, P. 13

AROMATHERAPY OILS

Tea tree, lavender, bergamot (bergapten-free), myrrh, chamomile (Roman and German), lemon, galbanum, grapefruit, eucalyptus blue gum, lemon eucalyptus.

BERGAMOT OIL

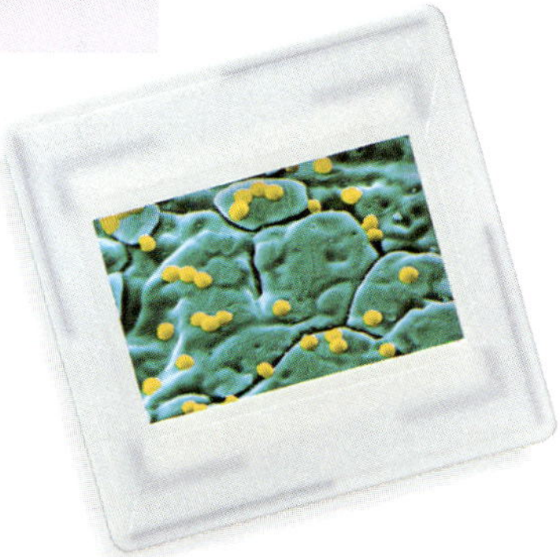

RIGHT
Staphylococci bacteria cause skin infections, such as acne or boils.

METHODS OF USE

Never wait for the boil or abscess to burst – treat as soon as it begins to appear by dabbing with neat tea tree oil. Repeat two or three times a day.

If the boil/abscess has already formed, apply a warm poultice of clay containing 3 to 4 drops of tea tree oil. Leave for 30 minutes to draw the liquid or pus, then bathe with water.

Apply a hot compress dipped in a solution of boiled water, a little cider vinegar, and a few drops of any of the recommended oils. Then dab with neat tea tree oil. Repeat the treatment two or three times daily.

If the boil/abscess is severe, apply a gauze pad that has been saturated with tea tree oil for 12 hours. Cover with a plaster.

Add 8 to 10 drops of tea tree, bergamot, or lavender oil (or one of the other recommended aromatherapy oils) to the bathwater as a general disinfectant measure.

ABOVE
Geranium oil may be added to apricot kernel oil to make a moisturizer to treat acne.

AROMATHERAPY OILS

Tea tree, bergamot, geranium, lavender, rosemary, cypress, sandalwood, lemongrass, juniper, palmarosa, petitgrain, chamomile, patchouli, lemon eucalyptus.

CLINICAL NOTES

Tea tree oil has been highlighted for use against acne in several scientifically controlled blind trials. In Australia (1990), it compared favorably with benzol peroxide, a widely used chemical acne treatment, and had fewer side effects.

SEE J. LAWLESS, TEA TREE OIL, P.15

Acne vulgaris

THIS CONDITION is characterized by a blemished complexion, enlarged pores, spots, pimples, and blackheads – sometimes boils or abscesses can develop. The face, neck, upper chest, and back are affected. The pores become congested due to overactivity of the sebaceous glands. This is especially common during adolescence, the menopause, and before or during menstruation. Acne can be exacerbated by poor diet (especially an excess of fat, oil, and sugar), too little exercise, lack of hygiene, stress, and other emotional factors.

DIETARY FACTORS

A good diet is important. Drink plenty of water and herb teas, such as chamomile, peppermint, echinacea, and lemon balm, and reduce tea, coffee and alcohol to a minimum. Vitamin A (retinol) deficiency can cause the pores to become blocked, causing whiteheads (goosepimply skin) and blackheads. Recommended nutritional supplements include evening primrose oil, garlic capsules, zinc, and vitamins A and B.

OTHER MEASURES

Take regular exercise and make time for relaxation. Moderate exposure to sunlight is also beneficial. Wash gently with an unscented pH-balanced soap, and avoid heavy make-up, especially face powders. *See also* Abscesses/boils, Oily skin, PMS/PMT, Stress.

METHODS OF USE

Apply neat tea tree oil night and morning using a cotton bud.

To stimulate the lymphatic system, aid elimination, and reduce stress, have a massage once a week, using 7 to 8 drops each of rosemary, geranium and fennel in 2fl oz/50ml of a light base oil.

To make a cleansing lotion, mix together 5 tsp/25ml witch hazel, 3fl oz/75ml lavender water, 1 tbs/15ml glycerine, 7 drops each of lavender and bergamot (bergapten-free), and 3 drops each of tea tree and chamomile oil. Shake well before using.

Make up a healing/nourishing moisturizing oil or cream by mixing 3 drops of lavender and 1 to 2 drops each of patchouli and geranium in 5 tsp/25ml of apricot kernel oil or a bland cream.

Once or twice a week, apply a deep-cleansing mask containing 5 tsp/25ml of wet clay paste and 2 to 3 drops each of tea tree, bergamot, and lavender oil.

Steam the face for 10 minutes, two or three times a week, using a few drops of tea tree, bergamot (bergapten-free), and lavender oil in a bowl of steaming hot water. Then apply cold water to which have been added 1 tbs/15ml of cider vinegar and a few drops of geranium or cypress oil.

Add 8 to 10 drops of any of the recommended oils to the bathwater, as a disinfectant measure. When washing the face, add a few drops of tea tree oil to the water in the basin.

LEFT
Acne is quite common during puberty, but it is generally agreed that eating plenty of fresh fruit and vegetables and avoiding sugary or fatty foods can help to control it.

Warts/verrucae

WARTS ARE BENIGN growths commonly occurring on hands, fingers, face, elbows, or knees. Plantar warts or verrucae usually occur on the soles of the feet, often at the base of the toes. Small black dots are visible at the center of the verruca. Both types are notoriously difficult to get rid of. Both are caused by a papilloma virus. Warts usually disappear of their own accord eventually, but because they are unsightly, most people resort to a cure.

DIETARY FACTORS

Vitamin E has been found to inhibit the formation of warts. Garlic builds up the immune system.

OTHER MEASURES

Verrucae are contagious. Wear rubber socks when swimming to prevent spreading infection.

METHODS OF USE

Treat warts with neat tree tea oil three times a day. This may take a month or more to be effective.

Verrucae should be covered daily with an equal-parts mixture of tea tree and lemon eucalyptus oil, then covered with a plaster. After a few days, the black roots of the verruca should be dug out with a needle. Treatment should be continued for about six weeks until the skin has healed over.

Add a few drops of any of the recommended oils to the bathtub or a footbath to speed up the process, and as a disinfectant measure.

Once the wart or verruca has gone, apply wheat germ or calendula cream or oil, with a few drops of myrrh added, to encourage healing and prevent reinfection.

ABOVE

Lemon is a traditional cure for warts, which are caused by a virus.

WARNING
Anal and genital warts, and those on the larynx, require medical attention.

AROMATHERAPY OILS

Tea tree, clove, cinnamon leaf, lemon eucalyptus, Virginian cedarwood, lemon, tagetes.

Corns/calluses

CORNS AND CALLUSES are areas of hard, thickened skin, generally found on the toes. A corn can form an inverted pyramid that presses into the deeper layers of skin, causing pain. Distorted nails and nail-bed infections often develop. Rheumatism or arthritic conditions, but especially poorly fitting footwear, can contribute to the problem.

DIETARY FACTORS

Lack of vitamin A in the diet can cause a build-up of dead skin cells, making the skin dry and thickened. Vitamin A is vital for the healthy functioning of the skin.

OTHER MEASURES

Correctly fitting footwear is essential for the prevention and treatment of corns and calluses. *See also* Nail infections, Warts.

AROMATHERAPY OILS

Tea tree, tagetes, carrot seed, lavender.

BELOW

Well-fitting shoes, and walking barefoot whenever possible, help to prevent corns and calluses.

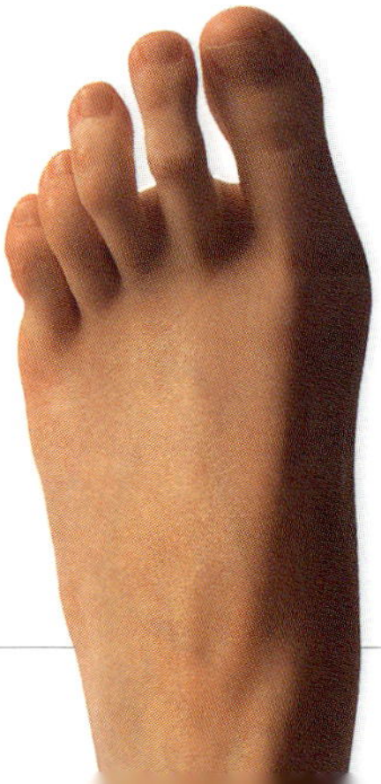

METHODS OF USE

Soak the feet daily in a bowl of warm water containing 1 tbs/15ml cider vinegar, a handful of sea salt and a few drops of tea tree oil. Dry thoroughly, then rub the dead skin away gently with a pumice stone or metal nailfile.

After bathing, apply pure tea tree or tagetes oil to the area, then cover with a plaster. Repeat daily – it may take several weeks to see any result, but the treatment is effective in the long run.

As the condition improves, to maintain and promote healthy skin, apply an ointment or oil made from 3 to 4 drops each of lavender, carrot seed and tea tree oil in 5 tsp/25ml of calendula cream or oil.

Nail infections

IN INFECTED NAILS the cuticle becomes inflamed, red and painful and there can be a slight pus discharge. The skin beneath the nail becomes discolored, and the nail itself furrowed and distorted. The most common infection Paronychia (whitlows), is often caused by contact with detergents. Onyxis is a fungal infection caused by a strain of *Candida albicans*.

DIETARY FACTORS

Adequate protein, and vitamins A and E are important for healthy nails.

OTHER MEASURES

Do not wear nail varnish. Use rubber gloves for washing up or using chemical cleaners to protect the hands.

AROMATHERAPY OILS

Tea tree, petitgrain, eucalyptus blue gum, lavender, tagetes, rosemary, carrot seed.

CLINICAL NOTES

Tree tree oil is very effective because of its penetrating, fungicidal, and antiseptic properties.

SEE J. LAWLESS, TEA TREE OIL, P14

METHODS OF USE

Rub the infected nails three times daily with pure tea tree oil for two or three minutes, massaging the oil into the nailbed.

Mix 1 tsp/5ml wheat germ oil, 4 tsp/20ml borage or carrot (base) oil and 5 to 6 drops each of lavender, rosemary, and carrot seed oil. Massage into nails and cuticles at least once a week as a preventive measure.

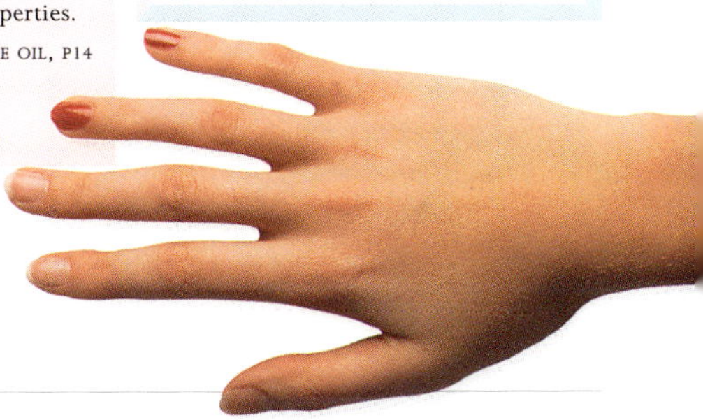

RIGHT
Nail infections can result from frequent wearing of nail varnish or from washing clothes and dishes without wearing rubber gloves.

Dhobi itch

INFLAMED PIMPLES appear on the inside of the upper thigh, and merge to form a scaly, red, and itchy patch with a clearly marked edge. The condition is properly called tinea cruris. This fungal infection usually affects men, especially in hot weather.

DIETARY FACTORS

Eat garlic or take garlic capsules to help build up the immune system.

OTHER MEASURES

Avoid wearing tight trousers, and let the skin breathe as much as possible. Wash towels and clothing thoroughly.

METHODS OF USE

Add 8 to 10 drops of tea tree and lemon eucalyptus or lemongrass oil to the bath water as a disinfectant measure on a regular basis.

Wash and dry thoroughly, and apply neat tea tree oil to the inflamed area twice a day.

As a preventive measure, apply an ointment or lotion made from 3 to 4 drops each of lavender, myrrh and tea tree oils in 5 tsp/25ml calendula cream or (infused) oil.

AROMATHERAPY OILS

Tea tree, myrrh, lavender, lemongrass, peppermint, patchouli, lemon eucalyptus, geranium.

CLINICAL NOTES

Scientific studies have shown both tea tree oil and lemongrass oil to be effective against tinea infections.

SEE M. LIS-BALCHIN, AROMASCIENCE, PP.68,100.

RIGHT
Eating garlic regularly helps to keep the immune system functioning well and so ward off many infections.

Heat rash

THIS RASH OF TINY red blisters can affect any part of the body, and is very itchy. It is the result of sweat glands being blocked through heat or humidity. An allergic reaction may also be implicated.

DIETARY FACTORS

Drink plenty of cold water to cool the body and prevent dehydration. If you are especially prone to heat rash, increase tolerance levels by taking para amino benzoic acid (PABA), a member of the B vitamin family.

OTHER MEASURES

Keep in the shade; expose the affected area to air; wear a hat, and cover up with light cotton clothing when going out in the sun. *See also* Eczema.

ABOVE
Anyone who spends time in the sun should wear a hat or some other form of protective head covering.

METHODS OF USE

Add 5 to 6 drops of blended rose (or tea tree), chamomile, and lavender oil to 5 tsp/25ml rose water, shake well, and gently dab the affected areas, using a saturated cotton pad.

Mix 4 to 5 drops of lavender with a handful (one cup) of baking powder, and add this to a lukewarm bathtub. Immerse the whole body in the water, and soak for at least 10 minutes.

CLINICAL NOTES

Clinical research has demonstrated that rose oil or water can help to alleviate heat rash.

SEE J. LAWLESS, ROSE OIL, P.70

AROMATHERAPY OILS

Lavender, chamomile (Roman and German), tea tree, rose.

Impetigo

TINY RED SPOTS, initially, turning into inflamed patches or pus-filled sores, which blister and then crust over. It usually affects the face, scalp, and neck, but sometimes the hands and knees. This highly infectious skin disease, which mainly affects children, is usually caused by an invasion of streptococcus or staphylococcus bacteria, often as a result of an infected scratch or insect bite.

DIETARY FACTORS

Eat plenty of garlic, or take a course of garlic capsules, to build up the immune system.

OTHER MEASURES

Immaculate hygiene is vital to prevent the infection spreading. *See also* Alopecia, Abscesses/Boils.

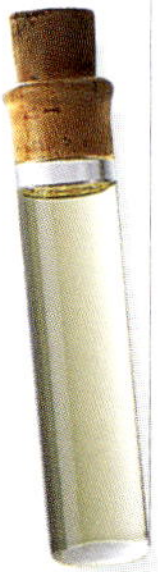

AROMATHERAPY OILS

Tea tree, lavender, myrrh, patchouli, chamomile (Roman and German), benzoin.

CLINICAL NOTES

Scientific studies have shown that tea tree oil is very effective in treating both the infection and the irritation of this contagious skin condition.

SEE J. LAWLESS, TEA TREE OIL, P.15

LEFT
Tea tree and lavender oils are powerful yet gentle antiseptics for a wide range of skin infections.

METHODS OF USE

Apply pure tea tree oil to the affected area using the tip of the finger or a cotton bud. Repeat the treatment twice a day.

If an open sore has developed, clean the area thoroughly with distilled water to which a few drops of tea tree oil have been added. Then cover with a lint or gauze compress or a dressing that has been saturated in a solution containing 5 tsp/25ml lavender water and 5 to 6 drops of tea tree oil. Fix this in place for an hour using adhesive tape (around the edge), then remove the dressing, allowing the sore exposure to air. Repeat as required.

Add 5 to 10 drops of lavender or tea tree oil and a cup of cider vinegar to the bathwater or washing water as a disinfectant measure.

Ulceration

WITH VARICOSE ULCERS, the skin initially takes on a papery-thin appearance, due to lack of blood and oxygen to the area. This fragile tissue can quickly develop into open, often painless, sores – usually on the lower legs or feet. Varicose ulcers can often form on the lower legs as a result of varicose veins. Elderly people are particularly prone to this condition, especially if they suffer from poor circulation – some merely have to scratch the skin on their lower legs and it develops into a sore which can be very slow to heal.

Tropical ulcers, or naga sores, also start with papery-thin skin. These ulcers usually occur in hot, humid climates. Again, a large, painless sore develops, often on the feet or legs, due to a bacterial infection, poor nutrition, or environmental factors.

DIETARY FACTORS

Eat plenty of fresh foods – especially those rich in fiber and vitamins E, C, D, and A. Cut down on dairy products, and avoid tea, coffee, and alcohol. Take zinc as a nutritional supplement, and a course of multivitamin tablets.

OTHER MEASURES

Keep the affected area raised as much as possible: bed rest is recommended. Avoid very hot baths. When sufficiently recovered, take gentle exercise as a preventive measure. *See also* Low blood pressure, Varicose veins.

AROMATHERAPY OILS

Tea tree, lavender, German chamomile, myrrh, bergamot (bergapten-free), geranium, yarrow.

METHODS OF USE

Bathe the sore gently with a warm, diluted solution of lavender, bergamot and/or tea tree oil by adding a few drops to a bowl of distilled or boiled water.

Apply neat lavender or tea tree oil to the sore. If the skin is very fragile, spray with distilled water to which have been added 3 to 4 drops each of bergamot, tea tree, and lavender oil per 5 tsp/25ml water (a new indoor plant spray is suitable). Shake well before use and reapply every hour. Keep the sore open to the air as much as possible.

Cover the ulcer with a clean melamine dressing, only when necessary (e.g. for sleeping).

To improve the circulation, and as a preventive measure, massage the feet regularly, using a blend of 3 to 4 drops each of rosemary, cypress, and geranium in 5 tsp/25ml carrot base oil or sweet almond oil.

As the condition improves, gently apply the following ointment, with upward strokes, once daily: 5 tsp/25ml calendula cream or oil, with 3 to 4 drops each of lavender (or bergamot), tea tree, and myrrh.

CLINICAL NOTES

Gattefossé and Valnet used lavender successfully for the treatment of long-standing varicose ulcers.

SEE J. LAWLESS, LAVENDER OIL, P.10)

Medical cases illustrate that lavender and tea tree oil are very effective. "Many cases of extreme ulcerations of the legs, with considerable suppurations, which have not responded to treatment by any other means, have been quickly cured with Ti-trol (tea tree oil)."

SEE J. LAWLESS, TEA TREE OIL, P.104

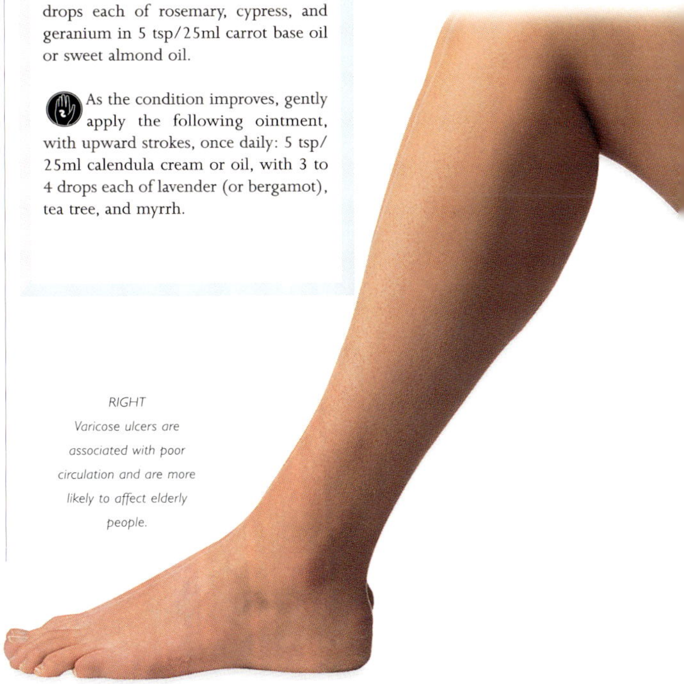

RIGHT Varicose ulcers are associated with poor circulation and are more likely to affect elderly people.

Psoriasis

PSORIASIS is a non-contagious skin disease that varies enormously in severity. Symptoms include chronic scaling, plaques, ringed lesions, smooth red areas, and acute pustules. It is believed to be caused by a dysfunction of skin enzymes, with increased turnover of epidermal cells and a dilation of dermal capillaries. Psoriasis can be precipitated by allergies, environmental factors, and stress.

DIETARY FACTORS

Assess diet for possible allergens. Take 6 x 500mg evening primrose oil daily.

OTHER MEASURES

Sunlight and sea water often give temporary relief. However, psoriasis is a difficult condition to treat, and may involve a variety of approaches. Psychotherapy, hypnotherapy, nutritional and allergy advice are particularly recommended. *See also* Alopecia, Stress.

ABOVE

Use avocado oil on the skin.

AROMATHERAPY OILS

Tea tree oil, cajeput, myrrh, lavender, Virginian cedarwood, angelica.

CLINICAL NOTES

In clinical studies 60 percent of sufferers benefited from taking evening primrose oil.

METHODS OF USE

Make up a thick lotion by blending 5 tsp/25ml avocado oil and 5 tsp/25ml borage seed or evening primrose oil with a little wheat germ oil, and adding 15 drops of tea tree, and 5 drops each of cajeput and myrrh oils. Apply at least twice daily to the affected area.

Mix together 5 tsp/25ml cider vinegar, 3fl oz/75ml lavender water, 10 drops each of lavender, cajeput, and tea tree oil. Shake well, and rub into the scalp several times a week.

Add a handful of Dead Sea salt and a few drops of the above essential oils to the bath as a general measure.

Ringworm

Ringworm (tinea capitis) usually affects the scalp, causing scaly skin and itching – temporary bald patches may also appear. It can also be found on elbows, knees, and other areas in the form of a characteristic, scaly ring. A number of different fungal organisms may be responsible, including *Trichophyton mentagrophytes* and *Microsporum audounii*. It can be picked up from pets and farm animals.

DIETARY FACTORS

Garlic builds up the immune system and combats infection.

OTHER MEASURES

Avoid wearing synthetic fibers. Expose the affected area to fresh air and sunlight as much as possible. Strict hygiene is essential to avoid reinfection. Combs, towels, clothes, and bedding should be disinfected by adding a few drops of tea tree oil to the wash. *See also* Alopecia.

AROMATHERAPY OILS

Tea tree, lemongrass, lavender, myrrh, peppermint, lemon eucalyptus, patchouli.

CLINICAL NOTES

Studies show that tea tree, lemongrass, lemon eucalyptus, and grapefruit oils are all effective.

BELOW

Ringworm can be carried by sheep.

METHODS OF USE

Apply neat tea tree oil to the affected areas. Repeat three or four times a day.

For ringworm of the scalp, apply neat tea tree oil in the same manner, then wash the hair daily with a tea tree oil shampoo.

Add 8 to 10 drops of tea tree oil, or any of the other recommended oils, to the bathwater regularly as a general disinfectant measure.

As the condition improves, make a healing and nourishing cream or oil using 3 to 4 drops each of tea tree, lavender, and myrrh oil in 5 tsp/25ml of calendula cream or infused oil. Apply morning and night.

Scabies

SMALL, RED, ITCHY PIMPLES, which can become infected. Common areas affected are the groin, penis, nipples, and skin between the fingers. This highly contagious skin disease is caused by the itch mite, *Sarcoptes scabiei*. In sheep-farming areas, it is commonly transmitted from the wool of the sheep to farm workers. It does not require close contact to pass from one person to another. The female mites lay eggs under the skin, and when hatched the mites burrow their way out, causing severe irritation and itching.

DIETARY FACTORS

Garlic builds up the immune system to combat infection.

OTHER MEASURES

Frequently wash linen and clothes using a few drops of tea tree oil in the washing water. Sponge the mattress down, using a 10 percent solution in alcohol.

AROMATHERAPY OILS

Tea tree, lavender, bergamot (bergapten-free), peppermint, clove, rosemary, lemon eucalyptus, eucalyptus blue gum, pine, thyme, lemongrass, cinnamon leaf, lemon.

METHODS OF USE

Add 8 to 10 drops of lavender or tea tree oil to bathing and washing water, as a disinfectant measure.

Wash the skin gently, then treat the affected area with a lotion made from 2fl oz/50ml glycerine, and 5 drops each of tea tree, lavender, lemon eucalyptus, clove, and peppermint oils – apply two or three times a day.

ABOVE

The scabies mite lays its eggs under the skin. When they hatch, the mites tunnel their way out, causing violent itching and blisters.

CLINICAL NOTES

Dr. Valnet cites Helmerich's Ointment as efficacious. This contains gum tragacanth, lemon, peppermint, lavender, clove, and cinnamon essential oils.

SEE J. VALNET, THE PRACTICE OF AROMATHERAPY, P.147.

Chilblains

SMALL, PAINFUL or itchy, reddish-blue swellings, mostly on the toes, fingertips, nose or ears. In extreme cases these can cause ulceration. They result from poor circulation, or extreme cold. The condition is aggravated by rubbing.

DIETARY FACTORS

Since vitamin and mineral deficiency (notably of calcium and silicon) can contribute to the problem of chilblains, it may be beneficial to take a multimineral and vitamin supplement daily. Rutin, a bioflavonoid, has also been used successfully in the treatment of circulatory disorders, and dietary supplements may help.

OTHER MEASURES

Exercise and warm clothing are important preventive measures. *See also* Low blood pressure.

AROMATHERAPY OILS

Black pepper, tea tree, lemon, lavender, rosemary, geranium, ginger, pine.

CLINICAL NOTES

The British Herbal Pharmacopoeia (1983) cites capsicum or cayenne pepper as specifics for chilblains, applied as an ointment. The essential oil of black pepper shares similar qualities.

LEFT

Poor circulation may cause chilblains and can be improved with dietary ginger, as illustrated, or ginger oil massage.

METHODS OF USE

For unbroken chilblains only, add 2 to 3 drops of black pepper oil to 1 tsp/5ml calendula or arnica cream and massage the area gently.

If the toes are affected, prepare a warm footbath to which a few drops of any of the recommended oils have been added. Soak the feet for 10 minutes at least once a day.

A regular massage treatment to improve the circulation is beneficial, using the following concentrated blend: 10 drops each of rosemary and pine, and 5 drops each of black pepper and ginger in 2fl oz/50ml of sweet almond oil. Add a little wheat germ oil as a preservative. Local blood supply can also be improved by massaging the feet or affected area with the above blend.

Cold sores

THESE PAINFUL blister-like sores are usually found on the lips or face. They are infectious and can be spread to other parts of the body or to other people quite readily. The cause is the virus *Herpes simplex I*, which can lie dormant in the body, only to flare up when the system is under stress. Some people are particularly prone to cold sores, especially when run-down or after exposure to cold winds, excessive heat, or illness.

DIETARY FACTORS

Take vitamin C and B in the diet or as supplements. Allergies can also be involved, so it is beneficial to assess any dietary indications.

OTHER MEASURES

Strict hygiene is vital to stop the infection spreading to other parts of the body or to other people. *See also* Stress.

AROMATHERAPY OILS

Tea tree, melissa, lavender, bergamot (bergapten-free), myrrh, geranium, lemon eucalyptus, chamomile (Roman and German).

METHODS OF USE

Use neat tea tree oil to dab the sore spot as soon as it begins to develop – this can stop the cold sore from developing altogether. Repeat frequently until the condition has cleared.

Add 3 drops of tea tree oil (or a blend of lavender, melissa and tea tree) to 1 tsp/5ml alcohol or cider vinegar. This astringent lotion may be used in place of pure tea tree oil during the initial stages of treatment, but only if the skin is unbroken.

In the later stages of healing, apply 3 to 4 drops each of tea tree, bergamot (bergapten-free) and lavender or myrrh in 5 tsp/25ml hypericum or calendula (infused) cream or oil.

CLINICAL NOTES

Clinical studies have shown that pure tea tree oil is a very effective remedy for cold sores, especially if they are treated early on.

SEE J. LAWLESS, TEA TREE OIL, P.16.

Genuine melissa oil is used clinically for treating cold sores in Germany by aromatherapy doctors.

ABOVE
Myrrh will ease painful cold sores and boost the immune system.

RIGHT
Early treatment with tea tree oil or a homemade blend of oils in cider vinegar can sometimes prevent cold sores from developing.

LEFT
Many people find that overwork and stress bring on attacks of cold sores. The sores can also flare up annoyingly before an important occasion.

THE SKIN
Beauty Care

Aging skin

CELL DIVISION slows down with age, and the epidermis (outer layer of the skin) becomes thinner, losing tone and suppleness. Wrinkles develop, and age spots and thread veins are also common. Smoking, drugs, poor diet, too much sun, central heating, and stress can all speed up the aging process.

DIETARY FACTORS

Overeating and overindulgence generally are implicated in hastening aging. A diet rich in fiber and fresh produce, with a minimum of additives, helps promote healthy skin. It is important to drink plenty of liquids daily, although alcohol, tea, and coffee should be drunk in moderation only. Recent research has shown that age degeneration largely results from oxidation caused by the highly reactive chemical compounds known as free-radicals. Antioxidants, notably vitamins A (beta-carotene), C, selenium, and E, can protect the body from this damage.

OTHER MEASURES

Aging is inevitable, but a healthy lifestyle with adequate exercise and relaxation, and a balanced disposition can certainly help to keep the signs of aging at bay. Despite our youth-oriented culture, age itself should not be rejected. *See also* Scarred skin, Sensitive skin.

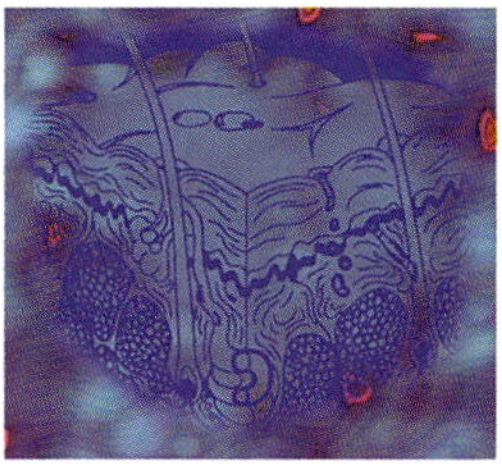

THE HUMAN SKIN

REFERENCES

CHAPPED SKIN
see **CRACKED SKIN**
page 115

GREASY SKIN
see **OILY SKIN**
page 114

MATURE SKIN
see **AGING SKIN**
page 113

THREAD VEINS
see **SENSITIVE SKIN**
page 116

WRINKLES
see **AGING SKIN**
page 113

ABOVE
Eating plenty of fresh fruit and vegetables gives vitality and helps to keep the face and body looking young.

AROMATHERAPY OILS

Rose, frankincense, sandalwood, neroli, geranium, lavender, carrot seed, elemi, galbanum, myrrh, palmarosa, patchouli.

CLINICAL NOTES

Marguerite Maury demonstrated that essential oils can do much to slow down the effects of aging by encouraging the skin cells to regenerate, as documented in *Guide to Aromatherapy: The Secret of Life and Youth.*

METHODS OF USE

Instead of soaps and alcohol-based products, use a natural toner/cleanser twice daily. In a dark, well-stoppered bottle mix 7 drops each of geranium and lavender oils and 3 drops each of frankincense and neroli (or petitgrain) oils in 3fl oz/75ml of rose water. After one month, filter into a similar container (use a coffee filter-paper). Add 5 tsp/25ml glycerine and shake well.

Regular use on face and neck of an oil or cream containing cytophylactic oils (stimulating new cell growth) is vital. A good basic blend for face and neck is as follows: to 5 tsp/25ml jojoba, almond or grapeseed oil (or a bland cream base), add 1 tbs/15ml wheat germ oil, 1 tbs/15ml rose-hip seed oil (or another rich vegetable oil, such as apricot kernel, avocado, hazelnut, borage, evening primrose, or peach kernel), and 10 to 15 drops (in total) of lavender, rose, neroli or petitgrain, and frankincense essential oils.

To treat and help prevent wrinkles around the eyes, apply a little wheat germ oil or rose-hip seed oil, gently to the area before retiring.

Gentle facial massage, avoiding the delicate area around the eyes, helps to improve the circulation and muscle tone. Use any of the recommended oils in a light base oil.

Use a face mask once a week. A basic mask can be made by mixing 2 tbs/30ml clay, 2 tsp/10ml runny honey, 1 tsp/5ml water, 4 to 5 drops (in total) of carrot seed, frankincense, and lavender oils.

Oily skin

OILY OR GREASY skin is especially common during adolescence, when hormonal changes promote the overproduction of sebum (the natural skin oil). Oily skin is more prone to developing large pores, blackheads, whiteheads, and pimples.

DIETARY FACTORS

Eating saturated fats contributes to the problem. Oily skin on the nose, forehead, and chin (combination skin) is associated with a lack of vitamin B2 (riboflavin) – found in lamb's liver, yeast, and wheat germ. Eat lots of fresh fruit and vegetables and drink plenty of water, fruit juices and herb teas.

OTHER MEASURES

Wash gently with an unscented pH-balanced soap. Adopt a suitable skin-care routine, and avoid heavy make-up. Moderate exposure to sunlight is also beneficial. *See also* Acne.

AROMATHERAPY OILS

Tea tree, bergamot (bergapten-free), geranium, lavender, rosemary, cypress, sandalwood, lemongrass, clary sage, juniper, palmarosa, petitgrain, chamomile (Roman and German), patchouli, lemon eucalyptus, cedarwood.

CLINICAL NOTES

Antiseborrheic oils are tea tree, geranium, bergamot, juniper, cedarwood, and lavender. Regulating oils are geranium, lavender, and palmarosa.

METHODS OF USE

To make a cleansing lotion mix together 5 tsp/25ml witch hazel, 3fl oz/75ml lavender water, 1 tbs/15ml glycerine, 7 drops each of lavender and geranium, 3 drops each of bergamot and sandalwood oil.

Make a moisturizing oil or cream by mixing 2 to 3 drops each of lavender, geranium, and patchouli or palmarosa oil, 1 tbs/15ml wheat germ oil, and 5 tsp/25ml apricot kernel oil or a bland cream. Use in moderation twice daily. Wipe away any excess after 15–20 minutes.

For a reviving cosmetic vinegar mix 4 tsp/20ml cider vinegar with 5 drops lavender oil, and add 4 tbs/60ml rose water and 4 tsp/20ml witch hazel.

Once or twice a week apply a mask made from 5 tsp/25ml wet clay paste with 6 to 7 drops (in total) of tea tree, bergamot, and lavender oils.

Dry skin

THIS TYPE of complexion is fine and close-textured, but it is also the most brittle, often having a fragile appearance. It becomes wrinkled more easily than greasy skin, and is also prone to flaking, and conditions such as eczema or psoriasis. In severe cases, thread veins or cracks can develop. Dry skin is aggravated by exposure to central heating and too much sun.

DIETARY APPROACH

Take a supplement of brewer's yeast, which is rich in biotin; assess the diet to check vitamin A content; if required, take a course of vitamin A supplements; use cold-pressed vegetable oils in food preparation: walnut, borage, and evening primrose oil especially.

OTHER MEASURES

Moisturize the skin regularly, and protect from extremes of cold and heat. *See also* Aging skin, Cracked skin.

AROMATHERAPY OILS

Rose, sandalwood, neroli, lavender, chamomile, palmarosa, rosewood, geranium, benzoin, myrrh.

CLINICAL NOTES

Rose oil, in the form of an ointment, is beneficial even for extremely dry skin, and has been used in clinical practice for the treatment of skin damaged by radiotherapy.

SEE J. LAWLESS, ROSE OIL, P.20

METHODS OF USE

Blend 2 to 3 drops each of rose, geranium or palmarosa and lavender, 5 tsp/25ml of apricot kernel oil, and 1 tbs/15ml of a rich oil such as avocado, borage, evening primrose, wheat germ, or rose-hip seed oil. Use as a moisturizer.

A good toner or cleanser for dry skin is made by mixing 7 to 8 drops each of chamomile, lavender, and sandalwood with 3fl oz/75ml of rose water in a dark, well-stoppered container. After one month, filter, using coffee filter-paper, then add 5 tsp/25ml glycerine and shake well. Use twice daily.

A mask for dry skin can be made by mixing 2 tbs/30ml clay, 2 tsp/10ml honey, 2 tsp/10ml cornstarch, 1 egg yolk, 1 tsp/5ml evening primrose oil or rose-hip seed oil, and a few drops of rose, lavender, or sandalwood oil. Leave on the skin for 15 minutes, then rinse off with cool water.

Cracked skin

CRACKED OR CHAPPED skin is a common problem on the feet and hands, but it can occur on the face, especially around the mouth, or on other parts of the body. The cracks can be painful. Exposure to cold, or skin complaints such as psoriasis or eczema can cause or aggravate the condition. Lack of vitamin B (especially B2, B6, and biotin), and of fatty acids may be associated with cracked skin.

DIETARY FACTORS

Include cold-pressed vegetable oils (especially walnut and borage oil), and natural sources of vitamin B, such as brewer's yeast, liver, and wheat germ.

OTHER MEASURES

Protect the skin from extreme cold, and treat exposed and affected skin with rich, moisturizing oils, such as unrefined avocado oil and wheat germ oil. *See also* Dry skin.

AROMATHERAPY OILS

Myrrh, patchouli, lavender, German chamomile, benzoin, tea tree, rose, sandalwood.

RIGHT German chamomile is soothing.

METHODS OF USE

Mix 3 to 4 drops each of myrrh, German chamomile, and patchouli/ benzoin oils with 5 tsp/25ml calendula cream. Massage the cream into the skin night and morning.

To nourish and moisturize very dry skin, add a few drops of rose oil to 5 tsp/25ml wheat germ, borage, walnut, avocado, or rose-hip seed oil (or a blend of these) and apply daily.

CLINICAL NOTES

German chamomile ointment is used medicinally for the treatment of cracked skin.

Scarred skin

SOME SCARS ARE pigmented – a common feature of birth marks – although most are flesh-colored. Most are caused by burns or deep wounds. However, a severe case of chickenpox can leave permanent pock marks, as can infected boils, spots, or abscesses. Stretch mark scars, following pregnancy or sudden weight loss, are also common.

DIETARY FACTORS

Lack of folic acid is associated with the slow healing of sores, and with a grayish-brown skin pigmentation. Vitamins C, E, and F or essential fatty acids (such as linoleic acid) are vital for the speedy healing of skin tissue.

OTHER MEASURES

To prevent scars and stretch marks, lubricate the skin, and treat wounds or boils with cicatrizant (healing, cell regenerating) oils immediately. *See also* Aging skin, Chicken pox, Pregnancy.

AROMATHERAPY OILS

Rose, frankincense, neroli, lavender, elemi, galbanum, sandalwood, palmarosa.

CLINICAL NOTES

Vegetable oils rich in vitamin E (such as borage and wheat germ) are especially good for repairing scarred skin. Rose oil, especially in combination with rose-hip seed oil, is also very beneficial for the treatment of all types of scars, including pigmented scars, stretch marks, old injuries, and surgical scars.

METHODS OF USE

Add 1 tsp/5ml of rose-hip seed, wheat germ, or borage oil to 1 tsp/ 5ml of a hypoallergenic cream base, with 1 drop of rose, lavender, or neroli oil. Apply at least twice daily.

To prevent stretch marks, mix 1 tbs/15ml each of wheat germ, borage and rose-hip seed oil in 5 tsp/ 25ml jojoba, grapeseed or sweet almond oil. Up to 6 drops of rose, neroli, frankincense, or lavender (or a combination of these) may also be added. After the fourth month, use this twice daily for light massage to the belly and breasts. This blend can also help to get rid of existing stretch marks.

Add 1 to 2 drops each of neroli, rose and lavender to 5 tsp/25ml of jojoba, apricot or peach kernel oil, or to an antiallergenic cream or lotion. Use as a daily moisturizer.

Sensitive skin and thread veins

SENSITIVE SKIN can be of any skin type, although it is usually fine-textured and delicate (like a baby's). It is easily irritated or sensitized by substances such as cosmetics, perfumes, or detergents. Thread veins mainly affect those with fair or sensitive complexions, though they can also be a sign of aging. They appear as very fine red lines on the cheeks, giving the face a ruddy appearance. Sensitive skin is commonly a hereditary condition, and may be associated with allergic tendencies. Thread veins are caused by a circulatory problem, which causes the capillary walls to dilate or stretch – like varicose veins.

DIETARY FACTORS

Sensitive skin will often react adversely to chemical food additives; alcohol, coffee, and tea should also be cut to a minimum.

OTHER MEASURES

Avoid exposure to harsh sunlight and extremes of heat or cold. For sensitive skin, it is important to avoid all possible irritants, such as lanolin or alcohol-based toiletries and perfumes, and to use only the most gentle essences. *See also* Aging skin, Varicose veins.

ABOVE
Coffee can aggravate a tendency to develop thread veins and should only be consumed in very small quantities.

CLINICAL NOTES

Rose is a remarkable ally in the fight against thread veins, due to its tonic and astringent effect – but it does require perseverance.

BELOW
Roses have long been associated with beauty, and rose oil makes an excellent treatment for sensitive skin.

METHODS OF USE

Avoid harsh soaps and products which dehydrate the skin. Instead make a natural cleanser by adding 5 to 6 drops each of chamomile and lavender, and 2 to 3 drops of rose to 3fl oz/75ml of rose water in a well-stoppered, dark container. Filter, using coffee filter-paper, after one month, add 5 tsp/25ml glycerine and shake well. Apply with a cotton pad, morning and night, before moisturizing the skin

For thread veins and sensitive skin, blend 2 to 3 drops each of rose, neroli or petitgrain, and lavender oils with 5 tsp/25ml witch hazel and 3fl oz/ 75ml orange flower water and apply to the cheeks twice a day.

For moisturizing the skin, add 5 to 6 drops (in total) of rose or chamomile or lavender oil to 5 tsp/25ml jojoba, apricot, or peach kernel oil or an antiallergenic cream or lotion. Use daily. For thread veins, mix 1 tbs/15ml of rose-hip seed oil or a hypoallergenic cream with 3 drops of rose oil and gently massage into the affected area twice daily.

For inflamed thread veins, apply soothing compresses of rose water to the cheeks.

Avoid clay masks, and instead use face packs containing honey, which is soothing and moisturizing, and suitable for thread veins, sensitive, and dehydrated skin.

AROMATHERAPY OILS

Rose, chamomile, lavender, jasmine, neroli, carrot seed, yarrow.

Perspiration

THE PRODUCTION OF perspiration or sweat is the body's natural cooling device. Vigorous exercise and heat cause an increase in perspiration rate. Stress, anxiety, or fear can cause the body to break out in a "cold sweat." Perspiration only becomes a problem when bacteria on the skin's surface cause it to break down, producing lactic acid – which has an offensive odor.

DIETARY FACTORS

Drinking plenty of water ensures that the body is constantly flushed out and cleansed. In hot climates, it is particulary important to drink plenty of water and to take extra salt to replace that which is lost in sweat.

OTHER MEASURES

Wash regularly, using bactericidal tea tree soaps; avoid wearing clothes made from synthetic fibers (nylon, polyester, lycra); wear footwear made from leather or other materials which allow the skin to breathe.

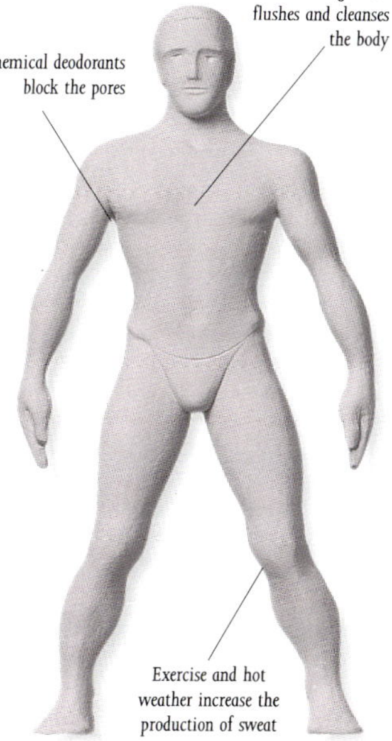

METHODS OF USE

Add 5 to 6 drops (in total) of lavender, tea tree, and/or rosemary oil, and 1 tbs/15ml of cider vinegar to a bowl of warm water, and soak the feet nightly for 5 minutes. Add 8 to 10 drops of any of the recommended oils to the bathwater.

A few drops of tea tree oil can be mixed with a little witch hazel and rubbed into the soles of the feet or beneath the arms in the morning.

A classic eau-de-Cologne can be made as follows: 100 drops/5ml bergamot, 50 drops/2.5ml lemon, 50 drops/2.5ml lavender, 30 drops/1.5ml neroli or petitgrain, 10 drops/0.5ml rosemary oils. Add to 5fl oz/150ml vodka and leave in a cool, dark place to mature for at least a month.

Add 10 drops bergamot, 5 drops lemon, 5 drops lavender, 3 drops neroli or petitgrain, and 1 drop rosemary oil to 2fl oz/50ml of a base oil such as sweet almond or grapeseed to make a cooling, refreshing body oil.

AROMATHERAPY OILS

Tea tree, petitgrain, cypress, rosemary, bergamot, grapefruit, myrtle, neroli, thyme, lemon, orange, lime, mandarin, lavender.

WARNING
Using chemical deodorants to prevent perspiration altogether is not healthy since it blocks the pores. Aluminum-based deodorants can cause dermal irritation.

EAU DE COLOGNE

CLINICAL NOTES

The classic eau-de-Cologne/deodorant oils are bergamot, neroli, lavender, and rosemary (sometimes with thyme, orange, lemon, and petitgrain added). This aromatic blend from Cologne rapidly became well known for its cooling, refreshing, deodorant and antiseptic properties.

SEE P. DAVIS, AROMATHERAPY: AN A–Z

BELOW
Lemon oil has a tangy, fresh citrus fragrance and is often used for its deodorant and refreshing actions.

RIGHT
Rosemary is used in many soaps, cosmetics and perfumes to refresh and invigorate the body.

Hair and scalp care

Greasy hair

THE CONDITION of the hair reveals a great deal about an individual's overall health and can affect a person's whole appearance. Greasy, lank hair not only looks unattractive, it is also difficult to style or control.

Greasy hair, like oily skin, is caused by overactivity of the sebaceous glands in the scalp. Frequent washing with harsh detergent shampoo strips the hair of its natural oils, and induces an ever greater production of sebum.

DIETARY FACTORS

Eating too many junk or fast foods such as potato chips, or fried foods, and especially saturated fats, can contribute to overproduction of sebum (oil) in the hair follicles and scalp. A nutritious diet, rich in minerals and vitamins (especially vitamins B, C, and F or essential fatty acids) is vital for the growth of healthy hair and for regulating seborrhea.

OTHER MEASURES

Use a mild pH-balanced shampoo that will not strip the hair of its protective acid mantle, and a natural bristle brush for brushing the hair. *See also* Dandruff, Alopecia.

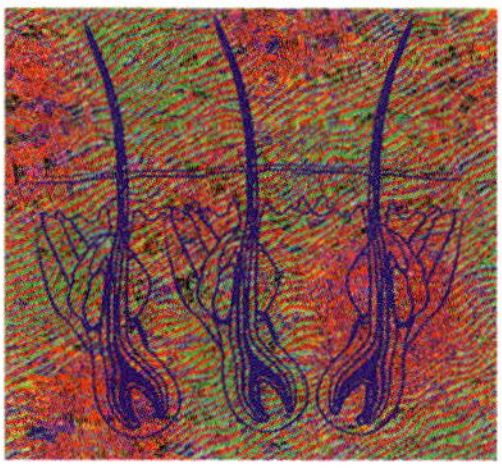

HUMAN HAIR

REFERENCES

DAMAGED HAIR see DRY/DAMAGED HAIR *page 120*

HAIR LOSS see ALOPECIA *page 119*

PEDICULOSIS see HEAD LICE *page 121*

SEBORRHEIC DERMATITIS see DANDRUFF *page 120*

METHODS OF USE

Choose a mild or pH-balanced shampoo that will not strip the hair of its protective acid mantle, and add 20 to 30 drops of rosemary, bay, and bergamot or sandalwood oil per 3½fl oz/ 100ml shampoo (or 2 to 3 drops to 1 tsp/5ml of shampoo). Try to leave at least three days between shampoos.

As a conditioner for oily hair, mix 10 to 12 drops (in total) of rosemary, sandalwood, and lavender with 5 tsp/25ml of slightly warmed jojoba oil (or sunflower seed oil) and massage thoroughly into the scalp. Wrap in warm towels and leave for an hour if possible. Wash out – applying the shampoo before the water, or the hair will remain oily. Repeat once a week.

Mix 2fl oz/50ml lavender water (rose water or orange flower water), 2fl oz/50ml witch hazel, 1 tbs/ 15ml cider vinegar, and 3 drops each of grapefruit, West Indian bay or rosemary, and lavender. Massage into the scalp between shampoos as required.

Add 3 drops of lavender, rosemary or bay and 1 tbs/15ml of cider vinegar to the final rinse water. This will help to remove detergent residue and restore the acid equilibrium of the scalp.

AROMATHERAPY OILS

Bergamot, cedarwood, cypress*, sandalwood, lemon*, lime*, grapefruit, rosemary, West Indian bay, juniper*, lavender, mandarin*, pine*, tea tree, patchouli, petitgrain, clary sage, Spanish sage, yarrow.*

*Note: The oils marked * are unstable in shampoo or detergent.*

CLINICAL NOTES

Tea tree and West Indian bay oil are used in commercial shampoos for greasy hair, while rosemary oil is used in pharmaceutically prepared lotions and liniments. Lavender oil also makes an excellent conditioning treatment for oily hair.

SEE J. LAWLESS, LAVENDER OIL, P.72

RIGHT
Washing hair too frequently encourages the overproduction of sebum – the oil that lubricates the skin – and in the long term this makes the problem worse.

Alopecia

ALOPECIA – hair loss – can be patchy, or it can result in total baldness. It mainly affects men, but some women are also prone, especially after middle age. In men, the condition is generally inherited. Poor nutrition, hormonal upheaval, and stress are also contributing factors. In women, the most common cause of hair loss is the overuse of hair dyes, permanents, and bleaches. Illness, and the side effects of chemotherapy and radiotherapy can cause dramatic hair loss.

BELOW
Overheating, even from modern hand-held driers, can severely damage the hair, as can strong chemical treatments.

DIETARY FACTORS

Cut down on tea, coffee, and alcohol and eat foods that are rich in vitamins and minerals. Vitamins B, C and F (essential fatty acids) are especially good for the hair, as is inositol, found in liver, wheat germ, oatmeal, molasses, and yeast. A course of yeast tablets and a lecithin supplement are recommended.

OTHER MEASURES

Avoid chemical treatments and wash the hair once a week only, using a mild pH-balanced shampoo. *See also* Hair care.

CLINICAL NOTES

Essential oils help combat hair loss by stimulating the hair follicles (roots), and, especially in combination with massage, by promoting the circulation: Studies have shown that… "pure lavender essence used as a scalp massage reduces hair loss and encourages regrowth."

SEE C. MEUNIER, LAVENDER AND LAVENDINS, P.198

RIGHT
Many essential oils are good for the hair and scalp.

METHODS OF USE

Local massage is effective if carried out regularly. Make a scalp massage oil by mixing 3 tbs/45ml coconut oil, 3 tbs/45ml wheat germ oil, and 7 to 8 drops each of West Indian bay, rosemary, and lavender oils.

To encourage hair growth and to treat baldness (alopecia), mix 10 to 12 drops of rosemary or lavender with 5 tsp/25ml of slightly warmed jojoba oil, castor oil or extra virgin olive oil and massage thoroughly into scalp. Wrap in warm towels and leave for an hour. Wash out – but apply shampoo before the water, or the hair will remain oily. Repeat once a week.

Mix 1 tbs/15ml cider vinegar with 3 drops each of West Indian bay, rosemary, and lavender oils, and add to 3½fl oz/100ml of lavender or rose or orange flower water. Shake well and massage the mixture into the scalp.

Alternatively rub a few drops of neat lavender oil into the scalp.

Add a few drops of any of the above oils to the shampoo at each wash, or to the final rinse water.

AROMATHERAPY OILS

West Indian bay, rosemary, lavender, German chamomile, clary sage, juniper, Spanish sage, yarrow.

RIGHT
As a herbal remedy, try rinsing with nettle infusion.

Dandruff

DANDRUFF CAN BE mild or severe. In pityriasis, and simple dandruff, small, dry flakes of dead skin are released into the hair from the scalp, spoiling its appearance. In seborrheic dermatitis, however, the greasy patches of skin may become infected, causing scabbing and inflammation. Seborrheic dermatitis is aggravated by overactive sebaceous glands. Chemical hair preparations, poor diet, and stress can contribute.

DIETARY FACTORS

Faulty diet and food allergies are often a major cause, especially when combined with greasy hair. Evening primrose oil capsules and vitamin E will help most cases of dandruff.

OTHER MEASURES

Use a natural bristle hair brush, and avoid brushing the hair when it is wet. If the condition persists, have a food allergy test.

CLINICAL NOTES

Scientific research has demonstrated that lemongrass oil is effective specifically against *P. ovale*, a fungus or yeast infection that causes dermatitis.

SEE M. LIS-BALCHIN, AROMASCIENCE, P.68

AROMATHERAPY OILS

Tea tree, chamomile, citronella, clary sage, lavender, lemongrass, lemon eucalyptus, rosemary.

METHODS OF USE

Mix 25 drops of tea tree oil (5 drops of lemongrass oil may also be added) with 2fl oz/50ml of slightly warmed jojoba or coconut oil. Massage thoroughly into scalp. Wrap in warm towels and leave for an hour. Wash out, using about 5 drops of tea tree oil to 1 tsp/5ml of a mild shampoo. Apply the shampoo before the water, to prevent the hair remaining oily. Repeat once a week.

Use up to 5 drops of tea tree oil to 1 tsp/5ml mild shampoo on a daily or regular basis.

Between washes, if required, rub a few drops of pure tea tree oil into the scalp using the fingertips.

Add a few drops of any of the recommended oils to the final rinsing water when washing the hair.

Dry/damaged hair

DRY, STRESSED, OR overtreated hair tends to become dull, frizzy, and difficult to manage. The hair becomes brittle, and the ends split more easily. It is often the result of frequently subjecting the hair to chemical treatments, such as permanents, bleaching, or artificial coloring. Exposure to the sun and heat treatments also dry out the hair.

DIETARY FACTORS

Protein deficiency results in brittle hair and nails, while a lack of essential fatty acids (found in cold-pressed vegetable oils) causes dry hair and a scaly scalp. A nutritious diet is vital for the growth of healthy hair.

OTHER MEASURES

Use a mild pH-balanced shampoo, which will not strip the hair of its protective acid mantle, and a natural bristle brush. *See also* Alopecia, Dandruff.

AROMATHERAPY OILS

Sandalwood, ylang ylang, lavender, chamomile (Roman and German), rose, geranium, petitgrain, neroli, clary sage, Spanish sage, yarrow, rosemary, tea tree.

Note: Ylang ylang is not stable in shampoo or detergent.

ABOVE
Chamomile is especially indicated for dry, irritated or sensitive scalp conditions.

METHODS OF USE

Choose a mild or pH-balanced shampoo and add 20 to 30 drops (in total) of chamomile, lavender, and geranium per 3½fl oz/100ml of shampoo (or 2 to 3 drops of essential oil to 1 tsp/5ml of shampoo).

Mix 10 to 12 drops (in total) of chamomile, petitgrain, and lavender with 5 tsp/25ml of slightly warmed jojoba oil, castor oil or extra virgin olive oil. Massage thoroughly into the scalp. Wrap in warm towels and leave for an hour. Wash out – but apply the shampoo before the water, or the hair will remain oily. Repeat once a week.

As a final rinse for dry hair, add 3 drops of lavender, petitgrain, geranium, or chamomile oil, and 1 tbs/15ml cider vinegar to the rinsing water. This will help to remove detergent residue and restore the acid equilibrium of the scalp.

HEAD LOUSE (PEDICULUS)

LEFT
Lice multiply rapidly in the hair, by laying tiny eggs. Their bites cause an uncomfortable itching sensation in the scalp.

Head lice

LICE ARE SMALL, grayish, blood-sucking insects that live in the hair. They keep very close to the scalp and can be difficult to see because they are no bigger than a pinhead. Lice can pass very quickly from one head of hair to the next. The first sign of their presence is often that the scalp starts to itch. This occurs after the lice have multiplied enough to cover the scalp with thousands of tiny bites. The lice also lay tiny, grayish-white eggs – the nits – which attach themselves firmly to the hair, usually near the scalp. The eggs are hard to see, and can also be quite difficult to remove.

DIETARY FACTORS

To prevent lice, eat plenty of garlic regularly.

OTHER MEASURES

Regular combing can usually keep lice infestations at bay. If any member of the family does get lice, it is vital that all family members check their hair and carry out preventive treatments. Brushes, combs, towels, and pillowcases should be thoroughly washed and disinfected, using a few drops of tea tree oil in the washing water.

CLINICAL NOTES

Several essential oils can kill lice, but do not prevent their eggs from hatching. Therefore, they must be used regularly (at three-day intervals) until all the eggs have hatched or been removed. These remedies are less toxic than commercial treatments, and actually improve the quality of the hair rather than damaging it.

AROMATHERAPY OILS

Eucalyptus blue gum, lavender, tea tree, cinnamon leaf, rosemary, geranium, clove, thyme.

METHODS OF USE

During an outbreak, use a lavender or tea tree oil shampoo daily to prevent contamination. Add 1 to 3 percent of lavender or tea tree oil to a mild or pH-balanced shampoo (use 20 to 60 drops per 3½fl oz/100ml of shampoo, or 2 to 3 drops to 1 tsp/5ml of shampoo). Leave for 10 minutes before rinsing. Also add a little lavender oil to the conditioner or final rinse water.

To counteract lice or eggs, make up an alcohol-based scalp rub by adding 1 tsp/5ml of lavender and tea tree oils to 5 tsp/25ml vodka, and 3fl oz/75ml water. Leave for at least an hour (overnight if possible), then wash out. Finally comb the hair carefully with a fine-toothed comb. Repeat every three days from the start of an infestation until the condition has cleared up.

If the scalp is too irritated or sensitive to use alcohol, replace the alcohol and water in the scalp rub with a vegetable oil.

FINE-TOOTHED COMB

ABOVE AND RIGHT
A scalp rub of a recommended oil and a special comb, available from pharmacies, can be used as part of the treatment.

ROSEMARY OIL

Bones, muscles, and joints

Rheumatism

GENERALLY, RHEUMATISM (like fibrositis) refers specifically to muscular pain, whereas arthritis is associated with pain located within the joints. The onset of rheumatic tendencies is often gradual, and the exact cause can be difficult to define – however, the condition nearly always signifies long-term friction, either of a purely physical, or of a more subtle, psychological nature. A slight, though progressive, aching in the muscles, can suddenly flare up, usually in association with stress, or environmental factors, such as exposure to cold or damp, or a change in diet.

DIETARY FACTORS

Since rheumatism, like arthritis, is aggravated by an accumulation of toxins in the system, the diet should be adjusted in a similar manner (*see* Arthritis).

OTHER MEASURES

It is most important to assess the overall lifestyle: "It is essential to treat the whole being, (for) when the unique picture of the individual is taken into account, it is possible to open the gates for quite a miraculous healing to occur."

SEE HOFFMAN, THE HOLISTIC HERBAL, P.83

See also Muscular pain

ABOVE
Fennel can be very helpful for rheumatic aches and pains, both as part of the diet, and as fennel seed oil rub, mixed with a base oil.

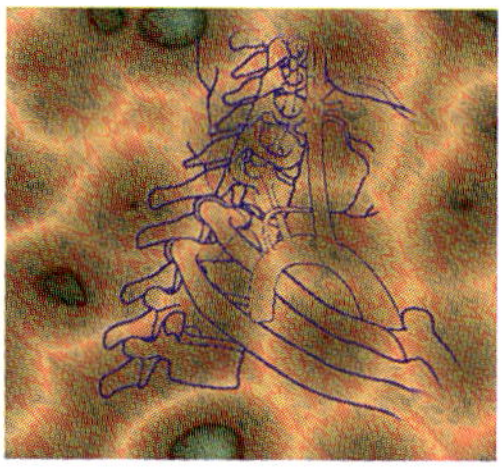

BONE TISSUE

REFERENCES

ACHES AND PAINS *see* **MUSCULAR PAIN** *page 124*

GOUT *see* **ARTHRITIS** *page 125*

HOUSEMAID'S KNEE *see* **BURSITIS** *page 127*

MUSCULAR SPASM *see* **CRAMP** *page 126*

OSTEOARTHRITIS *see* **ARTHRITIS** *page 125*

RHEUMATOID ARTHRITIS *see* **ARTHRITIS** *page 125*

SPORTS INJURIES *see* **SPRAINS/STRAINS** *page 123*

TENNIS ELBOW *see* **BURSITIS** *page 127*

CLINICAL NOTES

Spike lavender and juniper oil are current in the British *Herbal Pharmacopoeia* for the treatment of rheumatic pain, applied topically.

METHODS OF USE

Massage is helpful for rheumatic pains because it stimulates the circulation and helps remove toxins. For a concentrated massage oil mix 3 to 4 drops each of lavender, juniper, rosemary, and black pepper or ginger oil in 5 tsp/25ml Saint-John's-wort oil. Apply by massage to the area twice daily.

Add 8 to 10 drops of any of the recommended oils to the bathwater whenever required for pain relief, and to increase mobility.

Alternate hot and cold compresses, using a few drops of lavender or chamomile oil, can help relieve pain and swelling. Leave each compress in place for 10 minutes before changing.

AROMATHERAPY OILS

For detoxifying - fennel, juniper, carrot seed, celery seed, lemon, tea tree, angelica, grapefruit.
For inflammation – chamomile, lavender, yarrow.
Analgesic (pain killers) for stimulating greater mobility – pine, spike lavender, marjoram, rosemary, ginger, black pepper, eucalyptus blue gum, cardamom, peppermint, clove.

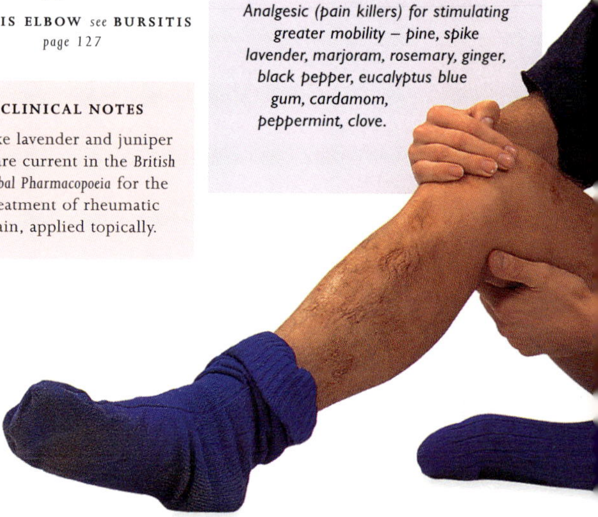

ABOVE
Pine is used in many ointments to treat sprains and strains.

Sprains/strains

SPRAINS CAUSE PAIN and tenderness around the joint, made worse by movement, with swelling and bruising. A strain is characterized by a sudden, sharp pain at the site of the injury. There can be swelling, stiffness, and cramp. A sprain occurs at a joint where the ligaments and surrounding tissues are wrenched or torn. A strain occurs when a muscle or group of muscles is over-stretched by a violent or sudden movement. It is most commonly caused by lifting heavy weights or by taking strenuous exercise.

DIETARY FACTORS

Adequate vitamin C in the diet is vital for the rapid healing of tissues and bones.

OTHER MEASURES

Rest and support the affected area. Elevate an injured limb, using cushions.

CLINICAL NOTES

The traditional remedy for application to slow-healing sprains, oleum spicae, was made by combining spike lavender oil and turpentine (pine oil).

LEFT
Sprains and strains are frequent sports injuries, and can be avoided to some extent by warming-up before exercise. When they do occur, aromatherapy can speed up the healing process.

METHODS OF USE

Apply a cold compress (with ice) to which a few drops of chamomile oil have been added. Repeat as often as possible to reduce the swelling. Do not massage. Wrap in a bandage moistened with witch hazel lotion, and rest as much as possible.

As the swelling subsides, gently apply the following cream or oil: 3 to 4 drops each of pine, lavender and rosemary oil in 5 tsp/25ml calendula cream or oil. Alternatively, use a liniment moistened with a few drops of any of the recommended oils (or a blend).

Apply arnica ointment to the skin locally for bruising – unless the skin is broken.

To encourage healing, soak in a warm bath containing 8 to 10 drops of one of the recommended oils and 3 tbs/ 45ml sea salt.

AROMATHERAPY OILS

Spike lavender, lavender, chamomile, pine, rosemary, eucalyptus blue gum, thyme, marjoram.

WARNING
Severe sprains or strains are difficult to distinguish from fractures: in all doubtful cases, seek medical help immediately.

Muscular pain

Muscular aches and pains can affect any part of the body. Many people carry tension in their necks and shoulders, which causes the muscles to become tight and painful. Muscular pain can be caused by overexertion, poor posture, cold or damp, injury, stress, and tension. It can also be related to other complaints, such as rheumatism, arthritis, lumbago (lower back pain), or a "slipped disk".

DIETARY FACTORS

Muscular aches and pains can indicate lack of biotin (this can be destroyed by taking antibiotics). The best natural source of biotin is yeast. Lack of vitamin E can also lead to muscular degeneration, causing stiffness and pain: supplements of evening primrose or borage oil are indicated.

OTHER MEASURES

Take gentle exercise (yoga, swimming); assess stress levels; avoid sudden, strenuous exercise without sufficient training. Alexander Technique can help improve habitual poor posture; osteopathy is indicated if there is a slipped disk or structural problem.

LEFT
While keeping fit with regular gentle exercise can help to prevent muscular aches and pains, sudden stressful exercise is a major cause of these problems.

METHODS OF USE

Muscular aches and pains respond well to local massage – make a massage oil by adding about 7 to 10 drops each of lavender, marjoram, and rosemary oil to 2fl oz/50ml of carrier oil, and rub into the affected area. Best after a warm shower or bath.

Soaking in a hot bathtub is an easy and effective way of relaxing the muscles and bringing instant pain relief. Adding 8 to 10 drops of any of the recommended oils to the water will increase the benefits further.

As a preventive treatment, and to tone the muscles before strenuous exercise, make a massage oil by mixing 10 drops each of rosemary and pine oils with 5 drops each of grapefruit and black pepper oils in 2fl oz/50ml of a vegetable carrier oil. Rub gently into the whole body, concentrating on the muscles that will have to work the most.

AROMATHERAPY OILS

Marjoram, rosemary, black pepper, chamomile, lavender, ginger, pine, juniper, bergamot, grapefruit.

ABOVE
Ginger warms the muscles and the oil is effective in sports massage.

CLINICAL NOTES

It is well known among keen sports players that the combination of essential oils and massage is very effective for muscular aches and pains, as well as a valuable preventive treatment:

"Rosemary is ... a very good oil to use for tired, stiff and overworked muscles. I have used it very successfully for massage [before and] after training or competing."

SEE P. DAVIS, AROMATHERAPY: AN A–Z, P.293

ROSEMARY

LEFT
Rosemary oil is widely used in the treatment of muscular aches and pains.

Arthritis

THERE ARE SEVERAL different kinds of arthritis, all forms of joint distress resulting in pain and progressive immobility. The three most common are rheumatoid arthritis, osteoarthritis, and gout. With the former, which can affect all age groups, the connective tissue around the joints (usually the wrists and knuckles) becomes swollen. The skin becomes tight and shiny around the joint, which gradually becomes stiff and sometimes deformed. With osteoarthritis, which usually occurs in the elderly, an aching pain and stiffness develop slowly, usually in the hips, knees, or fingers. Gout is characterized by severe pain and swollen joints, often with a burning sensation. It usually affects the joints of the toes, but also sometimes the fingers. All types signify an inability to eliminate toxic waste efficiently. Heredity, stress, emotional conflict, lack of exercise (or overuse, in the case of osteoarthritis), poor diet (or over-rich food, in the case of gout), or food allergies can all contribute to these conditions.

DIETARY FACTORS

Initially the diet should aim at eliminating toxic waste: drink plenty of water and herb teas; eat salads, fruit, green vegetables, whole wheat bread, pulses, white meat, and fish. Avoid red meat, tea, coffee, alcohol, fried foods, vinegar, spices, refined flour and sugar products, and all additives and preservatives. Vitamins A, C, D, and E are especially important for healthy bones and muscles. Take 1 tbs/15ml cod liver oil, and evening primrose oil supplements daily.

OTHER MEASURES

Take gentle exercise, especially yoga; reassess physical, emotional, and environmental factors – many cases of arthritis are brought on by underlying emotional issues. It is important to identify anything that aggravates the condition, such as stress, cold, and certain foods. It may be valuable to consult a dietary specialist to check for food allergies

CARROT

CARROT SEED

CLINICAL NOTES

Case studies show that aromatherapy is one of the most effective treatments for arthritis through helping to eliminate toxic waste, as well as providing considerable relief from pain and increased mobility.

ABOVE AND BELOW

Massage with carrot or carrot seed oil is one of the best forms of treatment.

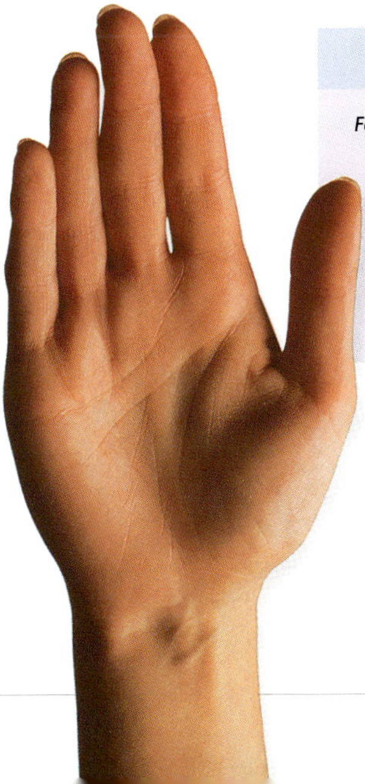

METHODS OF USE

As an excellent initial detoxifying treatment for all types of arthritis add 3 drops each of fennel, carrot or celery seed, and juniper oil (or up to 10 drops of any of the above detoxifying oils) to the bathwater, together with two handfuls of Epsom salt and one of rock salt. Repeat daily for two weeks. Oils (see below) for soothing pain or increasing mobility are also beneficial used in baths.

Make a massage oil to stimulate greater mobility and ease pain by mixing 7 to 10 drops each of lavender, rosemary, and marjoram oil with 2fl oz/50ml of a vegetable carrier oil. Rub into the area very gently twice daily.

To ease inflammation and pain, apply a cold compress with a few drops of lavender, and chamomile or yarrow oil. To reduce stiffness, a hot compress may be used with oils such as rosemary, marjoram, or black pepper.

AROMATHERAPY OILS

For detoxifying – fennel, juniper, carrot seed, celery seed, lemon, grapefruit.
For inflammation – chamomile, yarrow, lavender.
For stimulating greater mobility – pine, marjoram, rosemary, ginger, black pepper, eucalyptus blue gum, cardamom, lavender.

WARNING
Immediately after any kind of heat treatment (baths, massage, compress), the joint should be kept moving to avoid congestion. Never massage directly over a swollen joint.

Cramp

CRAMP OR MUSCULAR spasm causes sudden, intense pain. It can affect both the smooth (involuntary) muscle and the voluntary muscles with which we move our limbs. The calf or foot are most commonly affected (often at night), especially if there is anemia, or during pregnancy. Dysmenorrhea is also a form of cramp, caused by the contraction of the smooth muscles surrounding the uterus wall; stomach cramps often accompany severe indigestion or diarrhea. Poor circulation, exposure to cold, or other factors which cause an insufficient flow of blood to the muscle tissue can all cause spasm. An overworked muscle may also suddenly go into spasm, a common problem for keen sports players.

DIETARY FACTORS

A rich or heavy diet can induce cramps. Avoid swimming immediately after eating a big meal. Lack of pantothenic acid (found in yeast, liver and wheat germ) may be involved. Cramp can also be caused by a deficiency of salt, sodium, or other elements in the blood. Garlic capsules, calcium, and zinc supplements are recommended. The herb cramp bark, taken as a tea three times a day, is effective.

OTHER MEASURES

Stretch or flex the cramped muscle; then, gently stroke the affected area to warm it up, before applying deeper pressure, finally kneading the knotted muscles. *See also* Dysmenorrhea, Dyspepsia, Muscular pain, Pregnancy.

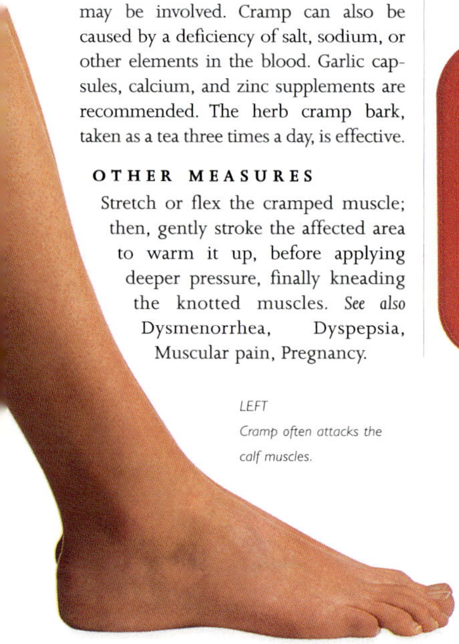

LEFT
Cramp often attacks the calf muscles.

CLINICAL NOTES

Many case histories bear witness to the fact that essential oils are very valuable for treating and preventing cramp or muscular spasm.
"I was troubled by acute pain and spasm in my neck muscles ... I massaged lavender into my neck which greatly reduced the pain and muscle spasm."

SEE INTERNATIONAL JOURNAL OF AROMATHERAPY, VOL. 3, NO. 1, 1991, P.24

BELOW
A hot water bottle can be used for cramp.

AROMATHERAPY OILS

Rosemary, clary sage, marjoram, black pepper, lavender, ginger, pine, bergamot, juniper, chamomile, coriander.

METHODS OF USE

To relieve muscular spasm of the limbs, or if a particular area is very tight or painful, massage with a concentrated blend containing 5 drops each of marjoram, rosemary, and lavender oil, and 3 of black pepper or ginger oil in 5 tsp/25ml base oil or cream.

For stomach cramp, period pains, or muscular spasm brought on by cold, apply a hot compress, using a few drops of clary sage or marjoram oil. Keep it warm with a hot water bottle.

As a preventive treatment after strenuous exercise, make a concentrated massage oil by mixing 7 to 10 drops each of rosemary, marjoram, and lavender oil with 2fl oz/50ml of a vegetable carrier oil. After a warm shower, rub the oil gently into the whole body, concentrating on the muscles that have worked the most.

Add 8 to 10 drops of any of the above aromatherapy oils to the bathwater after taking strenuous exercise as a preventive measure.

RIGHT
Massage with one of the recommended aromatherapy oils will help relieve cramp.

Bursitis

BURSITIS is characterized by hot, swollen, and tender skin at the elbow joint (tennis elbow), knee joint (housemaid's knee), shoulder, or hips. This is due to inflammation of the bursae – the small, water-filled cushions that enable muscles and tendons to move smoothly at the joint.

The condition may be caused by repeated use, friction, or accident involving a hard knock to the joint. It may also show a degenerative rheumatic or arthritic tendency.

DIETARY FACTORS

Boost the amounts of dietary calcium and magnesium, needed to form the synovial fluid which lubricates the joints. Rich sources of calcium include milk, leafy green vegetables, nuts, seeds, and grains. Foods rich in magnesium are whole grains, nuts, and seafood. Vitamin C is also vital for the rapid healing of tissues and bones. Take vitamin C supplements to aid recovery.

OTHER MEASURES

Rest the joint until the inflammation has subsided. *See also* Arthritis, Edema, Rheumatism.

METHODS OF USE

Mix 3 to 4 drops each of rosemary, pine, and marjoram or clove oil with 5 tsp/25ml of calendula cream or oil and apply gently, twice daily, to the affected part of the body.

Initially, if the joint is very swollen, apply a cold compress, using a few drops of lavender or chamomile oil. Repeat as required to reduce inflammation.

CLINICAL NOTES

Clove stem should not be used in aromatherapy treatments due to dermal toxicity.

Clove bud oil is officially: "patented for external use in the degeneration of bone, inflammation of joints, bursitis, and the treatment of sinuses."

SEE M. LIS-BALCHIN, AROMASCIENCE, P.45

AROMATHERAPY OILS

Clove bud, chamomile, spike lavender, yarrow, rosemary, marjoram, pine.

WARNING
Never massage directly over a swollen joint.

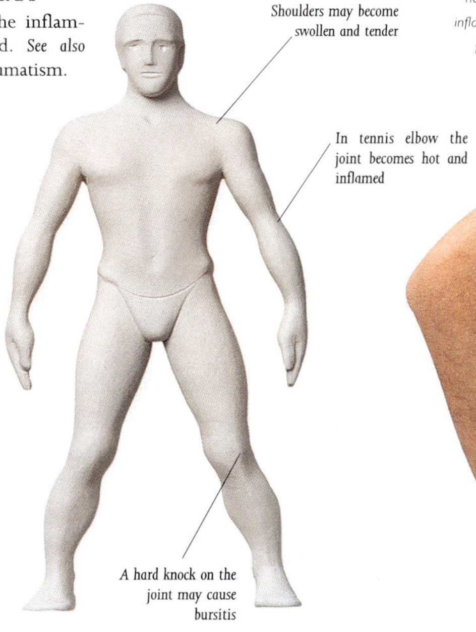

RIGHT
Inflamed joints respond well to treatment with the recommended oils. Rest helps induce inflammation.

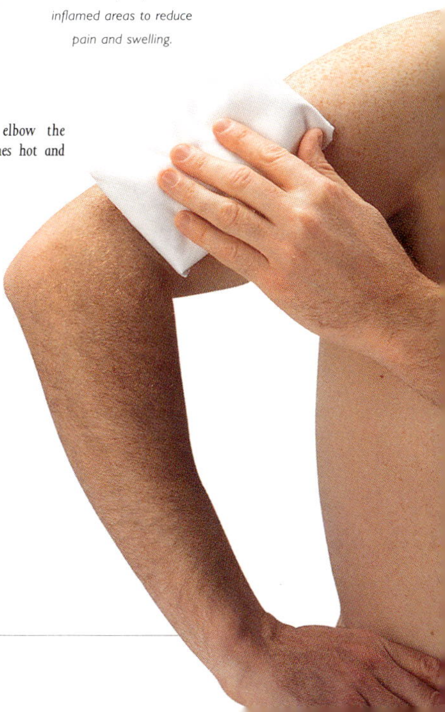

BELOW
A cold compress can be held over painful and inflamed areas to reduce pain and swelling.

The Circulatory System and Heart

Arteriosclerosis

MANY FORMS OF arteriosclerosis go unnoticed but one of the main symptoms of the most serious form, which affects the coronary arteries, is angina, a severe pain in the chest, and also breathlessness, usually brought on by stress or exercise. The danger of arteriosclerosis is that it can result in a coronary thrombosis (heart attack) or a stroke if the warning signs are not heeded in time. There may also be kidney damage. Arteriosclerosis is caused by a slow build-up of fatty deposits (atheroma) in the lining of the arteries (which carry blood from the heart). This leads to a thickening and hardening of the arterial walls, restricting the flow of blood and oxygen. Atheroma is linked to high blood cholesterol.

DIETARY FACTORS

Eat plenty of fresh, unrefined foods; avoid red meat, animal fats, dairy produce, and refined wheat and sugar products; alcohol, tea, and coffee should be drastically reduced – a glass or two of red wine is permitted. Cut out salt altogether. Raw onions, garlic, and rosemary, vitamin C and E supplements are all beneficial.

OTHER MEASURES

To reduce stress levels, a more relaxed lifestyle, which includes gentle exercise (yoga or swimming are ideal), should be taken up. Aromatherapy massage can help to reduce stress and anxiety levels. *See also* High blood pressure, Stress.

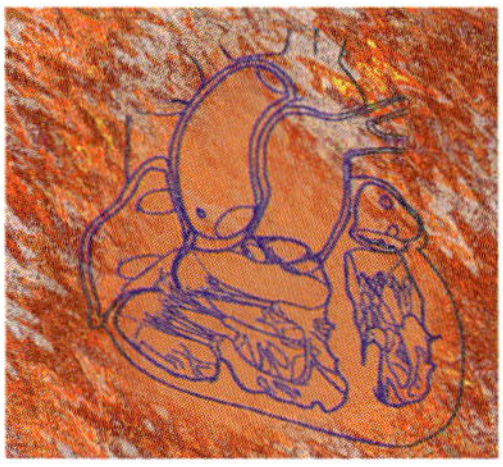

THE HEART

REFERENCES

ANGINA *see* ARTERIOSCLEROSIS *page* 128

BLOOD PRESSURE *see* HIGH BLOOD PRESSURE *page* 129, LOW BLOOD PRESSURE *page* 130

FLUID RETENTION *see* EDEMA *page* 133

HYPERTENSION *see* HIGH BLOOD PRESSURE *page* 129

HYPOTENSION *see* LOW BLOOD PRESSURE *page* 130

PILES *see* HEMORRHOIDS *page* 132

POOR CIRCULATION *see* LOW BLOOD PRESSURE *page* 130

TARCHYCARDIA *see* PALPITATIONS *page* 130

METHODS OF USE

Have a massage at least once a week using 7 to 10 drops each of rosemary and lavender oils and 5 drops of valerian oil in 2fl oz/50ml of vegetable carrier oil.

Rub the above blend of oils into the chest and soles of the feet on a daily basis.

Use relaxing oils such as lavender, marjoram, or chamomile for baths on a daily basis to help to reduce stress levels.

AROMATHERAPY OILS

Rosemary, lemon, yarrow, lavender, valerian, marjoram, juniper, chamomile.

CLINICAL NOTES

Yarrow is current in the British Herbal Pharmacopoeia as a specific for thrombotic conditions with hypertension.

Gentle exercise helps reduce stress levels

Yoga stretches the muscles gently without putting any strain on the body

RIGHT
Relaxation is a key to reducing stress and its damaging effects on the heart and blood vessels. Yoga is an ideal form of exercise to encourage relaxation as well as fitness.

ABOVE
Valerian, once known as "all heal," has been used as a herbal remedy since medieval times. It is now used to treat angina.

High blood pressure

HIGH BLOOD PRESSURE is a common side effect of the fast pace of 20th-century life. Symptoms may include headaches, palpitations, feelings of anxiety and restlessness – workaholics are especially prone. The condition, in the long term, may lead to serious kidney disease or heart failure. Prolonged stress, smoking, and arteriosclerosis (the thickening and hardening of the arterial walls); poor diet, especially too much alcohol, salt, animal fats, and caffeine, can all contribute to the problem.

DIETARY FACTORS

Diet should be reassessed: eat plenty of fresh, unrefined foods, especially those containing vitamin E; avoid red meat, animal fats, salt, and refined wheat and sugar products; stimulants such as alcohol, tea, and coffee should be drastically reduced. Intake of cholin and inositol should be reviewed. Garlic is beneficial.

OTHER MEASURES

General lifestyle, work, and ambitions need to be seriously reassessed for satisfactory long-term results. Other measures may include yoga, meditation, psychotherapy or counseling. *See also* Arteriosclerosis, Palpitations, Stress.

ABOVE AND RIGHT
Intake of stumulants such as alcohol and coffee, and salty foods such as smoked fish should be reduced.

ABOVE
Avoid foods containing animal fats, sugar and over-refined flour.

CLINICAL NOTES

Aromatherapy massage has been found to be especially effective in implementing change in this field.

GRANARY LOAF

SAVOY CABBAGE

COFFEE BEANS

METHODS OF USE

If possible, put aside some time each week to have a regular professional massage, using a blend of relaxing oils: 7 to 10 drops each of ylang ylang, lavender, and marjoram oil in 2fl oz/50ml jojoba oil. Self-massage or massage between partners or friends is also valuable.

Take a soothing bath every day, using 8 to 10 drops of relaxing oils such as lavender, ylang ylang, chamomile, or marjoram.

Use relaxing oils, singly or blended, in a vaporizer at home or in the office on a regular basis. Alternatively, put a few drops on a handkerchief for inhalation throughout the day.

AROMATHERAPY OILS

Lavender, marjoram, ylang ylang, chamomile (Roman and German), clary sage, vetiver, melissa, yarrow, bergamot, valerian, rose, neroli, jasmine.

LEFT
A good mixed diet, with plenty of fresh fruit and vegetables, fresh fish, cereals, and grains rather than red meat, and vegetable oils rather than animal fats, helps to ensure good health and normal blood pressure.

SMOKED MACKEREL

Low blood pressure

Although this condition (hypotension) has less potential danger than high blood pressure, it is often accompanied by debilitating symptoms such as dizziness, lightheadedness, constant feelings of tiredness, and sensitivity to the cold (especially the hands and feet). Nervous exhaustion, stress, poor circulation, anemia, and hereditary factors can all contribute.

DIETARY FACTORS

Eat foods rich in vitamins C and E; also use lots of onions and garlic. Spices such as ginger, coriander, and black pepper can help to stimulate the circulation.

OTHER MEASURES

Fresh air, sufficient exercise, and deep breathing exercises are beneficial. Brisk massage is particularly useful.

AROMATHERAPY OILS

Rosemary, pine, basil, fennel, peppermint, West Indian bay, thyme, angelica, Spanish sage, black pepper, caraway, ginger, cinnamon, coriander, clove, camphor.

ABOVE
Fresh garlic and garlic oil in capsule form help regulate blood pressure and protect against heart disease.

METHODS OF USE

Make a therapeutic massage oil by mixing 7 to 10 drops each of rosemary, pine, and basil (or 5 of black pepper) oils with 2fl oz/50ml of a vegetable carrier oil. Apply briskly to the entire body, paying particular attention to the hands and feet.

Add 8 to 10 drops of any of the above aromatherapy oils to the bathwater regularly.

Use stimulating oils in a vaporizer at home or in the office to uplift the mind and invigorate the body.

WARNING
Hypotension can be a symptom of a more serious health problem – if worried, seek medical advice.

Palpitations

This is a general term used to describe an irregular heartbeat, either "missing a beat" or a rapid fluttering or pounding of the heart. The condition (tachycardia) can be brought on by exercise (which is quite normal), but is also associated with high blood pressure, stress, and panic attacks. It is especially common in women during the menopause.

DIETARY FACTORS

Increase intake of the B vitamins; avoid stimulants, notably nicotine and caffeine; do not eat too much; use garlic in cooking (or take as a supplement); drink relaxing herbal teas, such as chamomile or verbena.

OTHER MEASURES

Training in yoga, meditation, deep breathing, or relaxation exercises can help to reduce stress levels and combat panic attacks.

AROMATHERAPY OILS

Ylang ylang, lavender, clary sage, rose, melissa, chamomile, neroli, valerian.

WARNING
Palpitations may be a sign of an underlying heart disorder – if worried, seek medical advice.

BELOW
A regular massage can reduce stress levels.

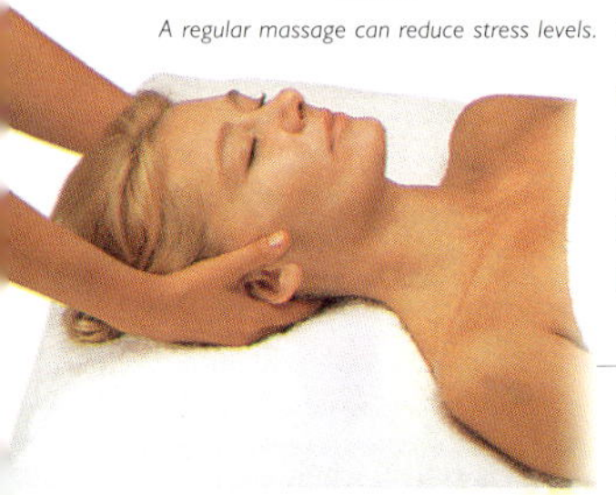

METHODS OF USE

A full-body massage is very effective in reducing stress levels. If possible, have a regular professional massage weekly, using a blend of 7 to 10 drops each of ylang ylang, lavender and clary sage oils in 2fl oz/50ml jojoba oil.

For self-massage, use the above blend and rub thoroughly into the soles of the feet. This is very therapeutic and relaxing.

Inhaling ylang ylang (or other relaxing oils) can help calm a rapidly beating heart.

Regular aromatic bathing using ylang ylang, lavender, neroli, rose, or chamomile essential oils helps reduce stress levels and anxiety, which often trigger tachycardia.

Cellulite

THIS FATTY, orange peel-like cell tissue commonly found on the thighs, legs, and upper arms, is very stubborn to shift even after considerable weight loss from other parts of the body has been achieved. There is a variety of causes: toxicity is a major factor, whether the cause is environmental or due to diet. Treatment, therefore, should focus on ridding the body of impurities. There is also a hereditary predisposition to developing cellulite.

DIETARY FACTORS

Correct diet is essential in the treatment of cellulite. Eliminate (or reduce) tea, coffee, alcohol, and refined products; use organically produced foods whenever possible; eat lots of raw fruit and vegetables, and drink plenty of spring water or herb teas. Zinc and vitamins C and B complex are also indicated.

OTHER MEASURES

Even severe cases of cellulite can be reversed if dietary changes are combined with the following measures:

- Plan an exercise routine which specifically targets the cellulite (as cellulite often gathers in places that tend to get no exercise).
- Give the area vigorous massage and use a loofah or scrubbing brush briskly while in the bath. This can help to break down congestion within the system, especially when combined with appropriate essential oils.
- Take up relaxation and deep breathing exercises to increase the supply of oxygen to the tissues, which is vital in shifting cellulite.
- Increase blood circulation with daily dry skin-brushing. Using a brush of real bristle, brush toward the heart, up legs, trunk, and arms, and down from the shoulders, starting with the feet and continuing all over the body.
- Have a full-body massage each week, if possible, concentrating on stimulating lymphatic drainage.

CLINICAL NOTES

There are many commercial creams and oils which claim to eliminate cellulite – often with dubious results. Essential oils are only effective if they are used in combination with the other measures stated here.

ABOVE
Celery seed helps eliminate the build-up of toxins in the body.

METHODS OF USE

A full-body massage, using 7 to 8 drops each of rosemary, geranium, and fennel to 2fl oz/50ml base oil, is very beneficial, helping to increase the circulation generally and improve lymphatic drainage

Make up a concentrated oil or cream using 3 to 4 drops of carrot seed, grapefruit and fennel oils in 5 tsp/25ml of jojoba or carrot carrier oil (or a bland cream) and rub into the affected areas vigorously.

Use 8 to 10 drops of any of the recommended oils (or a combination) in the bathtub. In addition, apply a few drops to a brush or loofah and rub the affected areas briskly in circular movements while bathing.

AROMATHERAPY OILS

Spanish sage, bergamot (bergapten-free), rosemary, juniper, thyme, grapefruit, celery seed, fennel, geranium, carrot seed, coriander, angelica, mandarin, orange, lime, petitgrain, lemon.

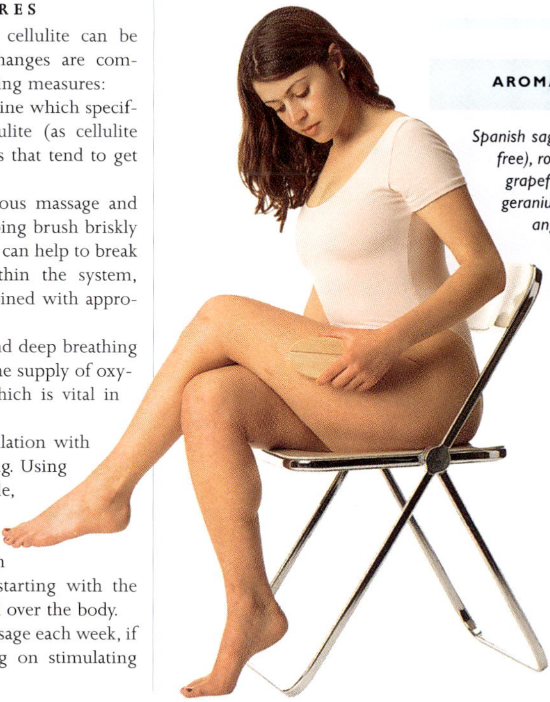

WARNING
Many citrus oils are phototoxic – do not use on the skin before exposing to direct sunlight or using a sunbed.

LEFT
Massage and dry skin-brushing help to improve the circulation and discourage toxic wastes from accumulating in the thigh area.

Hemorrhoids

HEMORRHOIDS OR PILES are swollen veins in the walls of the anus, which can appear on the inside or outside. They may be itchy or painful, and can bleed – surgery may be required in severe cases. Heredity, a sedentary lifestyle, overweight, sluggish circulation, pregnancy, constipation, and poor diet are all contributing factors.

DIETARY FACTORS

Include plenty of roughage in the diet, such as bran and whole wheat bread; salads and fruit also help to cleanse the digestive system. Drink plenty of liquids daily. Take a course of garlic capsules and vitamin E supplement.

OTHER MEASURES

Take more exercise, and keep the legs raised as much as possible. Inverted yoga positions are beneficial. *See also* Varicose veins.

AROMATHERAPY OILS

Cypress, geranium, yarrow, rose, Virginian cedarwood, clary sage, frankincense, myrrh, myrtle.

CLINICAL NOTES

Ranunculus (pilewort) is specific for this problem, used in topical application. Yarrow oil has well-documented vasoconstrictive properties.

FRANKINCENSE

METHODS OF USE

To alleviate symptoms and as a preventive, make up an ointment using 5 to 6 drops each of cypress or yarrow, and geranium oils in 5 tsp/25ml calendula cream (or a gel). Apply topically several times daily, or as required.

Add 8 to 10 drops of any of the above oils to the bathwater, or to a sitz or hip bath daily.

To soothe irritation, use cold witch hazel lotion applied on absorbent cotton.

LEFT AND BELOW Frankincense and yarrow are both recommended for circulatory problems.

Varicose veins

THESE ARE unsightly and sometimes painful, swollen, or knotted veins, usually in the legs. They are the result of poor circulation and inadequate elasticity in the walls of the veins. Heredity, lack of exercise, standing for long periods, overweight, pregnancy, and poor nutrition all make a contribution to this condition.

DIETARY FACTORS

Have a diet high in fiber; vitamins E, and C, and rutin (a riboflavonoid found in buckwheat and the pith of citrus fruits) are also indicated; use garlic in cooking (or take as a supplement).

OTHER MEASURES

Take gentle exercise; do not sit with legs crossed; avoid standing for long periods; rest with the legs raised (also when sleeping); inverted yoga postures are beneficial; do not take very hot baths. *See also* Hemorrhoids.

AROMATHERAPY OILS

Cypress, geranium, rose, yarrow, Virginian cedarwood, clary sage, frankincense, myrrh.

CLINICAL NOTES

Cypress and rose can do much to tone the blood vessels and reduce dilation.

YARROW

METHODS OF USE

Make up a massage oil or cream containing 7 to 10 drops each of geranium (or 5 of rose), yarrow and cypress oil in 2fl oz/50ml calendula oil or cream and rub gently into the area around and above the veins. DO NOT press directly on them or below them, and work up the legs toward the heart. The legs should be elevated after massage. Repeat this massage daily.

To help reduce swelling, apply local cold compresses soaked in witch hazel lotion.

Warm (not hot) baths with 8 to 10 drops of a circulatory stimulant such as rosemary or juniper can help improve the condition of the circulatory system as a whole.

Edema

IN EDEMA, excess fluid is retained in the body tissues, causing swelling or puffiness. Most commonly found in the ankles, it can also affect the hands, feet, abdomen, around the eyes – or the whole body. Edema or fluid retention is a common complaint, especially during pregnancy and in obesity, and is caused by fluids leaking from the tissues. Allergies, sprains, high blood pressure, PMS, jetlag, and taking oral contraceptives can contribute to this condition.

ABOVE
Massage with a recommended oil, such as celery seed, helps eliminate excess fluid.

DIETARY FACTORS

B vitamins are indicated; fennel, celery, parsley, garlic, and onions are beneficial. Drink fennel herb tea.

OTHER MEASURES

If the ankles or feet are affected, keep the legs raised as much as possible, and while sleeping. Massage is one of the best treatments for stimulating the circulation and lymphatic system, and thus eliminating excess fluids. Gentle exercise is a valuable preventive measure. *See also* Bursitis, Jetlag, PMS.

WARNING
Generalized edema is often a sign of serious kidney disease or progressive heart failure – seek medical help immediately.

METHODS OF USE

Add 3 to 4 drops each of rosemary, geranium, and fennel to 5tsp/25ml of carrier oil or cream. Massage into the affected area using upward strokes (always toward the heart).

If possible, have a full-body lymphatic drainage massage, once a week until the condition subsides.

Add 8 to 10 drops of any of the oils listed to a warm (not hot) bath, or to a footbath if the ankles are affected.

WARNING
Rosemary and juniper are contraindicated during pregnancy.

AROMATHERAPY OILS

Fennel, geranium, cypress, juniper, rosemary, celery seed, parsley seed, dill, angelica, carrot seed, grapefruit, thyme, lavender, clary sage, chamomile.

CLINICAL NOTES

In a venture combining aromatherapy and herbal medicine, a blend of six oils (juniper, lavender, clary sage, chamomile, rosemary, and thyme) was applied by neuromuscular and lymphatic drainage massage to three women suffering from PMS-associated edema twice a month:
"It was concluded that the treatment was successful for persistent edema and the synergy between two complementary disciplines was proven."

SEE DATA BASE, VOL. I, P.10.

BELOW
Edema, or fluid retention, often affects the feet and ankles.

The Respiratory System

Colds

THE SYMPTOMS of a cold include sore throat, coughing, feverishness, aching limbs, sneezing, fatigue, and catarrh. Secondary infections such as bronchitis, sinusitis, or ear infections may arise. There are at least thirty different strains of the virus which can cause the common cold, or in medical terms coryza. It is a highly contagious infection affecting the upper respiratory tract, and is picked up by breathing infected air. Exposure to cold, damp conditions, and to stuffy or smoky atmospheres, stress, and being generally run down are all contributory factors.

DIETARY FACTORS

Eating excessive amounts of dairy and wheat products encourages the formation of excess mucus. A cold is the body's attempt to cleanse the system of this congestion. To keep the system clean, eat plenty of fresh fruits and vegetables, particularly those high in vitamin C (especially lemons, oranges, strawberries) and lots of onions and garlic. Alternatively, if already infected, take a course of garlic capsules and vitamin C tablets. Cut down on alcohol, tea, and coffee: instead drink herbal teas – especially peppermint, rose-hip, and elderflower – or lemon with honey.

OTHER MEASURES

Rest and keep warm – staying in bed encourages faster recovery and prevents the germs from spreading. *See also* Coughs, Headaches, Influenza, Throat infections.

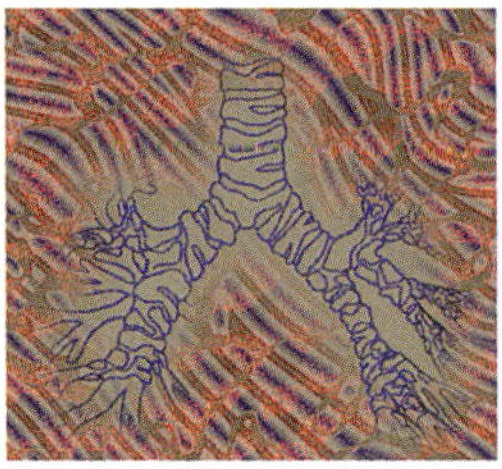

THE RESPIRATORY TRACT

REFERENCES

OTITIS
see EARACHE/OTITIS
page 140

RHINITIS
see HAY FEVER
page 138

SORE THROATS
see THROAT INFECTIONS
page 141

METHODS OF USE

For colds with a cough, or chills, make up a warming, concentrated chest rub by mixing 4 to 5 drops each of ginger, thyme, and lavender or hyssop in 5 tsp/25ml of carrier oil, and apply to the chest and upper back. Repeat at least twice a day.

Use tea tree, thyme, or eucalyptus oil in vaporizers throughout the duration of the illness, but especially at the onset of the cold – this may prevent it from developing at all. Add a few drops of one of these oils to a handkerchief for inhalation throughout the day. Use drops of soothing oils such as myrtle or lavender on the pillow at night.

Add 5 to 6 drops (in total) of tea tree, eucalyptus, or Spanish sage or thyme oil to a bowl of steaming water, cover the head with a towel and breathe deeply for 5–10 minutes, keeping the eyes closed. (Very hot steam is in itself a hostile environment for viruses.) Repeat at least twice a day.

Take a daily hot bath, adding 8 to 10 drops of tea tree, rosemary, or thyme to the water – this combats congestion and fights infection. Lavender, marjoram, or bergamot oil can also be used in baths to soothe aching limbs and encourage restful sleep.

For a sore throat, add 4 to 5 drops of tea tree or Spanish sage or clary sage or thyme to a glass of warm water, mix and gargle at least three times daily.

AROMATHERAPY OILS

Tea tree, eucalyptus blue gum, myrtle, rosemary, marjoram, lavender, cajeput, lemon, pine, thyme, peppermint, bergamot, black pepper, ginger, cinnamon leaf, clove, Spanish sage, hyssop.

RIGHT
Tea tree oil has a very potent antiseptic and antiviral action and is effective for colds.

Coughs

COUGHING IS A reflex action aimed at clearing the respiratory tract. A cough can be dry and unproductive, or can be accompanied by mucus discharge. Coughs can have several causes, including smoking, and exposure to dust, pollen, or a cold, damp atmosphere. They usually occur in association with an infection such as whooping cough, or with allergies such as hay fever or asthma.

DIETARY FACTORS

Dairy and wheat products encourage the formation of excess mucus. To cleanse the system, eat plenty of fresh fruits and vegetables, especially those high in vitamin C (including lemons, oranges, and strawberries) and lots of onions and garlic. Cut down on alcohol, tea, and coffee, and instead drink herbal teas – especially peppermint – and lemon with honey. The herb coltsfoot is excellent for persistent coughs, taken as a tea or syrup, three times a day.

OTHER MEASURES

Stop smoking, rest, and keep warm, especially the chest, throat, and neck area. Identify the type of cough (dry, infected, congested) and treat accordingly. *See also* Bronchitis, Colds, Fever, Headaches, Influenza, Sinusitis, Throat infections.

AROMATHERAPY OILS

Warming/tonic (for chills) – angelica, cinnamon, ginger, nutmeg, clove, aniseed.
Soothing/balsamic (for dry coughs) – benzoin, cedarwood, myrrh, frankincense, galbanum, sandalwood, marjoram.
Expectorant (for excess mucus) – myrtle, peppermint, hyssop, pine, rosemary, lavender.
Antimicrobial/antiviral (for infection) – eucalyptus blue gum, tea tree, bergamot, thyme, camphor, cajeput, Spanish sage.

STRAWBERRIES

METHODS OF USE

To loosen mucus and ease congestion, rub the chest, back, and throat with a blend of warming and expectorant oils: 3 to 4 drops each of lavender, thyme, ginger or hyssop in 5 tsp/ 25ml of a light base oil or cream.

Regular steam inhalations will help to soothe a dry cough. Add 2 to 3 drops each of sandalwood, and/or frankincense or benzoin to a bowl of steaming hot water and inhale for 5 to 10 minutes. For congestion, use 2 to 3 drops each of tea tree, lavender, thyme, peppermint, and/or eucalyptus oil. Repeat at least twice a day.

To combat infection, use tea tree, spike lavender, eucalyptus, or thyme (or a combination) in a vaporizer or humidifier in the home, and more soothing oils (sandalwood, benzoin, frankincense, cedarwood, or myrtle) for dry coughs and in the bedroom at night. A few drops of these essential oils may also be put on a handkerchief for inhalation throughout the day.

Hot baths with 8 to 10 drops of any of the recommended oils (or a combination) aid the body's natural response to infection. This also has a similar effect to steam inhalation.

ABOVE LEFT
Vitamin C is found in fresh fruit and vegetables. Strawberries are a particularly good source.

WARNING
Use no more than 3 drops of the spice oils (eucalyptus, camphor or peppermint) in the bathtub.

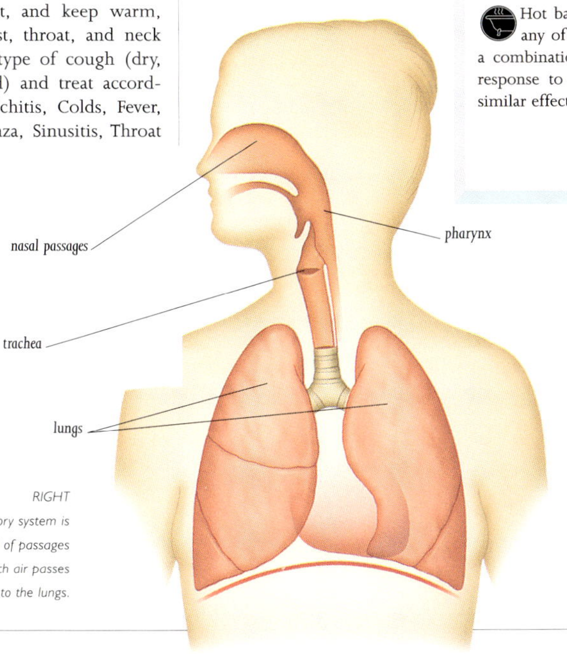

RIGHT
The respiratory system is composed of passages through which air passes to the lungs.

Bronchitis

BRONCHITIS indicates an inflammation of the bronchial tubes, and is accompanied by coughing, mucous congestion, chest pain, and aching muscles. Acute bronchitis usually starts with a cold or sore throat, which then develops into a fever that lasts a few days. Chronic bronchitis is a long-term condition, without fever, which is aggravated by smoking, a cold, damp climate, air pollution, and even bad posture, stress, and, sometimes, allergies.

DIETARY FACTORS

Dairy products, white flour products, and junk foods aggravate bronchitis. A wholesome, nutritious diet is essential for building up the body's defenses. Foods rich in vitamins A and C are especially indicated. Ginger, garlic, onions, and horseradish are good preventive additions to the diet. Take fresh ginger root tea three times a day throughout the winter. The herb coltsfoot, taken as a tea or syrup, is excellent for the treatment of long-term lung weakness.

OTHER MEASURES

Give up smoking. Rest, and keep the whole body warm, especially the chest and neck area. Avoid cold and damp, or very dry, air and open fires. *See also* Colds, Coughs, Fever, Headaches, Sinusitis, Sore throat.

AROMATHERAPY OILS

Soothing/balsamic – benzoin, cedarwood, myrrh, frankincense, galbanum, sandalwood, marjoram.
Expectorants – myrtle, peppermint, hyssop, pine, rosemary, lavender.
Antimicrobial/antiviral – eucalyptus blue gum, tea tree, bergamot, thyme, camphor, cajeput, Spanish sage.

CLINICAL NOTES

Chronic bronchitis has been successfully treated by inhalations of peppermint, lavender, and sage mixture.

WARNING
Use no more than 3 drops of the spice oils (eucalyptus, camphor, peppermint) in the bathtub.

METHODS OF USE

To loosen mucus and ease congestion, rub the chest, back, and throat with a blend of warming and expectorant oils: 4 to 5 drops each of lavender, peppermint, and Spanish sage or clary sage oil in 5 tsp/25ml of a light base oil or cream. Alternatively, use the same quantities of hyssop, thyme, and angelica oil.

If the cough is dry, regular steam inhalations will help to soothe irritation: add 6 drops (in total) of sandalwood, and/or frankincense or benzoin to a bowl of steaming hot water, and inhale for 5–10 minutes. If there is infection or congestion, use 6 drops of tea tree, thyme or hyssop, and/or eucalyptus oil. Repeat at least twice a day.

To combat infection, use tea tree, eucalyptus, or thyme in a vaporizer or humidifier in the home, and more soothing oils (marjoram, cedarwood, or myrtle) in the bedroom at night. A few drops of essential oil may also be put on a handkerchief for inhalation throughout the day.

Hot baths with 8 to 10 drops of any of the recommended oils (or a combination), aid the body's natural response to infection. This also has a similar effect to steam inhalation. When feverish, especially if the temperature is high, keep the bath water cool.

ABOVE
Coltsfoot is a herb traditionally used for the lungs.

LEFT
Smoking seriously harms the respiratory tract, and is a major cause of chronic bronchitis.

WARNING
Acute bronchitis can lead to complications (e.g. pneumonia), especially in the very young and elderly. Professional help should be sought immediately if the condition deteriorates.

Asthma

ASTHMA is characterized by wheezing and shortness of breath, caused by muscle spasm in the bronchi of the lungs. During an attack, the narrowing of the bronchial tubes makes breathing difficult, causing agitation and anxiety. It commonly appears during early childhood, and often ceases at puberty. It usually runs in families, and, as in many allergic conditions, an attack can be brought on by a number of factors, including: diet; contact with allergens such as dust, polish, hairspray, or feathers; cigarette smoke or climatic conditions, such as damp; strenuous exercise; and, especially, by anxiety, fear, or underlying emotional issues.

DIETARY FACTORS

Dairy products, notably cow's milk, are a common trigger for asthma attacks in children. Wheat products, refined sugar, red meat, fizzy drinks, and all types of additives and preservatives are also frequently implicated. The whole diet needs to be assessed carefully on an individual basis. Avoid stimulants (tea, coffee, chocolate), and replace with soothing herbal teas such as chamomile, linden, or lemon balm. Taking a course of vitamin B complex supplements is recommended.

OTHER MEASURES

Much can be done to alleviate and prevent asthma, if the cause of the attack and the pattern of the illness can be identified. Allergy testing; deep breathing exercises or yoga; psychotherapy, herbal, or homeopathic treatment are all beneficial. Regular massage to the chest, neck and shoulders, is also helpful. *See also* Bronchitis, Hay fever.

AROMATHERAPY OILS

Clary sage, cypress, sandalwood, rose, hyssop, melissa, sweet marjoram, benzoin, frankincense, lavender, chamomile, valerian. (With mucous congestion, as in bronchitis: eucalyptus blue gum, peppermint.)

METHODS OF USE

Mix 3 to 4 drops of lavender, clary sage, frankincense or benzoin oil with 5 tsp/25ml sweet almond oil, and use to massage the back in long, sweeping movements, starting at the base of the spine, up over the shoulders, then down the sides of the body.

Use lavender or peppermint (or other recommended oil) in vaporizers at home, and put a few drops on a tissue for inhalation throughout the day, especially at the onset of an attack.

Use 8 to 10 drops of any of the above oils in the bath on a regular basis as a general precautionary and preventive measure.

BIRD FEATHERS

SPRAY POLISH

ABOVE AND BELOW
Asthma attacks are frequently triggered by an allergen, which can sometimes be identified and avoided. Common allergens include pollen, scents, house dust, polish, feathers and animal fur.

CLINICAL NOTES

In one case history, a girl who suffered from frequent asthma attacks and coughs used lavender on a regular basis for massage, baths and inhalation: "... Despite a two-week camping holiday Jodie did not have to take any Triludan over the summer. Only one asthma attack was experienced."

SEE INTERNATIONAL JOURNAL OF AROMATHERAPY, VOL.3 NO.4, 1991, P.32

HOUSEHOLD POLISH

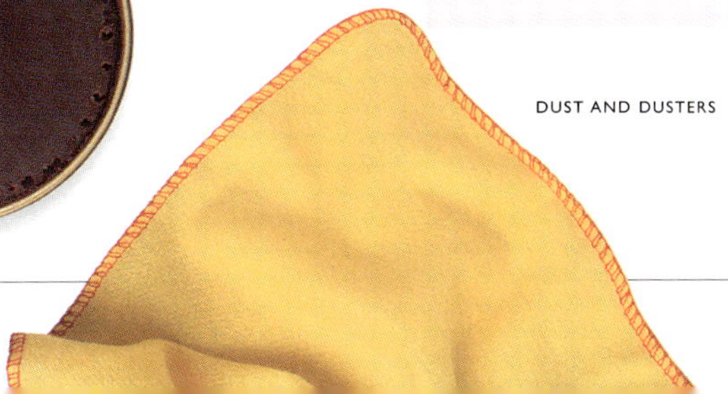

DUST AND DUSTERS

Hay fever

HAY FEVER is an allergic form of rhinitis, an inflammation of the lining of the nose. The symptoms are similar to those of the common cold. The eyes, throat and mucous membrane lining the nose are generally affected, resulting in sore or streaming eyes, headaches, sneezing, and a blocked or runny nose. Hay fever often starts in childhood but can also suddenly develop in later life. This is generally caused by airborne pollen or spores that are released during the spring and summer months. Different people react to specific allergens. Stress, or feeling run down, may also be a contributing factor.

DIETARY FACTORS

Cut down on milk and other dairy products. A high intake of vitamin C and garlic can help control the severity of the attack. Eating plenty of local honey also acts as a preventive in some cases. The following tea can be most effective, especially if the treatment starts at least a month before the person's particular hay fever season begins:
2 parts elderflowers, and 1 part each of eyebright, golden seal and ephedra – take one cupful 2–3 times a day.

OTHER MEASURES

Allergy testing; yoga and other forms of relaxation and deep-breathing exercises may be beneficial measures. *See also* Coughs, Sinusitis.

AROMATHERAPY OILS

Chamomile, melissa, rose, lemon eucalyptus, lavender, peppermint, clove, rosemary, lemon, eucalyptus blue gum, hyssop, cajeput, myrtle, basil, marjoram, pine, clary sage, Spanish sage, thyme.

CLINICAL NOTES

The most helpful oils for hay fever are those which combine an antiallergenic or antihistaminic action with balsamic and anti-inflammatory properties, notably rose, chamomile, melissa, lemon eucalyptus, lavender, and thyme – especially the milder citrol or linalol types. Thyme is current in the *British Herbal Pharmacopoeia* as specific for respiratory infections, including asthma. Rose is clinically indicated for inflamed mucous membranes and headaches:
"... a cream for dry mucous membranes in the nose (Bulgarian rose in eucerit) is very helpful."

SEE D. WABNER, "ROSE OIL: ITS USE IN THERAPY AND COSMETICS," INTERNATIONAL JOURNAL OF AROMATHERAPY, VOL.1, NO.4, P.29

METHODS OF USE

NOTE: Treatment can be a matter of trial and error. Experience has shown that often two or three oils need to be alternated or combined to provide the greatest benefit.

Apply one (or a combination) of the oils listed below left to a tissue to inhale throughout the day – additionally, use in room vaporizers.

Use a chosen oil for bathing on a regular basis.

Regular massage to the neck, chest and back with 4 to 5 drops each of chamomile and lavender, and 3 of rose or melissa oil in 5 tsp/25ml calendula or a light base oil can be beneficial, and may help to decrease the frequency or severity of an attack.

For sore, red eyes, apply cool compresses of rose water (not the essential oil).

For inflamed mucous membranes in the nose, mix 2 to 3 drops (in total) of rose, chamomile, and/or lavender oil with 1 tsp/5ml petroleum jelly (such as Vaseline). Apply a small amount to the nostrils 2–3 times a day.

BELOW
Hay fever is triggered by airborne allergens. It gets its name from grass pollens in the air at haymaking time.

ELDERFLOWER

BELOW
Drinking a herbal tea (see Dietary Factors) before the hay fever season begins may help alleviate the symptoms.

Sinusitis

AN INFECTION or inflammation of the mucous membranes lining the bony cavities behind, above, and on each side of the nose. An acute attack is often accompanied by congested headaches and catarrh, sometimes with fever. The complaint usually follows a cold, hay fever, or prolonged exposure to cold, damp air. Chronic or long-term sinusitis indicates a mild infection that causes the nose to be continually blocked, and a dull pain or feeling of tension to manifest in the area between the eyes. Sinusitis can be aggravated by working or living in overheated or stuffy rooms, and by neck-tension.

DIETARY FACTORS

People who suffer from constant or repeated attacks of sinusitis often suffer from allergies, especially to gluten and cow's milk. Cut down or eliminate these mucus-forming foods from the diet and eat plenty of fresh fruits and vegetables, especially those high in vitamin C (including lemons, oranges, and strawberries), and lots of onions and garlic. Alternatively, take a course of garlic capsules and vitamin C tablets.

OTHER MEASURES

Check for allergies. Fresh air, deep breathing, and gentle exercise can facilitate the easing of nasal congestion. If there is fever, stay in bed. *See also* Colds, Earache, Fever, Hay fever, Headaches.

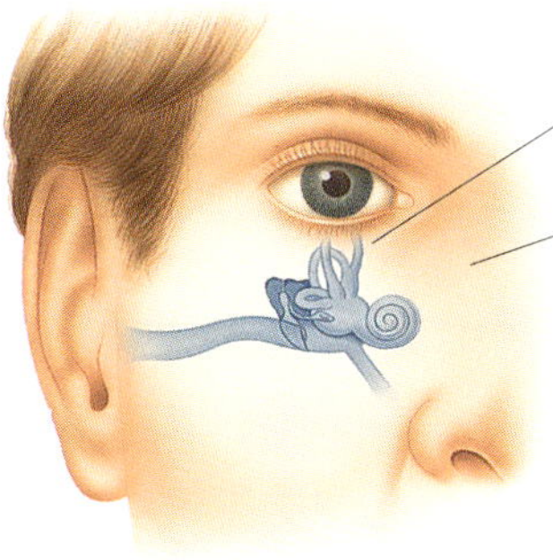

LEFT
In sinusitis, the mucous membranes lining the nasal cavities can become inflamed.

LEFT
Dairy products can cause a build-up of mucus, and many people find that chronic sinusitis and catarrh cease when these foods are avoided.

WARNING
Use no more than 3 drops of the spice oils (eucalyptus, camphor, peppermint) in the bathtub.

AROMATHERAPY OILS

Benzoin, cinnamon, ginger, nutmeg, clove, aniseed, marjoram, myrtle, peppermint, hyssop, pine, rosemary, lavender, eucalyptus blue gum, tea tree, bergamot, thyme, camphor, cajeput, Spanish sage, rose, lavender, chamomile.

WARNING
Sinusitis can lead to secondary infections, notably ear infections, and, very occasionally, meningitis. If in doubt seek professional advice immediately.

METHODS OF USE

Nasal decongestants relieve stuffiness and fight infection. Use 2 to 3 drops each of pine or rosemary, peppermint, and eucalyptus oil in a bowl of steaming water, cover the head with a towel, and inhale deeply for 5–10 minutes with the eyes closed. Repeat several times a day.

To ease congestion, massage the back of the neck, chest, and soles of the feet with 3 to 4 drops each of eucalyptus, pine or rosemary, and peppermint oil in 5 tsp/25ml of a light base oil or cream.

To combat infection, use tea tree, eucalyptus, and/or thyme in a vaporizer or humidifier during the day, and more soothing oils (marjoram, lavender, and/or myrtle) in the bedroom at night. A few drops of essential oil may also be put on a handkerchief for inhalation throughout the day.

Hot baths with 8 to 10 drops of any of the recommended oils (or a combination), aid the body's natural response to infection. This also has a similar effect to steam inhalation.

For inflamed mucous membranes in the nose, mix 2 to 3 drops (in total) of chamomile, lavender, and/or rose oil with 1 tsp/5ml petroleum jelly (such as Vaseline). Apply a small amount to the nostrils 2–3 times a day.

Earache/otitis

EAR INFECTIONS may affect the outer ear, middle ear, or inner ear. Middle ear infection, causing earache, is a common complaint, especially among children, often in association with a cold. Fever and partial loss of hearing are common symptoms. In some cases, earache can lead to a more serious infection of the inner ear. Earache may be a sign of dental decay, an abscess or boil, or it may herald the onset of mumps. Exposure to cold, damp, high winds, or loud noise can also bring on earache.

DIETARY FACTORS

If there is a cold, influenza, or sinusitis, avoid mucus-inducing foods such as dairy produce and white flour products. Drink warm lemon and honey, chamomile, or peppermint tea. Eat lots of garlic to combat infection. Echinacea is the most valuable herb for persistent ear infections: drink echinacea tea three times a day.

OTHER MEASURES

Keep the affected ear warm, and protect from wind by wrapping in a warm scarf. Check for dental decay – if necessary see a dentist. *See also* Abscesses/boils, Colds, Influenza, Sinusitis.

ABOVE
Garlic is a powerful antimicrobial plant which also strengthens the immune system. Peppermint tea can be soothing.

CLINICAL NOTES

The anti-inflammatory/analgesic effects of chamomile (especially German chamomile) have been extensively researched.

SEE DATA BASE, VOL. 1, PP.8–10.

METHODS OF USE

A hot compress applied gently to the ear, using a cloth treated with a few drops of lavender or chamomile (a hot water bottle can be used in this way) can help ease the pain.

Massage gently around the painful area using 2 to 3 drops each of lavender, chamomile, and/or tea tree oil diluted in 1 tbs/15ml carrier oil.

Soak an absorbent cotton ball in 1 tsp/5ml warm olive or almond oil to which have been added 3 drops (in total) of lavender and/or chamomile oil, and insert gently into the outer ear.

NOTE: This should be done only after a medical examination to ensure the eardrum is not perforated.

AROMATHERAPY OILS

Chamomile (Roman and German), lavender, tea tree.

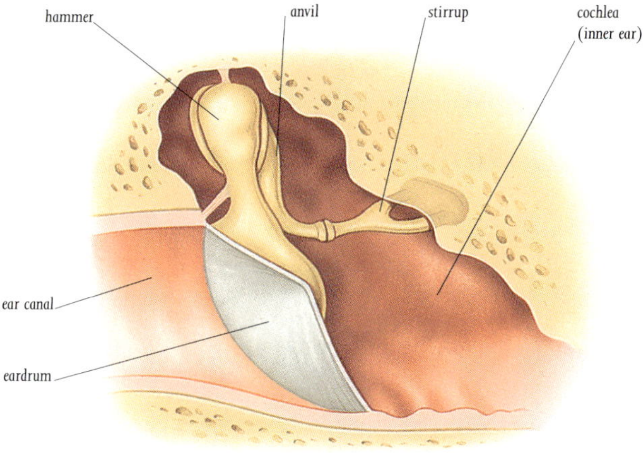

WARNING
Infection (as in a cold) can travel very rapidly from the nose via the Eustachian tube to cause middle ear infection. If untreated, this can damage the eardrum, or spread to the mastoid bone which projects from the skull. If there is a high temperature, blood, or pus, or if pain is severe or persistent, seek professional advice immediately.

LEFT
The middle ear is composed of the ear drum and three interconnecting bones: the hammer, anvil, and stirrup.

Throat infections

A SORE THROAT – inflammation of the membranes lining the mouth and throat – can be very painful. Laryngitis – inflammation of the larynx (voice box) – causes hoarseness, or a temporary loss of voice.

A sore throat usually accompanies other respiratory infections, such as flu, bronchitis, or the common cold. It is often the first sign of illness, and immediate treatment can prevent further infection from developing – or at least shorten the duration of the disease.

Laryngitis is brought on by an infection such as bronchitis or flu, or by overstraining the vocal chords, affecting singers, for example. Cold, damp or very dry air, smoking, stress, and poor nutrition can all be contributory factors.

DIETARY FACTORS

Eat plenty of fresh fruits and vegetables, especially those high in vitamin C (including lemons, oranges, and strawberries) and lots of onions and garlic. As a quick, short-term form of treatment, take a course of garlic capsules and vitamin C tablets. Sage or thyme tea, or lemon and honey are recommended.

OTHER MEASURES

Stop smoking; keep warm, especially the neck and chest area; rest the voice as much as possible, especially for laryngitis. *See also* Bronchitis, Colds, Influenza.

THYME

RIGHT
Gargling with a solution of tea tree oil (alone or mixed with oils such as thyme and sage) is an excellent treatment for sore throats.

CLINICAL NOTES

Tea tree is a very effective remedy for sore throats: "...came down with sore throats; we gargled with a few drops in water and within a few days the sore throat was gone."

SEE T. LORETTE, AS CITED IN C.W. OLSON, AUSTRALIAN TEA TREE OIL, P.18

ABOVE
Sage may be mixed with other oils to make a soothing gargle or massage oil for the chest and throat.

METHODS OF USE

Steam inhalation is the most effective treatment for laryngitis, and excellent for sore throats. If the throat is dry, regular steam inhalations will help to soothe irritation. Add 2 to 3 drops each of sandalwood, cedarwood or benzoin, and frankincense to a bowl of steaming hot water and inhale for 5–10 minutes. If there is infection, use 2 to 3 drops each of tea tree, lavender, thyme (or eucalyptus) oil. Repeat at least twice a day.

Add 2 drops each of tea tree, Spanish sage or clary sage, and thyme oil to a glass of warm water, mix well and gargle. Repeat three or more times a day.

For loss of voice, or a dry throat, make up a concentrated massage oil by mixing 3 to 4 drops each of thyme, Spanish sage or clary sage, benzoin, and sandalwood in 5 tsp/25ml of carrier oil. Apply to the chest and throat. Repeat at least twice a day.

To combat infection, and to soothe the throat, use bactericidal or balsamic oils in a vaporizer or humidifier or on a handkerchief during the day, and more soothing oils (marjoram or myrtle) in the bedroom at night.

AROMATHERAPY OILS

Bactericidal – tea tree, eucalyptus, thyme, Spanish sage, clary sage, bergamot, peppermint, cajeput, marjoram, myrtle, geranium, hyssop, lavender, pine.
Balsamic – sandalwood, benzoin, myrrh, cedarwood, frankincense.

Mouth, teeth, and gums

Toothache/ tooth abscess

TOOTHACHE is characterized by a persistent pain within the tooth itself. In the case of a tooth abscess, the surrounding gums become swollen, infected, and very painful. Poor dental hygiene, resulting in tooth decay, is the main causative factor in toothache and tooth abscesses. Stress and being run down contribute to the formation of abscesses, as these conditions weaken the immune system.

DIETARY FACTORS

Refined sugar products, candies, and sweet fizzy drinks contribute to tooth decay. Choose low-sugar products whenever possible and educate children to eat candies in moderation only. A sweet tooth, once acquired, can easily become a matter of habit. If an abscess has already developed, the herbs garlic and echinacea are indicated to combat the infection, and a course of vitamin C will help to encourage healing.

OTHER MEASURES

Improve dental hygiene, and visit a dentist regularly – prevention is better than cure. *See also* Abscesses/boils, Mouth and gum infections, Mouth ulcers, Stress.

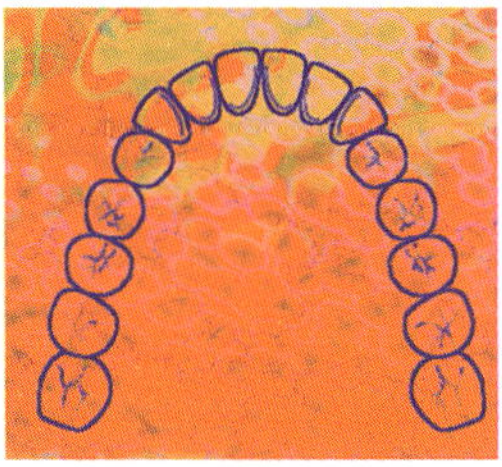

THE TEETH

REFERENCES

ABSCESS
see **TOOTHACHE/ TOOTH ABSCESS**
page 142

BAD BREATH
see **HALITOSIS**
page 144

GUMS
see **MOUTH AND GUM INFECTIONS**
page 143

ORAL THRUSH
see **MOUTH AND GUM INFECTIONS**
page 143

METHODS OF USE

As an emergency measure, to ease pain, apply 1 to 2 drops of clove oil directly to the tooth, using the fingertip or a cotton bud.

To ease swelling and aching pain, massage the outer cheek with the following blend: 1 to 2 drops each of chamomile (Roman or German), lavender, and peppermint oil in 1 tbs/15ml carrier oil or cream. Teething pain in babies and infants can be relieved by mixing 1 drop of lavender or chamomile (Roman or German) oil in 1 tsp/ 5ml of carrier oil, and massaging into the cheek.

As a general measure, and to combat infection, add 5 to 6 drops of tea tree oil to a glass of warm water, mix well, rinse the mouth, and/or gargle once or twice daily, morning and evening, after brushing the teeth.

AROMATHERAPY OILS

Clove, tea tree, thyme, lavender, chamomile (Roman and German), peppermint, myrrh, cinnamon leaf.

WARNING
Dental abscesses can be dangerous, as the infection can enter the bloodstream and may spread throughout the body. Seek medical advice, especially if there are signs of fever.

RIGHT
An old-fashioned remedy for toothache that still works as a short-term method is to apply clove oil.

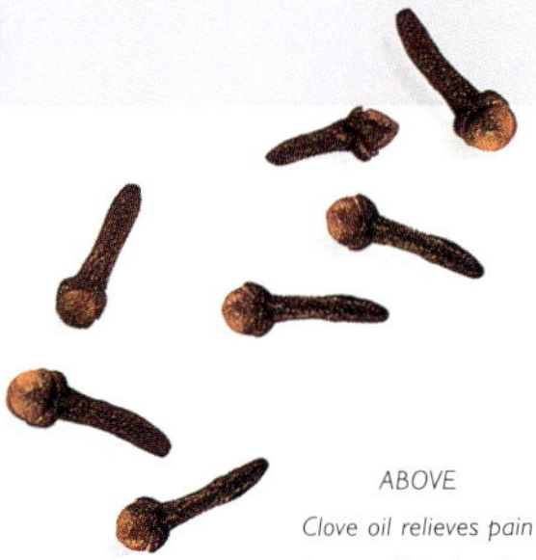

ABOVE
Clove oil relieves pain when applied directly on to the gums.

MYRRH

Mouth and gum infections

THE MOST COMMON types of mouth and gum infection are thrush and gingivitis. Thrush of the mouth is common among young children, but also sometimes occurs in adults, especially after a course of antibiotics. This appears as small white flecks on the inside of the cheeks or roof of the mouth – the breath is also often offensive. Gingivitis (gum disease) is characterized by a red, spongy swelling of the gums, which bleed easily, especially when cleaning the teeth. Thrush is caused by the fungal organism *Candida albicans*, the same organism that causes vaginal thrush. Gingivitis is caused by build-up of dental plaque. This can harden to form calcium deposits (calculus or tartar), and is aggravated by poor dental hygiene.

ABOVE
Live yogurt restores intestinal flora destroyed by taking prolonged broad-spectrum antibiotics.

DIETARY FACTORS

Reduce refined sugar and processed foods in the diet. Lack of vitamin C is associated with puffy or bleeding gums, and lack of vitamin B3 with bad breath. Eat plenty of live yogurt (or take lacto-bacillus tablets) to restore intestinal flora destroyed by antibiotics. To combat infection, the herbal teas of sage, fennel, thyme, and echinacea are especially useful – they may also be used as a mouthwash.

ABOVE
Thrush is caused by the fungus Candida albicans. It affects the moist mucous membranes of the body, including those in the mouth.

OTHER MEASURES

Improve dental hygiene – correct and regular brushing of the teeth, and flossing are vital; give up smoking; if necessary visit a dentist. *See also* Candida/thrush, Halitosis, Mouth ulcers, Toothache/tooth abscess.

TOP AND RIGHT
Tinctures of myrrh and cinnamon bark and leaf oils are often used in dental preparations.

METHODS OF USE

For gingivitis, thrush, or other mouth and gum infections add 4 to 5 drops of tea tree oil (or a blend of the oils listed) to a glass of warm water, mix well, rinse the mouth and/or gargle once or twice daily. Repeat morning and evening, after brushing the teeth.

Alternatively, for thrush, make up a solution containing 6 to 7 drops each of tea tree, geranium, and myrrh or lemon eucalyptus oil, dissolved in 1 tbs/ 15ml witch hazel and added to 2fl oz/ 50ml distilled water or lavender water. Put in a small spray bottle and shake well each time before using to spray the mouth.

For gingivitis, massage or rinse the gums before going to bed, using the following blend (it must be diluted): 2 tbs/30ml tincture of myrrh, 5 to 6 drops of tea tree, and 2 to 3 drops of lemon eucalyptus, peppermint and/or thyme oils. Add 6 to 8 drops of this mixture to a glass of lukewarm water and stir well before using – two or three times a day.

AROMATHERAPY OILS

Rose, thyme, clove, cinnamon leaf, tea tree, fennel, Spanish sage, clary sage, geranium, lemon eucalyptus, myrrh.

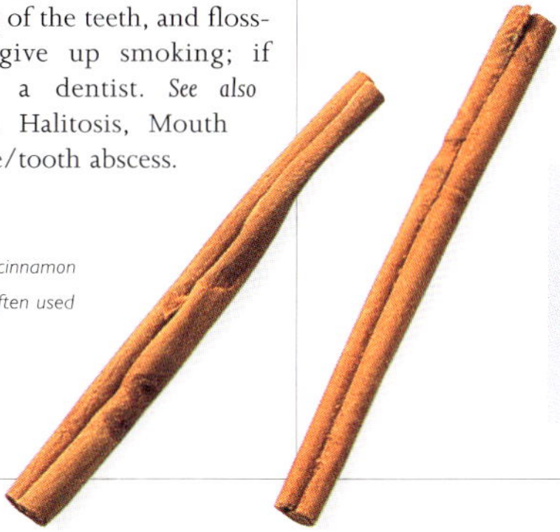

CINNAMON

WARNING
If left untreated, gingivitis can develop into periodontitis, which causes loss of teeth.

Mouth ulcers

MOUTH ULCERS are tiny blisters that burst to form painful sores inside the mouth. They may be caused by a mild viral infection, or food sensitivity. They tend to appear when the body is run down.

DIETARY FACTORS

Successful prevention and cure have been achieved by taking 1 to 2 tablets daily of 100mg zinc orotate tablets. Avoid alcohol and very spicy foods as they aggravate the condition. Drink plenty of water, and eat fresh fruit and vegetables. Increase vitamin C intake to speed healing, and eat plenty of live yogurt (or take lacto-bacillus tablets) to restore intestinal flora destroyed by antibiotics. Drink sage, thyme, or echinacea herbal tea regularly.

OTHER MEASURES

Check dental hygiene – regular brushing and flossing are vital. *See also* Halitosis, Mouth and gum infections, Stress.

CLINICAL NOTES

Research has shown that tea tree is very effective in the treatment of mouth ulcers or pockets of pus in the gums.

(SEE J. LAWLESS, TEA TREE OIL, PP.9–11)

AROMATHERAPY OILS

Cypress, myrrh, tea tree.

BELOW
Correct, regular brushing of the teeth and gums can help to prevent mouth infections of all sorts.

METHODS OF USE

For mouth ulcers, use tea tree oil direct, or dilute to 50 percent in water (dilute more for children). Mix well, and apply to spots or ulcers with a cotton bud. Repeat the treatment twice daily for three days.

As a general measure, add 5 to 6 drops of tea tree oil to a glass of warm water, mix well, rinse the mouth and/or gargle once or twice daily, morning and evening, after brushing the teeth.

Halitosis

HALITOSIS, OR offensive breath, is often the first sign of illness. Common causes include smoking, poor dental hygiene, infection, gastric disorders, or faulty diet.

DIETARY FACTORS

Lack of vitamin B3 is especially associated with bad breath and a coated tongue, while vitamin C deficiency results in weak gums. Chewing caraway seeds, coriander seeds, cardamoms (which neutralize the smell of garlic), clove buds, or candied ginger root are traditional remedies for sweetening the breath. Parsley, peppermint, spearmint, and basil help to freshen the breath after eating strong-smelling foods.

OTHER MEASURES

Dental hygiene with regular brushing and flossing is vital. *See also* Mouth and gum infections.

AROMATHERAPY OILS

Cardamom, coriander, thyme, clove, cinnamon leaf, tea tree, Spanish sage, clary sage, ginger, fennel.

CARDAMOM

ABOVE and RIGHT
Chewing cardamoms or fresh parsley is a traditional remedy for offensive breath. It neutralizes the odors caused by strong-smelling foods, and refreshes the mouth.

METHODS OF USE

Add 4 to 5 drops of tea tree (or a blend of antiseptic or germicidal oils) to a glass of lukewarm water. Stir well. Wash the mouth out and gargle with the mixture twice daily.

For general hygiene, dissolve 5 drops each of thyme, tea tree, clove or cinnamon leaf, fennel, and sage oil in 1 tbs/15ml vodka, and add to 8fl oz/250ml distilled water in a dark, well-stoppered container. Shake well. Leave for one month, then filter, using a coffee filter-paper. Use for rinsing the mouth twice daily.

PARSLEY

The Digestive System

Constipation

CONSTIPATION is a condition in which the normal rhythmic functioning of the digestive system breaks down. The stools are hard and compacted, so defecation becomes difficult and infrequent. This causes discomfort, tiredness, and feelings of bloatedness, sometimes with stomach pain. If the body is congested with waste matter for prolonged periods, this can lead to secondary problems, such as hemorrhoids, blemished skin, headaches, or colic. Constipation is not a disease but the symptom of an underlying condition. The principal immediate causes of constipation, however, are lack of dietary fiber, and insufficient fluid intake. Lack of exercise, stress, liver congestion, pregnancy, PMS, certain medications, and the long-term use of laxatives, are also common contributory factors.

DIETARY FACTORS

Increase the amount of roughage in the diet – eat plenty of fresh fruit, vegetables, and whole grains, especially bran and oats, and prunes. Avoid refined foods, and drink plenty of liquids, including fennel or ginger tea. Two or three glasses of spring water each morning will benefit the whole digestive system enormously. Lack of inositol or choline (found in wheat germ and yeast) and vitamin B (especially niacin and thiamin) is also associated with constipation and a sluggish digestive system. Eat meals at regular intervals. The herbal remedies senna and rhubarb root, taken as a tea, are also indicated.

OTHER MEASURES

Exercise regularly and review eating patterns. *See also* Dyspepsia, Liver congestion, PMS/PMT, Pregnancy.

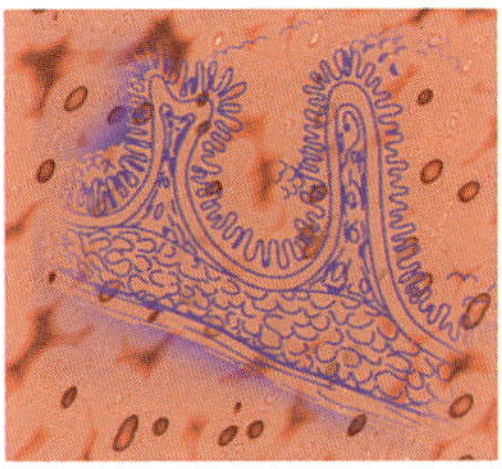

VILLI IN THE DIGESTIVE TRACT

REFERENCES

COLIC
see **DYSPEPSIA**
page 147
and **IRRITABLE BOWEL SYNDROME**
page 149

GASTRIC 'FLU
see **DIARRHEA**
page 146

INDIGESTION
see **DYSPEPSIA**
page 147

SICKNESS
see **NAUSEA/VOMITING**
page 149

PRUNES

AROMATHERAPY OILS

Depuratives – carrot seed, celery seed, juniper, bergamot, fennel, dill, aniseed, coriander, angelica, orange, neroli, grapefruit, tangerine, lime, palmarosa, petitgrain, lemon, geranium.
Digestive stimulants – ginger, rosemary, cinnamon leaf, peppermint, citronella, cardamom, black pepper.

METHODS OF USE

Mix 3 to 4 drops each of rosemary, peppermint, ginger or black pepper with 5 tsp/25ml almond oil (or other base oil) and massage the abdomen in a gentle, circular movement, in a clockwise direction. Repeat twice daily, or as required.

To reduce stress, boost the circulation and get rid of accumulated toxins in the system, have a full-body massage weekly, using a blend of depurative and digestive oils, such as 7 to 8 drops each of rosemary, neroli or petitgrain, and fennel or geranium oil in 2fl oz/50ml almond or grapeseed oil.

A warm compress placed over the abdomen, using a flannel soaked in hot water containing a few drops of the above oils, can help relieve pain. A hot water bottle (with the oils sprinkled on it) can be used instead, or the bottle can be placed on top of the compress to keep it warm.

In addition, add 8 to 10 drops of any of the recommended oils to the bathwater on a regular basis.

BRAN

RIGHT AND ABOVE
Cereals and the traditional prunes absorb moisture and swell up as they travel through the gut, so that the stools are passed gently and easily.

Diarrhea

DIARRHEA is characterized by frequent, loose bowel movements, with or without cramp. Other symptoms that may accompany diarrhea (e.g. with gastric flu) are nausea, vomiting, and fever. Like constipation, diarrhea is not in itself a disorder, but the symptom of an underlying condition, such as bacterial or viral infection, stress, gastric flu, food poisoning, or sudden change in diet. It can also be a side effect of certain medications.

DIETARY FACTORS

Assess the diet for possible causes (such as food poisoning or sudden dietary change). If a bacterial infection is suspected, eat plenty of garlic or take a course of garlic capsules. Avoid dairy products, and keep the diet simple (eat soups, rice, stewed fruits). Castor oil (1–2 tbs/15–30ml daily), fresh lemon juice, peppermint, meadowsweet, ginger, and cinnamon tea (with honey) are also indicated. Whatever the cause, drink plenty of water or other liquids to prevent dehydration – if severe, take extra salt.

OTHER MEASURES

If there is pain, vomiting, or fever, rest in bed. As a preventive measure, before going on vacation, find out about local customs. For example, it may be advisable to drink only bottled or boiled water, peel all fruit, and avoid uncooked food and ice in drinks. *See also* Fever, Nausea/vomiting, Stress.

CLINICAL NOTES

Cinnamon and nutmeg oil have been used successfully in treating diarrhea:
"...where the active constituent was identified as eugenol, which is also the main constituent of cloves."

SEE M. LIS-BALCHIN, AROMASCIENCE, PP.41, 81

WARNING
If symptoms are severe, or if they continue for more than three days, seek medical help.

METHODS OF USE

For stress-related diarrhea, take a warm bath with 3 drops each of geranium, lavender, and ginger oil added. If there is also fever or nausea, take a cool bath with 3 drops each of peppermint, tea tree or thyme, and ginger or nutmeg oil added to the water.

Make a massage oil by mixing 3 to 4 drops each of lavender, ginger or nutmeg, and geranium oil in 5 tsp/25ml of a light base oil. Rub gently into the abdomen in circular, clockwise movements. If viral or bacterial infection is suspected, add a few drops of tea tree or thyme oil to the blend.

A warm compress placed over the abdomen, using a flannel soaked in hot water containing a few drops of the above oils can help relieve pain. A hot water bottle can be used instead, or to keep the compress warm.

LEFT
Vacation diarrhea is a common occurrence.

RIGHT
Cinnamon leaf. Eugenol, one of the principal constituents of cinnamon oil, helps to relieve the symptoms of diarrhea.

AROMATHERAPY OILS

Geranium, peppermint, lavender, thyme, ginger, nutmeg, tea tree, cinnamon leaf, clove, chamomile.

RIGHT
Using a few drops of the recommended oils on a warm compress placed on the abdomen reduces the discomfort caused by diarrhea.

Dyspepsia

DYSPEPSIA (INDIGESTION) is a common complaint. Symptoms include heartburn, flatulence, colic, abdominal pain, and nausea. It is often associated with anxiety, stress, or underlying emotional tension. Eating too quickly or too much, bad food combinations, and food allergies are also common causes. Infantile colic is often caused by an allergy to cow's milk.

DIETARY FACTORS

Assess the diet for possible causes, and, if necessary, check for food allergies. Many herbs traditionally used in cooking aid digestion, notably garlic, rosemary, marjoram, sage, and spices (e.g. black pepper, ginger, coriander, cardamom). Herbs that have a soothing effect on the digestive system, and which may be drunk as a tea for indigestion and wind, include fennel, dill, aniseed, peppermint, and chamomile.

OTHER MEASURES

Wearing tight belts or restrictive clothing can induce stomach pains, as can remaining in a cramped position. Do not eat while feeling anxious or stressed, and relax immediately after eating a heavy meal to allow digestion to take place. *See also* Anxiety, Depression, Stress.

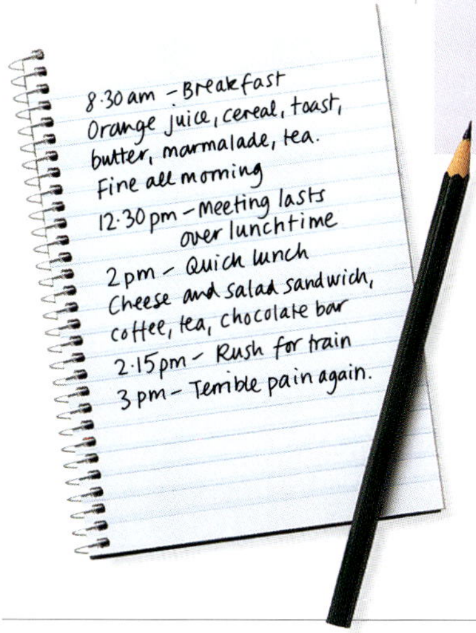

LEFT
Keep a note of what you eat and do, and of when attacks occur, to see if there is a correlation between your dyspepsia and your diet or other factors.

CLINICAL NOTES

Lavender is especially valuable for all types of digestive disorders, where there is a strong nervous or emotional element involved. In the British *Herbal Pharmacopoeia*, lavender is indicated specifically for "depressive states associated with digestive dysfunction." In clinical cases: "Lavender oil has carminative properties and has been used to treat flatulence and colic, given on a sugar lump or as a compound tincture."

SEE M. LIS-BALCHIN, AROMASCIENCE, P.65

WARNING
Abdominal pain can be associated with more serious digestive complaints, such as gastritis, gastric ulcers, enteritis, colitis, diverticulitis, or hiatus hernia. Although aromatherapy can offer preventive measures or complementary support for complaints of this type, such conditions require the attention of a medical herbalist, nutritionist or physician.

METHODS OF USE

Mix 3 to 4 drops each of lavender, Roman chamomile, and peppermint oil in 5 tsp/25ml of carrier oil and gently massage the abdomen in a clockwise direction. If there is flatulence, add a few drops of fennel or dill to the blend. Stomach ache or colic in babies, infants, and older children can be eased by mixing 1 to 3 drops (in total) of lavender, Roman chamomile, and dill in 1 tbs/ 15ml carrier oil, and gently massaging the lower back and stomach in a clockwise direction.

For stress-related indigestion, take a warm bath with 8 to 10 drops (in total) of Roman chamomile, lavender, and/or clary sage oil added.

If there is nausea, inhale peppermint oil from a tissue, or put a few drops in a vaporizer.

A warm compress placed over the abdomen, using a facecloth soaked in hot water containing a few drops of lavender, or chamomile, can help relieve pain. A hot water bottle can be used instead, or to keep the compress warm.

WARNING
Internal use of essential oils is not recommended for use at home except on the advice of a qualified physician.

AROMATHERAPY OILS

Lavender, Roman chamomile, peppermint, angelica, black pepper, fennel, dill, carrot seed, cardamom, nutmeg, marjoram, melissa, rose, neroli, clary sage, lemongrass, petitgrain, valerian, palmarosa.

Liver congestion

THE LIVER is involved, directly or indirectly, in all the physiological processes of the body. It plays a vital part in digestion – notably in the metabolism of carbohydrates, proteins, fats, and vitamins, as well as in the detoxification of drugs or potential poisons. It also excretes bile, a digestive juice essential for the digestive processes. Any congestion or dysfunction of the liver will thus manifest in all sorts of minor complaints, such as skin problems, digestive disturbances, or a general lack of vitality. Liver congestion can have a variety of causes – alcohol or drug abuse is the most common factor. Rich, fatty or heavy foods, and chemical additives, also put an undue strain on the liver. In conditions such as jaundice or hepatitis, physical damage and infection can also be causative factors.

DIETARY FACTORS

Avoid all fried and roasted food; reduce all fats and fatty foods to a minimum; cut out or reduce alcohol, and foods containing chemical additives. Use rosemary and garlic in cooking, and drink plenty of liquids. There are many folk remedies (e.g. silver birch sap and fresh lemon juice) that are used as spring tonics for general liverishness, to strengthen the liver and cleanse the body after a winter of heavy food. A good herbal spring tonic is to drink the following tea after each meal: 2 parts each of dandelion and meadowsweet; 1 part each of fringetree and golden seal.

OTHER MEASURES

Stop smoking – tar irritates the digestive system, and it has been shown that nicotine slows the healing of gastric ulcers. Take gentle exercise in the fresh air.

WARNING
Serious liver complaints such as all forms of jaundice and hepatitis, as well as problems related to the gall bladder, such as gall stones, require specialist attention.

METHODS OF USE

If there is pain in the liver area, a low dilution of rosemary oil (0.25 percent, or 2 drops per 2fl oz/50ml) can be applied to the nape of the neck, solar plexus, and soles of the feet.

Have a regular full-body massage using the following blend: 7 to 8 drops each of rosemary, carrot seed (or celery seed), and grapefruit oil in 2fl oz/50ml almond oil.

Use 8 to 10 drops of the above blend in baths on a regular basis.

AROMATHERAPY OILS

Rosemary, carrot seed, celery seed, parsley seed, lemon, rose, clary sage, thyme, Spanish sage, chamomile (Roman and German), lavender, geranium, yarrow, tea tree, lemon eucalyptus, grapefruit.

WARNING
Liver and pancreatic disorders call for a professional diagnosis before any course of aromatherapy treatment is embarked upon.

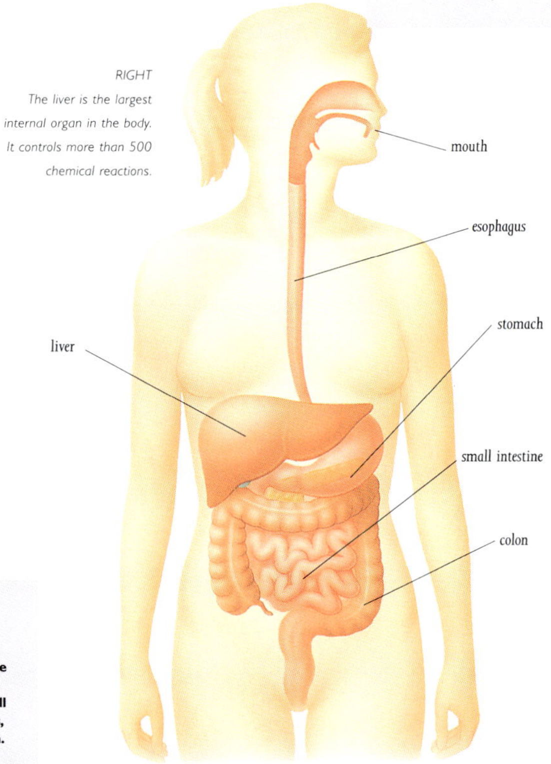

RIGHT The liver is the largest internal organ in the body. It controls more than 500 chemical reactions.

Irritable bowel syndrome

SYMPTOMS INCLUDE alternating bouts of constipation and diarrhea, stomach pain, colic, and flatulence. General feelings of tiredness and debility are also common. Stress, allergies, and too little fiber, are indicated.

DIETARY FACTORS

Eat fruits, vegetables, whole wheat bread, grains, and cereals – but not wheatbran, as it can irritate a sensitive digestive tract. Avoid or reduce alcohol, tea, and coffee. Take herbal teas, such as lemon balm, peppermint, valerian, chamomile, and hops. Peppermint oil capsules, available from health food stores, can also be helpful.

OTHER MEASURES

Relaxation exercises, massage, yoga, and meditation are beneficial. *See also* Stress.

ABOVE
Fruit is a good source of fiber and should be a regular part of your diet.

AROMATHERAPY OILS

Chamomile, lavender, marjoram, peppermint, melissa, rose, neroli, petitgrain.

WARNING
For any sudden change or irregularity in bowel habits in those over 40, seek medical advice.

METHODS OF USE

Mix 3 to 4 drops each of chamomile, peppermint, and lavender oil with 5 tsp/25ml almond oil (or other base oil) and massage the abdomen in a gentle, circular movement, in a clockwise direction.

To reduce stress, have a full-body massage weekly, using a blend of relaxing and carminative oils – mix 7 to 8 drops each of lavender, neroli or petitgrain, and peppermint oil in 2fl oz/50ml almond or grapeseed oil.

A warm compress placed over the abdomen, using a facecloth soaked in hot water containing a few drops of chamomile or lavender, can help relieve pain. A hot water bottle may be used instead, or to keep the compress warm.

Add 8 to 10 drops of any of the recommended oils to the bathwater on a regular basis.

Nausea/vomiting

NAUSEA IS A common complaint that can start as slight queeziness and progress to sickness or vomiting. With motion or travel sickness, the sense of balance, originating in the inner ear, is disturbed by the movement. Nausea can arise from many causes, including motion (as in travel sickness), viral infection, digestive problems, overeating, food poisoning, and emotional anxiety or tension.

DIETARY FACTORS

Do not eat while feeling nauseous. Peppermint, spearmint, lemon balm, and ginger teas relieve nausea. Herbal travel-sickness tablets are also available.

CLINICAL NOTES

Lavender is indicated specifically for sickness due to nerves or emotional upset, especially in combination with other digestive symptoms. Peppermint is used clinically where nausea is associated with fever, diarrhea, dyspepsia, or travel sickness.

RIGHT
Travel sickness is a common cause of nausea. There are several natural remedies that can help.

METHODS OF USE

Inhale lavender or peppermint directly from a tissue, or use in a vaporizer in the room.

For nausea with indigestion, gently massage the solar plexus or abdomen in a clockwise direction, using 3 to 4 drops of peppermint, ginger, and lavender oils in 5 tsp/25ml carrier oil.

AROMATHERAPY OILS

Peppermint, ginger, lavender, Roman chamomile, cardamom, coriander, fennel, nutmeg, melissa, aniseed.

Genitourinary/endocrine systems

Dysmenorrhea

MILD TO SEVERE cramping pains in the abdominal region, lasting from a matter of minutes to several days at a time. The pain is caused by uterine spasm during menstruation, although the frequency and severity of period pains is variable. Heredity, lack of exercise, being fitted with an intra-uterine device (IUD), underlying emotional problems, and faulty diet can all contribute to this condition.

DIETARY FACTORS

Constipation and poor nutrition are contributing factors, particularly lack of calcium in the diet – extra calcium is required by women using the contraceptive pill. Calcium supplements are recommended, and extra vitamin E and vitamin C are also indicated. A very effective long-term remedy for frequent attacks is the herb cramp bark, taken as a tea, three times a day.

OTHER MEASURES

Assess the lifestyle, aiming to reduce stress levels. If pain is severe, rest and keep warm. *See also* Cramp, PMS/PMT.

BELOW
Cramp bark is a natural herbal remedy that is often helpful.

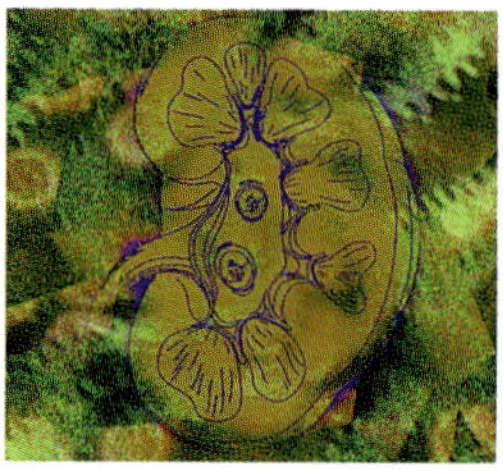

KIDNEY

REFERENCES

CHANGE IN LIFE *see* **MENOPAUSE** *page 152*

HEAVY PERIODS *see* **MENORRHAGIA** *page 151*

LABOR *see* **CHILDBIRTH** *page 160*

MISSING PERIODS *see* **AMENORRHEA** *page 153*

PAINFUL PERIODS *see* **DYSMENORRHEA** *page 150*

THRUSH *see* **CANDIDA/THRUSH** *page 155*

URETHRITIS *see* **CYSTITIS AND URETHRITIS** *page 156*

VAGINAL ITCHING *see* **LEUCORRHEA AND PRURITUS** *page 157*

"WHITES" *see* **LEUCORRHEA AND PRURITUS** *page 157*

CLINICAL NOTES

Many oils, notably clary sage, chamomile (Roman and German), marjoram, peppermint, lavender, valerian, ginger, and nutmeg, have been demonstrated clinically to have a strong anti-spasmodic action – valuable in all types of muscular spasm.

SEE DATA BASE, VOL. 3, P.25

METHODS OF USE

Gentle massage to the abdomen and lower back with 4 to 5 drops each of clary sage, marjoram, and lavender in 5 tsp/25ml of base oil, with 1 tbs/15ml evening primrose oil can be very effective.

Hot compresses, using a few drops of any of the oils listed below on a facecloth (or on a hot water bottle) can be placed on the abdomen as an aid to relieving pain.

Relaxing in a hot aromatic bath (using 8 to 10 drops of a relaxant oil) eases pain, and also soothes away stress and tension.

AROMATHERAPY OILS

Chamomile (Roman and German), clary sage, lavender, rose, marjoram, melissa, nutmeg, geranium, neroli, peppermint, ginger, valerian, rosemary, cardamom, cinnamon leaf.

WARNING
Very severe or persistent pain may indicate a gynecological disorder such as endometriosis.

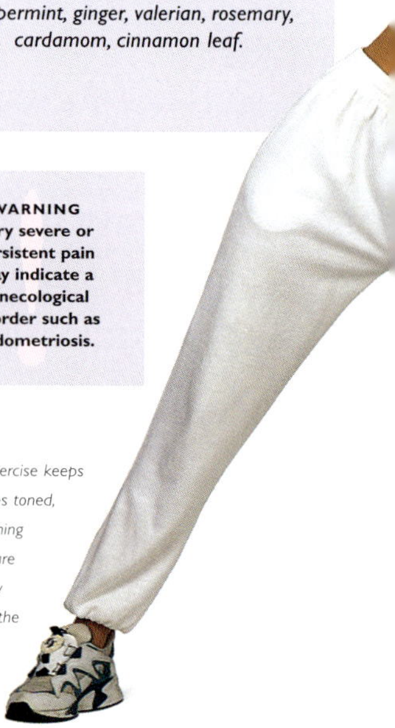

RIGHT
Regular exercise keeps the muscles toned, and stretching exercises are particularly helpful at the onset of a period.

Menorrhagia

EXCESSIVE MENSTRUAL flow, often in association with cramping pains. There are many possible causes of these symptoms, including endometriosis, fibroids, stress, poor diet, excessive exercise, and muscular strain.

DIETARY FACTORS

A diet containing too many saturated oils and refined carbohydrates, together with a lack of fresh fruit and vegetables, can contribute to menstrual problems and make the flow congested. To balance the loss of additional blood, a diet rich in iron (or iron supplements) is recommended. Improve the diet, cut down on alcohol, and drink plenty of water and herbal teas – especially raspberry leaf, American cranesbill, lady's mantle, and yarrow.

OTHER MEASURES

Make time for relaxation; take gentle exercise; assess lifestyle and emotional factors. *See also* Dysmenorrhea, Stress.

WARNING
Prolonged or heavy bleeding may indicate a more serious gynecological problem – seek medical advice.

METHODS OF USE

Gently massage the abdomen and lower back with the following blend each day, especially on the days immediately prior to menstruation: 3 to 4 drops of geranium, cypress or yarrow, and rose in 5 tsp/25ml base oil.

Use 8 to 10 drops of any of the recommended oils in the bathtub regularly, especially on the days just before and during menstruation.

Have a regular massage, using a blend of stress-relieving oils – for example use from 7 to 10 drops of chamomile or rose, geranium, and lavender in 2fl oz/50ml base oil.

AROMATHERAPY OILS

Cypress, geranium, rose, yarrow, chamomile, lavender.

CLINICAL NOTES

Cypress and yarrow are both recognized medicinally for their astringent action: "Tincture of cypress, like that of hamamelis (witch hazel) is given for hemorrhoids, varicose veins, menorrhagia, menopausal problems etc..."

SEE J. VALNET, THE PRACTICE OF AROMATHERAPY, P.121

Rose is also helpful for menorrhagia. Case histories show that: "Rose has a regulating effect on the cycle, and is a uterine tonic."

SEE P. DAVIS, AROMATHERAPY: AN A–Z, P.224

BELOW
Taking a warm, relaxing bath containing a few drops of the recommended oils, prior to and during menstruation, relieves pain associated with menorrhagia.

Menopause

THE MENOPAUSE can sometimes be accompanied by unpleasant emotional and physical symptoms, such as headaches, hot flushes, depression, rapid mood swings, irritability, edema, and the tendency to put on weight. Nevertheless, a recent survey indicates that only 25 percent of women suffer menopausal problems, hot flushes being the most common symptom. Hormonal changes, notably a decrease in estrogen and progesterone levels, are the main physiological causative factors of these symptoms. Underlying psychological attitudes to the change in life also need to be taken into account, since anxiety about the future or fear of growing older can contribute to the discomfort and duration of menopausal symptoms.

DIETARY FACTORS

Nutrition can have a profound influence on the menopausal experience – it is very important to have a healthy, wholesome diet. Supplements of evening primrose oil, minerals, and trace elements (especially calcium, to prevent bones becoming brittle), as well as multivitamin tablets (incorporating especially vitamins D, E, and the B complex vitamins) can be very helpful. Specifically formulated menopausal herbal supplements (e.g. Phytesterol) are available from some pharmacies/health food stores – ginseng root, sage, and fennel tea are also found to help in many cases.

OTHER MEASURES

Gentle exercise, such as yoga, swimming, or walking, and some form of spiritual nourishment (prayer or meditation) are beneficial. Relaxation techniques, the Bach flower remedies, counseling, psychotherapy, or homeopathy can all be valuable supports at this time. *See also* Anxiety, Depression, Edema, Faintness/shock, Headaches, Palpitations, Stress.

CLINICAL NOTES

Fennel tea helps to regulate hormonal change, and boosts estrogen levels during the menopause. Clinical studies have demonstrated that fennel oil is also estrogenic.

SEE M. LIS-BALCHIN, AROMASCIENCE, P.84

Trials have also demonstrated the benefits of ginseng root.

SEE B. SALMON, NATURE'S SECRETS, P.72

BELOW
The time of the menopause can be a time of many changes in a woman's life. As her children grow up, she can spend more time alone with her husband, and find time for herself, too. A positive attitude helps to lessen any problems that may be experienced.

METHODS OF USE

Massage is very comforting and relaxing in itself. The following blend has in addition a regulating effect: 4 to 5 drops each of geranium or rose, fennel, and clary sage oils in 5 tsp/25ml of a light base oil, plus 1 tbs/15ml of evening primrose oil or borage oil may be added for their high gamma linoleic acid (GLA) content.

Choose oils to scent the environment, according to specific moods or symptoms (e.g. lavender for headaches, or to soothe anxiety).

For hot flushes, use cold compresses of chamomile, lavender, or rose water on the face and body.

Add 8 to 10 drops of any of the recommended oils to a warm bath on a daily basis. To help prevent night sweats, take a warm (not hot) bath before retiring, using a blend of grapefruit, clary sage, and geranium (8 to 10 drops in total).

AROMATHERAPY OILS

Geranium, rose, chamomile, bergamot, clary sage, jasmine, lavender, neroli, sandalwood, ylang ylang, fennel, grapefruit.

ABOVE
Ginseng root, taken as a tea or in tablet form, has been found by many women to help them overcome the symptoms of the menopause.

Amenorrhea

AMENORRHEA can take several forms, ranging from the total absence of menstruation over an extended period, to a scanty or missed period. Amenorrhea is common at the onset of puberty, and during the menopause, when the menstrual cycle is irregular. (Pregnancy also causes menstrual periods to cease.) A woman's menstrual cycle can become irregular as a result of emotional stress, shock, excessive exercise, nutritional deficiency, hormonal imbalance, or a serious illness.

DIETARY FACTORS

Girls and women suffering from anorexia nervosa often stop menstruating, due to lack of the nutrients needed to synthesize the body's hormones. Protein deficiency, and lack of vitamin B12 and folic acid result in anemia (insufficient red blood corpuscles) and scanty or irregular menstruation. It is therefore important to improve the diet: liver, leafy greens, and yeast products (e.g. spreads such as Marmite) are especially indicated. Avoid tea, coffee, and alcohol, and drink the herb teas yarrow, rose-hip, chasteberry, mugwort, or marigold (all uterine tonics).

OTHER MEASURES

Assess lifestyle, and, if necessary, seek psychotherapeutic help: stress and emotional disharmony are commonly implicated in amenorrhea. *See also* Menopause, Shock, Stress.

METHODS OF USE

Gently massage the abdomen and lower back with 3 to 4 drops each of carrot seed, clary sage, and myrrh or rose oil in 5 tsp/25ml carrier oil daily, especially before menstruation is due.

Use a few drops of any of the recommended oils in the bath regularly (best used in combination) – always check contraindications first: *see Safety data for each oil on pp. 178–210.*

If possible, put aside some time each week to have a professional massage, using a blend of relaxing or stress-relieving oils – e.g. 6 to 7 drops each of marjoram, lavender, rose, and clary sage oil in 2fl oz/50ml carrier oil.

CLINICAL NOTES

Case histories have shown that the use of rose oil can help to promote and reassert a natural rhythm: "Rose is of great help to women who have been trying to conceive, as it makes it possible to predict the time of ovulation more accurately."

SEE P. DAVIS, AROMATHERAPY: AN A–Z, P.224

AROMATHERAPY OILS

Angelica, carrot seed, celery seed, cinnamon leaf, clary sage, dill, sweet fennel, hyssop, juniper, marjoram, myrrh, parsley seed, rose, Spanish sage.

WARNING
Amenorrhea can lead to fertility problems – if the condition persists, seek medical advice.

LEFT
Diet generally plays its part when periods are irregular or absent. It is also important to cut down alcohol consumption, and substitute herbal teas for tea and coffee.

BELOW
Many teenagers have irregular meals, eaten in a rush and short on fresh green vegetables. This, and a demanding way of life, may result in problems of missing periods.

PMS/PMT

THE SYMPTOMS of pre-menstrual syndrome or tension are various: on a physical level they may include fluid retention, tender breasts, headaches, weight gain, spots, nausea, or a swollen abdomen; while on an emotional level, symptoms may include depression, sudden mood swings, weepiness, or unpredictable behavior. Onset of symptoms varies from two days to two weeks prior to menstruation. PMS is fundamentally caused by a temporary hormonal imbalance – notably inadequate amounts of progesterone in the body – in the days prior to menstruation. The condition is also aggravated by other factors, including stress, poor diet, viral infection, smoking, and overwork.

DIETARY FACTORS

A nutritional approach to PMS has been found to have a 70 percent success rate. Cut out refined sugar altogether, and reduce dairy products, tea, coffee, chocolate, alcohol, salt, and red meat. Foods containing vitamin E, magnesium, and the B vitamins (especially B6) are particularly indicated (and these can be taken as supplements). However, the most successful single remedy is evening primrose oil, because it contains essential fatty acids, including GLA (gamma linoleic acid), which stimulate the body's production of prostaglandins, natural hormone-like substances. Take 2 to 4 capsules daily, or on each day during the ten days prior to menstruation. The herb chaste tree (*Vitex agnus-castus*) can also help to regulate hormonal imbalance (also available in tablet form).

OTHER MEASURES

These depend on the particular symptoms. *See also* Acne, Anxiety, Depression, Edema, Headaches, Stress.

CLINICAL NOTES

Case studies show that aromatherapy can be a great aid in combating pre-menstrual tension: "I blended the following oils for her: chamomile, lavender, geranium and melissa (to be used in the bath and in a massage oil for two weeks before her period) ... she has now had four periods and says that both mentally and physically it has been a huge success."

SEE J. GINGELL, "P.M.T.," IN AROMATHERAPY QUARTERLY, NO.8, 1985, P.12

BELOW
Smoking can make the symptoms worse.

METHODS OF USE

Use 8 to 10 drops of a chosen oil (see below) in baths during the ten days prior to menstruation, and throughout the duration of the period.

A regular full-body massage treatment can be a great aid in combating PMS. The oils need to be selected according to the specific symptoms (e.g. 7 to 10 drops of lavender, geranium, and chamomile in 2fl oz/50ml base oil, plus 1 tbs/15ml of evening primrose oil, can be very helpful for moodiness/irritability).

For self-treatment to help regulate hormonal imbalance, mix 4 to 5 drops each of rose/lavender, fennel, and geranium in 5 tsp/25ml light carrier oil, plus 1 tbs/15ml evening primrose oil. Apply by gentle massage to the abdomen and lower back.

Use any of the recommended oils (according to mood) in burners during the ten days prior to menstruation, and throughout the duration of the menstrual period.

AROMATHERAPY OILS

Fennel, rose, geranium, clary sage, bergamot, nutmeg, grapefruit, jasmine, chamomile, palmarosa, melissa, parsley seed, lavender, neroli, vetiver, ylang ylang.

BELOW
A change in diet may help alleviate the symptoms of PMS. Cut down on foods that contain a lot of sugar.

CREAM CAKE

SUGAR

CHOCOLATE

Candida/thrush

THRUSH, ALSO KNOWN as candidiasis or moniliasis, can manifest in several forms. It is caused by the yeast-like fungus *Candida albicans*, which thrives in moist, warm parts of the body. In its most common form, however, thrush affects the vagina, causing severe itching, redness, and a milky white discharge. The organism *Candida albicans* (formerly called *Monila albicans*) causes problems of infection only when it proliferates above a certain level. Some people are more prone to this infection than others, and this can be connected to food allergies, low immunity levels, and stress. Quite commonly, it is a result of antibiotic treatment. This is because antibiotics kill some of the intestinal flora that keep the candida organisms under control. Balanitis (affecting the penis) is usually passed to the male by sexual contact with a woman suffering from vaginal thrush.

DIETARY FACTORS

To encourage beneficial intestinal flora, eat plenty of live yogurt (or take acidophilus capsules), avoid alcohol, and keep sugary and starchy foods to a minimum. Garlic is also indicated to help build up resistance to infection.

OTHER MEASURES

Do not wear underwear made from synthetic fibers (e.g. nylon or lycra), which do not let the skin breathe, and avoid harsh chemical soaps and toiletries. Both male and female partners must be treated simultaneously before renewing sexual relations to avoid reinfection occurring. *See also* Eczema, Mouth and gum infections.

CLINICAL NOTES

Tea tree is very effective for treating thrush, due to its powerful fungicidal action, combined with its mildness on the skin, even when applied to the delicate mucous membranes.

SEE J. LAWLESS, TEA TREE OIL, PP.13,14

In clinical tests, Algerian geranium and lemon eucalyptus oil showed very effective fungicidal activity against *Candida albicans*.

SEE M. LIS-BALCHIN, AROMASCIENCE, PP.51,58

AROMATHERAPY OILS

Tea tree, geranium, lemon eucalyptus, lavender.

GERANIUM LEAVES

METHODS OF USE

A simple way of treating vaginal thrush is to soak a tampon in a 1 percent tea tree/water solution (20 drops of tea tree oil to $3^{1}/_{2}$fl oz/100ml purified or distilled water) and insert into the vagina. Replace every 8 hours. (This is the routine method employed at the Annandale Women's Centre in Sydney, Australia.)

Alternatively, a pessary can be made with a 1 percent dilution of tea tree oil in a cocoa butter base, 10 drops of oil to 2fl oz/50ml melted cocoa butter cooled slightly and formed into pellets, then left to harden. One of these can be inserted into the vagina once or twice a day.

For a vaginal douche, add 20 to 25 drops of tea tree oil to 8fl oz/200ml of purified or distilled water. This helps reduce infection, irritation, and discomfort, and may be used between the treatments described above.

As a wash, add 8 to 10 drops of tea tree or geranium or lemon eucalyptus oil to a bowl or shallow bath of warm water and soak in this for 5–10 minutes daily.

Balanitis may be treated by washing the area carefully with a 1 percent solution (20 drops to $3^{1}/_{2}$fl oz/100ml water) of tea tree oil in distilled water. Shake well, and apply four times a day.

As an adjunct to treatment, or as a general precautionary measure, add 8 to 10 drops of any recommended oil to the bathwater.

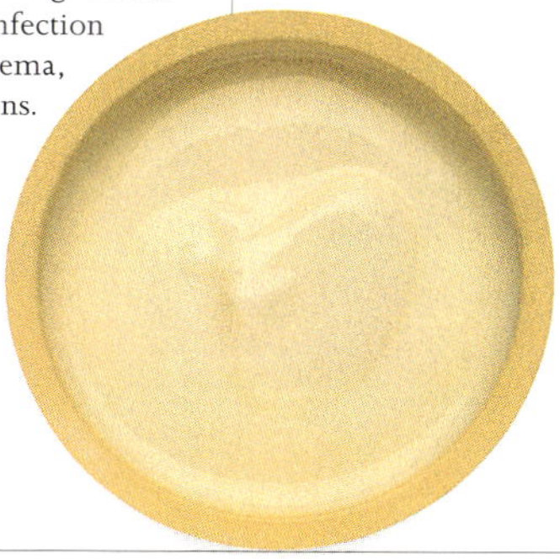

RIGHT
Yogurt is well established as a treatment for candida infections. Fresh live yogurt should be taken as part of the diet and can also be used as a local treatment for thrush.

ABOVE
Geranium oil is a powerful fungicide and is also pleasantly scented and mild on the skin when used in the standard dilution.

WARNING
Although it is normal to experience a temporary, warm sensation when tea tree is used in the vaginal area, discontinue the treatment if a burning irritation develops.

Cystitis and urethritis

CYSTITIS IS A bacterial infection causing inflammation of the bladder, more common among women than men. It is characterized by a frequent need to urinate (even when the bladder is empty), a painful, burning sensation while passing water (which is often cloudy), a pain in the groin, and sometimes fever. Many attacks of cystitis start as urethritis – an infection of the urethra. Bacterial infection, inhalation of industrial chemical fumes, a physical injury, catching a chill, or prolonged stressful circumstances can all trigger an attack. Some individuals are more prone than others, especially those who have undergone surgery to the urethra or (in men) who suffer from an enlarged prostate gland. So-called honeymoon cystitis can occur as a result of prolonged sexual activity.

DIETARY FACTORS

Occasionally, food allergies are implicated in chronic cystitis. If in doubt, check with an allergy specialist for possible dietary causes. Whatever the case, drink plenty of water and herbal teas (especially echinacea, fennel, yarrow, golden seal, or thyme) to flush out the kidneys and dilute the urine. In addition, eat lots of garlic (or take as capsules) to build up the immune system.

OTHER MEASURES

Avoid tightly fitting clothes and nylon underwear. Assess the lifestyle, and make appropriate changes if stress could be a causative factor. Rest as much as possible, especially if there is fever. *See also* Fever, Stress.

WARNING
If symptoms do not improve within a few days, or if there is blood or pus in the urine, seek professional help immediately.

AROMATHERAPY OILS

Bergamot, lavender, chamomile, tea tree, sandalwood, juniper, frankincense, parsley seed, celery seed, thyme, yarrow.

CLINICAL NOTES

Tea tree oil has been successful taken internally as part of treatment for cystitis but this requires clinical prescription and supervision.

METHODS OF USE

Make up a solution of 10 to 12 drops of tea tree oil in $3^{1}/_{2}$fl oz/ 100ml of cooled, boiled water. Using soaked absorbent cotton (cotton wool) swab the opening of the urethra frequently and each time after passing water. Shake the solution well before each application.

Bathe frequently, using bactericidal oils, as a general disinfectant and preventive measure. Add 8 to 10 drops of a recommended oil (or a combination) to the bathwater.

Make up a massage oil using 3 to 4 drops each of tea tree, sandalwood, bergamot (or lavender) in 5 tsp/ 25ml of a light carrier oil (such as sweet almond or grapeseed) and rub gently into the lower abdomen and back. Repeat at least twice daily.

FENNEL

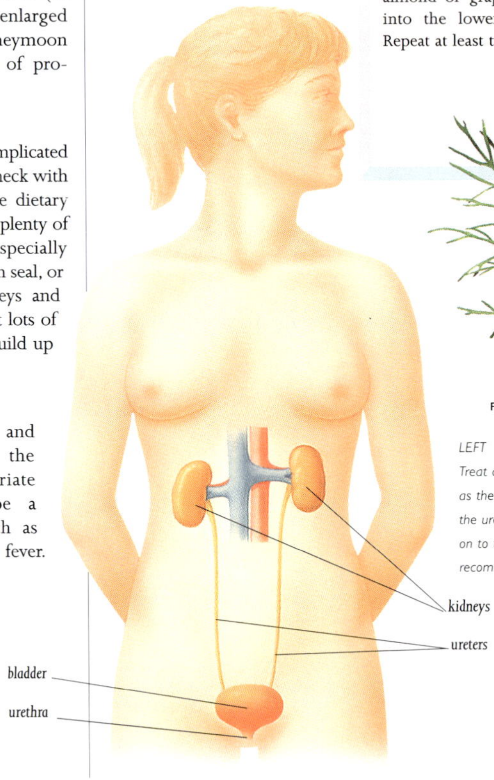

LEFT
Treat cystitis as soon as it occurs, as the infection can spread from the urethra to the bladder and on to the kidneys. Fennel tea is recommended.

WARNING
Do not take tea tree oil internally without medical supervision.

Leucorrhea and pruritus

THE MAIN SYMPTOM of leucorrhea is a thick white or yellow discharge, and severe itching of the vaginal area. Pruritus, or itching, generally accompanies any type of mild vaginal infection. Leucorrhea is an inflammation of the vagina caused by a proliferation of a variety of bacteria or fungi (e.g. candida or other nonspecified organisms). Infections of this kind often occur during times of stress.

DIETARY FACTORS

Boost intake of vitamin C and B complex vitamins. Take garlic capsules, and keep consumption of tea, coffee, alcohol, and spices to a minimum.

OTHER MEASURES

Avoid tight clothing, nylon underwear, and harsh bubble baths. *See also* Cystitis, Genital herpes, Stress, Thrush.

CLINICAL NOTES

Tea tree has been found to be very effective for the treatment of these conditions.

ABOVE AND BELOW
A dietary supplement of garlic capsules and a few drops of lavender oil in the bath are a good preventative measure.

AROMATHERAPY OILS

Tea tree, lavender, geranium, lemon eucalyptus, myrrh.

METHODS OF USE

Add 8 to 10 drops of tea tree or lavender oil to a bowl or shallow bath of warm water and soak for 5–10 minutes daily to treat the condition.

Add 8 to 10 drops of any of the recommended oils to the bathwater on a daily basis as a general preventive and antiseptic measure.

Genital herpes

GENITAL HERPES is an infection transmitted by sexual contact. The first attack is generally the worst: the skin of the genital region becomes red and itchy and then erupts into small, very painful blisters that can last for several weeks. This tends to be followed by recurrent attacks that take a milder form, often precipitated by stress, sexual activity, or an infection, and lasting only a few days. This is caused by the virus *Herpes simplex II*, which, like *Herpes simplex I* (the cause of cold sores), often lies dormant in the body, flaring up during times of stress.

DIETARY FACTORS

Take garlic and vitamin C and B complex vitamins in the diet or as supplements.

OTHER MEASURES

Avoid sexual activity during attacks. Reduce stress levels. *See also* Chicken pox, Cold sores, Stress.

AROMATHERAPY OILS

Lavender, bergamot (bergapten-free), tea tree, chamomile, yarrow, peppermint, geranium, melissa, myrrh, eucalyptus blue gum, bergamot.

WARNING
Although it is normal to experience a temporary, warm sensation in using tea tree oil, discontinue this method if irritation occurs.

LAVENDER

METHODS OF USE

At the very first signs of infection, make a concentrated solution by mixing 10 to 12 drops of tea tree oil with $3\frac{1}{2}$fl oz/100ml of warm water. Using this solution to douche or wash the genital area frequently will soothe irritation and prevent the infection from developing. Shake or stir well before use.

Use neat tea tree oil to dab any blisters as soon as they begin to develop – check for sensitivity first. Repeat frequently over a period of several days, or until the condition has cleared.

Add 8 to 10 drops of tea tree oil to the bathwater as a general disinfectant measure.

Sexual problems

DEBILITY, FRIGIDITY, impotence, inability to conceive, and lack of confidence are all commonly encountered. Many physical problems, such as frigidity or impotence, have a psychological basis, and may be accompanied by depression, anxiety, or other stress-related conditions.

DIETARY FACTORS

A wholesome, nutritious diet is required for optimum health and the maintenance of sexual vitality. Although alcohol can act as an aphrodisiac in small doses, in excess it is soporific, depressant, and damaging to the whole system. Zinc and beta carotene are specifically indicated to increase sexual vigor. Ginseng, is also recommended as a general sexual stimulant, due to its ability to increase the production of hormones, and can be taken as capsules.

WARNING
Essential oils should not be allowed to come into contact with condoms, as they can have a detrimental effect on the rubber.

OTHER MEASURES

Make time for relaxation; adequate exercise is also a basic requirement for a healthy body. Psychotherapy, hypnotherapy, Bach flower remedies, and nutritional advice may also be valuable aids. *See also* Stress.

LEFT
Neroli oil can help to relieve psychological tension and is said to be aphrodisiac.

WARNING
Deep-seated sexual problems may require professional help.

BELOW
Aromatic oils can be relaxing and confidence-building.

METHODS OF USE

Wear essential oils such as rose, ylang ylang, or sandalwood (or a personalized blend) as a perfume to create a sensual mood.

Make up a massage oil using 5 to 7 drops each of rose, sandalwood, and ylang ylang in 2fl oz/50ml of a light base oil. Massage between partners can be a very intimate experience and a means of enhancing sexual communication.

Aromatic bathing can be a mood-setting sensual experience in itself – select a favorite scent (or a blend) from the recommended oils.

Set the scene for seduction by using aphrodisiac oils in a vaporizer, or light a scented candle, and simply enjoy the erotic aroma.

AROMATHERAPY OILS

Aphrodisiacs – rose, neroli, clary sage, patchouli, ylang ylang, jasmine, black pepper, cardamom, sandalwood. Regulators – lavender, geranium.

BLENDED PERFUME

Pregnancy

PROBLEMS DURING pregnancy can arise for all kinds of reasons, both physical and psychological. Common complaints include edema, lower back pain, constipation, fatigue, hemorrhoids, morning sickness, leg cramps, and feelings of anxiety or depression.

DIETARY FACTORS

Eat nourishing food – everything which goes into the body directly affects the growing child, whether it is carbohydrates, fats, minerals, vitamins, or toxic chemicals, alcohol, or tobacco. It is now recognized that the nutritional foundations of good health are laid down during prenatal life. Although it is common to have specific food fads during the early stages of pregnancy, it is important to establish good eating habits – eat plenty of fresh fruit and vegetables, whole grains, adequate protein, and cold-pressed vegetable oils on a daily basis. Avoid refined products, and cut down on tea, coffee, and alcohol.

OTHER MEASURES

Do not overwork – adequate rest is essential for the health of the growing child, and relaxation ensures that the mother and child enjoy their prenatal togetherness. Nonstrenuous daily exercise is also important, such as stretching, walking, yoga, or swimming. Stop smoking. *See also* Anxiety, Constipation, Childbirth, Debility, Depression, Edema, Hemorrhoids, Muscular pain, Nausea/vomiting, Stress.

RIGHT
Using essential oils during pregnancy can be very beneficial in a variety of ways. However, it is best to choose those oils which are of low toxicity, nonirritant, and nonsensitizing.

WARNING
All essential oils should be used in half the usual quantities, or less, during pregnancy.

AROMATHERAPY OILS

Lavender, rose, grapefruit, bergamot, neroli, mandarin, vetiver, chamomile, jasmine, ylang ylang, petitgrain, sandalwood, patchouli, geranium, frankincense.

WARNING
Some essential oils should be avoided altogether during pregnancy. These include basil, clove, cinnamon leaf, hyssop, juniper, marjoram, myrrh, Spanish sage, and thyme. The following oils are best avoided during the first four months of pregnancy: fennel, rose, peppermint, Atlas cedarwood, and rosemary.

METHODS OF USE

To prevent stretch marks (or to get rid of existing stretch marks), prepare the following blend: 1 tbs/15ml each of wheat germ, borage, and/or rose-hip seed oil in 5 tsp/25ml jojoba or grapeseed or sweet almond oil. A few drops (not more than 10 drops in total) of rose, neroli, frankincense, and lavender (singly, or in combination) may also be added. Use this twice daily for light massage to the belly and breasts, especially after the fourth month. The blend can also be rubbed into the perineum for 5–10 minutes daily in the last six weeks before the birth.

Aromatic bathing is a great pleasure and relief, especially toward the end of pregnancy. Add 4 to 5 drops of any of the recommended oils to a warm bath, according to mood, and relax in the aromatic vapors. For weary muscles, use equal amounts of chamomile and lavender oil.

Gentle massage, using mild essential oils such as rose, neroli, petitgrain, lavender, or chamomile can help with a wide variety of problems, such as back pain, anxiety, depression, or fatigue. Keep the concentration of the blend low (10 to 12 drops of essential oil to 2fl oz/50ml base oil).

Cooling compresses of lavender, chamomile, or rose water can be very refreshing during the latter stages of pregnancy. Alternatively, add the flower water to a fine mist spray for regular application throughout the day.

Postnatal depression can be helped by the use of rose, bergamot, neroli, lavender, mandarin, vetivert, or ylang ylang in burners or worn as a perfume.

ABOVE
Every mother-to-be hopes for an easy birth and a happy, healthy baby.

Childbirth

CHILDBIRTH (LABOR) is one of the most moving yet demanding experiences that a woman can undergo. More and more women are choosing a natural or active birth, whether it is in a hospital or at home. Whatever the case, good preparation is the key to coping with the experience, and playing an active role in the birth.

There are many problems that can arise during childbirth – but the key point is to be prepared. Breech birth, methods for coping with severe pain or a long labor, the possible need for Caesarean section or an episiotomy (cutting the perineum), are all options that need to be discussed in advance.

DIETARY FACTORS

It is vital to have a nourishing diet throughout pregnancy. In addition, in preparation for childbirth, take raspberry leaf tea 2–3 times daily during the final three months of pregnancy. It is a marvelous aid to easy childbirth, toning the whole reproductive system and the uterine muscles. Use 1oz/30g of dried herb to 18fl oz/500ml boiled water, infused for 15 minutes (tablets are also available). This also makes an excellent postnatal tonic to restore normal function and tone. An adequate milk supply can be ensured by drinking plenty of fennel, dill, or aniseed tea immediately prior to the birth and afterward.

AROMATHERAPY OILS

Chamomile (Roman and German), clary sage, lemon eucalyptus, eucalyptus blue gum, frankincense, jasmine, lavender, lemon, mandarin, peppermint, rose, bergamot, ylang ylang, cypress, neroli.

CLINICAL NOTES

Many mothers, midwives, and nurses are now using essential oils during pregnancy and for childbirth. Aromatherapy is well regarded as a noninvasive aid to natural birth and of great benefit in promoting rapid recovery.

In hospital trials, over a six-month period, the use of essential oils during labor was studied and recorded. The trials involved over five hundred women. The essential oils used were chamomile, clary sage, eucalyptus, frankincense, jasmine, lavender, lemon, mandarin, peppermint, and rose, used in different combinations and at different stages. The results showed "a high degree of overall satisfaction by mothers and midwives on the use of aromatherapy during labor/delivery."

SEE BURNS AND BLAMEY, "USING AROMATHERAPY IN CHILDBIRTH," CITED IN DATA BASE, VOL.3, P.24

METHODS OF USE

Two weeks prior to the delivery, use the following blend daily to help prepare for the birth and strengthen the uterine muscles: 2 to 3 drops each of rose, jasmine, and black pepper or nutmeg in 5 tsp/25ml light carrier oil, rubbed into the lower abdomen.

During labor, a firm massage to the lower abdomen, and to the whole lower back region, between contractions can be very comforting and can provide good pain relief. Make the following blend in preparation: 2 to 3 drops each of clary sage, rose or lavender, and ylang ylang or nutmeg oils in 5 tsp/25ml carrier oil.

A hot compress applied to the lower abdomen, using warm water and a few drops of clary sage oil – frequently replaced – can act as a natural anesthetic during labor.

Relaxing in an aromatic bath during the early stages of labor and/or soon after the birth can be a great aid and comfort.

During the birth, and in preparing to bring the baby home, the use of vaporized oils (such as bergamot, chamomile, or lavender) to scent the environment can be very conducive to creating an uplifting or relaxing mood. These oils also help to prevent the spread of airborne bacteria.

To help heal the perineum after the birth, add a few drops of rose, cypress, or lavender to a sitz bath, or a shallow bath and soak for at least 10 minutes. Up to a handful of sea salt added to the water will aid healing and prevent infection.

After the birth, the breasts can become engorged by the sudden flow of milk. Massage the hard, swollen lumps with a mixture of 3 to 4 drops (in total) of geranium, rose, or peppermint oil in 1 tbs/15ml carrier oil or a nonallergenic cream.

IMMUNE SYSTEM

Infectious Diseases

Immune system

THE IMMUNE SYSTEM is supported by and closely related to other body systems, especially the lymphatic and nervous systems. Recent research suggests that emotional and psychological factors play a vital role in the efficiency of immune response. This may help to account for the fact that viral infections and conditions involving suppressed immune systems are becoming an increasing problem today. The immune response is orchestrated by three distinct groups of cells – the phagocytes, the T cells, and the B cells. These all originate from white blood cells in the bone marrow, and serve to protect the body from infection. If this defensive barrier breaks down for some reason, the body becomes vulnerable to invasion from all sorts of pathogenic organisms. There are many factors that lead to a damaged immune system – notably the overuse of antibiotics.

DIETARY FACTORS

Insecticides and other additives found in many food products can contribute to the breakdown of the immune system. In extreme cases, this can lead to all types of allergies and sensitization reactions, with symptoms such as headaches, stomach pains, or general fatigue. To maintain optimum health, it is important to follow an organic and additive-free diet as much as possible. To boost the immune system, a course of garlic capsules, vitamin E, and vitamin C are also indicated.

OTHER MEASURES

Since stress contributes to a depressed immune system, it is vital to assess general lifestyle, including work and emotional environment. Psychotherapy, counseling, yoga, meditation, and even allergy testing can all be valuable aids in this field.

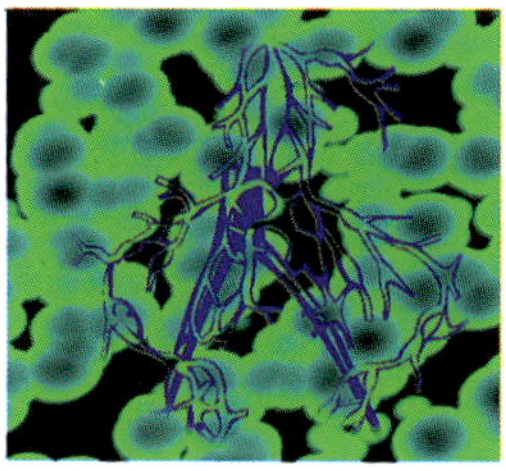

LYMPH IN THE DIGESTIVE TRACT

REFERENCES

EPIDEMIC PAROTITIS
see **MUMPS**
page 162

'FLU
see **INFLUENZA**
page 165

GERMAN MEASLES (RUBELLA)
see **MEASLES** *page* 164

PERTUSSIS
see **WHOOPING COUGH**
page 162

ZONA (SHINGLES)
see **CHICKEN POX**
page 163

AROMATHERAPY OILS

Tea tree, cinnamon leaf, clove, eucalyptus, thyme, rosemary, lavender, pine.

CLINICAL NOTES

Many essential oils, particularly tea tree oil, stimulate the immune system and assist the body in resisting and fighting infection.

METHODS OF USE

To help build up resistance levels, use 8 to 10 drops of tea tree oil in the bathwater at least twice a week.

To strengthen the immune system, have a massage once a week using 7 to 8 drops each of tea tree and rosemary, and 2 to 3 drops of cinnamon leaf oil in 2fl oz/50ml base oil. If this is not possible, make up a 5 percent tea tree concentrated massage oil blend (50 drops per 2fl oz/50ml base oil), and rub this firmly into the palms of the hands and soles of the feet once a day.

Use tea tree and any of the other essential oils listed above as room fragrancers on an everyday basis.

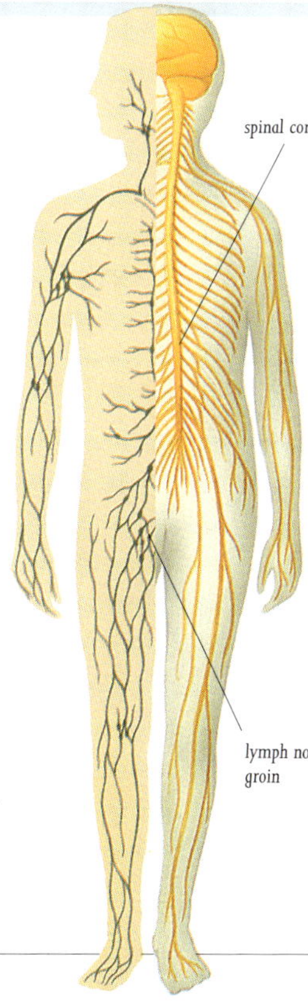

RIGHT
The lymphatic and nervous systems support the body's immune system.

Mumps

NORMALLY A childhood illness, mumps (epidemic parotitis) is often preceded by a slight fever and a sore throat. This is followed by an egg-like swelling of one or both of the salivary glands in front of the ears. High fever, earache, and headache can accompany the main swelling, and these symptoms usually subside after a few days. Mumps is caused by an airborne virus that can be passed via saliva or the breath. It is contagious from one day before symptoms appear to one week after all swelling has gone, and the disease has an incubation period of two to three weeks.

DIETARY FACTORS

Give soft, easily eaten foods since the pain is made worse by chewing and swallowing. Do not give acids such as vinegar, oranges, or lemons. Rinse the mouth with water to prevent dryness.

CLINICAL NOTES

Due to its low toxicity, lavender is especially suited to the treatment of childhood complaints such as mumps.

SEE J. LAWLESS, LAVENDER OIL, PP.31–38

WARNING
Mumps can cause complications in adults, as the infection can spread to other glands such as the testes, ovaries, or pancreas. Seek medical help immediately.

AROMATHERAPY OILS

Tea tree, lavender, coriander, lemon, cajeput, chamomile, eucalyptus, myrtle.

METHODS OF USE

Use lavender and tea tree, or eucalyptus and myrtle in vaporizers, or on a handkerchief or pillow.

Give a daily hot bath, with a few drops of lavender (for older children), or chamomile (for young children) in the water. This soothes aching limbs and acts as a steam inhalation. A high temperature can be reduced by immersing the whole body in a lukewarm bath to which a few drops of lavender or tea tree oil have been added.

Apply a warm lavender or chamomile compress to the swollen cheeks.

Gargle with 2 drops of tea tree or lemon oil, and 2 drops Roman chamomile in a glass of distilled water (children over six only).

Whooping cough

WHOOPING COUGH is characterized by a sudden intake of breath or "whoop" after a bout of coughing. Coughing is sudden, frequent, and violent; there may also be vomiting. It is highly infectious and can last up to 12 weeks. It usually affects children under eight. Despite immunization, it is possible to contract a mild form of this viral disease, especially after an infection such as a cold or influenza. It is contagious for at least two weeks after the onset of symptoms.

DIETARY FACTORS

Cut out dairy products and red meats, which encourage formation of mucus. Give a diet that is light, nutritious, and easy to digest, with vegetable soups, chicken broth, fruit juices, mineral water, and herb teas – especially mouse ear, sundew, coltsfoot, thyme, and white horehound. Give additional vitamin C and cod liver oil.

AROMATHERAPY OILS

Thyme, hyssop, cinnamon leaf, cypress, cajeput, tea tree, lavender.

WARNING
Whooping cough can be extremely dangerous, especially for babies and children under five years of age. Always seek medical advice.

RIGHT Hyssop is beneficial for respiratory problems.

METHODS OF USE

Use a few drops of lavender, thyme, or hyssop in vaporizers in the bedroom during the course of the illness, and in steaming hot inhalations to soothe bouts of coughing. A humid atmosphere is essential.

Apply a hot compress to the chest, using a few drops of lavender oil on a cotton pad (this can be kept warm with a hot water bottle), to facilitate breathing.

Make up a blend of lavender, thyme (white), and tea tree oil (dilution according to age, *see Safety Data, p.211*) and rub onto the child's throat and chest.

Add a few drops of lavender and/or tea tree oil to the bath-water (according to age).

Chicken pox

CHICKEN POX is a highly contagious viral infection, most commonly affecting children. A fever develops, and itchy spots appear in crops, progressing to blisters and then to crusts. Eruption usually starts on the trunk, and spreads to face and limbs, beginning one day after the onset of symptoms and lasting for one to two weeks. In the related shingles (zona), the virus affects the sensory nerves and clusters of blisters appear along the line of a nerve, often in the form of a band around the torso. The condition can be accompanied by severe pain, usually beginning before the rash appears, and there may be fever.

Chicken pox is caused by the same virus as shingles, *Herpes zoster*. It usually occurs in epidemics and spreads through contact at school or play-groups. Its incubation period (the time from first contact to appearance of symptoms) is two to three weeks, and it is contagious from one day before symptoms appear, until all lesions have crusted over. The virus can also lie dormant and return as shingles later in life.

DIETARY FACTORS

It is vital to drink plenty of liquids – water, fruit juices, peppermint, yarrow, chamomile, or elderflower tea (with honey) – to avoid dehydration. Fever is usually accompanied by loss of appetite. As the fever subsides, light, nutritious foods such as soup, rice, or fruit are recommended. Garlic and vitamin C increase resistance to infection and aid in recovery. *See also* Fever.

LEFT
Fluids are essential during any illness, especially where there is fever or high temperature. Fruit juice provides added vitamin C which helps to fight infection and elderflower tea is beneficial.

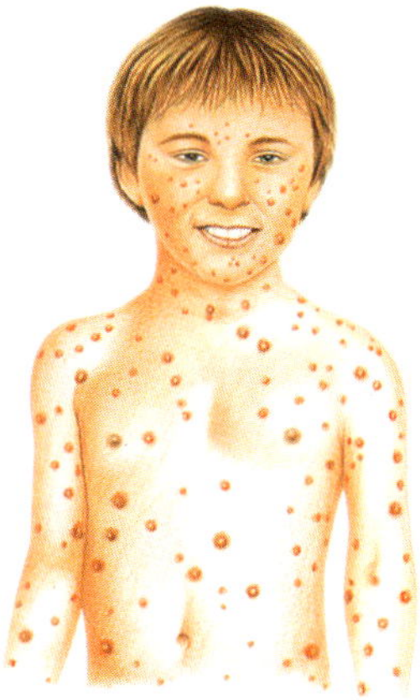

ABOVE
The intensely itchy rash of chicken pox usually starts on the trunk. Tea tree and chamomile oils can both help to soothe the rash and prevent the scratching that can lead to permanent scarring.

CLINICAL NOTES

Tea tree is a very effective remedy for chicken pox due to its combined properties. It soothes itching and promotes rapid healing of spots, thus helping to prevent possible infection or scarring due to scratching. German chamomile oil can be added for its soothing qualities.

ELDERFLOWER

METHODS OF USE

Soak frequently for 10–15 minutes in tepid water, every few hours if possible. For babies, add 2 drops of tea tree and 1 drop of chamomile or lavender oil dissolved in 1 tsp/5ml of alcohol or witch hazel; for children add 3 drops of tea tree and 2 drops of chamomile or lavender oil in 1 tsp/5ml alcohol or witch hazel); for adults add 5 drops of tea tree and 5 drops of chamomile or lavender oil in 1 tsp/5ml alcohol or witch hazel. A handful of colloidal oatmeal (available from most pharmacies), may also be added to the bathwater to soothe the skin and encourage healing.

Dissolve 20 (10 for children) drops of tea tree and 10 (5 for children) drops each of lavender and chamomile oils in 2 tsp/10ml alcohol, and mix with 2fl oz/50ml rose water and 2fl oz/50ml witch hazel. Apply the lotion frequently to the spots. Shake well before each use.

NOTE: This treatment is not suitable for young babies.

AROMATHERAPY OILS

Tea tree, lavender, chamomile, yarrow, peppermint, eucalyptus blue gum, bergamot.

WARNING
In adults, chicken pox or shingles can be dangerous, with high temperatures and pain. Seek medical advice immediately.

Measles and rubella

MEASLES IS A common childhood illness. Its symptoms include fever; barking cough; sensitivity to light; white spots in the mouth, and a blotchy rash on the face and behind the ears. The rash begins three to five days after the appearance of the first symptoms, and lasts up to a week, spreading downward. The symptoms of German measles include fever, catarrh, headache, swollen, tender lymph nodes behind the ears, and a rash of pink spots, which begin on the face and neck, and then spread. The rash appears on the first or second day and lasts for up to three days. Both conditions are spread by the rubella virus. Measles is contagious five days before and after the first appearance of the rash, and the incubation period is one to two weeks. German measles is contagious from one day before the appearance of the symptoms until one day after the disappearance of the rash; incubation is two to three weeks.

ABOVE AND BELOW Lavender or myrtle oil in a steam inhalation helps soothe coughing.

DIETARY FACTORS

It is vital to drink plenty of liquids to avoid dehydration. Give water, fruit juices, or lukewarm peppermint, yarrow, chamomile, or elderflower tea (with honey). There is usually loss of appetite, but as the fever subsides, light, nutritious foods such as soup, rice, or fruit are recommended. Garlic and vitamin C increase resistance to infection and aid recovery.

OTHER MEASURES

During the fever stage, bed rest is advisable. Keep lighting dim in cases of measles. *See also* Fever, Sore throat.

CLINICAL NOTES

Lavender is a useful children's remedy during any infectious illness, due to its ability to ease both physical and psychological discomfort, and because of its balancing nature or two-way effect, which is both calming and stimulating.

This effect is put to use simultaneously at signs of the onset of an infection, such as fever, sore throat, headache, aches and pains, and unrest. Lavender's calming actions as an anti-inflammatory, analgesic, antipyretic, and nervous system sedative will relieve these symptoms early. However, its stimulating actions as a diaphoretic, antiinfective and antiseptic will work directly on the source of the infection itself.

WARNING

German measles can be dangerous to unborn babies. Pregnant women who have not had rubella should seek immediate medical advice if they have been exposed to the disease. Measles in adults can also lead to serious complications. Medical advice should always be sought.

MYRTLE

METHODS OF USE

Use lavender and tea tree, or eucalyptus and myrtle, in vaporizers throughout the duration of the illness, or add a few drops to a handkerchief for inhalation throughout the day, and to the pillow at night.

Give a daily hot bath with a few added drops of lavender (for older children) or chamomile (for young children) to the water. This soothes aching limbs and also acts as a steam inhalation. A high temperature can be reduced by immersing the whole body in a lukewarm bath to which a few drops of lavender or tea tree oil have been added.

For a sore throat, add 3 to 4 drops of lavender or tea tree to a glass of warm water, mix well and use the mixture as a gargle. Repeat at least two or three times a day.

If the fever is very high, it can be reduced by applying cold compresses, and sponging the body at regular intervals, using $3^{1}/_{2}$fl oz/100ml distilled water, with 2fl oz/50ml witch hazel, and 5 drops each of tea tree, lavender, and chamomile oil.

For older children, regular steam inhalations will help to soothe coughing. Add 3 to 6 drops (in total) of tea tree or eucalyptus or myrtle oil to a bowl of steaming hot water and get the child to inhale for 5–10 minutes.

AROMATHERAPY OILS

Chamomile (Roman and German), lemon eucalyptus, eucalyptus blue gum, lavender, cajeput, tea tree, myrtle.

Influenza

INFLUENZA IS THE most common single cause of fever, although the term is often used to include various unidentified viral infections. All are characterized by a raised temperature, aching limbs, fatigue, sore throat, and other respiratory symptoms, such as catarrh or a dry cough. Flu is caused by a virus, and often occurs in epidemics during the winter. New strains of the virus seem to emerge each year, despite the availability of flu vaccines.

DIETARY FACTORS

Drink plenty of liquids, especially peppermint or elderflower teas, and sliced ginger or lemon and honey in hot water. Once the fever has subsided, eat foods which are easy to digest such as soups, rice, or steamed vegetables. Garlic and vitamin C increase resistance to infection and aid recovery.

OTHER MEASURES

Stay in bed and keep warm. Contact with other people should be kept to a minimum as influenza is highly contagious (incubation is from 12 to 24 hours; contagion lasts for the first three days of symptoms). *See also* Congested headaches, Coughs, Fever, Sore throat.

METHODS OF USE

Use tea tree, eucalyptus, and/or rosemary oils, or another recommended oil, in vaporizers especially at the onset of influenza. Sprinkle a few drops of marjoram or bergamot oil onto the pillow at night.

At the very first sign of infection, take a hot bath with 8 to 10 drops of tea tree added to the water, and go straight to bed. Repeated each evening, this is often enough to avert a full-blown attack. Lavender, marjoram, or chamomile oil can also be used in the bathtub to soothe aching limbs and encourage restful sleep.

To combat respiratory infection, add 2 to 3 drops each of tree tree, Spanish sage or clary sage, and thyme oil to a glass of warm water, mix well and gargle. Repeat the treatment at least two or three times a day.

Massage the back of the neck, chest and soles of the feet with 4 to 5 drops each of tea tree, lemon eucalyptus, and cinnamon or clove oil in 5 tsp/25ml base oil. Repeat twice daily.

AROMATHERAPY OILS

Lemon eucalyptus, peppermint, lavender, bergamot, tea tree, rosemary, thyme, basil, citronella, ginger, marjoram, lemongrass, lemon, cinnamon, yarrow, cajeput, Spanish sage, camphor, clove, nutmeg.

ABOVE
Vaporized oils can help to kill germs in the air.

WARNING
Influenza can be dangerous in that bacterial pneumonia may develop.

LEFT
It is important to take plenty of fluids. Herbal teas of peppermint or elderflower are particularly recommended.

CLINICAL NOTES

Essential oils can do much to prevent an attack of flu, or to reduce the severity of the illness. The most effective is tea tree through its powerful antiviral, bactericidal, and immunostimulant qualities. It is also a diaphoretic in cases of fever, and helps the body to sweat out the fever. (However, when the body is in its normal state, these diaphoretic qualities are absent.)

SEE J. LAWLESS, TEA TREE OIL, P.69

Fever

A FEVER IS ANY condition in which the body temperature is higher than normal (i.e. above 37°C/98.4°F). A raised temperature is a vital and healthy response to infection because it speeds up the body's metabolic rate and strengthens its defense systems. In many instances, a fever should be allowed to take its course. This process often includes shivering or feelings of cold, and culminates in a period of profuse sweating that eventually subsides at the same time as a lowering of the fever. Fever can result from numerous viral or bacterial infections, ranging from influenza – the most common cause – to tropical diseases such as malaria or typhoid.

DIETARY FACTORS

Eating is not beneficial while the fever is high because vital energy can be diverted into the digestive process – as opposed to fighting the infection. Feverish people rarely feel like eating anything anyway. However, it is vital to drink plenty of liquids – water, fruit juices, peppermint or elderflower tea – to avoid dehydration. As the fever subsides, light, nutritious foods such as soup, rice, or fruit are recommended. Garlic and vitamin C increase resistance to infection and aid recovery.

OTHER MEASURES

A feverish person must be kept in bed – rest is essential for the body to recuperate. Eat plenty of live yogurt afterward, if antibiotic treatment has been necessary.

LEFT
A patient with fever may have little appetite. Light soups will provide nourishment and much-needed fluids.

Seek professional help if temperature rises to 40°C/104°F

Normal temperature

LEFT
There is a range of acceptable "normal" temperatures, and the temperature also usually varies a little during the day.

AROMATHERAPY OILS

Eucalyptus blue gum, peppermint, lavender, bergamot, tea tree, rosemary, thyme, basil, lemon eucalyptus, citronella, lemongrass, lemon, cinnamon, yarrow, cajeput, Spanish sage, camphor, clove.

WARNING
If the fever remains high, or rises to a dangerous level, seek professional medical advice immediately.

WARNING
Use no more than 3 drops of the spice oils, eucalyptus, camphor, or peppermint in the bathtub.

METHODS OF USE

Use tea tree, eucalyptus (lemon or blue gum) and/or rosemary (or another recommended oil) in vaporizers throughout the duration of the illness.

To help control a high temperature, immerse the whole body in a tepid bath containing 3 to 10 drops in total of the following cooling oils: peppermint, basil, tea tree or eucalyptus (lemon or blue gum). If the person is too weak to get into a bathtub, sponge the body using a facecloth soaked in tepid water to which a few drops of the above oils have been added.

Massage the back of the neck, chest, and soles of the feet with 4 to 5 drops each of tea tree, lemon eucalyptus, cinnamon or clove oil in 5 tsp/ 25ml base oil. Repeat twice daily.

BELOW
People with fever should keep well-wrapped and stay in a warm room.

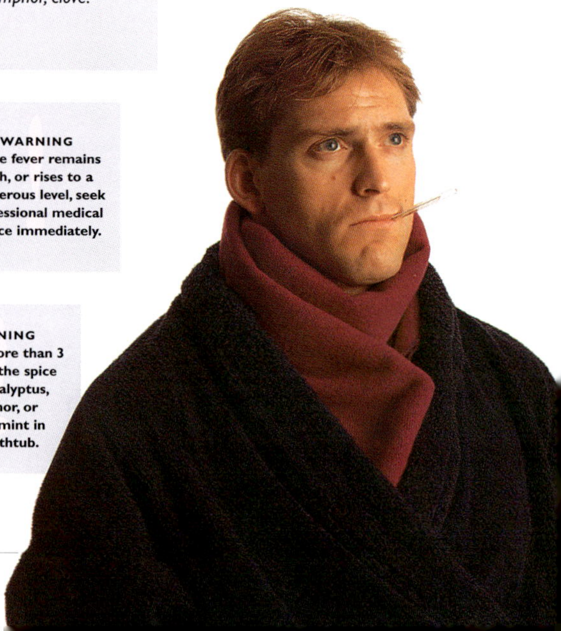

The Nervous System

Anxiety

ANXIETY IS ONE of the most common stress-related conditions encountered today. It is accompanied at the physical level by such symptoms as high blood pressure and palpitations, and at the mental level by insomnia, and irritability. Some people are more prone to worrying than others, although a certain degree of anxiety can also be a natural response to a stressful situation. Anxiety becomes a problem when it is not expressed or released, and when the psychological factors underlying the anxiety are not addressed. Food allergies or the side effects of certain drugs can promote anxiety.

DIETARY FACTORS

Cut down on stimulants such as tea, coffee, alcohol, and on sweet carbonated drinks and refined sugar products. Drink herb teas such as chamomile, lemon balm, lime flowers (linden), hops, or verbena. Oatmeal or porridge oats as a regular part of the diet is one of the best tonics for the nerves.

OTHER MEASURES

Gentle exercise, yoga, meditation, and, if necessary, psychotherapy can all be helpful. Bach flower remedies can be beneficial for chronic worriers or those prone to unpredictable panic attacks. *See also* Depression, High blood pressure, Insomnia, Stress.

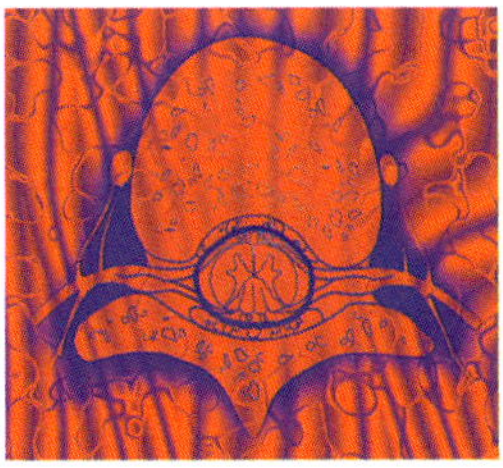

CROSS-SECTION OF SPINAL COLUMN

REFERENCES

LISTLESSNESS
see **DEPRESSION**
page 170

MIGRAINE
see **HEADACHES**
page 168

NERVE PAIN
see **NEURALGIA**
page 175

NERVOUS FATIGUE
see **DEBILITY**
page 171

SHOCK
see **FAINTNESS/SHOCK**
page 173

METHODS OF USE

Add 8 to 10 drops of lavender (or any combination of the recommended oils) to a warm evening bath to relieve insomnia, restlessness, anxiety, and tension.

Regular massage can dramatically reduce anxiety levels. A suitable blend of oils would be 7 to 8 drops each of clary sage, ylang ylang, and lavender in 2fl oz/50ml base oil.

For self-treatment, blend 2 to 3 drops of lavender or chamomile oil with 1 tsp/5ml sweet almond oil, and massage the oil into the hands and the soles of the feet.

For a soothing room fragrance, use lavender, frankincense, or bergamot oil in a vaporizer. Put a few drops of any of these oils on a handkerchief for inhalation throughout the day. Use rose, ylang ylang, or neroli oil (or a blend) neat as a perfume.

AROMATHERAPY OILS

Bergamot, chamomile, neroli, ylang ylang, lavender, valerian, vetiver, rose, clary sage, frankincense, cedarwood, melissa.

WARNING
If the state of anxiety is allowed to persist over a prolonged period, it can lead to secondary, more serious complaints, such as stomach ulcers or heart failure. Chronic anxiety requires professional help.

LEFT
Lavender is a favorite oil for dispelling anxiety and tension.

RIGHT
Time spent in contemplative meditation, particularly in pleasant surroundings, does much to reduce stress-related complaints.

Headaches

HEADACHES ARE a common complaint among both adults and children. They can vary in intensity from a mild ache to severe and lasting pain. Headaches can be caused, or aggravated, by sinus congestion, nervous stress, muscular spasm, physical injury, structural misalignment, inhaling toxic fumes, eye strain, too much sun, or too much alcohol.

DIETARY FACTORS

Recurrent headaches may be related to food allergies. Migraine is most commonly a food-related complaint, and is often triggered by foods containing tyramine. These include chocolate, citrus fruits, cheese, caffeine, alcohol, peanut butter, vinegar, yogurt, yeast, and cured meats. Relaxing herbal remedies such as chamomile, hops, linden, lemon balm, or verbena can help soothe tension headaches when taken as tea. Peppermint tea can help ease congested headaches. Feverfew is recommended for migraine headaches.

OTHER MEASURES

Try to identify the cause of the headache and treat accordingly. This may involve assessing lifestyle, aiming to reduce stress; avoiding the sun; visiting an osteopath or chiropractor to check for structural misalignment; consulting an allergy specialist; avoiding fumes and odors which trigger an attack. *See also* Anxiety, High blood pressure, Sinusitis, Stress.

CLINICAL NOTES

Clinical evidence and CNV data (contingent negative variation curve – a device for measuring electrical brainwave patterns created by anticipation) have demonstrated that several essential oils have a combined sedative and antispasmodic effect which can help in reducing nervous tension. These include lavender, Roman chamomile, marjoram, and melissa.

SEE M. LIS-BALCHIN, AROMASCIENCE, PP.38,65,74

WARNING
Persistent headaches and migraines require professional diagnosis and treatment.

BELOW
Many people find that migraines are triggered by eating certain foods. Chocolate, cheese, citrus fruits and alcohol are common culprits.

METHODS OF USE

For tension headaches, inhale a few drops of lavender or rose and/or melissa oil from a tissue, or apply a drop direct to the temples.

Nasal decongestants can relieve stuffiness and congested headaches. Use 2 to 3 drops each of peppermint and/or eucalyptus oil in a bowl of steaming water, cover the head with a towel, and inhale deeply for 5–10 minutes, keeping the eyes closed.

Headaches brought on by tension or stress can be eased by a firm neck and shoulder massage, using 4 to 5 drops each of lavender, peppermint and marjoram oil in 5 tsp/25ml carrier oil.

For eye strain, apply a cold compress of rose water, chamomile, water, or lavender water (not the essential oil) to the eyelids. A cold compress may also be applied to the forehead or the back of the neck to soothe tension headaches and sunstroke.

Relax in a warm aromatic bath to ease away tension, using 8 to 10 drops (in total) of lavender, chamomile, and/or rose oil; to promote decongestion, use a few drops of peppermint, eucalyptus, and/or marjoram oil.

AROMATHERAPY OILS

Rose, lavender, melissa, chamomile, peppermint, eucalyptus, marjoram.

CITRUS FRUITS

ALCOHOL

CHEESE

Insomnia

INABILITY TO SLEEP (insomnia) is another common stress-related complaint that everyone suffers from at some time. When insomnia continues over a period of time, however, it can lead to secondary problems such as reduced concentration, irritability, depression, and chronic fatigue.

DIETARY FACTORS

Reduce intake of stimulants such as tea or coffee, especially in the evening, and do not eat a heavy meal just before retiring. Lack of vitamin B is associated with poor sleep patterns. Three of the B group are known as antistress vitamins, because they are especially required during periods of stress. A vitamin B complex supplement, and chamomile, hops, skullcap or valerian taken as a tea (or in tablet form) last thing at night can help induce relaxation.

OTHER MEASURES

Check that the mattress is comfortable; make sure the bedroom is neither too cold nor too stuffy; assess lifestyle and work patterns, aiming to reduce stress levels – yoga, meditation, relaxation exercises or tapes can be useful. *See also* Anxiety, Debility, High blood pressure, Stress.

METHODS OF USE

Massage a few drops of neat lavender or chamomile oil into the soles of the feet before retiring. This will quickly be absorbed into the bloodstream to act as a natural sedative. For more stubborn cases of insomnia, valerian oil can be used instead.

To encourage relaxation or a restful night (also excellent during pregnancy, and for children), put a few drops of lavender oil on the pillow or on pajamas. Scenting the sheets with lavender oil also helps to induce sleep. Alternatively, use the vaporized oil of lavender, marjoram, valerian, and/or chamomile in the bedroom.

Relax for at least 10 minutes before retiring for the night in a warm bath to which you have added 8 to 10 drops of lavender, or one of the other recommended oils. Restlessness, hyperactivity, and insomnia in babies, infants and older children can be helped by adding a few drops of lavender or chamomile oil to the bathtub at bedtime.

A regular massage, using soothing oils such as lavender, chamomile, clary sage, and marjoram is also very beneficial in reducing stress and helping to induce sleep.

AROMATHERAPY OILS

Lavender, chamomile, vetiver, valerian, marjoram, neroli, clary sage.

WARNING

Do not use valerian oil for more than two weeks at a stretch, since it is a depressant to the central nervous system.

CLINICAL NOTES

Several studies in British hospitals have shown that vaporized lavender oil helps to induce sleep – in some cases with better effect than night medication.

SEE J. LAWLESS, LAVENDER OIL, PP.22–25

LEFT
Meditation helps to calm the mind, and this enables you to relax and fall asleep instead of worrying uselessly about problems or letting the mind race.

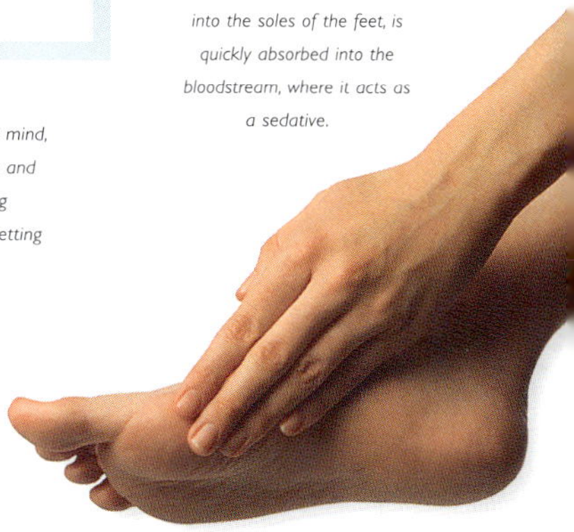

BELOW
A few drops of neat lavender or chamomile oil, massaged into the soles of the feet, is quickly absorbed into the bloodstream, where it acts as a sedative.

Depression

DEPRESSION can take many forms: it is often associated with lack of energy and listlessness, but can also be accompanied by restlessness or agitation, and sometimes alternates between the two. It can be triggered by a traumatic event such as a bereavement, a divorce, or even moving house. It may also be caused by ongoing problems such as emotional or financial difficulties.

DIETARY FACTORS

To speed recovery, it is vital to eat balanced, nutritious food when suffering from depression. It is easy to slip into bad food habits, or simply not to eat enough, during such times. A course of good multimineral and multivitamin supplements (especially the B complex vitamins) can be helpful. Ginseng or damiana (taken as a tea or as tablets) are valuable restorative herbal remedies.

OTHER MEASURES

Bach flower remedies, yoga, meditation, and psychotherapy, counseling or attending support groups can all help. *See also* Anxiety, Debility, Faintness/shock, Stress.

LEFT AND BELOW
Making a major change in life, such as moving house, can result in listlessness and depression. Sandalwood and ginseng are valuable restorative remedies.

METHODS OF USE

Add 8 to 10 drops of lavender oil and any of the other recommended oils in the bath.

Receiving a regular professional massage, using a blend of antidepressant oils, can help encourage feelings of self-worth and well-being. A suitable blend would be 7 to 8 drops (in total) of lavender, neroli or petitgrain, and bergamot in 2fl oz/50ml base oil.

For an uplifting or soothing room fragrance use oils such as bergamot or lavender in a vaporizer. Wear rose, jasmine, or neroli oil as a perfume.

WARNING
Chronic depression, or deep depression that has no apparent cause, requires professional treatment.

CLINICAL NOTES

Mild depression responds well to aromatherapy treatment, as does depression arising from having to cope with difficult life situations involving grief, loss, or fear. In one case history, a doctor describes her own reasons for using aromatherapy after the death of her mother as follows:
"I didn't want tranquilizers and didn't feel antidepressants were needed as mine was a perfectly normal reaction to the stress I was living through. I didn't want to take alcohol and yet craved relief from what I was experiencing. I knew these pharmacological treatments did not work for real-life situations of stress ... [whereas] a combination of massage and essential oils is more powerful than either one alone, and [makes for] a valuable form of relaxation therapy."

SEE DR. ANN COXON, "PRESCRIBING AROMATHERAPY," AROMATHERAPY QUARTERLY, 1991, NO.31, P.9

GINSENG TEA

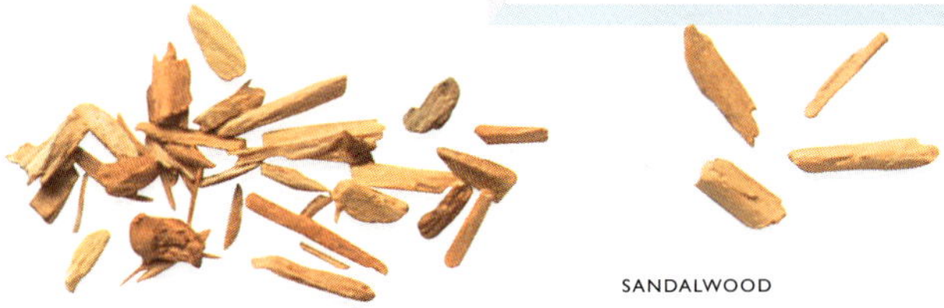

SANDALWOOD

AROMATHERAPY OILS

Basil, bergamot, neroli, jasmine, melissa, rose, sandalwood, lavender.

CLINICAL NOTES

Rosemary is still specific in the *British Herbal Pharmacopoeia* for "depressive states with general debility." Dr. Valnet recommended rosemary in "fortifying morning baths," especially for children, and for adults with general fatigue. Lemon, grapefruit, and lime oils have been used as an air spray in Japanese offices to increase concentration levels: "...typing mistakes were reduced by 54% when lemon oil was disbursed in the room."

SEE J. LAWLESS, AROMATHERAPY AND THE MIND, P.172

BELOW
Uplifting and stimulating essential oils (see Aromatherapy Oils) can be inhaled from a handkerchief for a pick-me-up.

Put a few drops of recommended oil on a tissue and inhale

Debility

DEBILITY (nervous fatigue) is often characterized by both physical and mental languor. Symptoms include low spirits, feeling constantly tired, dizziness or faintness, and a general sense of malaise. The causes of debility are various: common contributing factors include emotional or physical exhaustion due to long working hours, VDU strain (low-level radiation from computer screens), a severe or long-term illness, or emotional pressure.

DIETARY FACTORS

Nervous fatigue and weakness are associated with insufficient folic and pantothenic acid (both found in liver and yeast) and vitamin B1 (thiamine), which regulates the release of energy in the body. Eat plenty of unrefined carbohydrates and complete proteins that produce energy gradually, since excessively high or low blood sugar levels ultimately lead to exhaustion and depression – as in diabetes. Drink fresh ginger root tea with honey for an excellent restorative herbal remedy.

OTHER MEASURES

Assess lifestyle and work patterns; take gentle exercise; perform deep breathing in the fresh air; consider psychotherapy; if necessary, take a complete break to rest and recuperate. *See also* Anxiety, Depression, Faintness/shock, Stress.

ABOVE
Spending long hours at work can lead to low energy and low spirits.

METHODS OF USE

Add 8 to 10 drops of rosemary or pine oil to the daily bath, or to a footbath, as a reviving "pick-me-up."

Inhaling eucalyptus, lemon, or rosemary from a tissue can help counteract feelings of weakness or nervous fatigue. Alternatively, use any of the recommended oils in a vaporizer, at home or in the workplace.

Use fortifying oils for massage to strengthen the whole nervous system. For example, 7 to 8 drops each of rosemary, pine, and black pepper or basil in 2fl oz/50ml base oil.

AROMATHERAPY OILS

Peppermint, pine, geranium, rosemary, basil, ginger, eucalyptus, angelica, lavender, lemon, grapefruit, bergamot, orange, and most spice oils.

Epilepsy

EPILEPSY is the most common serious neurological disorder. Epileptic fits can vary from momentary attacks (inattention), without loss of consciousness (minor epilepsy) to muscular spasm and convulsions (major epilepsy). Caused by a disturbance in the central nervous system, epilepsy is associated with brief disruptions in the normal electrical activity of the brain. It may start in childhood, or may come on unexpectedly, but the precipitating factor is often a traumatic or stressful life event with high anxiety levels.

BELOW
During an epileptic seizure, the normal electrical activity of the brain is interrupted. This brain scan shows one such episode.

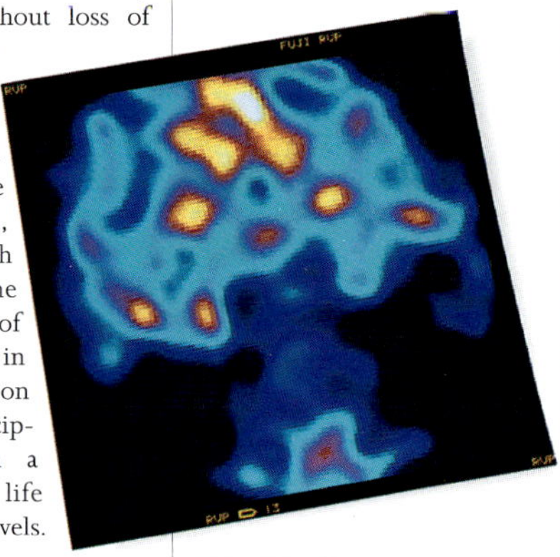

DIETARY FACTORS

Certain substances, when ingested in significant doses, are known to promote epilepsy because they are neurotoxic: these are notably ketones found in herbs such as tansy, mugwort, rue, thuja, pennyroyal, and wormwood (and, to a lesser degree, in common sage, fennel, hyssop, and rosemary). Relaxing herbs such as hops, chamomile, and lemon balm (melissa) are beneficial taken as a tea.

OTHER MEASURES

Do not try to restrain, move, or wake an individual during an epileptic fit. On regaining consciousness after an attack, the person needs to rest quietly for a period, in order to establish equilibrium.

CLINICAL NOTES

One patient using chamomile oil in a series of clinical trials "showed a 90% reduction in seizures" and it was found that: "Intervention with the use of essential oils in individuals who have epilepsy can significantly reduce seizure rates, although maintenance of treatments might be necessary."

SEE INTERNATIONAL JOURNAL OF AROMATHERAPY, P.23, CITED IN T. CLOUSTON, OILS FOR EPILEPSY

METHODS OF USE

If you suffer from epilepsy, if possible, have a full-body massage once a week using a chosen oil (from the list below) diluted to 2.5 percent in sweet almond oil (25 drops per 2fl oz/ 50ml base oil. Alternatively, practice self-massage on the hands and feet with a similar blend.

Inhale neat lavender oil (or other chosen oil) from a tissue, or use in a vaporizer. Wearing neroli or rose oil as a perfume can help allay anxiety and provide comfort.

Add 8 to 10 drops of lavender, chamomile, or ylang ylang oil to a warm bath to help restore equilibrium and cope with the emotional aftereffects of an attack.

AROMATHERAPY OILS

Chamomile, lavender, melissa, ylang ylang, rose, neroli.

BELOW
Tansy and rue should be avoided in epilepsy, while hops and chamomile are relaxing and beneficial.

RUE

TANSY

HOPS

CHAMOMILE

Faintness/shock

THIS CAN vary from a mild feeling of faintness to complete collapse. Symptoms may include nausea, vomiting, restlessness, a pale and clammy skin, and a racing pulse. Slight faintness or dizziness can result from a number of causes, such as sunstroke, hangover, nervous exhaustion, or very low blood pressure. It is common during the menopause and with PMS. Shock can cause faintness due to a reduced volume of blood or body fluid through either physical injury or fear.

DIETARY FACTORS

Faintness may also be due to anemia (low red blood corpuscle count), anorexia, bulimia, hunger, or poor nutrition. It is important to eat regular, balanced meals.

OTHER MEASURES

Rest, keep warm and loosen any tight clothing. Breath deeply, remain calm.

AROMATHERAPY OILS

Lavender, neroli, rose, geranium, palmarosa, ylang ylang, clary sage, jasmine.

WARNING
Traumatic (injury) shock is a serious condition which requires immediate medical attention.

METHODS OF USE

Inhale neat lavender oil from a tissue, or use in a vaporizer. Neroli, jasmine, or rose oil can be inhaled to help allay anxiety and provide comfort.

Add 8 to 10 drops of lavender, clary sage, or geranium oil to a warm bath to help restore equilibrium and cope with the emotional aftereffects of a shock.

Rose, lavender, or orange flower water, applied to the temples and face, is reviving to the spirits, and helpful in cases of emotional shock, as well as good for hangovers, nervous exhaustion, and sunstroke.

LEFT
Neroli can be used to help with problems of an emotional origin.

Jetlag

THE SYMPTOMS of jetlag after a long flight, are well recognized: sleep disturbance, swollen ankles, disorientation, nervous fatigue, and dehydration. The problems are caused by disruption of the body's biological clock due to crossing time zones; change in altitude; being in a compressurized atmosphere, and, often, anxiety or nausea brought on by traveling.

DIETARY FACTORS

Drink plenty of bottled water or other liquids (not alcohol) to avoid dehydration during the flight. If stress is involved, take extra vitamins C and B complex to aid recovery.

OTHER MEASURES

Keep the feet raised as much as possible to avoid swollen ankles. *See also* Anxiety, Edema, Nausea/vomiting, Stress.

AROMATHERAPY OILS

Lavender, chamomile, geranium, rosemary, bergamot, grapefruit, peppermint, lemon, clary sage.

ABOVE
Using a blackout mask can help you to sleep on long journeys by air.

METHODS OF USE

To prevent jetlag, freshen up frequently during the flight using a little lavender water, or inhale lavender or geranium oil from a tissue.

Use a lavender or rose moisturizing cream on the face and hands to prevent skin dryness.

On arrival, if possible, take a long bath containing 8 to 10 drops of lavender or geranium or chamomile oil for relaxing, or rosemary or bergamot or grapefruit oil for an enlivening effect. This helps readjust physiological and psychological rhythms.

Stress

STRESS IS A multidimensional syndrome that can cause a wide range of physical ailments and psychological problems, from high blood pressure, headaches, or digestive complaints, to feelings of constant tiredness, depression, or nervous anxiety. Stress weakens the immune system, and, in the long term, makes an individual more susceptible to all kinds of disease.

It occurs when excessive demands are placed on an individual's physical, mental, or emotional resources. The body reacts by boosting levels of adrenaline – the hormone that prepares us for fight or flight in situations of danger. Many potentially stressful events are dealt with on a day-to-day basis and can provide interest and challenge in life. When unresolved demanding situations build up over a period of time, this causes what we call stress.

DIETARY FACTORS

There may be a deficiency in trace elements such as copper, cobalt, manganese or iron, in minerals such as phosphorus and potassium, or in vitamins, and especially vitamin B6 (pyridoxine) and vitamin B3 (niacin). It is important to have a wholesome mixed diet, containing adequate protein, fats, carbohydrates, vitamins, and minerals, and to avoid processed foods and foods containing chemical additives. Nervine and relaxant herbs such as chamomile (suitable for children), valerian, hops, or skullcap are recommended, taken as teas or in tablets.

OTHER MEASURES

Take regular exercise, if possible in the fresh air, as this helps work out physical and emotional tension, and aids relaxation. Find time to practice yoga, meditation, deep breathing, and pleasurable hobbies. Make clear boundaries between work and free time. Assess work and lifestyle – psychotherapeutic help or counseling may be beneficial. *See also* Anxiety, Debility, Depression, High blood pressure, Insomnia, Palpitations.

METHODS OF USE

Add 8 to 10 drops of lavender (or any combination of the recommended oils) to a warm evening bath to relieve insomnia, restlessness, anxiety, and nervous tension.

Receiving a regular professional massage can dramatically reduce stress levels. A blend of oils such as clary sage, ylang ylang, and lavender is often found to be helpful.

For self-treatment, mix 2 to 3 drops of lavender or Roman chamomile oil with 1 tsp/5ml sweet almond oil, and massage the blend into the hands and the soles of the feet.

For a soothing room fragrance, use lavender, frankincense, or bergamot oil in a vaporizer or put a few drops on a handkerchief for inhalation throughout the day. In addition, rose, ylang ylang, or neroli oil may be used as a perfume.

AROMATHERAPY OILS

Lavender, chamomile, valerian, bergamot, clary sage, marjoram, frankincense, melissa, nutmeg, neroli, rose, jasmine.

CLINICAL NOTES

Clinical research has shown that the synergistic combination of smell and touch can have a profoundly nourishing and comforting effect on the psyche.

Several oils have been shown in clinical tests to have destressing effects, including valerian, nutmeg, neroli, rose, and lavender.

SEE R. TISSERAND, INTERNATIONAL JOURNAL OF AROMATHERAPY, VOL.4, NO.2, P.16

headaches often occur as a result of stress

RIGHT There are many ways of dealing with stress. The most important thing is to take time to assess all the factors involved and be prepared to make changes in your life.

Neuralgia

NERVE PAIN or neuralgia can take many forms. It may run the whole length of a nerve, or may affect a localized point on the skin's surface. Sciatica is a form of neuralgia that is characterized by an intense shooting pain or tenderness felt along the length of the sciatic nerve, which runs from the back of the thigh to the lower calf. The term is also often used to describe nerve pain which radiates from the lower back to the thigh. This distressing condition can result from a variety of causes, including an infection, an accident, or an osteopathic problem, but more commonly it occurs through general debility, poor diet, lack of exercise, and stress. Facial neuralgia can be triggered by cold wind. Although sciatica is often associated with a misalignment of the hips or lower spine, causing pressure on the sciatic nerve, the root cause of the problem frequently lies in abdominal congestion and constipation.

DIETARY FACTORS

It is vital to tackle the root of the problem, and this often means a change of diet. Include plenty of roughage, green vegetables, fruit, oats, and a course of vitamin B complex. Relaxant herbs, and nervines such as hops, skullcap, valerian, and peppermint, taken as a tea (or as tablets) are also recommended.

OTHER MEASURES

Assess lifestyle to reduce stress levels; if necessary, consult an osteopath or chiropractor; take gentle exercise. *See also* Constipation, Debility, Stress.

AROMATHERAPY OILS

Lavender, peppermint, rosemary, marjoram, chamomile, ginger.

CLINICAL NOTES

Rosemary can be of great relief to those suffering from sciatica or neuralgia. It also acts as a stimulant for the whole system, including the abdominal region, thus helping to relieve any congestion in this area. Case studies have also shown that: "Where there is neuralgia or nerve pain, relaxing nervines and tonics will help ... massage of the lower back and legs may help a lot."

SEE D. HOFFMAN, THE HOLISTIC HERBAL, P.85

METHODS OF USE

Simply soaking in a hot bath is an easy and effective way of bringing pain relief. Use 8 to 10 drops of any of the above oils added to the bathwater to increase the benefits.

Gentle massage is itself very helpful for sciatica and neuralgia. Add about 25 drops (in total) of rosemary, lavender, marjoram, and/or peppermint to 2fl oz/50ml of Saint-John's-wort oil and rub gently into the affected area.

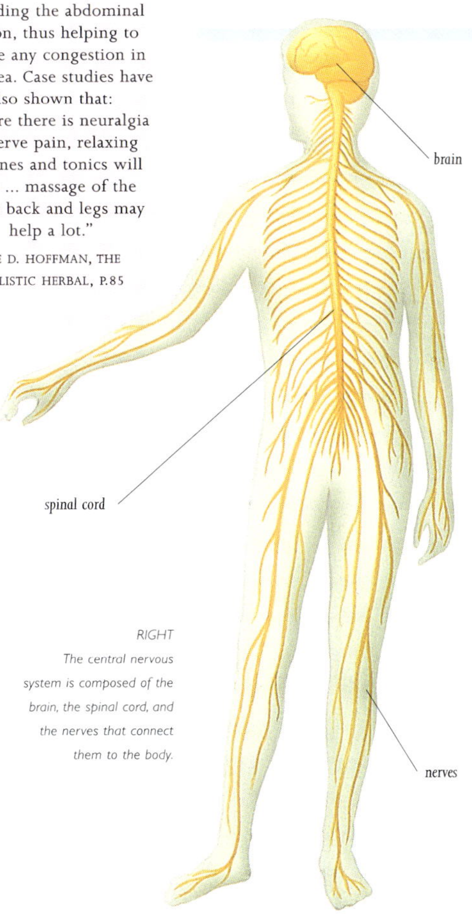

RIGHT
The central nervous system is composed of the brain, the spinal cord, and the nerves that connect them to the body.

PART FOUR

Index of Essential Oils

In the following pages a profile is given for each of the oils in the three groups listed on page 18 and mentioned in the uses, remedies, and treatments suggested throughout this book. Each profile describes the plant from which the oil is derived, the quality of the oil in appearance and scent, its general actions, and the ways in which it is used.

The bars in the center column of each profile show the scent properties of the oil and the general effect it has in use, both physiologically and psychologically. These are a useful guide to understanding the nature of the oil, but the qualities and effects of essential oils are extremely subtle, and vary both according to the particular source and also with the physical and emotional state of the person using them. Intuition and experience can be used in selecting oils for use. The group number (indicating general usefulness), and the part used for extraction of the oil are indicated in boxes in the top heading. A third symbol highlights oils that can be used for children.

The oil profiles are arranged in botanical name order. For a quick reference, the entries are listed below in common name order.

All essential oils are very strong and some can be toxic in various ways if incorrectly used. Before using any oil, check its profile, look out especially for Safety data and Warning boxes, which describe ways in which the oil must be used, and give contraindications for its use.

WHERE TO FIND THE OILS

KEY TO SYMBOLS

Roots | Flowers | Parts of plants | Fruit or peel | Leaves | Whole plant | Seeds | Wood | Resin | Good for children

Yarrow

ACHILLEA MILLEFOLIUM **FAMILY** *ASTERCEAE* (COMPOSITAE)

DESCRIPTION

A perennial herb with simple stems, up to 3ft/1m high, with finely dissected leaves, and bearing numerous, pinky-white, dense flower heads.

ACTIONS

Anti-inflammatory, antipyretic, anti-rheumatic, antiseptic, antispasmodic, astringent, carminative, cicatrizant, diaphoretic, digestive, expectorant, hemostatic, hypotensive, stomachic, tonic.

EXTRACTION

The oil is extracted by steam distillation from the dried herb.

CHARACTERISTICS

A dark blue or greenish-olive liquid, with a fresh, green, sweet, herbaceous, slightly camphoraceous odor. It blends well with cedarwood, pine, chamomile, valerian, vetivert, and myrrh.

SAFETY DATA

Nontoxic, nonirritant, but there is possible sensitization in some individuals. The oil can cause skin irritation in concentration.

SCENT SCALE
Top *Middle* *Base*

PSYCHOLOGICAL SCALE
Uplifting *Balancing* *Soothing*

PHYSIOLOGICAL SCALE
Stimulating *Regulating* *Sedative*

PERFUME

Scent: *Warm, fresh, green, sweet, herbaceous, slightly camphoraceous.*
Key qualities: *Balancing, restorative, tonic (nerve), strengthening, opening, grounding, revitalizing, mildly stimulating.*
Odor intensity: *High.*

AROMATHERAPY USE

Skin care: *Acne, burns, cuts, eczema, hair rinse, inflammation, rashes, scars, wounds.* **Circulation, muscles and joints:** *Arteriosclerosis, high blood pressure, rheumatoid arthritis, thrombosis, varicose veins.* **Digestive system:** *Constipation, cramp, flatulence, hemorrhoids, indigestion.* **Reproductive system:** *Amenorrhea, dysmenorrhea.* **Immune system:** *Colds, fever, 'flu.* **Urinary system:** *Cystitis, and other infections.* **Nervous system:** *Hypertension, insomnia, stress-related conditions.*

Dill seed

ANETHUM GRAVEOLENS **FAMILY** *APIACEAE* (UMBELLIFERAE)

DESCRIPTION

Annual or biennial herb, up to 3ft/1m high, with a smooth stem, feathery leaves, and umbels of yellowish flowers followed by flat, small seeds.

ACTIONS

Antispasmodic, bactericidal, carminative, digestive, emmenagogue, galactagogue, hypotensive, stimulant, stomachic.

EXTRACTION

The oil is extracted by steam distillation (sometimes water) from the seeds.

CHARACTERISTICS

Seed oil is a colorless to pale yellow, mobile liquid, with a light, fresh, warm-spicy scent. Weed oil is colorless or pale yellow, mobile liquid, with a powerful, sweet-spicy aroma. It blends well with mint, nutmeg, spice, and the citrus oils.

SAFETY DATA

Nontoxic, nonirritant, nonsensitizing.

SCENT SCALE
Top *Middle* *Base*

PSYCHOLOGICAL SCALE
Uplifting *Balancing* *Soothing*

PHYSIOLOGICAL SCALE
Stimulating *Regulating* *Sedative*

PERFUME

Scent: *Herbaceous, fresh, peppery, spicy, warm.*
Key qualities (mind): *Reviving, clearing, tonic.*
Odor intensity: *Medium.*

AROMATHERAPY USE

Digestive system: *Colic, dyspepsia, flatulence, indigestion.* **Reproductive and endocrine systems:** *Amenorrhea, galactagogue.*

Angelica root

ANGELICA ARCHANGELICA **FAMILY** *APIACEAE* (UMBELLIFERAE)

DESCRIPTION

A large, hairy plant with rhizome-like roots, ferny leaves, and umbels of white flowers. The whole plant has a strong, aromatic scent.

ACTIONS

Antispasmodic, carminative, depurative, diaphoretic, digestive, diuretic, emmenagogue, expectorant, febrifuge, nervine, stimulant, stomachic, tonic, bactericidal, fungicidal.

EXTRACTION

The essential oil is produced by steam distillation from the roots.

CHARACTERISTICS

The root oil is colorless, or pale yellow, turning yellowy-brown with age. It has a rich, herbaceous-earthy body note. The seed oil is a colorless liquid, with a fresher, spicy top note. Blends well with patchouli, clary sage, vetivert, and citrus oils.

SAFETY DATA

Not to be used during pregnancy or by young children or people with diabetes. The root oil is phototoxic. Use with care, in low dilutions only (1%).

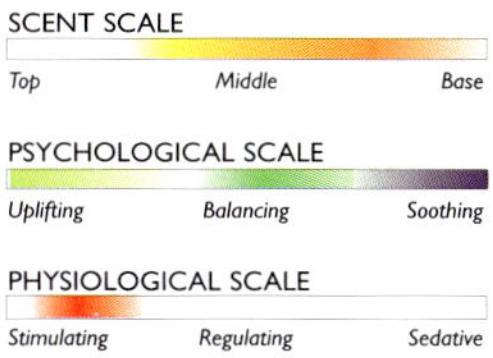

PERFUME

Scent: *Balsamic, musky, herbaceous, bitter-sweet, powerful, earthy, spicy, long-lasting. Acts as a fixative.* **Key qualities:** *Restorative, revitalizing, tonic, purifying, comforting, stimulating (in small quantities), sedating (in large quantities), warming, grounding, aphrodisiac.* **Odor intensity:** *High.*

AROMATHERAPY USE

Skin care: *Dull and congested skin, irritated conditions, psoriasis.* **Circulation, muscles, and joints:** *Accumulation of toxins, arthritis, gout, rheumatism, water retention.* **Respiratory system:** *Bronchitis, colds, coughs.* **Digestive system:** *Anemia, anorexia, flatulence, indigestion.* **Nervous system:** *Fatigue, migraine, nervous tension, stress-related disorders.*

Rosewood/bois de rose

ANIBA ROSAEODORA. **FAMILY** *LAURACEAE*

DESCRIPTION

Medium-size, tropical evergreen tree, with a reddish bark and heartwood, bearing yellow flowers; used extensively for timber.

ACTIONS

Mildly analgesic, anticonvulsant, antidepressant, antimicrobial, antiseptic, aphrodisiac, bactericidal, cellular stimulant, cephalic, deodorant, immune system stimulant, tissue regenerator, tonic.

EXTRACTION

The oil is extracted by steam distillation of the wood chippings.

CHARACTERISTICS

Colorless to pale yellow liquid, with a very sweet, woody-floral fragrance that has a spicy hint. Blends well with most oils, especially citrus, woods, and florals; it helps give body, and rounds off sharp edges.

SAFETY DATA

Nontoxic, nonirritant, nonsensitizing.

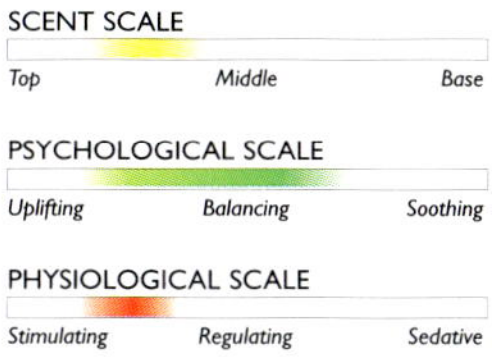

PERFUME

Scent: *Rosy, woody, dry, floral, slightly green, fresh, mild.* **Key qualities (mind):** *Warming, comforting, pleasing.* **Odor intensity:** *Low.*

AROMATHERAPY USE

Skin care: *Acne, dermatitis, scars, wounds, wrinkles, and good for general skin care of all skin types.* **Immune system:** *Colds, coughs, fever, infections, immune system stimulant.* **Nervous system:** *Frigidity, headaches, nausea, nervous tension, stress-related conditions.*

Celery seed

APIUM GRAVEOLENS **FAMILY** *APIACEAE* (UMBELLIFERAE)

DESCRIPTION

A familiar biennial plant, 2–3ft/30–60cm high, with a grooved, fleshy, erect stalk, shiny pinnate leaves, and umbels of white flowers.

ACTIONS

Antioxidant, antirheumatic, antiseptic (urinary), antispasmodic, aperitif, depurative, digestive, diuretic, carminative, cholagogue, emmenagogue, galactagogue, hepatic, nervine, sedative (to nervous system), stimulant (uterine), stomachic, tonic (digestive).

EXTRACTION

The oil is extracted by steam distillation from the whole or crushed seeds.

CHARACTERISTICS

A pale yellow, or orange, spicy-warm, sweet, long-lasting odor. It blends well with lavender, pine, tea tree, coriander, and other spices.

SAFETY DATA

Nontoxic, nonirritant, possible sensitization.

SCENT SCALE

Top *Middle* *Base*

PSYCHOLOGICAL SCALE

Uplifting *Balancing* *Soothing*

PHYSIOLOGICAL SCALE

Stimulating *Regulating* *Sedative*

PERFUME

Scent: *Spicy-warm, sweet, long-lasting.*
Key qualities (mind): *Warming, refreshing, reviving.*
Odor intensity: *Medium.*

AROMATHERAPY USE

Circulation, muscles and joints: *Arthritis, build-up of toxins in the blood, gout, rheumatism.* **Digestive system:** *Dyspepsia, flatulence, indigestion, liver congestion, jaundice.* **Reproductive and endocrine systems:** *Amenorrhea, glandular problems, increases milk flow.* **Urinary system:** *Cystitis.* **Nervous system:** *Neuralgia, sciatica.*

WARNING
Avoid using during pregnancy.

Frankincense/olibanum

BOSWELLIA CARTERI **FAMILY** *BURSERACEAE*

DESCRIPTION

A small tree or shrub, with pinnate leaves, and white or pale pink flowers. It yields a natural oleo-gum resin.

ACTIONS

Anti-inflammatory, antiseptic, astringent, carminative, cicatrizant, cytophylactic, digestive, diuretic, emmenagogue, expectorant, sedative, tonic, uterine, vulnerary.

EXTRACTION

The oil is extracted by steam distillation from selected oleo-gum resin (around 3–10% oil to 60–70% resin).

CHARACTERISTICS

A pale yellow or greenish, mobile liquid, with a fresh terpeney top note, and a warm, rich, sweet-balsamic undertone. It blends well with sandalwood, pine, vetivert, geranium, lavender, neroli, orange, bergamot, and other citrus oils, camphor, basil, pepper, cinnamon, and other spice oils.

SAFETY DATA

Nontoxic, nonirritant, nonsensitizing.

SCENT SCALE

Top *Middle* *Base*

PSYCHOLOGICAL SCALE

Uplifting *Balancing* *Soothing*

PHYSIOLOGICAL SCALE

Stimulating *Regulating* *Sedative*

PERFUME

Scent: *Balsamic, long-lasting, woody, slightly camphoraceous, resinous, rich, sweet, incense-like, dry. This oil is a fixative, and preservative.* **Key qualities:** *Clearing, purifying, restorative, warming, sedative, uplifting, tonic, cephalic, revitalizing.*
Odor intensity: *High.*

AROMATHERAPY USE

Skin care: *Blemishes, dry and mature complexions, scars, wounds, wrinkles.* **Respiratory system:** *Asthma, bronchitis, catarrh, colds, coughs, flu, laryngitis.* **Genitourinary system:** *Cystitis, dysmenorrhea, leukorrhea, metrorrhagia.* **Nervous system:** *Anxiety, nervous tension, stress-related conditions. Frankincense has the ability to slow down, and deepen, the breath – very conducive to prayer and meditation.*

Ylang ylang

CANANGA ODORATA, FORMA GENUINA **FAMILY** *ANNONACEAE*

DESCRIPTION

A tall tropical tree up to 68ft/20m high, with large, tender, fragrant flowers, that can be pink, mauve, or yellow.

ACTIONS

Aphrodisiac, antidepressant, anti-infectious, anti-seborrheic, antiseptic, euphoric, hypotensive, nervine, regulator, sedative (nervous), stimulant (to the circulatory system), tonic.

EXTRACTION

The oil is extracted by water or steam distillation from freshly picked flowers. Yellow flowers yield the best oil.

CHARACTERISTICS

A colorless to pale yellow liquid with a light, fresh balsamic, slightly spicy scent. A good oil has a creamy, rich top note. A very intriguing perfume oil in its own right, it also blends well with sandalwood, jasmine, bois de rose, vetiver, bergamot, rose, and floral and oriental bases. It is also an excellent fixative.

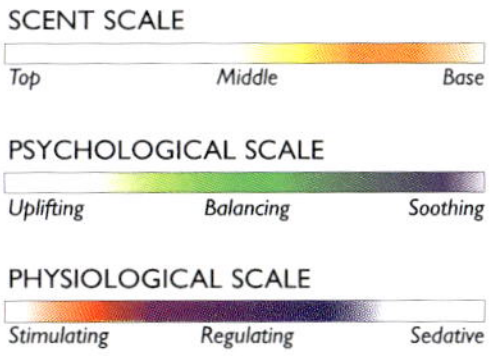

PERFUME

Scent: *Exotic, sweet, balsamic, floral, slightly spicy, sensual, heady, oriental, rich, voluptuous.*
Key qualities: *Powerfully sedative, soothing, calming, regulating, euphoria-inducing, and narcotic when used in large quantities; aphrodisiac.*
Odor intensity: *High.*

AROMATHERAPY USE

Skin care: *Acne, hair growth, hair rinse, insect bites, irritated and oily skin, general skin care.*
Circulation: *High blood pressure, hyperpnoea (abnormally fast breathing), tachycardia, palpitations.*
Nervous system: *Depression, frigidity, impotence, insomnia, nervous tension, and stress-related disorders.*

SAFETY DATA

Nontoxic, nonirritant, but a few cases of sensitization have been reported. Use in moderation, since the oil's heady scent can cause headaches or nausea.

Elemi

CANARIUM LUZONICUM **FAMILY** *BURSERACEAE*

DESCRIPTION

A tropical tree up to 100ft/30m high, which yields a resinous exudation from its trunk. This has a green, pungent odor, and although it is called a gum, it is made up almost entirely of resin and essential oil.

ACTIONS

Antiseptic, balsamic, cicatrizant, expectorant, fortifying, regulator, stimulant, stomachic, tonic.

EXTRACTION

The oil is extracted by steam distillation from the resin.

CHARACTERISTICS

A colorless to pale yellow liquid, with a light, fresh, balsamic-spicy, lemon-like odor. It blends well with myrrh, frankincense, rosemary, lavender, sage, cinnamon, and other spices.

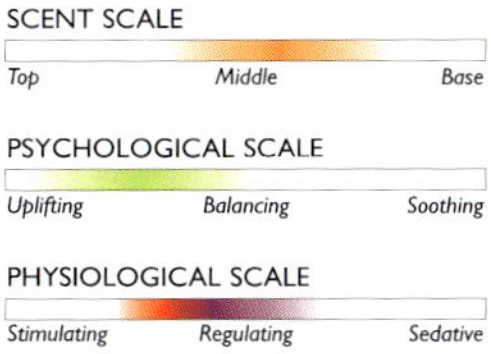

PERFUME

Scent: *Light, fresh, soft, balsamic, slightly camphoraceous, incense-like, spicy, green, diffusive.* **Key qualities:** *Restorative, stimulating, drying, fortifying, warming, refreshing.*
Odor intensity: *High.*

AROMATHERAPY USE

Skin care: *Aging skin, infected cuts and wounds, inflammation, wrinkles (rejuvenator).* **Respiratory system:** *Bronchitis, catarrhal conditions, unproductive coughs.* **Nervous system:** *Nervous exhaustion, stress-related conditions.*

SAFETY DATA

Nontoxic, nonirritant, nonsensitizing.

Cedarwood, Atlas

CEDRUS ATLANTICA **FAMILY** PINACEAE

DESCRIPTION

Pyramidal evergreen tree, with a majestic stature, up to 130ft/40m high. The wood is hard, and strongly aromatic, due to its high essential oil content.

ACTIONS

Antiseptic, antiputrescent, antiseborrheic, astringent, diuretic, expectorant, fungicidal, mucolytic, sedative (to nervous system), stimulant (to circulatory system), tonic.

EXTRACTION

The oil is extracted by steam distillation from the wood, stumps, and sawdust.

CHARACTERISTICS

A yellow, orange, or deep amber, viscous oil with a warm, camphoraceous top note, and sweet, tenacious, woody-balsamic undertone. It blends well with bois de rose, bergamot, cypress, jasmine, juniper, neroli, mimosa, frankincense, clary sage, vetiver, rosemary, ylang ylang, oriental, and floral bases.

WARNING
This oil is best avoided during pregnancy.

SAFETY DATA
Nontoxic, nonirritant, nonsensitizing.

SCENT SCALE
Top — *Middle* — *Base*

PSYCHOLOGICAL SCALE
Uplifting — *Balancing* — *Soothing*

PHYSIOLOGICAL SCALE
Stimulating — *Regulating* — *Sedative*

PERFUME

Scent: *Balsamic, sweet, smoky, slightly camphoraceous, dry-woody, tenacious, turpentine-like, long-lasting, and acts as a fixative.* **Key qualities:** *Aphrodisiac, warming, tonic, uplifting, elevating, grounding, opening, comforting, reviving.*
Odor intensity: *Medium–low.*

AROMATHERAPY USE

Skin care: *Acne, dandruff, dermatitis, eczema, fungal infections, greasy skin, hair loss, skin eruptions, ulcers.*
Circulation, muscles and joints: *Arthritis, rheumatism.* **Respiratory system:** *Bronchitis, catarrh, congestion, coughs.*
Genitourinary system: *Cystitis, leukorrhea, pruritus.* **Nervous system:** *Nervous tension, stress-related conditions.* **Other:** *Insect repellent (moths).*

Chamomile, Roman

CHAMAEMELUM NOBILIS/ANTHEMIS NOBILIS **FAMILY** ASTERACEAE (COMPOSITAE)

DESCRIPTION

A small, stocky, perennial herb, up to 10in/25cm high, with a much-branched, hairy stem, half spreading or creeping. It has feathery, pinnate leaves, and daisy-like, white flowers.

ACTIONS

Analgesic, anti-anemic, antineuralgic, antiphlogistic, antiseptic, antispasmodic, bactericide, carminative, cholagogue, cicatrizant, digestive, emmenogogue, febrifuge, hepatic, hypnotic, nerve sedative, stomachic, sudorific, tonic, vermifuge, vulnerary.

EXTRACTION

The oil is produced by steam distillation from the flower heads.

CHARACTERISTICS

A pale blue liquid (turning yellow on keeping), with a warm, sweet, fruity-herbaceous scent. It blends well with bergamot, clary sage, jasmine, neroli, rose, geranium, and lavender.

SAFETY DATA
Nontoxic, generally nonirritant, but can cause dermatitis in some individuals.

SCENT SCALE
Top — *Middle* — *Base*

PSYCHOLOGICAL SCALE
Uplifting — *Balancing* — *Soothing*

PHYSIOLOGICAL SCALE
Stimulating — *Regulating* — *Sedative*

PERFUME

Scent: *Slightly fruity, sweet, fresh, warm, herbaceous, rich, grassy, fragrant, apple-like.*
Key qualities: *Restorative, calming, sedative, relaxing, soothing, warming, balancing, comforting, mild, slightly soporific or hypnotic in large doses.* **Odor intensity:** *High.*

AROMATHERAPY USE

Skin care: *Acne, boils, burns, cuts, chilblains, dermatitis, earache, eczema, inflammation, insect bites, rashes, sensitive skin, wounds.*
Circulation, muscles and joints: *Arthritis, inflamed joints, muscular pain, neuralgia, rheumatism, sprains.*
Digestive system: *Dyspepsia, colic, indigestion, nausea.* **Reproductive system:** *Dysmenorrhea, menopausal problems, menorrhagia.* **Nervous system:** *Headache, insomnia, nervous tension, migraine and stress-related complaints.*

Chamomile, German/blue

CHAMOMILLA MATRICARIA/MATRICARIA RECUTITA **FAMILY** ASTERACEAE

DESCRIPTION

A strongly aromatic annual herb, up to 2ft/60cm tall, with a hairless, erect, branching stem. It has delicate feathery leaves, and daisy-like, white flowers.

ACTIONS

Analgesic, anti-allergenic, anti-inflammatory, antiphlogistic, antispasmodic, bactericide, calminative, cicatrizant, cholagogue, digestive, febrifuge, fungicidal, hepatic, nerve sedative, stimulant of leukocyte production, stomachic, sudorific, vermifuge, vulnerary.

EXTRACTION

The oil is extracted by steam distillation from the flower heads.

CHARACTERISTICS

An inky-blue, viscous liquid, with a strong, sweetish, warm-herbaceous odor. It blends well with geranium, lavender, patchouli, rose, benzoin, neroli, bergamot, marjoram, lemon, ylang ylang, jasmine, and clary sage.

SCENT SCALE
Top *Middle* *Base*

PSYCHOLOGICAL SCALE
Uplifting *Balancing* *Soothing*

PHYSIOLOGICAL SCALE
Stimulating *Regulating* *Sedative*

PERFUME

Scent: *Warm, herbaceous, sweet, slightly bitter, green.* **Key qualities:** *Relaxing, soothing, balancing, calming, tonic (nerve).* **Odor intensity:** *Very high.*

AROMATHERAPY USE

Skin care: *Acne, allergies, boils, burns, cuts, chilblains, dermatitis, earache, eczema, hair care, inflammation, insect bites, rashes, sensitive skin, teething pain, toothache, wounds.* **Circulation, muscles and joints:** *Arthritis, inflamed joints, muscular pain, neuralgia, rheumatism, sprains.* **Digestive system:** *Dyspepsia, colic, indigestion, nausea.* **Reproductive system:** *Dysmenorrhea, menopausal problems, menorrhagia.* **Nervous system:** *Headache, insomnia, nervous tension, migraine, stress-related complaints.*

SAFETY DATA

Generally nontoxic, nonirritant, but causes dermatitis in some individuals.

Camphor, white

CINNAMOMUM CAMPHORA **FAMILY** LAURACEAE

DESCRIPTION

A tall, handsome, evergreen tree, up to 100ft/30m high. It has many branches, bearing clusters of small white flowers followed by red berries.

ACTIONS

Anti-inflammatory, antiseptic, antiviral, bactericidal, counterirritant, diuretic, expectorant, stimulant, vermifuge.

EXTRACTION

Crude camphor is collected from the trees in crystalline form. The essential oil is produced by steam distillation from the wood, rootstumps, and branches.

CHARACTERISTICS

White camphor is the lightest (lowest boiling) fraction, and is a colorless to pale yellow liquid, with a sharp, pungent, camphoraceous odor. Brown camphor is the middle fraction, and yellow camphor, a blue-green or yellowish liquid, is the heaviest. Camphor blends with herb and spice oils.

SAFETY DATA

White camphor, which does not contain safrole, is relatively nontoxic, nonsensitizing, and nonirritant. Avoid using it for children, however.

SCENT SCALE
Top *Middle* *Base*

PSYCHOLOGICAL SCALE
Uplifting *Balancing* *Soothing*

PHYSIOLOGICAL SCALE
Stimulating *Regulating* *Sedative*

PERFUME

Scent: *Clear, sharp, penetrating, camphoraceous, pungent.* **Key qualities:** *Anaphrodisiac, restorative, balancing, refreshing.* **Odor intensity:** *High.*

AROMATHERAPY USE

Skin care: *Acne, inflammation, oily conditions, spots.* **Circulation, muscles and joints:** *Arthritis, muscular aches and pains, rheumatism, sprains.* **Respiratory system:** *Bronchitis, chills, coughs.* **Immune system:** *Colds, fever, flu, infectious disease.* **Other:** *Insect prevention (flies, moths).*

WARNING

Brown and yellow camphor (containing safrole) are toxic and carcinogenic. They should not be used in therapy, either internally or externally.

Cinnamon leaf

CINNAMOMUM ZEYLANICUM **FAMILY** LAURACEAE

DESCRIPTION

A tropical evergreen tree, up to 50ft/15m high, with stiff sharp spines, smooth ovate leaves, and small white flowers and bluish-white berries.

ACTIONS

Anthelmintic, antidiarrheal, antidote, antimicrobial, antiseptic, antispasmodic, antiputrescent, astringent, digestive, emmenagogue, hemostatic, parasiticide, refrigerant, spasmolytic, stimulant, stomachic, vermifuge.

EXTRACTION

Essential oil is extracted by water or steam distillation from the leaves and twigs.

CHARACTERISTICS

Leaves and twigs yield a yellow to brownish oil, with a warm-spicy, somewhat harsh odor. It blends well with frankincense, ylang ylang, orange, mandarin, and benzoin.

SAFETY DATA

The leaf oil is relatively nontoxic, though possibly a skin irritant. Its major component, eugenol, causes irritation to the mucous membrane. Use in moderation. The bark oil should not be used on the skin.

SCENT SCALE

Top *Middle* *Base*

PSYCHOLOGICAL SCALE

Uplifting *Balancing* *Soothing*

PHYSIOLOGICAL SCALE

Stimulating *Regulating* *Sedative*

PERFUME

Scent: *Sweet-spicy, peppery, hot, dry, tenacious, slightly woody, herbaceous, diffusive, powerful, oriental, warm.*
Key qualities (mind): *Warming, reviving, tonic, strengthening, aphrodisiac, restorative, uplifting.*
Odor intensity: *High.*

AROMATHERAPY USE

Skin care: *Lice, scabies, tooth and gum care, warts, wasp stings.*
Circulation, muscles and joints: *Poor circulation, rheumatism..*
Digestive system: *Anorexia, colitis, diarrhea, dyspepsia, intestinal infection, sluggish digestion, spasm.*
Reproductive system: *Childbirth (stimulates contractions), frigidity, leukorrhea, metrorrhagia (scanty periods).* **Immune system:** *Chills, colds, flu, infectious diseases.*
Nervous system: *Debility, nervous exhaustion, stress-related conditions.*

Lime

CITRUS AURANTIFOLIA **FAMILY** RUTACEAE

DESCRIPTION

A small evergreen tree, up to 15ft/4.5m high, with stiff, sharp spines, smooth, ovate leaves, and small white flowers. The bitter fruit is a pale green color, about half the size of a lemon.

ACTIONS

Antirheumatic, antiscorbutic, antiseptic, antiviral, aperitif, bactericidal, febrifuge, restorative, tonic.

EXTRACTION

The oil is extracted by cold expression from the peel of the unripe fruit, or by steam distillation of the whole, ripe, crushed fruit.

CHARACTERISTICS

The peel oil is a pale yellow or olive-green liquid, with a fresh, sweet citrus-peel odor. The fruit oil is a water-white or pale yellow liquid, with a fresh, sharp, fruity-citrus scent. It blends well with neroli, citronella, lavender, rosemary, clary sage, and other citrus oils.

SCENT SCALE

Top *Middle* *Base*

PSYCHOLOGICAL SCALE

Uplifting *Balancing* *Soothing*

PHYSIOLOGICAL SCALE

Stimulating *Regulating* *Sedative*

PERFUME

Scent: *Fresh, bitter, citrus, penetrating, green, fruity, clean.*
Key qualities (mind): *Refreshing, uplifting, active.* **Odor intensity:** *High.*

AROMATHERAPY USE

Skin care: *Acne, anemia, brittle nails, boils, chilblains, corns, cuts, greasy skin, herpes, insect bites, mouth ulcers, spots, warts.* **Circulation, muscles and joints:** *Arthritis, cellulitis, high blood pressure, nosebleeds, obesity (congestion), poor circulation, rheumatism.* **Respiratory system:** *Asthma, bronchitis, catarrh.*
Digestive system: *Dyspepsia.*
Immune system: *Colds, flu, fever, throat infections, infections.*

SAFETY DATA

Generally non-toxic, non-irritant, non-sensitizing. However the expressed peel oil (but not the steam-distilled whole fruit oil) is phototoxic.

Petitgrain, orange

CITRUS AURANTIUM, VAR. AMARA **FAMILY** RUTACEAE

DESCRIPTION

The oil of orange petitgrain is produced from the leaves and twigs of the same tree that produces both bitter orange oil and neroli oil (see below).

ACTIONS

Antiseptic, antispasmodic, deodorant, digestive, nervine, stimulant (to both digestive, and nervous systems), stomachic, tonic.

EXTRACTION

The oil is extracted by steam distillation from the leaves and twigs.

CHARACTERISTICS

A pale yellow to amber liquid, with a fresh-floral citrus scent, and a woody-herbaceous undertone. It blends well with rosemary, lavender, geranium, bergamot, orange, neroli, clary sage, jasmine, benzoin, palmarosa, and clove, and is a classic ingredient in eau-de-Cologne and toilet waters.

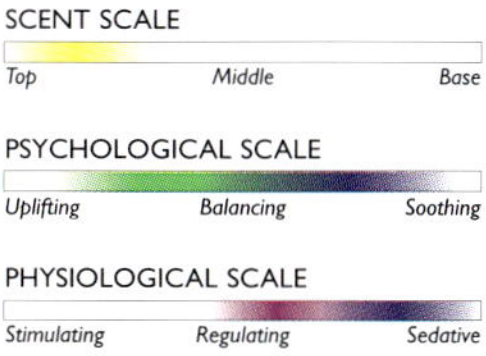

PERFUME

Scent: *Citrus and floral.* **Key Qualities:** *Calming and refreshing.* **Odor intensity:** *Medium.*

AROMATHERAPY USE

Skin care: *Acne, excessive perspiration, greasy skin and hair, toning.* **Digestive system:** *Dyspepsia, flatulence.* **Nervous system:** *Convalescence, insomnia, nervous exhaustion, stress-related conditions.*

SAFETY DATA
Nontoxic, nonirritant, nonsensitizing, nonphototoxic.

Neroli

CITRUS AURANTIUM VAR. AMARA **FAMILY** RUTACEAE

DESCRIPTION

An evergreen tree, up to 33ft/10m high, with dark green, glossy, oval leaves, paler beneath, and with long, but not very sharp, spines. It has a smooth, grayish trunk and branches, and very fragrant white flowers. The fruits are smaller and darker than those of the sweet orange.

ACTIONS

Antiseptic, antispasmodic, bactericidal, carminative, cicatrizant, cordial, deodorant, digestive, mildly fungicidal, stimulant (nervous), tonic.

EXTRACTION

Essential oil is extracted by steam distillation from the freshly picked flowers.

CHARACTERISTICS

The oil is a pale yellow, mobile liquid, with a light, sweet-floral fragrance and terpeney top note. Blends well with virtually all oils, especially jasmine, lavender, rose, lemon, and other citrus oils.

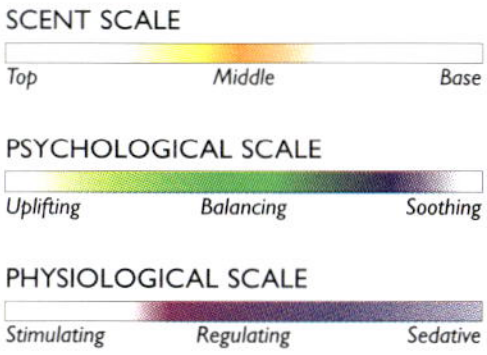

PERFUME

Scent: *Floral, soft, delicate, pervasive, sweet, warm, rich.* **Key qualities:** *Aphrodisiac, hypnotic, sedative, soothing, tonic, restorative, uplifting, antidepressant.* **Odor intensity:** *Medium–high.*

AROMATHERAPY USE

Skin care: *Scars, stretch marks, thread veins, mature and sensitive skin, wrinkles, tones the complexion.* **Circulatory system:** *Palpitations, poor circulation.* **Digestive system:** *Diarrhea(chronic), colic, flatulence, spasm, nervous dyspepsia.* **Nervous system:** *Anxiety, depression, nervous tension, PMS, shock, stress-related conditions, and especially problems of emotional origin.*

SAFETY DATA
Nontoxic, nonirritant, nonsensitizing, nonphototoxic.

Bergamot 2

CITRUS BERGAMIA **FAMILY** *RUTACEAE.*

DESCRIPTION

A small tree, about 15ft/4.5m high, with smooth, oval leaves, bearing small, round fruit that ripens from green to yellow.

ACTIONS

Analgesic, anthelmintic, antiseptic, antispasmodic, antitoxic, carminative, digestive, diuretic, deodorant, febrifuge, laxative, parasiticide, rubefacient, stimulant, stomachic, tonic, vermifuge, vulnerary, insecticide.

EXTRACTION

Bergamot oil is extracted from the peel of the nearly ripe fruit by cold expression. Bergapten-free oil is produced by a process known as fractionation.

CHARACTERISTICS

A light greenish-yellow liquid, with a fresh, sweet-fruity scent, and slightly spicy-balsamic undertone. It blends well with lavender, neroli, jasmine, cypress, geranium, clary sage, chamomile, juniper, coriander, and other citrus oils.

WARNING
Phototoxic: extreme care must be taken when using the oil in dermal applications, or a rectified, bergapten-free oil should be substituted.

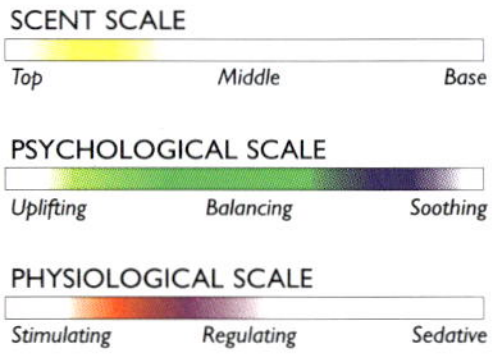

PERFUME

Scent: *Fresh, citrus, sweet, light, warm, slightly spicy-floral, green.*
Key qualities: *Reviving, refreshing, calming, soothing, uplifting, sedative, regulating, balancing, anti-depressant.*
Odor intensity: *Low.*

AROMATHERAPY USE

Skin care: *Acne, boils, cold sores, eczema, insect bites, oily complexion, psoriasis, scabies, spots, varicose ulcers, wounds.* **Respiratory system:** *Halitosis, mouth infections, sore throat, tonsillitis.* **Digestive system:** *Flatulence, loss of appetite.* **Genitourinary system:** *Cystitis, leukorrhea, pruritus, thrush.* **Immune system:** *Colds, fever, flu, infectious diseases.* **Nervous system:** *Anxiety, depression, stress-related conditions. The oil has a refreshing and uplifting quality.* **Other uses:** *Insect repellent.*

Lemon 3

CITRUS LIMON **FAMILY** *RUTACEAE*

DESCRIPTION

A small evergreen tree, up to 20ft/6m high, with serrated oval leaves, stiff thorns, and fragrant flowers. The fruit ripens from green to yellow.

ACTIONS

Anti-anemic, antimicrobial, antirheumatic, antisclerotic, antiseptic, antispasmodic, antitoxic, astringent, bactericide, carminative, cicatrizant, depurative, diaphoretic, diuretic, febrifuge, hemostatic, hypotensive, insecticide, rubefacient, tonic, vermifuge.

EXTRACTION

The oil is extracted by cold expression from the outer part of the fresh peel.

CHARACTERISTICS

A pale greeny-yellow liquid, with a light, fresh, citrus scent. It blends well with lavender, neroli, ylang ylang, rose, sandalwood, olibanum, chamomile, benzoin, fennel, geranium, eucalyptus, juniper, elemi, and other citrus oils.

WARNING
This oil is phototoxic – do not use on skin before exposing to direct sunlight or sun beds. May cause irritation or sensitization. Use in moderation.

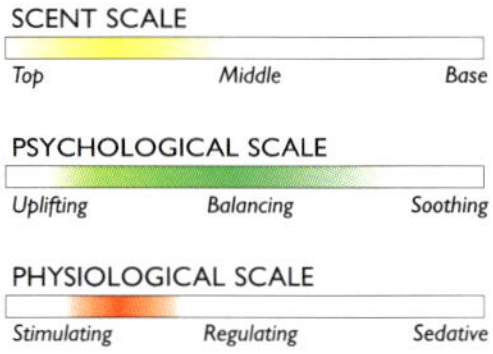

PERFUME

Scent: *Fresh, clean, lemony, light, penetrating, fruity, diffusive.* **Key qualities:** *Refreshing, mental stimulant, cephalic, purifying, reviving, strengthening, soothing.*
Odor intensity: *Medium.*

AROMATHERAPY USE

Skin care: *Acne, anemia, brittle nails, boils, chilblains, corns, cuts, greasy skin, herpes, insect bites, mouth ulcers, spots, throat infections, warts.* **Circulation, muscles and joints:** *Arthritis, cellulitis, high blood pressure, nosebleeds, obesity (congestion), poor circulation, varicose veins, rheumatism.* **Respiratory system:** *Asthma, bronchitis, catarrh.* **Digestive system:** *Dyspepsia.* **Immune system:** *Colds, flu, fever, infections.*

Grapefruit

CITRUS X *PARADISI* **FAMILY** RUTACEAE

DESCRIPTION

A cultivated tree, often over 33ft/10m high, with glossy leaves, and familiar large yellow fruits.

ACTIONS

Antiseptic, antitoxic, astringent, bactericidal, diuretic, depurative, stimulant (to lymphatic and digestive systems), tonic.

EXTRACTION

The oil is extracted by cold expression from the fresh peel.

CHARACTERISTICS

A yellow or greenish, mobile liquid, with a fresh, sweet, citrus aroma. It blends well with lemon, palmarosa, bergamot, neroli, rosemary, cypress, lavender, geranium, cardamom, and other spice oils.

SAFETY DATA

Nontoxic, nonirritant, nonsensitizing, but slightly phototoxic. This oil has a short shelf life – it oxidizes quickly.

SCENT SCALE

Top *Middle* *Base*

PSYCHOLOGICAL SCALE

Uplifting *Balancing* *Soothing*

PHYSIOLOGICAL SCALE

Stimulating *Regulating* *Sedative*

PERFUME

Scent: *Citrus, fruity, bitter, powerful, lemony, fresh.* **Key qualities (mind):** *Cleansing, stimulating, refreshing, uplifting.*
Odor intensity: *Medium.*

AROMATHERAPY USE

Skin care: *Acne, congested and oily skin, promotes hair growth, tones the skin and tissues.* **Circulation, muscles and joints:** *Cellulitis, exercise preparation, muscle fatigue, obesity, stiffness, water retention.* **Immune system:** *Chills, colds, flu.* **Nervous system:** *Depression, headaches, nervous exhaustion, performance stress.*

Mandarin

CITRUS RETICULATA **FAMILY** RUTACEAE

DESCRIPTION

A small evergreen tree, up to 20ft/6m high, with glossy leaves, fragrant flowers, and bearing fleshy fruit. The tangerine is larger than the mandarin, and is rounder, with a more yellowy skin.

ACTIONS

Antiseptic, antispasmodic, carminative, digestive, diuretic (mild), laxative (mild), sedative, stimulant (to digestive and lymphatic systems), tonic.

EXTRACTION

The oil is extracted by cold expression from the outer peel.

CHARACTERISTICS

Mandarin oil is a yellowy-orange, mobile liquid with a blue-violet hint. It has a sweet, almost floral, citrus scent. It blends well with other citrus oils, especially neroli, and spice oils such as nutmeg, cinnamon and clove.

SAFETY DATA

Nontoxic, nonirritant, nonsensitizing, but slightly phototoxic.

SCENT SCALE

Top *Middle* *Base*

PSYCHOLOGICAL SCALE

Uplifting *Balancing* *Soothing*

PHYSIOLOGICAL SCALE

Stimulating *Regulating* *Sedative*

PERFUME

Scent: *Fresh, warm, sweet, fruity, soft, mild.* **Key qualities (mind):** *Warming, comforting, soothing, uplifting.* **Odor intensity:** *Low.*

AROMATHERAPY USE

Skin care: *Acne, congested and oily skin, scars, spots, stretch marks, toner.* **Circulatory system:** *Fluid retention, obesity.* **Digestive system:** *Digestive problems, dyspepsia, hiccoughs, intestinal problems.* **Nervous system:** *Insomnia, nervous tension, restlessness.*

Orange, sweet 3

CITRUS SINENSIS/CITRUS AURANTIUM, VAR. DULCIS **FAMILY** RUTACEAE

DESCRIPTION

An evergreen tree, smaller than the bitter variety, less hardy, and with fewer, or no, spines. The fruit has a sweet pulp, and nonbitter membranes.

ACTIONS

Antidepressant, anti-inflammatory, antiseptic, bactericidal, carminative, choleretic, digestive, fungicidal, hypotensor, sedative (to the nervous system), stimulant, stomachic, tonic.

EXTRACTION

The oil is extracted by cold expression (by hand or machine), or by steam distillation, of the fresh, ripe, or almost ripe outer peel.

CHARACTERISTICS

The oil is a yellowy-orange or dark orange, mobile liquid, with a sweet, fresh-fruity scent. It blends well with lavender, neroli, lemon, clary sage, myrrh, and spice oils such as nutmeg, cinnamon, and cloves.

WARNING
Distilled orange oil should not be used on the skin before exposure to sunlight or use of a sun bed.

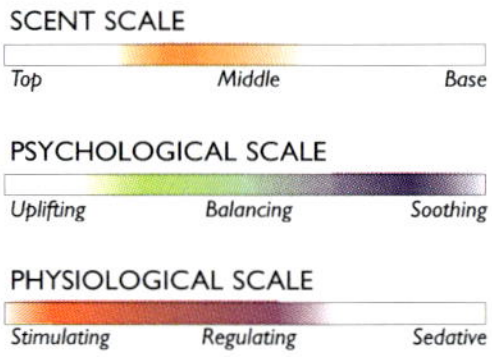

PERFUME

Scent: *Sweet, warm, sensual, radiant, fresh, citrus, fruity, tangy.* **Key qualities:** *Tonic (to the nervous system), refreshing, warming, uplifting, soothing, sedative, comforting.* **Odor intensity:** *Medium–low.*

AROMATHERAPY USE

Skin care: *Dull and oily complexions (nonirritant, generally nonsensitizing, but can cause dermatitis in some individuals).* **Circulatory system:** *Obesity, palpitations, water retention.* **Respiratory system:** *Bronchitis, chills, colds, flu.* **Digestive system:** *Constipation, dyspepsia, spasm.* **Nervous system:** *Nervous tension, stress-related conditions.* **Other uses:** *Used to treat mouth ulcers.*

Myrrh 2

COMMIPHORA MYRRH **FAMILY** BURSERACEAE

DESCRIPTION

Shrubs or small trees up to 33ft/10m high, with knotted branches, aromatic leaves, and small white flowers The trunk yields oleo-resin (myrrh).

ACTIONS

Anti-inflammatory, antimicrobial, antiphlogistic, antiseptic, astringent, balsamic, carminative, cicatrizant, expectorant, fungicidal, sedative, stimulant, stomachic, tonic, uterine, vulnerary.

EXTRACTION

Resinoid (and resin absolute) are obtained by solvent extraction from the crude myrrh. The oil is extracted by steam distillation.

CHARACTERISTICS

The essential oil is a pale yellow to amber, oily liquid with a warm, slightly spicy-medicinal odor. It blends well with frankincense, sandalwood, benzoin, cypress, juniper, mandarin, geranium, patchouli, thyme, mints, lavender, pine.

WARNING
This oil is not to be used during pregnancy. Do not use in high concentrations.

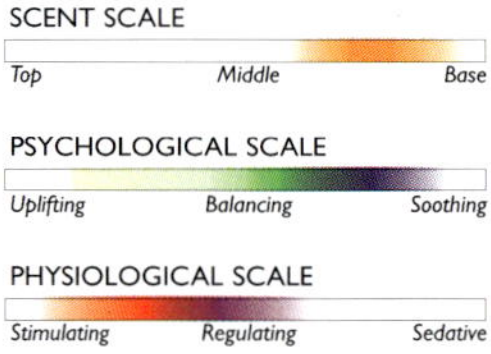

PERFUME

Scent: *Bitter-spicy, rich, balsamic, resinous, long-lasting.* **Key qualities:** *Purifying, uplifting, revitalizing, sedative (to nervous system), restorative, soothing.* **Odor intensity:** *High.*

AROMATHERAPY USE

Skin care: *Athlete's foot, chapped and cracked skin, eczema, ringworm, wounds, wrinkles, mature complexions (nonirritant, nonsensitizing).* **Circulation, muscles and joints:** *Arthritis.* **Respiratory system:** *Asthma, bronchitis, catarrh, colds, coughs, sore throat, voice loss.* **Digestive System:** *Diarrhea, dyspepsia, flatulence, hemorrhoids, loss of appetite.* **Genitourinary system:** *Amenorrhea, leukorrhea, pruritus, thrush.* **Other uses:** *Treats gum infections, mouth ulcers.*

Coriander

CORIANDRUM SATIVUM **FAMILY** *APIACEAE* (*UMBELLIFERAE*)

DESCRIPTION

A strongly aromatic annual herb, about 3ft/1m high, with bright green, delicate leaves, and umbels of lace-like, white flowers, followed by a mass of green (turning brown) round seeds.

ACTIONS

Analgesic, aperitif, antioxidant, anti-rheumatic, antispasmodic, bactericidal, depurative, digestive, carminative, cytotoxic, fungicidal, larvicidal, lipolytic activity, stimulant, stomachic.

EXTRACTION

The oil is extracted by steam distillation from the crushed ripe seeds.

CHARACTERISTICS

A colorless to pale yellow liquid, with a sweet, woody-spicy, slightly musky fragrance. It blends well with clary sage, bergamot, jasmine, frankincense, neroli, petitgrain, citronella, sandalwood, cypress, pine, ginger, cinnamon, and other spice oils.

SAFETY DATA

Generally nontoxic, nonirritant, nonsensitizing, but stupefying in large doses. Use in moderation.

SCENT SCALE

Top *Middle* *Base*

PSYCHOLOGICAL SCALE

Uplifting *Balancing* *Soothing*

PHYSIOLOGICAL SCALE

Stimulating *Regulating* *Sedative*

PERFUME

Scent: *Fresh, herbal, sweet-spicy, bitter, woody, slightly musky, diffusive.* **Key qualities:** *Aphrodisiac, stimulating, soporific (in excess), refreshing, warming, comforting, revitalizing, strengthening, purifying, soothing, active.* **Odor intensity:** *Medium.*

AROMATHERAPY USE

Circulation, muscles and joints: *Accumulation of fluids or toxins, arthritis, gout, muscular aches and pains, poor circulation, rheumatism, stiffness.* **Digestive system:** *Anorexia, colic, diarrhea, dyspepsia, flatulence, nausea, piles, spasm.* **Immune system:** *Colds, flu, infections (general), measles.* **Nervous system:** *Debility, migraine, neuralgia, nervous exhaustion.*

Cypress

CUPRESSUS SEMPERVIRENS **FAMILY** *CUPRESSACEAE*

DESCRIPTION

A tall evergreen tree, with slender branches and a statuesque, conical shape. It bears small flowers, and round, brownish-gray cones or nuts.

ACTIONS

Anti-rheumatic, antiseptic, antispasmodic, antisudorific, astringent, deodorant, diuretic, hepatic, styptic, tonic, vasoconstrictive.

EXTRACTION

The oil is extracted by steam distillation from the needles and twigs. An oil from the cones is available occasionally.

CHARACTERISTICS

A pale yellow to greenish-olive, mobile liquid, with a smoky, sweet-balsamic, tenacious odor. It blends well with cedarwood, pine, lavender, mandarin, clary sage, lemon, cardamom, juniper, benzoin, bergamot, orange, marjoram, and sandalwood.

SAFETY DATA

Nontoxic, nonirritant, nonsensitizing.

SCENT SCALE

Top *Middle* *Base*

PSYCHOLOGICAL SCALE

Uplifting *Balancing* *Soothing*

PHYSIOLOGICAL SCALE

Stimulating *Regulating* *Sedative*

PERFUME

Scent: *Smoky, sweet, balsamic, tenacious, woody, dry, slightly nutty, austere, spicy.* **Key qualities:** *Refreshing, purifying, relaxing, warming, reviving, restorative, comforting, protective, soothing.* **Odor intensity:** *Medium–low.*

AROMATHERAPY USE

Skin care: *Oily, and over-hydrated skin, perspiration, wounds, bruises.* **Circulation, muscles and joints:** *Hemorrhoids, varicose veins, cellulitis, muscular cramp, edema, poor circulation, rheumatism.* **Respiratory system:** *Asthma, bronchitis, spasmodic coughing.* **Reproductive system:** *Dysmenorrhea, menopausal problems, menorrhagia.* **Nervous system:** *Nervous tension, stress-related conditions.* **Other uses:** *Treats pyorrhea (inflamed/bleeding gums); insect repellent.*

Lemongrass, West Indian

CYMBOPOGON CITRATUS **FAMILY** POACEAE (GRAMINACEAE)

DESCRIPTION

A fast-growing, tall, aromatic, perennial grass, up to 5ft/1.5m high, producing a network of roots and rootlets that rapidly exhaust the soil.

ACTIONS

Analgesic, antidepressant, antimicrobial, antioxidant, antipyretic, antiseptic, astringent, bactericidal, carminative, deodorant, febrifuge, fungicidal, galactagogue, insecticide, nervine, sedative (nervous system), tonic.

EXTRACTION

The oil is extracted by steam distillation from the fresh, and partially dried, leaves (grass), finely chopped.

CHARACTERISTICS

A yellow, amber, or reddish-brown liquid, with a fresh, grassy-citrus scent, and an earthy undertone. Blends well with geranium, bergamot and the other citrus oils.

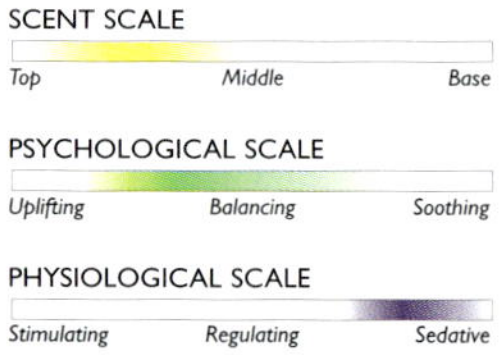

PERFUME

Scent: *Citrus, clean, green, hay-like, slightly bitter, lemony, pungent.* **Key qualities (mind):** *Refreshing, active, stimulating, soothing.* **Odor intensity:** *High.*

AROMATHERAPY USE

Skin care: *Acne, athlete's foot, excessive perspiration, open pores, pediculosis, scabies, tissue toner.* **Circulation, muscles and joints:** *Muscular pain, poor circulation and muscle tone, slack tissue.* **Digestive system:** *Colitis, indigestion, gastro-enteritis.* **Immune system:** *Fevers, infectious diseases.* **Nervous system:** *Headaches, nervous exhaustion, stress-related conditions.*
Other uses: *Insect repellent (fleas, lice, ticks).*

SAFETY DATA

Nontoxic, but possible dermal irritation and/or sensitization in some individuals – use with care.

Palmarosa

CYMBOPOGON MARTINII, VAR. MARTINII **FAMILY** GRAMINACEAE

DESCRIPTION

A wild herbaceous plant, with long, slender stems and terminal flowering tops; the grassy leaves are very fragrant.

ACTIONS

Antiseptic, bactericidal, cicatrizant, digestive, febrifuge, hydrating, stimulant (to the digestive and circulatory systems), tonic.

EXTRACTION

The oil is extracted by steam or water distillation of the fresh or dried grass.

CHARACTERISTICS

A pale yellow or olive liquid, with a sweet, floral, rosy, geranium-like scent. It blends well with ylang ylang, rose geranium, bois de rose, sandalwood, cypress, cedarwood, and floral oils.

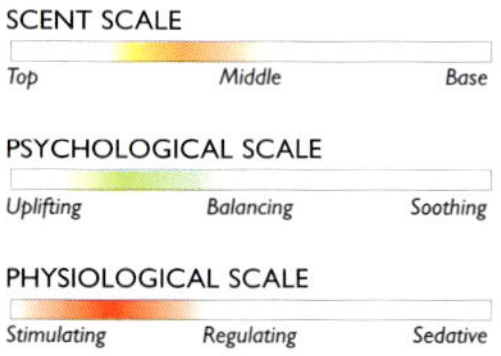

PERFUME

Scent: *Rosy, sweet, fresh, warm, slightly-green, floral.* **Key qualities (mind):** *Refreshing, balancing, comforting.* **Odor intensity:** *Medium–high.*

AROMATHERAPY USE

Skin care: *Acne, dermatitis and minor skin infections, scars, sores, wrinkles: valuable for all types of treatment for the face, hands, feet, neck and lips (moisturizes the skin, stimulates cellular regeneration, regulates sebum production).* **Digestive system:** *Anorexia, digestive atonia, intestinal infections.* **Nervous sytem:** *Nervous exhaustion, stress-related conditions,*

SAFETY DATA

Nontoxic, nonirritant, nonsensitizing.

Citronella

CYMBOPOGON NARDUS **FAMILY** POACEAE (GRAMINACEAE)

DESCRIPTION

A tall, cultivated aromatic, perennial grass, derived from the wild managrass found in Sri Lanka.

ACTIONS

Antiseptic, antispasmodic, bactericidal, deodorant, diuretic, emmenagogue, febrifuge, fungicidal, insecticide, stomachic, tonic, vermifuge.

EXTRACTION

The oil is extracted by steam distillation of the fresh, part-dried, or dried grass. Java citronella yields twice as much oil as the Sri Lanka type.

CHARACTERISTICS

A yellowy-brown, mobile liquid, with a fresh, powerful, lemony scent.The Java oil is colorless to pale yellow, with a fresh, woody-sweet fragrance; it is considered of superior quality in perfumery work. It blends well with geranium, lemon, bergamot, orange, cedarwood, and pine.

SAFETY DATA

Nontoxic, generally nonirritant, but may cause dermatitis in some individuals.

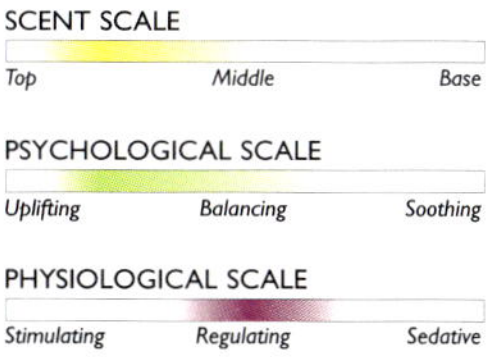

PERFUME

Scent: *Fresh, lemony, slightly-herbaceous, green, powerful.* **Key qualities (mind):** *Refreshing, active, penetrating.* **Odor intensity:** *High.*

AROMATHERAPY USE

Skin care: *Excessive perspiration, oily skin.* **Immune system:** *Colds, flu, minor infections.* **Nervous system:** *Fatigue, headaches, migraine, neuralgia.* **Other:** *Insect repellent. Mixed with Virginia cedarwood oil, it is a popular remedy against mosquitoes.*

WARNING
Avoid using this oil during pregnancy.

Carrot seed

DAUCUS CAROTA **FAMILY** APIACEAE (UMBELLIFERAE)

DESCRIPTION

Annual or biennial herb, with a small, inedible, tough whitish root. It has a much-branched stem, up to 5ft/1.5m high, with hairy leaves, and umbels of white, lacy flowers.

ACTIONS

Anthelmintic, antiseptic, carminative, depurative, diuretic, emmenagogue, hepatic, stimulant, tonic, vasodilatory, smooth muscle relaxant.

EXTRACTION

The oil is extracted by steam distillation from the dried seeds.

CHARACTERISTICS

A yellow or amber liquid, with a warm, dry, woody-earthy odor. It blends well with cedarwood, geranium, citrus, and with the spice oils.

SAFETY DATA

Nontoxic, nonirritant, nonsensitizing.

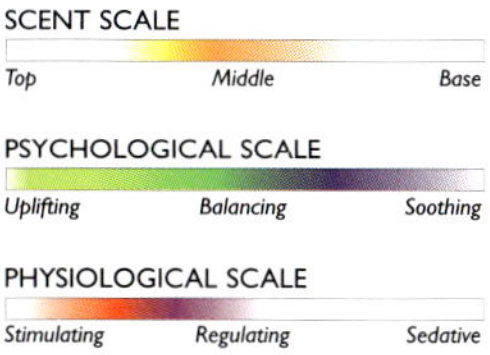

PERFUME

Scent: *Woody-earthy, herbaceous, slightly spicy, strong, warm.* **Key qualities (mind):** *Clearing, comforting, reviving.* **Odor intensity:** *Medium–high.*

AROMATHERAPY USE

Skin care: *Dermatitis, eczema, oily skin, psoriasis, rashes, wrinkles, mature complexions – revitalizing and toning.* **Circulation, muscles and joints:** *Anemia, accumulation of toxins, arthritis, gout, edema, rheumatism.* **Digestive system:** *Anorexia, colic, indigestion, liver congestion.* **Reproductive and endocrine system:** *Amenorrhea, dysmenorrhea, glandular problems, PMS.*

Cardamom

ELETTARIA CARDAMOMUM **FAMILY** ZINGIBERACEAE

DESCRIPTION

A reed-like perennial herb, up to 13ft/4m high, with long, silky, blade-shaped leaves. Its long, sheathing stems bear small, yellowish flowers with purple tips, which are followed by oblong red-brown seeds.

ACTIONS

Antiseptic, antispasmodic, carminative, digestive, diuretic, orexigenic, sialagogue, stimulant, stomachic, tonic.

EXTRACTION

The oil is extracted by steam distillation from the dried ripe seeds.

CHARACTERISTICS

A colorless to pale yellow liquid, with a sweet-spicy, warming fragrance, and a woody-balsamic undertone. It blends well with rose, frankincense, orange, bergamot, cinnamon, cloves, ylang ylang, cedarwood, neroli, and with oriental bases in general.

SAFETY DATA

Nontoxic, nonirritant, nonsensitizing.

SCENT SCALE

Top *Middle* *Base*

PSYCHOLOGICAL SCALE

Uplifting *Balancing* *Soothing*

PHYSIOLOGICAL SCALE

Stimulating *Regulating* *Sedative*

PERFUME

Scent: *Pleasing, camphoraceous, warm, sweet, spicy, powerful, soft, rich, oriental. Has a high odor intensity – easily overshadows other smells.* **Key qualities (mind):** *Cephalic, aphrodisiac, warming, comforting, refreshing, uplifting, penetrating, soothing.* **Odor intensity:** *Very high.*

AROMATHERAPY USE

Digestive system: *Anorexia, colic, cramp, dyspepsia, flatulence, griping pains, halitosis (bad breath), heartburn, indigestion, vomiting.* **Nervous system:** *Mental fatigue, nervous strain.*

Lemon eucalyptus

EUCALYPTUS CITRIODORA **FAMILY** MYRTACEAE

DESCRIPTION

An attractive, tall evergreen tree, with a smooth, dimpled bark, blotched in gray, cream, and pink, cultivated as an ornamental plant. The trunk grows fast, straight, and to considerable height, and is used for timber. The young leaves are oval, while the mature leaves are narrow and tapering.

ACTIONS

Antiseptic, antiviral, bactericidal, deodorant, expectorant, fungicidal, insecticide.

EXTRACTION

The oil is extracted by steam distillation from the leaves and twigs.

CHARACTERISTICS

A colorless or pale yellow, mobile liquid, with a strong, fresh, citronella-like odor, and sweet, balsamic undertone. It blends well with both citrus and floral oils.

SCENT SCALE

Top *Middle* *Base*

PSYCHOLOGICAL SCALE

Uplifting *Balancing* *Soothing*

PHYSIOLOGICAL SCALE

Stimulating *Regulating* *Sedative*

PERFUME

Scent: *Lemony, fresh, clean, penetrating.* **Key qualities (mind):** *Invigorating, active, stimulating.* **Odor intensity:** *High.*

AROMATHERAPY USE

Skin care: *Athlete's foot and other fungal infections (such as candida), cuts, dandruff, herpes, infectious skin conditions (such as chicken pox), scabs, sores, wounds.* **Respiratory system:** *Asthma, laryngitis, sore throat.* **Immune system:** *Colds, fevers, infectious diseases.* **Other uses:** *Insect repellent.*

SAFETY DATA

Nontoxic, nonirritant, but there is possible sensitization in some individuals.

Eucalyptus blue gum

EUCALYPTUS GLOBULUS VAR. GLOBULUS. **FAMILY** *MYRTACEAE*

DESCRIPTION

An evergreen tree, up to 50ft/15m high. Mature trees have long, narrow, yellowish leaves, creamy-white flowers, and a smooth, pale gray bark often covered in a white powder.

ACTIONS

Analgesic, antineuralgic, antiseptic, antiviral, cicatrizant, decongestant, deodorant, depurative, diuretic, expec-torant, febrifuge, hypoglycemic, parasiticide, prophylactic, rubefacient, stimulant, vermifuge, vulnerary, insecticide.

EXTRACTION

The oil is extracted by steam distillation from the leaves and young twigs.

CHARACTERISTICS

A colorless, mobile liquid that yellows on aging, with a somewhat harsh, camphoraceous odor, and woody-sweet undertone. It blends well with thyme, rosemary, lavender, marjoram, pine, cedarwood, and lemon.

WARNING
Apply in dilution only: in concentration, eucalyptus oil can irritate the skin. The oil should not be used on young children. When taken internally eucalyptus oil is toxic.

SCENT SCALE
Top *Middle* *Base*

PSYCHOLOGICAL SCALE
Uplifting *Balancing* *Soothing*

PHYSIOLOGICAL SCALE
Stimulating *Regulating* *Sedative*

PERFUME

Scent: *Woody-camphoraceous, penetrating, fresh, slightly sweet.* **Key qualities:** *Stimulating, refreshing, clearing, purifying, balsamic, regulating.* **Odor intensity:** *High.*

AROMATHERAPY USE

Skin care: *Burns, blisters, cuts, herpes, insect bites, lice, skin infections, wounds.* **Circulation, muscles and joints:** *Muscular aches and pains, poor circulation, rheumatoid arthritis, sprains.* **Respiratory system:** *Asthma, bronchitis, catarrh, coughs, sinusitis, throat infections.* **Immune system:** *Chicken pox, colds, epidemics, flu, measles.* **Genitourinary system:** *Cystitis, leukorrhea.* **Nervous system:** *Debility, headaches, neuralgia.* **Other uses:** *Insect repellent*

Galbanum

FERULA GUMBOSA **FAMILY** *APIACEAE (UMBELLIFERAE)*

DESCRIPTION

A large perennial herb, with a smooth stem, shiny leaflets, and small flowers. It contains resin ducts that exude a milky juice, an oleoresin.

ACTIONS

Analgesic, anti-inflammatory, antimicrobial, antiseptic, antispasmodic, aphrodisiac, balsamic, carminative, cicatrizant, digestive, diuretic, emmenagogue, expectorant, hypotensive, restorative, tonic.

EXTRACTION

The oil is extracted by water or steam distillation from the oleoresin (gum). Only the Levant or soft type is used for oil production.

CHARACTERISTICS

A colorless, pale yellow, or olive liquid with a fresh, green top note, and woody-dry balsamic undertone. It blends well with lavender, geranium, pine, frankincense, and oriental bases.

SCENT SCALE
Top *Middle* *Base*

PSYCHOLOGICAL SCALE
Uplifting *Balancing* *Soothing*

PHYSIOLOGICAL SCALE
Stimulating *Regulating* *Sedative*

PERFUME

Scent: *Sharp, green-woody, penetrating, turpentine-like, balsamic, musky, earthy, herbaceous, spicy, bitter, clean, powerful.* **Key qualities:** *Uplifting, clearing, purifying, soothing.* **Odor intensity:** *Very high.*

AROMATHERAPY USE

Skin care: *Abscesses, acne, boils, cuts, scar tissue, inflammation, mature skin, wrinkles, wounds – tones, softens and preserves the skin.*
Circulation, muscles and joints: *Poor circulation, muscular aches and pains, rheumatism.* **Respiratory system:** *Asthma, bronchitis, catarrh, chronic coughs.* **Digestive system:** *Cramp, flatulence, indigestion.*
Nervous system: *Nervous tension, stress-related complaints.* **Other uses:** *Insect repellent.*

SAFETY DATA
Nontoxic, nonirritant, nonsensitizing.

Fennel, sweet 2

FOENICULUM VULGARE **FAMILY** APIACEAE (UMBELLIFERAE)

DESCRIPTION

Biennial or perennial herb, up to 6ft 6in/2m high, with feathery leaves, and golden yellow flowers. There are two varieties of fennel: bitter and sweet. Bitter fennel is not recommended for aromatherapy use.

ACTIONS

Aperitif, anti-inflammatory, antimicrobial, antiseptic, antispasmodic, carminative, depurative, diuretic, emmenagogue, expectorant, galactagogue, laxative, stimulant (to circulation), splenetic, stomachic, tonic, vermifuge.

EXTRACTION

The oil is extracted by steam distillation from the crushed seeds.

CHARACTERISTICS

Sweet fennel is a colorless to pale yellow liquid, with a very sweet, anise-like, slightly earthy-peppery scent. It blends well with rose geranium, lavender, rose, and sandalwood.

WARNING
Use in moderation – this oil should not be used by people who suffer from epilepsy, children under six, or pregnant women.

SCENT SCALE
Top — *Middle* — *Base*

PSYCHOLOGICAL SCALE
Uplifting — *Balancing* — *Soothing*

PHYSIOLOGICAL SCALE
Stimulating — *Regulating* — *Sedative*

PERFUME

Scent: *Sweet, anise-like, earthy, peppery. The name derives from the Latin foenum, meaning hay, descriptive of the plant's musty fragrance.* **Key qualities:** *Stimulating, balancing, restorative, revitalizing, purifying, cleansing.*
Odor intensity: *High.*

AROMATHERAPY USE

Skin care: *Bruises; dull, oily, mature complexions.* **Circulation, muscles and joints:** *Cellulitis, obesity, edema, rheumatism.* **Respiratory system:** *Asthma, bronchitis.* **Digestive system:** *Anorexia, colic, constipation, dyspepsia, flatulence, hiccoughs, nausea.*
Reproductive system: *Amenorrhea, insufficient milk in nursing mothers, menopausal problems.* **Other uses:** *Treats pyorrhea.*

Hyssop 3

HYSSOPUS OFFICINALIS **FAMILY** LAMIACEAE (LABIATAE)

DESCRIPTION

An attractive perennial, almost evergreen, sub-shrub, up to 2ft/60cm high, with a woody stem, small, lance-shaped leaves, and purplish-blue flowers.

ACTIONS

Astringent, antiseptic, antispasmodic, antiviral, bactericide, carminative, cephalic, cicatrizant, digestive, diuretic, emmenagogue, expectorant, febrifuge, hypertensive, nervine, sedative, sudorific, tonic (to heart and circulation), vermifuge, vulnerary.

EXTRACTION

The oil is extracted by steam distillation from the leaves and flowering tops.

CHARACTERISTICS

A colorless to pale yellowy-green liquid, with a sweet, camphoraceous top note, and warm, spicy-herbaceous undertone. It blends well with lavender, rosemary, myrtle, bay, sage, clary sage, geranium, and the citrus oils.

WARNING
This oil should be used only in moderation, and should be avoided in pregnancy, and by people suffering from epilepsy. Do not use on children.

SCENT SCALE
Top — *Middle* — *Base*

PSYCHOLOGICAL SCALE
Uplifting — *Balancing* — *Soothing*

PHYSIOLOGICAL SCALE
Stimulating — *Regulating* — *Sedative*

PERFUME

Scent: *Sweet, warm, herbaceous, slightly camphoraceous.* **Key qualities:** *Tonic, cephalic, nervine, warming, calming, purifying, cleansing, aphrodisiac, mental stimulant, balancing.* **Odor intensity:** *High.*

AROMATHERAPY USE

Skin care: *Bruises, cuts, dermatitis, eczema, inflammation, wounds (nonirritant, nonsensitizing).*
Circulatory system: *Low or high blood pressure, rheumatism.*
Respiratory system: *Asthma, bronchitis, catarrh, cough, flu, sore throat, tonsillitis, whooping cough.*
Digestive system: *Colic, indigestion.*
Reproductive system: *Amenorrhea, leukorrhea.* **Nervous system:** *Anxiety, fatigue, nervous tension, stress-related conditions.*

Jasmine

JASMINUM OFFICINALE **FAMILY** *OLEACEAE*

DESCRIPTION

An evergreen shrub or vine up to 33ft/10m high, with delicate, bright green leaves, and star-shaped, very fragrant white flowers.

ACTIONS

Analgesic (mild), anti-inflammatory, antiseptic, antispasmodic, carminative, cicatrizant, expectorant, galactagogue, parturient, sedative, tonic (uterine).

EXTRACTION

A concrete is produced from the flowers by solvent extraction. The absolute is obtained from the concrete by separation with alcohol. A second essential oil is produced by steam distillation of the absolute.

CHARACTERISTICS

The absolute is a dark orange-brown, viscous liquid, with an intensely rich, warm, floral scent, and a tea-like undertone. It blends well with rose, sandalwood, clary sage, and all citrus oils.

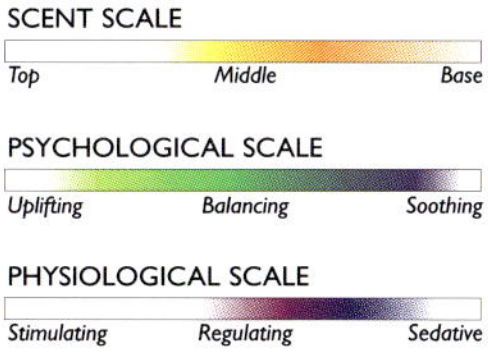

PERFUME

Scent: *Rich, warm, floral, sweet, tea-like, exquisite, exotic, long-lasting.* **Key qualities:** *Intoxicating, uplifting, anti-depressant, euphoric, aphrodisiac, tonic, balancing, warming.*
Odor intensity: *High.*

AROMATHERAPY USE

Skin care: *Dry, greasy, irritated, sensitive skin.* **Circulation, muscles and joints:** *Muscular spasm, sprains.* **Respiratory system:** *Catarrh, coughs, hoarseness, laryngitis.* **Reproductive system:** *Dysmenorrhea, frigidity, labor pains, uterine disorders.* **Nervous system:** *Depression, nervous exhaustion, stress-related conditions.*

SAFETY DATA

Nontoxic, nonirritant, generally nonsensitizing, although an allergic reaction has been known to occur in some individuals.

Juniper

JUNIPERUS COMMUNIS **FAMILY** *CUPRESSACEAE*

DESCRIPTION

An evergreen shrub or tree, up to 20ft/6m high, with bluish-green, narrow, stiff needles. It has small flowers, and little round, black berries.

ACTIONS

Antirheumatic, antiseptic, antispasmodic, antitoxic, aphrodisiac, astringent, carminative, cicatrizant, depurative, diuretic, emmenagogue, nervine, parasiticide, rubefacient, sedative, stomachic, sudorific, tonic, vulnerary.

EXTRACTION

The oil is extracted by steam distillation from the berries, the needles or the wood.

CHARACTERISTICS

Juniper berry oil is a water-white or pale yellow, mobile liquid, with a sweet, fresh, woody-balsamic odor. It blends well with vetiver, sandalwood, cedarwood, galbanum, elemi, cypress, clary sage, pine, lavender, rosemary, benzoin, geranium, and citrus oils.

WARNING

This oil stimulates the uterine muscle (an abortifacient) and must not be used during pregnancy. It should not be used by those with kidney disease, as it is nephrotoxic. It is not suitable for young children. Use in moderation.

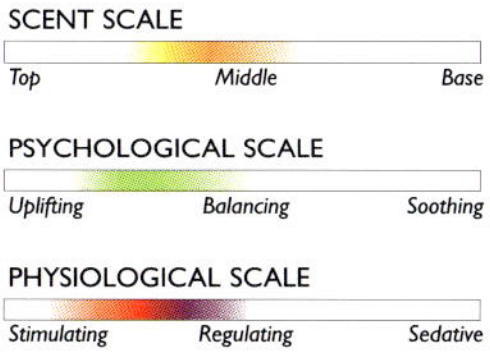

PERFUME

Scent: *Sweet, fresh, woody, balsamic, turpentine-like, peppery, smoky.* **Key qualities:** *Aphrodisiac, purifying, clearing, depurative, tonic (nerve), reviving, protective, restorative.*
Odor intensity: *Medium.*

AROMATHERAPY USE

Skin care: *Acne, dermatitis, eczema, hair loss, hemorrhoids, wounds, tonic for oily complexions (nonsensitizing, but may be slightly irritating).* **Circulation, muscles and joints:** *Accumulation of toxins, arteriosclerosis, cellulite, gout, obesity, rheumatism.* **Immune system:** *Colds, flu, infections.* **Genitourinary system:** *Amenorrhea, cystitis, dysmenorrhea, leukorrhea.* **Nervous system:** *Anxiety, nervous tension, stress-related conditions.*

Cedarwood, Virginian

JUNIPERUS VIRGINIANA **FAMILY** CUPRESSACEAE

DESCRIPTION

A slow-growing, evergreen coniferous tree, up to 180ft/33m high, with a narrow, dense, and pyramidal crown, a reddish heartwood, and brown cones.

ACTIONS

Abortifacient, antiseborrheic, antiseptic (pulmonary, genitourinary), antispasmodic, astringent, balsamic, diuretic, emmenagogue, expectorant, insecticide, sedative (to the nervous system), stimulant (to the circulation).

EXTRACTION

The oil is extracted by steam distillation from lumber waste, sawdust, and shavings.

CHARACTERISTICS

A pale yellow, or orange, oily liquid, with a mild, sweet-balsamic, pencil-wood scent. It blends well with sandalwood, rose, juniper, cypress, vetiver, patchouli, and benzoin.

WARNING
Use this oil in dilution only, with care, and in moderation. The oil is a powerful abortifacient – avoid during pregnancy.

SCENT SCALE
Top *Middle* *Base*

PSYCHOLOGICAL SCALE
Uplifting *Balancing* *Soothing*

PHYSIOLOGICAL SCALE
Stimulating *Regulating* *Sedative*

PERFUME

Scent: *Sweet-balsamic, pencil-wood, tenacious, tobacco, clean, sporty.* **Key qualities (mind):** *Restorative, uplifting, warming.* **Odor intensity:** *Medium–low.*

AROMATHERAPY USE

Skin care: *Acne, dandruff, eczema, greasy hair, oily skin, psoriasis (can cause acute local irritation in some individuals).* **Circulation, muscles and joints:** *Arthritis, rheumatism.* **Respiratory system:** *Bronchitis, catarrh, congestion, coughs, sinusitis.* **Genitourinary system:** *Cystitis, leukorrhea.* **Nervous system:** *Nervous tension, stress-related disorders.* **Other:** *Insect repellent.*

Lavender, true

LAVANDULA ANGUSTIFOLIA/L.OFFICINALIS **FAMILY** *LAMIACEA* (*LABIATAE*)

DESCRIPTION

An evergreen, woody shrub, up to 3ft/1m tall, with gray-green, narrow, linear leaves, and blue flower spikes.

ACTIONS

Analgesic, anticonvulsive, antimicrobial, antirheumatic, antiseptic, antispasmodic, antitoxic, carminative, cholagogue, choleretic, cytophylactic, deodorant, diuretic, emmenagogue, hypotensor, insecticide, nervine, parasiticide, rubefacient, sedative, stimulant, sudorific, tonic, vermifuge, vulnerary.

EXTRACTION

The oil is extracted from the fresh flowering tops by steam distillation.

CHARACTERISTICS

The oil is colorless to pale yellow, with a sweet, floral-herbaceous scent, and balsamic-woody undertone. Blends well with most oils, especially citrus, florals, cedarwood, clove, clary sage, pine, geranium, vetivert, and patchouli.

SAFETY DATA
Nontoxic, nonirritant, nonsensitizing.

SCENT SCALE
Top *Middle* *Base*

PSYCHOLOGICAL SCALE
Uplifting *Balancing* *Soothing*

PHYSIOLOGICAL SCALE
Stimulating *Regulating* *Sedative*

PERFUME

Scent: *Light, floral, classic, soft, mellow.*
Key qualities: *Soothing, sedative, antidepressant, calming, relaxing, balancing, restorative, cephalic, appeasing, cleansing, purifying.*
Odor intensity: *Medium.*

AROMATHERAPY USE

Skin care: *Abscess, acne, allergies, athlete's foot, boils, bruises, burns, dermititis, eczema, inflammation, insect bites and stings, lice, psoriasis, ringworm, scabies, spots, sunburn, wounds.* **Circulation, muscles and joints:** *Lumbago, rheumatism, sprains.* **Respiratory system:** *Asthma, bronchitis, catarrh, flu, halitosis, throat infections, whooping cough.* **Digestive system:** *Colic, dyspepsia, flatulence, nausea.* **Genitourinary system:** *Cystitis, dysmenorrhea, leukorrhea.* **Nervous system:** *Depression, headache, hypertension, insomnia, migraine, nervous tension, stress.*

Tea tree

MELALEUCA ALTERNIFOLIA **FAMILY** MYRTACEAE

DESCRIPTION

A small tree or shrub (the smallest of the melaleuca family), with needle-like leaves, similar to those of cypress, and heads of stalkless yellow or purplish colored flowers.

ACTIONS

Anti-infectious, anti-inflammatory, antiseptic, antiviral, bactericidal, balsamic, cicatrizant, diaphoretic, expectorant, fungicidal, immunostimulant, parasiticide, vulnerary.

EXTRACTION

The oil is extracted by steam or water distillation from the leaves and twigs.

CHARACTERISTICS

A pale yellowy-green or water-white, mobile liquid, with a warm, fresh, spicy-camphoraceous odor. It blends well with lavender, clary sage, rosemary, pine, ylang ylang, geranium, marjoram, and spice oils, especially clove and nutmeg.

SAFETY DATA

Nontoxic, nonirritant, although there are indications of possible sensitization in some individuals.

SCENT SCALE
Top — Middle — Base

PSYCHOLOGICAL SCALE
Uplifting — Balancing — Soothing

PHYSIOLOGICAL SCALE
Stimulating — Regulating — Sedative

PERFUME

Scent: *Medicinal, fresh, powerful, camphoraceous, pungent, slightly spicy.* **Key qualities:** *Penetrating, medicinal, stimulating, refreshing.* **Odor intensity:** *High*

AROMATHERAPY USE

Skin care: *Abscess, acne, athlete's foot, blisters, burns, bruises, chicken pox rash, cold sores, dandruff, herpes, insect bites, oily skin, rashes (nappy rash), spots, verrucae, warts, wounds (infected).* **Respiratory system:** *Asthma, bronchitis, catarrh, coughs, sinusitis, tuberculosis, whooping cough.* **Reproductive system:** *Thrush (vaginal), vaginitis.* **Immune system:** *Colds, fever, flu, infectious illnesses.* **Urinary system:** *Cystitis, pruritus.*

Cajeput

MELALEUCA CAJEPUTI **FAMILY** MYRTACEAE

DESCRIPTION

A tall evergreen tree, up to 100ft/30m high, with thick, pointed leaves, and white flowers. The flexible trunk has a whitish, spongy bark that flakes easily.

ACTIONS

Mildly analgesic, antimicrobial, antineuralgic, antispasmodic, antiseptic (pulmonary, urinary, intestinal), anthelmintic, diaphoretic, carminative, expectorant, febrifuge, insecticide, sudorific, tonic.

EXTRACTION

The oil is extracted by steam distillation from the fresh leaves and twigs.

CHARACTERISTICS

A pale yellowy-green, mobile liquid (the green tinge derives from traces of copper found in the tree), with a penetrating, camphoraceous-medicinal odor. Compared to eucalyptus oil, it has a slightly milder, fruity body note. It blends well with herb and spice oils.

SAFETY DATA

Nontoxic, nonsensitizing, but may irritate the skin in high concentration.

SCENT SCALE
Top — Middle — Base

PSYCHOLOGICAL SCALE
Uplifting — Balancing — Soothing

PHYSIOLOGICAL SCALE
Stimulating — Regulating — Sedative

PERFUME

Scent: *Fresh, camphoraceous, slightly medicinal, fruity-sweet.* **Key qualities (mind):** *Clearing, refreshing, reviving, anaphrodisiac.* **Odor intensity:** *Medium–high.*

AROMATHERAPY USE

Skin care: *Insect bites, oily skin, spots.* **Circulation, muscles and joints:** *Arthritis, muscular aches and pains, rheumatism.* **Respiratory system:** *Asthma, bronchitis, catarrh, colds, coughs, flu, sinusitis, sore throat.* **Genitourinary system:** *Cystitis, urethritis, urinary infection.* **Immune system:** *Colds, flu, infections.*

Melissa/lemon balm

MELISSA OFFICINALIS **FAMILY** LABIATAE (LAMIACEAE)

DESCRIPTION

A sweet-scented herb about 2ft/60cm high, soft and bushy, with bright green, serrated leaves, square stems, and tiny white or pink flowers.

ACTIONS

Antidepressant, antihistaminic, antispasmodic, bactericidal, carminative, cordial, diaphoretic, emmenagogue, febrifuge, hypertensive, nervine, sedative, stomachic, sudorific, tonic, uterine, vermifuge, insect-repellent.

EXTRACTION

The oil is extracted by steam distillation from the leaves and flowering tops.

CHARACTERISTICS

A pale yellow liquid, with a light, fresh, lemony fragrance. It blends well with lavender and geranium oil and with all floral, and citrus oils.

SAFETY DATA

Available information suggests possible sensitization and skin irritation. See Warning box.

SCENT SCALE

Top *Middle* *Base*

PSYCHOLOGICAL SCALE

Uplifting *Balancing* *Soothing*

PHYSIOLOGICAL SCALE

Stimulating *Regulating* *Sedative*

PERFUME

Scent: *Lemony, light, fresh, green, herbaceous, honey-sweet.* **Key qualities:** *Soothing, calming, uplifting, regulating, sedative, appeasing, comforting, heart tonic, strengthening, revitalizing, protecting, antidepressant.* **Odor intensity:** *High.*

AROMATHERAPY USE

Skin care: *Allergies, insect bites.* **Respiratory system:** *Asthma, bronchitis, chronic coughs.* **Digestive system:** *Colic, indigestion, nausea.* **Reproductive system:** *Menstrual problems.* **Nervous system:** *Anxiety, depression, hypertension, insomnia, migraine, nervous tension, shock, vertigo.* **Other uses:** *Insect repellent.*

WARNING

Skin irritant. Use in low dilutions (up to 1%). Narcotic in large doses, causing headaches.

Peppermint

MENTHA X PIPERITA **FAMILY** LAMIACEAE (LABIATAE)

DESCRIPTION

A perennial herb, up to 3ft/1m high. White peppermint has green stems and leaves; black peppermint has dark green, serrated leaves, purplish stems, and reddish-violet flowers.

ACTIONS

Analgesic, anti-inflammatory, antimicrobial, antiphlogistic, antipruritic, antiseptic, antispasmodic, antiviral, astringent, diaphoretic, carminative, cephalic, cordial, emmenagogue, expectorant, febrifuge, hepatic, nervine, stomachic, sudorific, vasoconstrictor, vermifuge.

EXTRACTION

The oil is extracted by steam distillation from the flowering herb.

CHARACTERISTICS

A pale yellow or greenish liquid, with a highly penetrating, grassy-minty, camphoraceous odor. It blends well with benzoin, rosemary, lavender, marjoram, lemon, eucalyptus, and bergamot.

SAFETY DATA

Nontoxic, nonirritant, but possible sensitization due to the menthol content. Do not use oil with homeopathic remedies. Use in low dilutions on the skin. Suitable for use with children (with care) as described in this book.

SCENT SCALE

Top *Middle* *Base*

PSYCHOLOGICAL SCALE

Uplifting *Balancing* *Soothing*

PHYSIOLOGICAL SCALE

Stimulating *Regulating* *Sedative*

PERFUME

Scent: *Fresh, bright, minty, penetrating, clean.* **Key qualities:** *Refreshing, restorative, nerve tonic, cephalic, aphrodisiac, stimulant (mental).* **Odor intensity:** *High.*

AROMATHERAPY USE

Skin care: *Acne, dermatitis, ringworm, scabies, toothache.* **Circulation, muscles and joints:** *Neuralgia, muscular pain, palpitations.* **Respiratory system:** *Asthma, bronchitis, sinusitis, spasmodic cough.* **Digestive system:** *Colic, cramp, dyspepsia, flatulence, nausea.* **Immune system:** *Colds, flu, fevers.* **Nervous system:** *Fainting, headache, mental fatigue, migraine, nervous stress, vertigo.* **Other uses:** *Treats halitosis, insect repellent.*

Nutmeg

MYRISTICA FRAGRANS **FAMILY** MYRISTICACEAE

DESCRIPTION

An evergreen tree, up to 70ft/20m high, with dense foliage, and small, dull-yellow flowers.

ACTIONS

Analgesic, antiemetic, antioxidant, anti-rheumatic, antiseptic, antispasmodic, carminative, digestive, emmenagogue, orexigenic, prostaglandin inhibitor, stimulant, tonic.

EXTRACTION

The oil is extracted by steam (or water) distillation from the dried, worm-eaten nutmeg seed, or the dried, orange-brown aril or husk (mace).

CHARACTERISTICS

Nutmeg oil is a water-white or pale yellow, mobile liquid, with sweet, warm-spicy odor with terpeney top note. It blends well with lavender, bay, orange, geranium, clary sage, rosemary, lime, petitgrain, mandarin, coriander, and other spice oils.

WARNING
Used in large doses nutmeg oil shows signs of toxicity. Use in moderation. Do not use during pregnancy, or on young children.

SCENT SCALE
Top *Middle* *Base*

PSYCHOLOGICAL
Uplifting *Balancing* *Soothing*

PHYSIOLOGICAL SCALE
Stimulating *Regulating* *Sedative*

PERFUME

Scent: *Rich, spicy, oriental, sensual, sweet, warm.* **Key qualities:** *Aphrodisiac, analgesic, narcotic, tonic (nerve and heart), comforting, soothing, calming, elevating, cephalic, euphoric.* **Odor intensity:** *High.*

AROMATHERAPY USE

Circulation, muscles and joints: *Arthritis, gout, muscular aches and pains, poor circulation, rheumatism.* **Digestive system:** *Flatulence, indigestion, nausea, sluggish digestion.* **Immune system:** *Bacterial infection.* **Nervous system:** *Frigidity in women, impotence in men, neuralgia, nervous fatigue.*

SAFETY DATA
Nutmeg is generally nontoxic, nonirritant, and nonsensitizing. (See Warning box.)

Myrtle

MYRTUS COMMUNIS **FAMILY** MYRTACEAE

DESCRIPTION

A large bush or small tree, with many tough but slender branches, a brownish-red bark, and small, sharp, pointed leaves. It has white flowers, followed by small, black berries; both leaves and flowers are very fragrant.

ACTIONS

Anticatarrhal, antiseptic, astringent, balsamic, bactericidal, expectorant, regulator, slightly sedative.

EXTRACTION

The oil is extracted by steam distillation from the leaves and twigs (and sometimes the flowers).

CHARACTERISTICS

A pale yellow or orange liquid, with a clear, fresh, camphoraceous, sweet-herbaceous scent somewhat similar to eucalyptus. It blends well with bergamot, lavender, rosemary, clary sage, hyssop, bay, lime, ginger, clove, and other spice oils.

SAFETY DATA
Nontoxic, nonirritant, nonsensitizing.

SCENT SCALE
Top *Middle* *Base*

PSYCHOLOGICAL SCALE
Uplifting *Balancing* *Soothing*

PHYSIOLOGICAL SCALE
Stimulating *Regulating* *Sedative*

PERFUME

Scent: *Clear, fresh, balsamic, camphoraceous, floral, spicy, diffusive.* **Key qualities:** *Mildly stimulating, tonic (nerve), antiseptic, clarifying, cleansing, uplifting, aphrodisiac, refreshing.* **Odor intensity:** *Medium–high.*

AROMATHERAPY USE

Skin care: *Acne, hemorrhoids, oily skin, open pores.* **Respiratory system:** *Asthma, bronchitis, catarrhal conditions, chronic coughs, tuberculosis. Because of its relative mildness, this is a very suitable oil for children's coughs and chest complaints.* **Immune system:** *Colds, flu, infectious disease.*

Basil, sweet/French

OCIMUM BASILICUM **FAMILY** *LAMIACEAE (LABIATAE)*

DESCRIPTION

A tender annual herb up to 2.5in/60cms high, with dark green, ovate leaves, grayish-green beneath. It bears whorls of two-lipped, greenish or pinky-white flowers. The whole plant has a powerful aromatic scent.

ACTIONS

Antiseptic, antispasmodic, carminative, digestive, emmenagogue, expectorant, febrifuge, galactagogue, nervine, prophylactic, stimulant of adrenal cortex, stomachic, tonic, insecticide.

EXTRACTION

The oil is extracted by steam distillation from the flowering herb.

CHARACTERISTICS

Sweet basil oil is a colorless or pale yellow liquid, with a light, fresh, sweet-spicy scent, and balsamic undertones. It blends well with bergamot, clary sage, lime, citronella, geranium, hyssop, and other green notes.

WARNING
Possible sensitization. Avoid prolonged use, and do not use during pregnancy.

SCENT SCALE
Top — Middle — Base

PSYCHOLOGICAL SCALE
Uplifting — Balancing — Soothing

PHYSIOLOGICAL SCALE
Stimulating — Regulating — Sedative

PERFUME

Scent: *Fresh, slightly spicy, clove-like.*
Key qualities: *Restorative, tonic, antidepressant, refreshing, uplifting, fortifying, purifying, clearing, warming, cephalic, stupefying (in excess).*
Odor intensity: *High.*

AROMATHERAPY USE

Skin care: *Insect bites (mosquito, wasp), insect repellent.* **Circulation, muscles and joints:** *Gout, muscular aches and pains, rheumatism.* **Respiratory system:** *Bronchitis, colds, coughs, earache, sinusitis.* **Digestive system:** *Dyspepsia, flatulence, nausea.* **Reproductive system:** *Cramps, scanty periods.* **Immune system:** *Colds, fever, flu, infectious disease.* **Nervous system:** *Anxiety, depression, fatigue, insomnia, migraine, nervous tension.*

SAFETY DATA
Possible sensitization in some individuals. Use in moderation.

Marjoram, sweet

ORIGANUM MARJORANA/MARJORANA HORTENSIS
FAMILY *LAMIACEAE (LABIATAE)*

DESCRIPTION

A tender, bushy perennial plant, up to 2ft/60cm high, with a hairy stem, dark green oval leaves, and small grayish-white flowers growing in clusters.

ACTIONS

Analgesic, anaphrodisiac, antioxidant, antiseptic, antispasmodic, antiviral, bactericidal, carminative, cephalic, cordial, diaphoretic, digestive, diuretic, emmenagogue, expectorant, fungicidal, hypotensor, laxative, nervine, sedative, tonic, vasodilatator, vulnerary.

EXTRACTION

The oil is extracted by steam distillation from the dried flowering herb.

CHARACTERISTICS

A pale yellow or amber-colored, mobile liquid with a warm, woody, spicy-camphoraceous odor. Blends well with lavender, rosemary, bergamot, chamomile, cypress, tea tree, and eucalyptus.

WARNING
This oil should not be used during pregnancy.

SAFETY DATA
Nontoxic, nonirritant, nonsensitizing.

SCENT SCALE
Top — Middle — Base

PSYCHOLOGICAL SCALE
Uplifting — Balancing — Soothing

PHYSIOLOGICAL SCALE
Stimulating — Regulating — Sedative

PERFUME

Scent: *Warm, woody, spicy, nutty, camphoraceous, herbaceous, penetrating.* **Key qualities:** *Anaphrodisiac, stupefying in large doses, cephalic, sedative, nervine, restorative, warming, comforting.*
Odor intensity: *Medium.*

AROMATHERAPY USE

Skin care: *Chilblains, bruises, tics.* **Circulation, muscles and joints:** *Arthritis, lumbago, muscular aches and stiffness, rheumatism, sprains, strains.* **Respiratory system:** *Asthma, bronchitis, colds, coughs.* **Digestive system:** *Colic, constipation, dyspepsia, flatulence.* **Reproductive system:** *Amenorrhea, dysmenorrhea, leukorrhea, PMS.* **Nervous system:** *Headache, hypertension, insomnia, migraine, nervous tension, stress-related conditions.*

Geranium, rose

PELARGONIUM GRAVEOLENS **FAMILY** *GERANIACEAE*

DESCRIPTION

A perennial hairy shrub, up to 3ft/1m high, with lobed leaves, serrated at the edges, and small pink flowers. The whole plant is aromatic.

ACTIONS

Antihemorrhagic, anti-inflammatory, antiseptic, astringent, cicatrizant, deodorant, diuretic, fungicidal, hemostatic, stimulant (to adrenal cortex and lymphatic system), styptic, tonic, vermifuge, vulnerary.

EXTRACTION

The oil is extracted by steam distillation from the leaves, stalks and flowers.

CHARACTERISTICS

Greenish-olive liquid with a green, rosy-sweet, minty scent. (The Bourbon oil is generally preferred in perfumery work.) It blends well with lavender, patchouli, clove, rose, sandalwood, jasmine, juniper, neroli, bergamot, and other citrus oils.

SAFETY DATA

Nontoxic, nonirritant, generally nonsensitizing, but may cause contact dermatitis in hypersensitive individuals (especially the Bourbon type).

SCENT SCALE

Top *Middle* *Base*

PSYCHOLOGICAL SCALE

Uplifting *Balancing* *Soothing*

PHYSIOLOGICAL SCALE

Stimulating *Regulating* *Sedative*

PERFUME

Scent: *Green, rosy-sweet, floral-minty, fresh, strong, powerful.* **Key qualities:** *Tonic, antidepressant, uplifting, balancing, refreshing, soothing, warming, regulating.*
Odor intensity: *Medium–high.*

AROMATHERAPY USE

Skin care: *Acne, bruises, broken capillaries, burns, congested skin, cuts, dermatitis, eczema, hemorrhoids, lice, oily complexion, mature skin, ringworm, ulcers, wounds.*
Circulatory system: *Cellulitis, engorgement of breasts, edema, poor circulation.* **Respiratory system:** *Sore throat, tonsillitis.* **Reproductive and endocrine system:** *Adrenocortical glands and menopausal problems, PMS.* **Nervous system:** *Nervous tension, neuralgia, stress-related conditions.* **Other uses:** *Insect repellent (especially mosquitoes).*

Parsley seed

PETROSELINUM CRISPUM **FAMILY** *APIACEAE* (*UMBELLIFERAE*)

DESCRIPTION

A biennial or short-lived perennial herb, up to 28in/70cm high, with crinkly, bright green foliage, and small, greenish-yellow flowers producing small brown seeds (when ripe).

ACTIONS

Antimicrobial, antirheumatic, antiseptic, astringent, carminative, diuretic, depurative, emmenagogue, febrifuge, hypotensive, laxative, stimulant (mild), stomachic, tonic (uterine).

EXTRACTION

This oil is extracted by steam distillation from the seeds. (A different oil with slightly different properties is also produced from the herb.)

CHARACTERISTICS

A yellow, amber or brownish liquid, with a warm, woody-spicy, herbaceous odor. It blends well with rose, neroli, ylang ylang, tea tree, clary sage, and spice oils.

SAFETY DATA

Although the oil is moderately toxic and irritant – apiol has been shown to have irritant properties – it is nonsensitizing when used in moderation.

SCENT SCALE

Top *Middle* *Base*

PSYCHOLOGICAL SCALE

Uplifting *Balancing* *Soothing*

PHYSIOLOGICAL SCALE

Stimulating *Regulating* *Sedative*

PERFUME

Scent: *Herbaceous, spicy, fresh, warm, pungent.* **Key qualities (mind):** *Refreshing, stimulating, warming.* **Odor intensity:** *Medium.*

AROMATHERAPY USE

Circulation, muscles and joints: *Accumulation of toxins, arthritis, broken blood vessels, cellulitis, rheumatism, sciatica.* **Digestive system:** *Colic, flatulence, indigestion, hemorrhoids.* **Reproductive system:** *Amenorrhea, dysmenorrhea, to aid labor.* **Urinary system:** *Cystitis, urinary infection.*

WARNING
Avoid using this oil during pregnancy.

Bay, West Indian

PIMENTA ACRIS **FAMILY** MYRTACEAE

DESCRIPTION

A tropical evergreen tree up to 28ft/8m high, with large, leathery leaves, and aromatic fruits.

ACTIONS

Analgesic, anticonvulsant, antineuralgic, antirheumatic, antiseptic, astringent, expectorant, stimulant, hair tonic.

EXTRACTION

The oil is extracted by water or steam distillation from the leaves.

CHARACTERISTICS

A dark yellow, mobile liquid with a fresh-spicy top note, and a sweet-balsamic undertone. It blends well with lavender, rosemary, geranium, ylang ylang, citrus, and spice oils.

WARNING
Use in moderation only.

SCENT SCALE
Top *Middle* *Base*

PSYCHOLOGICAL SCALE
Uplifting *Balancing* *Soothing*

PHYSIOLOGICAL SCALE
Stimulating *Regulating* *Sedative*

PERFUME

Scent: *Fresh, penetrating, slightly camphoraceous, spicy-medicinal.*
Key qualities (mind): *Reviving, warming, clearing, refreshing.*
Odor intensity: *Medium.*

AROMATHERAPY USE

Skin care: *Scalp stimulant; treats dandruff, greasy, lifeless hair; promotes hair growth.* **Circulation, muscles and joints:** *Rheumatism, arthritis, aches and pains, strains, neuralgia, poor circulation.* **Immune system:** *Colds, flu, infectious diseases.*

SAFETY DATA
Moderately toxic due to high eugenol content, but generally nonirritant, nonsensitizing. Use in moderation.

Aniseed

PIMPINELLA ANISUM **FAMILY** *APIACEAE* (UMBELLIFERAE)

DESCRIPTION

An annual herb, less than 3ft/1m high, with delicate leaves, and white flowers.

ACTIONS

Antiseptic, antispasmodic, carminative, diuretic, expectorant, galactagogue, stimulant, stomachic.

EXTRACTION

The oil is extracted by steam distillation from the seeds.

CHARACTERISTICS

A colorless to pale yellow liquid, with a characteristic warm, spicy-sweet scent. Bay is a good masking agent. It blends well with other spice oils.

WARNING
Use in moderation only.

SCENT SCALE
Top *Middle* *Base*

PSYCHOLOGICAL SCALE
Uplifting *Balancing* *Soothing*

PHYSIOLOGICAL SCALE
Stimulating *Regulating* *Sedative*

PERFUME

Scent: *Spicy-sweet, liquorice-like, rich, very pervasive.* **Key qualities:** *Warming, purifying, aphrodisiac, uplifting, reviving, soothing, comforting, stimulant (in small doses), stupefying (in excess).* **Odor intensity:** *Very high.*

AROMATHERAPY USE

Circulation, muscles and joints: *Muscular aches and pains, rheumatism.* **Respiratory system:** *Bronchitis, colds, coughs.*
Digestive system: *Colic, cramp, flatulence, indigestion.*

SAFETY DATA
The major component, anethole, is known to cause dermatitis in some individuals – avoid in allergic and inflammatory skin conditions. In large doses it is narcotic, slows down the circulation, and can lead to cerebral disorders.

Pine needle, Scotch

PINUS SYLVESTRIS **FAMILY** PINACEAE

DESCRIPTION

A tall evergreen tree, up to 130ft/40m high. It has reddish-brown, deeply fissured bark, long, stiff needles growing in pairs, and pointed, brown cones.

ACTIONS

Antimicrobial, antineuralgic, antirheumatic, antiscorbutic, antiseptic, antiviral, bactericidal, balsamic, cholagogue, choleretic, deodorant, diuretic, expectorant, hypertensive, insecticide, restorative, rubefacient, stimulant (circulatory and nervous systems), vermifuge.

EXTRACTION

The oil is extracted by dry distillation from the needles.

CHARACTERISTICS

Pine needle oil is a colorless or pale yellow, mobile liquid, with a strong, dry-balsamic, turpentine-like aroma. It blends well with cedarwood, rosemary, tea tree, sage, lavender, juniper, lemon, cajeput, eucalyptus, and marjoram.

WARNING
Do not use this oil if there are allergic skin conditions. It is a skin irritant in concentration – use in low dilutions only.

SCENT SCALE
Top *Middle* *Base*

PSYCHOLOGICAL SCALE
Uplifting *Balancing* *Soothing*

PHYSIOLOGICAL SCALE
Stimulating *Regulating* *Sedative*

PERFUME

Scent: *Fresh, camphoraceous, balsamic, woody, penetrating, strong.* **Key qualities:** *Strengthening, cleansing, restorative, reviving, refreshing, stimulant (nerve), soothing (mental).* **Odor intensity:** *Medium–high.*

AROMATHERAPY USE

Skin care: *Cuts, lice, excessive perspiration, scabies, sores.* **Circulation, muscles and joints:** *Arthritis, gout, muscular aches and pains, neuralgia, poor circulation, rheumatism.* **Respiratory system:** *Asthma, bronchitis, catarrh, colds, coughs, flu, sinusitis, sore throat.* **Urinary system:** *Cystitis, urinary infection.* **Nervous system:** *Fatigue, nervous exhaustion, stress-related conditions.*

Pepper, black

PIPER NIGRUM **FAMILY** PIPERACEAE

DESCRIPTION

A perennial woody vine, up to 16.5ft/5m high, with heart-shaped leaves, and small white flowers. The berries turn from red to black as they mature – black pepper is the dried, unripe fruit.

ACTIONS

Analgesic, antimicrobial, antiseptic, antitoxic, aperitif, bactericidal, carminative, diaphoretic, digestive, diuretic, febrifuge, laxative, rubefacient, stimulant, stomachic, tonic.

EXTRACTION

The oil is extracted by steam distillation from the black peppercorns, which have been dried and crushed.

CHARACTERISTICS

A water-white to pale olive, mobile liquid, with a fresh, dry-woody, warm, spicy scent. It blends well with frankincense, sandalwood, lavender, rosemary, marjoram, spices, and florals when used in minute quantities.

WARNING
This oil is toxic and irritant in concentration – use in low dilutions only (not more than 1% in a blend).

SCENT SCALE
Top *Middle* *Base*

PSYCHOLOGICAL SCALE
Uplifting *Balancing* *Soothing*

PHYSIOLOGICAL SCALE
Stimulating *Regulating* *Sedative*

PERFUME

Scent: *Spicy, camphoraceous, fresh, woody, active, masculine, oriental, sensual, warm.* **Key qualities:** *Aphrodisiac, stimulant (mental), tonic (nerve), restorative, strengthening, comforting, analgesic, antiseptic.* **Odor intensity:** *High.*

AROMATHERAPY USE

Skin care: *Chilblains.* **Circulation, muscles and joints:** *Anemia, arthritis, muscular aches and pains, neuralgia, poor circulation, poor muscle tone, rheumatic pain, sprains, stiffness.* **Respiratory system:** *Catarrh, chills.* **Immune system:** *Colds, flu, infections, viruses.* **Digestive system:** *Colic, constipation, diarrhea, flatulence, heartburn, loss of appetite, nausea.*

Patchouli

POGOSTEMON PATCHOULI **FAMILY** *LAMINACEAE (LABIATAE)*

DESCRIPTION

A perennial bushy herb, up to 3ft/1m high, with large, fragrant, furry leaves, and white flowers tinged with purple.

ACTIONS

Antidepressant, antiinflammatory, antiemetic, antimicrobial, antiphlogistic, antiseptic, antitoxic, antiviral, astringent, bactericidal, carminative, cicatrizant, deodorant, digestive, diuretic, febrifuge, fungicidal, nervine, prophylactic, stimulant, stomachic, tonic.

EXTRACTION

The oil is extracted by steam distillation of the dried leaves.

CHARACTERISTICS

An amber or dark orange, viscous liquid, with a sweet, rich, herbaceous-earthy odor that improves with age. It blends well with vetivert, sandalwood, cedarwood, geranium, clove, lavender, rose, neroli, bergamot, myrrh, frankincense, clary sage, and oriental bases.

SAFETY DATA
Nontoxic, nonirritant, nonsensitizing. However, its overuse can cause loss of appetite, insomnia and nervous attacks.

SCENT SCALE
Top — Middle — Base

PSYCHOLOGICAL SCALE
Uplifting — Balancing — Soothing

PHYSIOLOGICAL SCALE
Stimulating — Regulating — Sedative

PERFUME

Scent: *Earthy, musky, spicy, woody, diffusive, warm, oriental, medicinal, powerful.* **Key qualities:** *Stimulant in small amounts, sedative in large doses, aphrodisiac, nerve tonic, appeasing, calming, uplifting.*
Odor intensity: *Very high.*

AROMATHERAPY USE

Skin care: *Acne, athlete's foot, cracked and chapped skin, dandruff, dermatitis, eczema (weeping), fungal infections, hair care, impetigo, sores, oily hair and skin, open pores, wounds, wrinkles.* **Nervous system:** *Frigidity, nervous exhaustion, stress-related complaints.* **Other uses:** *Insect repellent (moths).*

Rose maroc

ROSA CENTIFOLIA/R. GALLICA **FAMILY** *ROSACEAE*

DESCRIPTION

The rose that is generally used for oil production is a hybrid between *R. centifolia* and *R. gallica*. It grows to 8ft/2.5m and produces pink or rosy-purple flowers.

ACTIONS

Antidepressant, antiphlogistic, antiseptic, antispasmodic, antiviral, aphrodisiac, astringent, bactericidal, choleretic, cicatrizant, depurative, hemostatic, hepatic, laxative, appetite regulator, sedative, stomachic, tonic.

EXTRACTION

The oil or otto is extracted by water or steam distillation from the fresh petals. Concrete and absolute are produced by solvent extraction from the fresh petals.

CHARACTERISTICS

The oil is pale yellow, while the absolute is red-orange. Blends well with jasmine, orange flower, geranium, bergamot, lavender, clary sage, sandalwood, patchouli, benzoin, chamomile, clove, and palmarosa.

WARNING
Although generally safe, this oil is best avoided during the first 4 months of pregnancy.

SCENT SCALE
Top — Middle — Base

PSYCHOLOGICAL SCALE
Uplifting — Balancing — Soothing

PHYSIOLOGICAL SCALE
Stimulating — Regulating — Sedative

PERFUME

Scent: *Floral, rosy, rich, tenacious, sweet, tender, warm.* **Key qualities:** *Aphrodisiac, soothing, comforting, anti-depressant, sedative (to the nervous system), uplifting, appeasing, regulating, tonic (heart).*
Odor intensity: *Very high.*

AROMATHERAPY USE

Skin care: *Thread veins, dry, mature and sensitive skin, wrinkles, eczema, herpes, (nonirritant, nonsensitizing).*
Circulation, muscles and joints: *Palpitations, poor circulation.*
Respiratory system: *Asthma, coughs, hay fever.* **Digestive system:** *Cholecystitis, liver congestion, nausea.*
Reproductive system: *Irregular menstruation, leukorrhea, menorrhagia, uterine disorders.*
Nervous system: *Depression, impotence, insomnia, frigidity, headache, nervous tension, stress-related complaints.*

Rosemary

ROSMARINUS OFFICINALIS **FAMILY** LAMIACEAE (LABIATAE)

DESCRIPTION

An aromatic, shrubby evergreen bush, up to 6ft/2m high, with silvery-green leaves, and pale blue flowers.

ACTIONS

Analgesic, antimicrobial, antioxidant, antiseptic, antispasmodic, astringent, carminative, choleretic, cicatrizant, cordial, diaphoretic, digestive, diuretic, emmenagogue, fungicidal, hepatic, hypertensor, restorative, rubefacient, stimulant, stomachic, sudorific, tonic.

EXTRACTION

The oil is extracted by steam distillation from the fresh flowering tops, or, in Spain, from the whole plant.

CHARACTERISTICS

A colorless or pale yellow, mobile liquid with a strong, minty-herbaceous, woody-balsamic scent. It blends well with frankincense, lavender, citronella, basil, thyme, pine, peppermint, elemi, cedarwood, petitgrain, and spice oils.

WARNING
This oil should not be used by people suffering from epilepsy, or during pregnancy.

SCENT SCALE
Top *Middle* *Base*

PSYCHOLOGICAL SCALE
Uplifting *Balancing* *Soothing*

PHYSIOLOGICAL SCALE
Stimulating *Regulating* *Sedative*

PERFUME

Scent: *Penetrating, fresh, camphoraceous, woody-balsamic, strong.* **Key qualities:** *Stimulant (nervous and mental), analgesic, tonic (to the nervous system), strengthening, restorative, purifying, protective, reviving, refreshing.*
Odor intensity: *Medium–high.*

AROMATHERAPY USE

Skin care: *Acne, dermatitis, eczema, lice, scabies, hair, and scalp.*
Circulation, muscles and joints: *Arteriosclerosis, fluid retention, gout, muscular pain, neuralgia, palpitations, poor circulation, varicose veins, rheumatism.* **Respiratory system:** *Asthma, bronchitis, whooping cough.*
Digestive system: *Colitis, dyspepsia, flatulence, hepatic disorders, jaundice.*
Reproductive system: *Dysmenorrhea, leukorrhea.* **Immune system:** *Colds, flu, infections.*
Nervous system: *Headaches, hypotension, nervous exhaustion, stress-related disorders.*

Sage, Spanish

SALVIA LAVANDULIFOLIA **FAMILY** LAMIACEAE (LABIATAE)

DESCRIPTION

An aromatic evergreen shrub, similar to the garden sage, but with narrower leaves, and small purple flowers. The oil is mainly produced in Spain.

ACTIONS

Antidepressant, antiinflammatory, antimicrobial, antiseptic, antispasmodic, astringent, carminative, deodorant, depurative, digestive, emmenagogue, expectorant, febrifuge, hypotensive, nervine, stimulant, stomachic, tonic.

EXTRACTION

The oil is extracted by steam distillation from the leaves.

CHARACTERISTICS

A pale yellow, mobile liquid, with a fresh-herbaceous, camphoraceous, slightly pine-like odor. It blends well with rosemary, lavender, pine, eucalyptus, juniper, clary sage, and cedarwood.

WARNING
Do not use during pregnancy. Always use in moderation only.

SCENT SCALE
Top *Middle* *Base*

PSYCHOLOGICAL SCALE
Uplifting *Balancing* *Soothing*

PHYSIOLOGICAL SCALE
Stimulating *Regulating* *Sedative*

PERFUME

Scent: *Camphoraceous, fresh, herbaceous, penetrating, powerful.* **Key qualities (mind):** *Refreshing, invigorating, clearing.*
Odor intensity: *High.*

AROMATHERAPY USE

Skin care: *Acne, cuts, dandruff, dermatitis, eczema, excessive sweating, hair loss, sores.* **Circulation, muscles and joints:** *Arthritis, debility, fluid retention, muscular aches and pains, poor circulation, rheumatism.*
Respiratory system: *Asthma, coughs, laryngitis.* **Digestive system:** *Jaundice, liver congestion.*
Reproductive system: *Amenorrhea, dysmenorrhea, sterility.* **Immune system:** *Colds, fevers, flu.* **Nervous system:** *Headaches, nervous exhaustion, stress-related conditions.*
Other uses: *Treats gingivitis and other gum infections.*

Sage, clary

SALVIA SCLARIA **FAMILY** LABIATAE (LAMIACEAE)

DESCRIPTION

Stout biennial or perennial herb, up to 3ft/1m high, with large, hairy leaves, green with a hint of purple, and small blue flowers.

ACTIONS

Anticonvulsive, antidepressant, antiphlogistic, antiseptic, aphrodisiac, astringent, bactericidal, carminative, cicatrizant, deodorant, digestive, emmenagogue, hypotensive, nervine, sedative, stomachic, uterine tonic.

EXTRACTION

The oil is extracted by steam distillation from the flowering tops, and leaves.

CHARACTERISTICS

A colorless or pale yellowy-green liquid, with a sweet, nutty-herbaceous scent. It blends well with juniper, lavender, coriander, cardamom, geranium, sandalwood, cedarwood, pine, jasmine, frankincense, bergamot, and all the citrus oils.

WARNING
Nontoxic in normal use, but avoid during pregnancy. Do not use clary sage oil while drinking alcohol, since it can induce a narcotic effect, and exaggerated drunkenness.

SCENT SCALE
Top *Middle* *Base*

PSYCHOLOGICAL SCALE
Uplifting *Balancing* *Soothing*

PHYSIOLOGICAL SCALE
Stimulating *Regulating* *Sedative*

PERFUME

Scent: *Musky-amber, mellow, rich, warm, herbaceous, sweet; imperative in eau-de-Cologne.* **Key qualities:** *Relaxing, rejuvenating, balancing, inspiring, sedative (to the nervous system) revitalizing, aphrodisiac, intoxicating, euphoric, warming.* **Odor intensity:** *Medium–high.*

AROMATHERAPY USE

Skin care: *Acne, boils, dandruff, hair loss, inflamed conditions, oily skin and hair, ulcers, wrinkles.* **Circulation, muscles and joints:** *High blood pressure, muscular aches and pains.* **Respiratory system:** *Asthma, throat infections, whooping cough.* **Digestive system:** *Colic, cramp, dyspepsia, flatulence.* **Reproductive system:** *Amenorrhea, labor pain, dysmenorrhea, leukorrhea.* **Nervous system:** *Depression, frigidity, impotence, migraine, nervous tension, stress-related disorders.*

Sandalwood

SANTALUM ALBUM **FAMILY** SANTALACEAE

DESCRIPTION

A small, evergreen, parasitic tree, up to 30ft/9m high, with brown-gray trunk, and many smooth, slender branches.
It has small, pinky-purple flowers.

ACTIONS

Antidepressant, antiphlogistic, antiseptic, antispasmodic, aphrodisiac, astringent, bactericidal, carminative, cicatrizant, diuretic, expectorant, fungicidal, insecticide, sedative, tonic.

EXTRACTION

The oil is extracted by water or steam distillation from the powdered and dried roots and heartwood.

CHARACTERISTICS

A pale yellow, greenish or brownish, viscous liquid, with a deep, soft, sweet-woody, balsamic scent. It blends well with rose, clove, lavender, black pepper, bergamot, rosewood, geranium, benzoin, vetivert, patchouli, myrrh, and jasmine.

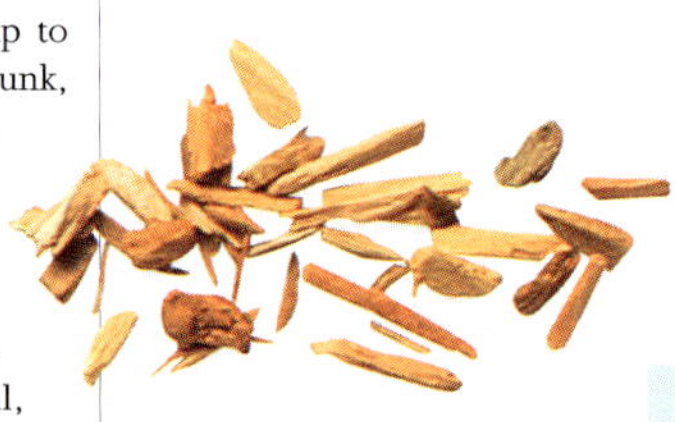

SAFETY DATA
Nontoxic, nonirritant, nonsensitizing.

SCENT SCALE
Top *Middle* *Base*

PSYCHOLOGICAL SCALE
Uplifting *Balancing* *Soothing*

PHYSIOLOGICAL SCALE
Stimulating *Regulating* *Sedative*

PERFUME

Scent: *Dry-woody, amber, balsamic, musky, oriental, sensual, masculine, tenacious, warm.* **Key qualities:** *Aphrodisiac, soothing, relaxing, uplifting, purifying, warming, grounding, opening, elevating, sedative (to the nervous system).* **Odor intensity:** *Low–medium.*

AROMATHERAPY USE

Skin care: *Acne; dry, cracked, and chapped skin, after-shave (for barber's rash), greasy skin, moisturizer.* **Respiratory system:** *Bronchitis, catarrh, coughs (dry, persistent), laryngitis, sore throat.* **Digestive system:** *Diarrhea, nausea.* **Urinary system:** *Cystitis.* **Nervous system:** *Depression, insomnia, nervous tension, stress-related complaints.*

Benzoin

STYRAX BENZOIN **FAMILY** STYRACACEAE

DESCRIPTION

A large tropical tree, up to 66ft/20m high, with hard-shelled fruit. When cut, the trunk exudes a balsamic resin.

ACTIONS

Anti-inflammatory, antioxidant, antiseptic, astringent, carminative, cordial, deodorant, diuretic, expectorant, sedative, styptic, vulnerary.

EXTRACTION

Benzoin resinoid, or resin absolute, is prepared from the crude benzoin using solvents such as benzene and alcohol, which are then removed. Commercial benzoin is usually sold dissolved in ethyl glycol, or similar solvent.

CHARACTERISTICS

Benzoin resinoid is an orange-brown, viscous mass, with an intensely rich, sweet-balsamic odor. It blends well with sandalwood, rose, jasmine, frankincense, myrrh, cypress, juniper, lemon, coriander, and other spice oils.

WARNING
Do not use on babies.

SCENT SCALE
Top *Middle* *Base*

PSYCHOLOGICAL SCALE
Uplifting *Balancing* *Soothing*

PHYSIOLOGICAL SCALE
Stimulating *Regulating* *Sedative*

PERFUME

Scent: *Sweet, balsamic, vanilla-like, resinous, rich, intense. Acts as a fixative, and preservative.* **Key qualities:** *Warming, energizing, uplifting, comforting, purifying, elevating, stimulant, soothing, antidepressant.* **Odor intensity:** *Medium.*

AROMATHERAPY USE

Skin care: *Cuts, chapped skin, inflamed and irritated conditions.* **Circulation, muscles and joints:** *Arthritis, gout, poor circulation, rheumatism.* **Respiratory system:** *Asthma, bronchitis, chills, colic, coughs, flu, laryngitis.* **Nervous system:** *Nervous tension and general stress-related problems.*

SAFETY DATA
Nontoxic, nonirritant, but can cause possible sensitization, due to the solvents used.

Clove bud

SYZYGIUM AROMATICUM **FAMILY** MYRTACEAE

DESCRIPTION

A slender evergreen tree with a smooth, gray trunk, up to 40ft/12m high. It has large bright green leaves, standing in pairs on short stalks. At the start of the rainy season, long buds appear, with a rosy-pink corolla at the tip; as the corolla fades, the calyx slowly turns deep red.

ACTIONS

Anthelmintic, antibiotic, anti-emetic, antirheumatic, antineuralgic, antioxidant, antiseptic, antiviral, carminative, expectorant, larvicidal, spasmolytic, stimulant, stomachic, vermifuge.

EXTRACTION

The oil is obtained by water distillation from the flower buds.

CHARACTERISTICS

Clove bud oil is a pale yellow liquid, with a sweet-spicy odor that has a fruity-fresh top note. Used in perfumery, it blends well with rose, lavender, clary sage, bergamot, bay, and ylang ylang.

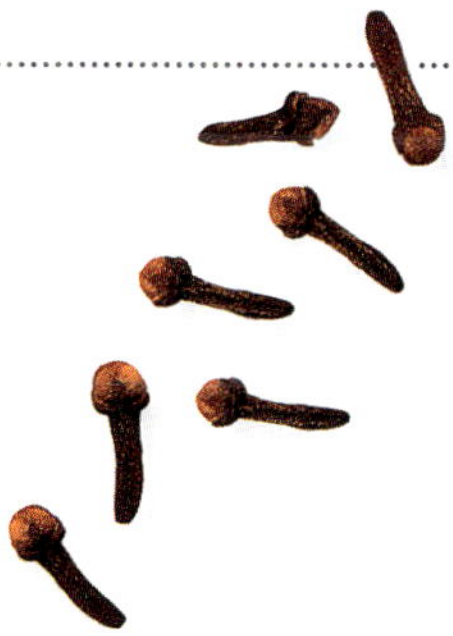

SAFETY DATA
Clove bud oil can cause skin and mucous membrane irritation, and may cause dermatitis in some individuals. See Warning box.

SCENT SCALE
Top *Middle* *Base*

PSYCHOLOGICAL SCALE
Uplifting *Balancing* *Soothing*

PHYSIOLOGICAL SCALE
Stimulating *Regulating* *Sedative*

PERFUME

Scent: *Hot, fruity, floral, fresh, fragrant, peppery, sweet-spicy, diffusive, powerful, clean, medicinal, oriental.* **Key qualities:** *Tonic, stimulating, revitalizing, aphrodisiac, warming, comforting, purifying, active.* **Odor intensity:** *High.*

AROMATHERAPY USE

Skin care: *Acne, athlete's foot, bruises, burns, cuts, toothache, ulcers, wounds.* **Circulation, muscles and joints:** *Arthritis, rheumatism, sprains.* **Respiratory system:** *Asthma, bronchitis.* **Digestive system:** *Colic, dyspepsia, nausea.* **Immune system:** *Colds, flu, minor infections.* **Other:** *Insect repellent (mosquitoes).*

WARNING
Use this oil in moderation only, and in low dilution (less than 1%).

Tagetes

TAGETES MINUTA **FAMILY** ASTERACEAE (COMPOSITAE)

DESCRIPTION

A strongly scented annual herb, about 1ft/30cm high, with bright orange, daisy-like flowers, and soft green feathery leaves.

ACTIONS

Anthelmintic, antispasmodic, bactericide, carminative, diaphoretic, emmenagogue, fungicidal, stomachic.

EXTRACTION

The oil is extracted by steam distillation from the fresh flowering herb.

CHARACTERISTICS

A dark orange or yellow, mobile liquid, which slowly solidifies on exposure to air and light. It has a bitter-green, herby odor, and blends well with clary sage, lavender, jasmine, bergamot, and other citrus oils in very small percentages.

SAFETY DATA
It is quite possible that the main constituent, tagetone, is toxic. There have been some reported cases of dermatitis with the tagetes species.

SCENT SCALE
Top — *Middle* — *Base*

PSYCHOLOGICAL SCALE
Uplifting — *Balancing* — *Soothing*

PHYSIOLOGICAL SCALE
Stimulating — *Regulating* — *Sedative*

PERFUME

Scent: *Bitter-green, herbaceous, fruity, powerful, citrus-like.* **Key qualities:** *Penetrating, hypotensive, soothing, relaxing, narcotic (in excess).* **Odor intensity:** *Very high.*

AROMATHERAPY USE

Skin care: *Bunions, calluses, corns, fungal infections.*

WARNING
Use with care, and in moderation.

Thyme, white

THYMUS VULGARIS. **FAMILY** LAMIACEAE (LABIATAE)

DESCRIPTION

A perennial evergreen sub-shrub, up to 18in/45cm high, with small, gray-green, oval, aromatic leaves, and pale purple or white flowers.

ACTIONS

Anthelmintic, antimicrobial, antioxidant, antirheumatic, antiseptic, antispasmodic, antitussive, antitoxic, astringent, bactericidal, balsamic, carminative, cicatrizant, diuretic, emmenagogue, expectorant, fungicidal, hypertensive, nervine, rubefacient, stimulant, sudorific, aphrodisiac, tonic, vermifuge.

EXTRACTION

The oil is extracted by water or steam distillation from the fresh, or partially dried, leaves and flowering tops.

CHARACTERISTICS

White thyme oil is a clear, pale yellow liquid, with a sweet, green-fresh scent. It blends well with bergamot, lemon, rosemary, melissa, lavender, marjoram, pine, and spice oils.

WARNING
Some thyme oils contain large amounts of toxic phenols. Use all thyme oils in moderation and in low dilution. Avoid during pregnancy.

SCENT SCALE
Top — *Middle* — *Base*

PSYCHOLOGICAL SCALE
Uplifting — *Balancing* — *Soothing*

PHYSIOLOGICAL SCALE
Stimulating — *Regulating* — *Sedative*

PERFUME

Scent: *Warm, spicy-herbaceous, powerful, penetrating, fresh, sporty, medicinal, green.* **Key qualities (mind):** *Stimulating, restorative, warming, reviving, refreshing, purifying, antidepressant.* **Odor intensity:** *High.*

AROMATHERAPY USE

Skin care: *Abscess, acne, bruises, burns, cuts, dermatitis, eczema, insect bites, lice.* **Circulation, muscles and joints:** *Arthritis, gout, muscular aches and pains, obesity, edema, poor circulation, rheumatism, sprains.* **Respiratory system:** *Asthma, bronchitis, catarrh, coughs, laryngitis, sinusitis, tonsillitis.* **Digestive system:** *Diarrhea, dyspepsia, flatulence.* **Immune system:** *Chills, colds, flu, infectious diseases.* **Urinary system:** *Cystitis, urethritis.* **Nervous system:** *Headaches, insomnia, and stress-related complaints.*

Valerian

VALERIANA OFFICINALIS, **FAMILY** *VALERIANACEAE*

DESCRIPTION

A perennial herb, up to 5ft/1.5m high, with a hollow, erect stem, deeply dissected dark leaves, and many purplish-white flowers. It has short, thick, grayish roots, showing above ground; these have a strong odor.

ACTIONS

Anodyne (mild), anti-dandruff, anti-diuretic, antispasmodic, bactericidal, carminative, depressant of the central nervous system, hypnotic, hypotensive, regulator, sedative, stomachic.

EXTRACTION

The oil is extracted by steam distillation from the roots.

CHARACTERISTICS

An olive to brown liquid, darkening with age, with a warm-woody, balsamic, musky odor; fresh oils have a green top note. It blends well with patchouli, pine, lavender, cedarwood, mandarin, petitgrain, and rosemary.

SAFETY DATA

Nontoxic, nonirritant, but can cause possible sensitization.

SCENT SCALE

Top — *Middle* — *Base*

PSYCHOLOGICAL SCALE

Uplifting — *Balancing* — *Soothing*

PHYSIOLOGICAL SCALE

Stimulating — *Regulating* — *Sedative*

PERFUME

Scent: *Warm, woody, balsamic, musky, earthy, green.* **Key qualities (mind):** *Sedative (mental and nervous), depressant of the central nervous system, mildly hypnotic, regulator, calming, soothing, grounding.* **Odor intensity:** *Very high.*

AROMATHERAPY USE

Nervous system: *Insomnia, nervous indigestion, migraine, restlessness, tension states.*

WARNING

In large amounts, valerian can cause headaches, mental agitation, and delusions. Use in moderation, and do not use over long periods of time (more than a month) without a break.

Vetivert

VETIVERIA ZIZANOIDES/ANDROPOGON MURICATUS

FAMILY *POACEAE (GRAMINEAE)*

DESCRIPTION

A tall, tufted, perennial, scented grass, with a straight stem, long, narrow leaves, and an abundant, complex lacework of undergound white rootlets.

ACTIONS

Antiseptic, antispasmodic, depurative, rubefacient, sedative (to the nervous system), stimulant (circulatory, and to blood itself), tonic, vermifuge.

EXTRACTION

The oil is extracted by steam distillation from the roots and rootlets – which have been washed, chopped, dried, and soaked.

CHARACTERISTICS

A dark brown, olive, or amber, viscous oil, with deep, smoky, earthy-woody odor, and a sweet, persistent undertone. The color and scent can vary according to the source. It blends well with sandalwood, rose, jasmine, patchouli, lavender, clary sage, and ylang ylang.

SCENT SCALE

Top — *Middle* — *Base*

PSYCHOLOGICAL SCALE

Uplifting — *Balancing* — *Soothing*

PHYSIOLOGICAL SCALE

Stimulating — *Regulating* — *Sedative*

PERFUME

Scent: *Smoky, rich, earthy, dry-woody, sweet, green, diffusive, masculine, sporty, warm.* **Key qualities:** *Sedative (nervous and mental), soothing, calming, tonic (nervous), grounding, uplifting, protective.* **Odor intensity:** *High.*

AROMATHERAPY USE

Skin care: *Acne, cuts, oily skin, wounds.* **Circulation, muscles and joints:** *Arthritis, muscular aches and pains, rheumatism, sprains, stiffness.* **Nervous system:** *Debility, depression, insomnia, nervous tension – known as the oil of tranquillity.*

SAFETY DATA

Nontoxic, nonirritant, nonsensitizing.

Ginger

ZINGIBER OFFICINALE **FAMILY** ZINGIBERACEAE

DESCRIPTION

An erect perennial herb, up to 3ft/1m high, with a thick, spreading, tuberous rhizomatous root, which is very pungent. The green, reed-like stalk, with narrow, spear-shaped leaves, and white or yellow flowers grows up from the root.

ACTIONS

Analgesic, antioxidant, antiseptic, antispasmodic, aperitif, aphrodisiac, bactericidal, carminative, cephalic, expectorant, febrifuge, laxative, rubifacient, stimulant, stomachic, tonic.

EXTRACTION

The oil is extracted by steam distillation from the unpeeled, dried, ground root.

CHARACTERISTICS

A pale yellow, amber, or greenish liquid, with a warm, slightly green, fresh, woody-spicy scent. It blends well with sandalwood, vetiver, patchouli, frankincense, rosewood, cedarwood, coriander, rose, lime, neroli, orange, and lemon.

SAFETY DATA
Nontoxic, nonirritant (except in high concentration), but may cause some sensitization – use in low dilutions only. Slightly phototoxic.

SCENT SCALE
Top *Middle* *Base*

PSYCHOLOGICAL SCALE
Uplifting *Balancing* *Soothing*

PHYSIOLOGICAL SCALE
Stimulating *Regulating* *Sedative*

PERFUME

Scent: *Fresh, woody-spicy, rich, slightly green, peppery, fiery, penetrating, diffusive, exotic.*
Key qualities: *Tonic, aphrodisiac, stimulating, warming, cephalic, comforting.* **Odor intensity:** *High.*

AROMATHERAPY USE

Circulation, muscles and joints: *Arthritis, fatigue, muscular aches and pains, poor circulation, rheumatism, sprains, strains.* **Respiratory system:** *Catarrh, congestion, coughs, sinusitis, sore throat.* **Digestive system:** *Diarrhea, colic, cramp, flatulence, indigestion, loss of appetite, nausea, travel sickness.* **Immune system:** *Chills, colds, flu, fever, infectious disease.* **Nervous system:** *Debility, nervous exhaustion.*

BELOW
An aromatherapy kit can be assembled to suit the needs of each individual family. Start with the five most essential oils, peppermint, Roman chamomile, lavender, tea tree, and rosemary, and add to these gradually as you become more familiar with the oils and their uses.

Appendix

SAFETY DATA

Safety guidelines
In general, all the essential oils listed in this book are safe to use for aromatherapy or household purposes. However, it is necessary to be aware of the following safety measures.

Safety data
Always check with specific safety data before using a new oil (see information on individual oils, pages 177–210).

Internal use
Do not take essential oils internally. Essential oils may damage the lining of the digestive tract and some essential oils are toxic if taken internally.

Toxicity
Essential oils that should be used in moderation because of toxicity levels when absorbed through the skin are: aniseed, West Indian bay, white camphor, clove bud, coriander, eucalyptus blue gum, hyssop, nutmeg, sweet fennel, parsley seed, Spanish sage, tagetes, thyme. Pennyroyal, mustard, sassafras, rue, and mugwort should not be used at all and are not included in this book.

Neat application
In general, essential oils should not be applied neat to the skin. Exceptions are lavender and tea tree, for applications described in this book. Non-irritant oils such as jasmine, ylang ylang, or sandalwood may be applied neat for use as a perfume.

Patch test
Before applying any new oil to the skin, do a patch test. Put a few drops on the back of your wrist, cover with a plaster, and leave for an hour. If irritation or redness occurs, bathe with cold water. For future use, reduce the recommended concentration level by half or avoid using the oil altogether.

Sensitive skin
Neat tea tree may cause skin irritation in people with very sensitive skins. These people should dilute it first in a non-oily cream or gel. Oils that may cause an adverse reaction on very sensitive skin, even when diluted, include benzoin, lemon eucalyptus, melissa, tagetes, valerian, yarrow, and skin irritant oils.

Skin irritation
Oils that may irritate the skin, especially in high concentrations are: aniseed, sweet basil, black pepper, cajeput, white camphor, Virginian cedarwood, cinnamon leaf, clove bud, eucalyptus blue gum, ginger, juniper, lemon, lemongrass, parsley seed, peppermint, pine needle, and thyme. Do not use more than 3 drops of these oils in the bath.

Phototoxicity
Oils that can cause adverse reaction if used before exposure to sunlight or ultraviolet light (e.g. sunbeds) are: angelica root, bergamot, lime, bitter orange, lemon, grapefruit, sweet orange, and tangerine.

Babies and children
Always increase the dilution for babies and infants to at least half the recommended amount. For babies, avoid the possibly toxic and irritant oils altogether. For babies 0–12 months: use only 1 drop of lavender, rose, or chamomile oil, diluted in 1 tsp/5ml carrier oil for massage or bathing (do not use other oils).
For infants 1–5 years: use only 2–3 drops of any of the nontoxic and nonirritant oils, diluted in 1 tsp/5ml carrier oil for massage or bathing.
For children 6–12 years: use as for adults but in half the stated concentration.

Pregnancy
During pregnancy, use essential oils in half the stated amount. Do not use oils that are potentially toxic or have emmenagogue properties. Avoid altogether: basil, Virginian cedarwood, celery seed, clary sage, clove, cinnamon leaf, citronella, hyssop, juniper, marjoram, myrrh, nutmeg, Spanish sage, thyme. Avoid during the first four months: angelica root, Atlas cedarwood, sweet fennel, rose, rosemary.

High blood pressure
Avoid using the following oils in any form in cases of high blood pressure: rosemary, Spanish sage, thyme.

Epilepsy
Avoid using the following oils in cases of epilepsy: fennel, hyssop, rosemary, Spanish sage.

Alcohol
Clary sage should not be used in any form within a few hours (before or after) of drinking alcohol. It can cause nausea and exaggerated drunkenness.

Homeopathy
Homeopathic treatment is not compatible with the following oils, due to their strength: black pepper, camphor, eucalyptus, peppermint.

Storage
Store essential oils and blends in dark, well-stoppered bottles, kept away from light and heat, and well out of reach of children. Label bottles clearly.

CHEMICAL CONSTITUENTS

This appendix shows the chief chemical constituents of each of the essential oils described in this book. For each oil, the major chemical groups and their approximate proportions are shown, linked to the principal effects of the oil. Constituents that are mainly stimulating in their effect are shown in red, those that are mainly relaxing/sedating are shown in blue, and those that are mainly balancing are shown in purple. These are for standard samples, but it must be borne in mind that the chemical make-up of essential oils can vary enormously, depending on the source. Small quantities of trace elements may also be present.

	RELAXING			BALANCING	STIMULATING				
	ESTERS	ALDEHYDES	KETONES	SEQUISTERPENES	OXIDES	ACIDS	MONOTERPENES	ALCOHOLS	PHENOLS
YARROW *Achillea millefolium*				34%	11%		25%	9%	
DILL *Anethum graveolens*			UP TO 55%	UP TO 21%			UP TO 69%	UP TO 4%	UP TO 18%
ANGELICA ROOT *Angelica archangelica*	UP TO 15%			UP TO 34%	14%		UP TO 80%	UP TO 19%	
ROSEWOOD *Aniba rosaeodora*								70%	
CELERY SEED *Apium graveolens*				21%			75%		
FRANKINCENSE *Boswellia carteri*	UP TO 10%						UP TO 50%	UP TO 12%	
YLANG YLANG *Cananga odorata forma genuina*	UP TO 16%			16%			UP TO 47%	20%	
ELEMI *Canarium luzonicum*							UP TO 85%		
CEDARWOOD, ATLAS *Cedrus atlantica*			3%	86%				10%	
CHAMOMILE, ROMAN *Chamaemelum nobilis, Anthemis nobilis*	UP TO 70%			4%			10%	35%	
CHAMOMILE, GERMAN/BLUE *Chamomilla matricaria Matricaria recutita*				47%	19%				
CAMPHOR *Cinnamomum camphora*			37%				UP TO 58%	10%	
CINNAMON LEAF *Cinnamomum zeylanicum*				6%				5%	74%
LIME *Citrus aurantifolia*					3%		UP TO 84%	11%	
PETITGRAIN ORANGE *Citrus aurantium var. amara*	75%							UP TO 40%	
NEROLI *Citrus aurantium var. amara*	13%						29%	UP TO 40%	
BERGAMOT *Citrus bergamia*	28%						UP TO 52%	13%	
LEMON *Citrus limon*							80%		
GRAPEFRUIT *Citrus x paradisi*							88%	3%	

CHEMICAL CONSTITUENTS

	ESTERS	ALDEHYDES	KETONES	SEQUISTERPENES	OXIDES	ACIDS	MONOTERPENES	ALCOHOLS	PHENOLS
MANDARIN *Citrus reticulata*							89%		
ORANGE, SWEET *Citrus sinensis, Citrus aurantium var. dulcis*	3%	UP TO 39%	5%				UP TO 95%	UP TO 15%	
MYRRH *Commiphora myrrh*				UP TO 32%				43%	
CORIANDER *Coriandrum sativum*	2%		4%				9%	81%	
CYPRESS *Cupressus sempervirens*				3%			UP TO 77%	10%	
LEMONGRASS, WEST INDIAN *Cymbopogon citratus*		74%					3%	10%	
PALMAROSA *Cymbopogon martinii,*	10%			2%				83%	
CITRONELLA *Cymbopogon nardus*		UP TO 49%		2%			UP TO 11%	UP TO 25%	1%
CARROT SEED *Daucus carota*	UP TO 19%		10%	UP TO 30%	UP TO 31%		UP TO 35%	UP TO 85%	
CARDOMOM *Elettaria cardamomum*	52%				31%		4%	5%	
LEMON EUCALYPTUS *Eucalyptus citriodora*	3%	82%			2%			9%	
EUCALYPTUS BLUE GUM *Eucalyptus globulus*					96%		4%		
GALBANUM *Ferula gumosa*							70%		
FENNEL, SWEET *Foeniculum vulgare*		2%	14%				2%		77%
HYSSOP *Hyssopus officinalis*			48%	16%			13%		
JASMINE *Jasminum officinale*	70%							8%	
JUNIPER *Juniperus communis*				2%			70%		
CEDARWOOD, VIRGINIAN *Juniperus virginiana*				56%				33%	
LAVENDER, TRUE *Lavandula angustifolia/ L.officinalis*	43%			2%	6%		37%		
TEA TREE *Melaleuca alternifolia*				2%	3%		36%	48%	
CAJEPUT *Melaleuca cajeputi*				11%	35%		23%	21%	2%

CHEMICAL CONSTITUENTS

	ESTERS	ALDEHYDES	KETONES	SEQUISTERPENES	OXIDES	ACIDS	MONOTERPENES	ALCOHOLS	PHENOLS
MELISSA *Melissa officinalis*	UP TO 6%	UP TO 92%	UP TO 9%	UP TO 10%		UP TO 9%		UP TO 3%	
PEPPERMINT *Mentha x piperata*			UP TO 40%				6%	UP TO 48%	
NUTMEG *Myristica fragrans*				2%			UP TO 88%	8%	7%
MYRTLE *Myrtus communis*	25%				37%		31%	3%	
BASIL, SWEET/ FRENCH *Ocimum basilicum*	8%				7%			64%	3%
MARJORAM, SWEET *Origanum majorana/ Marjorana hortensis*				2.4%			30%	52%	
GERANIUM, ROSE *Pelargonium graveolens*	30%		6%				2%	54%	
PARSLEY SEED *Petroselinum crispum*							45%		UP TO 59%
BAY, WEST INDIAN *Pimenta acris*	4%						21%	2%	64%
ANISEED *Pimpinella anisum*		UP TO 2%					2%		UP TO 96%
PINE NEEDLE, SCOTCH *Pinus sylvestris*	27%			2%			UP TO 61%	3%	
PEPPER, BLACK *Piper nigrum*				7%			77%		
PATCHOULI *Pogostemon patchouli*				UP TO 60%				25%	
ROSE MAROC *Rosa centifolia*		UP TO 38%						UP TO 93%	3%
ROSEMARY *Rosmarinus officinalis*			13%				69%		
SAGE, SPANISH *Salvia lavandulifolia*	9%		26%				30%	23%	
SAGE, CLARY *Salvia sclarea*	72%			3%				14%	
SANDALWOOD, EAST INDIAN *Santalum album*				3%				68%	
BENZOIN *Styrax benzoin*	80%	2%			17%				
CLOVE *Syzygium aromaticum*	5%			4%					84%
TAGETES *Tagetes minuta*			UP TO 95%				UP TO 35%		
THYME, WHITE (COMMON) *Thymus vulgaris*							40%	50%	
VALERIAN *Valeriana officinalis*	30%			5%			12%	2%	
VETIVERT *Vetiveria zizanoides*			12%	6%		5%		20%	
GINGER *Zinziber officinale*		3%		60%	5%		15%		

VITAMINS AND DIETARY SOURCES

Vitamin A (Retinol)

- Needed for vision, skin health, resistance to infection, growth, reproduction. Needs oils and fats for absorption into body. Not affected by heat.
- Found in meat, fish, dairy produce, fortified spreads, carrots, greens, sweet potatoes, endive, tomatoes, green beans, dried apricots, cantaloup, prunes.

Vitamin B1 (Thiamine)

- Needed for release of energy from food. Aids appetite and digestion.
- Found in unrefined foods, cereals (wheat germ, soy flour, whole wheat flour, brown rice), nuts, seeds, brewer's yeast, molasses, fortified foods.
- More may be needed by pregnant or breastfeeding women, the elderly, drinkers, smokers.

Vitamin B2 (Riboflavin)

- Needed for vitality, release of energy from food, healthy eyes and skin.
- Found in meat (liver, lamb, beef, pork, chicken, kidney), cereals (wheat germ), nuts and seeds, molasses, brewer's yeast.

B3 (Niacin/Nicotinic Acid)

- Needed for production of energy.
- Found in: meat, fish, cereal, nuts, seeds, molasses, brewer's yeast.
- Extra may be needed by pregnant and breastfeeding women, those suffering from stress, and the elderly.

B6 (Pyridoxine)

- Needed for normal functioning of brain and nerves, in utilization of essential fatty acids, production of many enzymes; regulating magnesium levels.
- Found in meat (especially offal), yeast, cereals (wheat bran and germ), molasses.
- Extra needed in pregnancy, when taking oral contraceptives; may help with epilepsy, diabetes, anemia, kidney stones.

Biotin

- Needed for fat metabolism; deficiency of biotin may be involved in dermatitis and hair loss.
- Found in egg yolk and liver; also made in the intestine.

B12 (Cobalamine)

- Needed by rapidly dividing cells such as those in the bone marrow that form red blood cells.
- Found in meat (especially liver), dairy produce, fortified products (e.g. breakfast cereals). (Only in animal foods.)
- Vegetarians, vegans, the elderly, and those pregnant or breastfeeding should check they have adequate B12.

Folic Acid (Bc)

- Needed for cell division; production of red blood cells; growth and healing; utilization of pantothenic acid.
- Found in meat (especially liver), nuts, green vegetables, yeast.
- Important in and before pregnancy.

Pantothenic Acid

- Needed for cell growth and utilization of energy from foods. Needed for synthesis of hormones by adrenal glands.
- Found in meat (especially offal), cereals, vegetables, yeast. Lost in cooking, canning, exposure to light, and storage.
- Those suffering from stress, allergies, or injury may have increased need.

Inositol

- Combines with choline to make lecithin in the liver. This keeps cholesterol in small particles to prevent clogging of blood vessels. Inositol also aids the digestion.
- Found in meat, cereals, molasses, yeast.
- Those with high blood pressure or high cholesterol levels, and smokers may need extra inositol and choline.

Choline

- Used to form lecithin with inositol.
- Found in meat (including brains, liver, kidneys), egg yolk, wheat germ, yeast. Can be made in the blood, given adequate folic acid and B12.
- Those with high blood pressure or high cholesterol levels may need more.

Vitamin C (Ascorbic acid)

- Needed for resistance to infection and allergies, healing, strong gums, teeth, and bones, skin elasticity, strong connective tissue. Detoxifies harmful substances. Aids iron absorption.
- Found in fruit (especially strawberries, oranges, lemons), greens, raw sweet pepper, meat (especially liver).
- Vitamin C cannot be stored in the body. Extra needed in illness. Destroyed in food preparation and storage.

Vitamin D

- Needed for absorption, retention, and utilization of calcium (essential for strong bones and teeth, relaxes nerves, decreases pain sensitivity, aids sound sleep). Vitamin D is fat-soluble and can only be absorbed if fat is present in the diet. Excessive amounts can be toxic.
- Found in oily fish, fish-liver oils, fortified products; also formed by the action of sunlight on the skin.
- Important for those with low exposure to sunlight, children, vegetarians, vegans.

Vitamin E

- Prevents oxidation of unsaturated fatty acids, vitamin A, various hormones; for glands, hormones, reproduction. Prevents thrombosis in legs. Aids liver function. Fat and bile need to be present in the intestine for absorption.
- Found in oils of all cereals, nuts and seeds, stoneground flour, cold-pressed oils. Destroyed by cooking and storage.

General Glossary

Abortifacient: capable of inducing abortion.
Absolute: a highly concentrated, semi-solid or solid perfume material, usually obtained by alcohol extraction from the concrete.
Acrid: leaving a burning sensation in the mouth.
Adaptogen: a substance that causes beneficial adaptive change to take place in the body.
Allergy: hypersensitivity to a foreign substance.
Alliaceous: garlic- or onion-like.
Alterative: corrects disordered bodily function.
Amebicidal: having the power of destroying amebae.
Analgesic: remedy or agent that deadens pain.
Anaphrodisiac: reduces sexual desire.
Anemia: deficiency of red corpuscles in the blood.
Anesthetic: loss of feeling or sensation; substance that causes such a loss.
Annual: a plant that completes its life cycle in one year.
Anodyne: stills pain and quiets disturbed feelings.
Anorexia: condition of being without appetite.
Anthelmintic: a vermifuge, destroying or expelling intestinal worms.
Antianemic: an agent that combats anemia.
Antiarthritic: an agent that combats arthritis.
Antibilious: an agent that helps remove excess bile.
Antibiotic: prevents the growth of, or destroys, bacteria.
Anticatarrhal: helps remove excess catarrh.
Anticonvulsant: helps arrest or prevent convulsions.
Antidepressant: helps alleviate depression.
Antidiarrheal: efficacious against diarrhea.
Antiemetic: an agent which reduces the incidence and severity of nausea or vomiting.
Antihemorrhagic: an agent that prevents or combats hemorrhage or bleeding.
Antihistamine: counteracts effects of histamine.
Anti-inflammatory: alleviates inflammation.
Antilithic: prevents the formation of a calculus or stone.
Antimicrobial: an agent that resists or destroys pathogenic micro-organisms.
Antineuralgic: relieves or reduces nerve pain.
Antioxidant: prevents or delays oxidation.
Antiphlogistic: checks or counteracts inflammation.
Antipruritic: relieves or prevents sensation of itching.
Antiputrescent: prevents and combats decay.
Antipyretic: reduces fever; *see also* febrifuge.
Antirheumatic: helps prevent and relieve rheumatism.
Antisclerotic: helps prevent the hardening of tissue.
Antiscorbutic: a remedy for scurvy.
Antiscrofula: combats the development of tuberculosis of lymph nodes (scrofula).
Antiseborrheic: helps control the products of sebum.
Antiseptic: destroys and prevents the development of microbes.
Antispasmodic: prevents and eases spasms or convulsions.
Antitoxic: counteracts the effects of poison.
Antitussive: relieves coughs.
Antiviral: substance that inhibits the growth of a virus.
Aperient: a mild laxative.
Aperitif: a stimulant of the appetite.
Aphonia: loss of voice.
Aphrodisiac: increases or stimulates sexual desire.
Aril: the husk or membrane covering the seed of a plant.
Aromachology: the study of the use of aromas, both natural and synthetic.
Aromatic: a substance with a strong aroma or smell.
Asthenia: *see* debility.
Astringent: causes contraction of organic tissues.
Atony: lessening or lack of muscular tone or tension.
Axil: upper angle between a stem and leaf or bract.
Bactericidal: an agent that destroys bacteria.
Balsam: a resinous semi-solid mass or viscous liquid exuded from a plant, characterized by its high content of benzoic acid, benzoates, cinnamic acid, or cinnamates.
Balsamic: a soothing medicine or application having the qualities of a balsam.
Bechic: anything that relieves or cures coughs; or referring to coughs.
Biennial: a plant which completes its life cycle in two years, without flowering in the first year.
Biliousness: condition caused by excessive secretion of bile.
Bitter: a tonic component which stimulates the appetite and promotes the secretion of saliva and gastric juices.
Blenorrhea: abnormally free secretion and discharge of mucus, sometimes from the genitals (as in gonorrhea).
Blepharitis: inflammation of the eyelids.

Calculus: a solid pathological concentration (or "stone"), formed in any part of the body.
Calmative: a sedative.
Calyx: the sepals or outer layer of floral leaves.
Cardiac: pertaining to the heart.
Cardiotonic: having a stimulating effect on the heart.
Carminative: settles the digestive system, relieves flatulence.
Catarrh: inflammation of mucous membranes, usually associated with an increase in secretion of mucus.
Cathartic: a purgative.
Cellulite: "orange-peel" skin.
Cephalic: remedy for disorders of the head; referring or directed toward the head.
Cerebral: pertaining to the largest part of the brain, the cerebrum.
Chemotype: the same botanical species occurring in other forms due to different conditions of growth.
Chlorosis: a rare form of anemia.
Cholagogue: stimulates the secretion and flow of bile.
Cholecystokinetic: agent that stimulates the contraction of the gall bladder.
Choleretic: aids excretion of bile by the liver, so there is a greater flow of bile.
Cholesterol: a naturally occurring steroid alcohol. Excess can lead to gallstones.
Cicatrizant: an agent that promotes healing by the formation of scar tissue.
Cirrhosis: degenerative change in any organ (specially liver), resulting in fibrous tissue overgrowth.
Colic: pain due to contraction of the involuntary muscle of the abdominal organs.
Colitis: inflammation of the colon.
Compress: a lint or substance applied hot or cold to an area of the body, for relief of swelling and pain, or to produce localized pressure.
Concrete: a concentrate, waxy, solid or semi-solid perfume material prepared from previously live plant matter, usually using a hydrocarbon type of solvent.
Constipation: congestion of the bowels; incomplete or infrequent action of the bowels.
Contagious disease: a disease spreading from person to person by direct contact.
Cordial: a stimulant and tonic.
Corolla: the petals of a flower considered as a whole.
Counterirritant: applications to the skin that relieve deep-seated pain, usually applied in the form of heat.

Cutaneous: pertaining to the skin.
Cytophylactic: increasing the activity of leucocytes in defense of the body against infection.
Cytotoxic: toxic to all cells.

Debility: weakness, lack of tone.
Decoction: a herbal preparation, where the plant material (usually hard or woody) is boiled in water and reduced to make a concentrated extract.
Decongestive: an agent for the relief or reduction of congestion, e.g., mucus.
Demulcent: a substance that protects mucous membranes and allays irritation.
Depurative: helps combat impurity in the blood and organs; detoxifying.
Deodorant: an agent that corrects, masks, or removes unpleasant odors.
Dermal: pertaining to the skin.
Diaphoretic: *see* sudorific.
Digestive: substance that promotes or aids the digestion of food.
Disinfectant: prevents and combats spread of germs.
Diuretic: aids production of urine, promotes urination.
Dropsy: excess of fluid in the tissues.
Drupe: a fleshy fruit, with one or more seeds, each surrounded by a stony layer.
Dysmenorrhea: painful and difficult menstruation.
Dyspepsia: difficulty with digestion associated with pain, flatulence, heartburn, and nausea.

Edema: a painless swelling caused by fluid retention.
Elliptical: shaped like an ellipse, or regular curve.
Emetic: induces vomiting.
Emmenagogue: induces or assists menstruation.
Emollient: softens and soothes the skin.
Engorgement: congestion of a part of the tissues, or fullness (as in the breasts).
Enteritis: inflammation of the mucous membrane of the intestine.
Enzyme: complex proteins that are produced by the living cells, and catalyze specific biochemical reactions.
Erythema: a superficial redness of the skin due to excess of blood.
Essential oil: a volatile and aromatic liquid (sometimes semi-solid), which generally constitutes the odorous principles of a plant, and is obtained by a process of expression or distillation.
Estrogen: a hormone produced by the ovary, necessary for development of female secondary sexual characteristics.
Expectorant: helps promote the removal of mucus from the respiratory system.

Febrifuge: combats fever.
Fixative: a material that slows down the rate of evaporation of the more volatile components in a perfume.
Fixed oil: vegetable oil obtained from plants that, unlike essential oils, are fatty, dense and nonvolatile.
Florets: the small individual flowers in the flower heads of the Compositae family.
Follicle: a dry, one-celled, many seeded fruit.
Fungicidal: prevents and combats fungal infection.

Galactagogue: increases secretion of milk.
Gastritis: inflammation of stomach lining.
Genitourinary: referring to both genital and reproductive systems.
Germicidal: destroys germs or micro-organisms.
Gingivitis: inflammation of the gum.
Gout: a disease that involves excess uric acid in the blood.
Gums: the term is often applied to "resins," specially with relation to turpentines. Strictly speaking, gums are natural or synthetic water-soluble materials, such as gum arabic.

Halitosis: offensive breath.
Hallucinogenic: causes visions or delusions.
Heartwood: the central portion of a tree trunk.
Hematuria: blood in the urine.
Hemorrhoids: piles, dilated rectal veins.
Hemostatic: arrests bleeding.
Hepatic: relating to the liver, tones and aids its function.
Herpes: inflammation of the skin or mucous membrane with clusters of deep-seated vesicles.
Hormone: a product of living cells that produces a specific effect on the activity cells remote from its point of origin.
Hybrid: a plant originating by fertilization of one species or subspecies by another.
Hypertension: raised blood pressure.
Hypertensive: agent which raises blood pressure.
Hypnotic: causing sleep.
Hypocholesterolemia: lowering the cholesterol content of the blood.
Hypoglycemia: lowered blood sugar levels.
Hypotension: low blood pressure.
Hypotensive: agent that lowers blood pressure.
Hysteria: a psychoneurosis manifesting itself in various disorders of the mind and body.

Inflorescence: flowering structure above the last stem leaves (including bracts and flowers).
Infusion: a herbal remedy prepared by steeping the plant material in water.
Insecticide: repels insects.
Insomnia: inability to sleep.

Lanceolate: lance-shaped, oval, and pointed at both ends (usually a leaf shape).
Larvicidal: an agent that prevents and kills larvae.
Laxative: promotes evacuation of the bowels.
Legume: a fruit consisting of one carpel, opening on one side, such as a pea.
Leucocyte: white blood cells responsible for fighting disease.
Leucocytosis: an increase in the number of white blood cells above the normal limit.
Leucorrhea: white discharge from the vagina.
Ligulet: a narrow protection from the top of a leaf sheath in grasses.
Linear: of leaves, narrow and more or less parallel-sided.
Lipolytic: causing lipolysis, the chemical disintegration or splitting of fats.
Lithuria: a morbid condition marked by the presence of excessive amounts of uric acid in the urine.
Lumbago: a painful rheumatic affliction of the muscles and fibrous tissue of the lumbar region of the back.
Lymphatic: pertaining to the lymph system.

Macerate: soak until soft.
Metrorrhagia: uterine bleeding outside the menstrual cycle.
Microbe: a minute living organism, specially pathogenic bacteria, viruses, etc.
Mucilage: a substance containing gelatinous constituents that are demulcent.
Mucolytic: dissolving or breaking down mucus.

Narcotic: a substance that induces sleep; intoxicating or poisonous in large doses.

Nervine: strengthening and toning to the nerves and nervous system.
Nephritis: inflammation of the kidneys.
Neuralgia: a stabbing pain along a nerve pathway.
Neurasthenia: nervous exhaustion.
Oleo gum resin: a natural exudation from trees and plants that consists mainly of essential oil, gum, and resin.
Oleoresin: a natural resinous exudation from plants, or an aromatic liquid preparation, extracted from botanical matter using solvents. They consist almost entirely of a mixture of essential oil and resin.
Olfaction: the sense of smell.
Ophthalmia: inflammation of the eye, a term usually applied to conjunctivitis.
Orexigenic: appetite stimulant.
Ovate: egg-shaped.

Panacea: a cure-all.
Pappus: the calyx in a composite flower having feathery hairs, scales, or bristles.
Parasiticide: prevents and destroys parasites such as fleas, lice, etc.
Parturient: aiding childbirth.
Pathogenic: causing or producing disease.
Pathological: unnatural or destructive process on living tissue.
Pediculicide: an agent that destroys lice.
Peptic: applied to gastric secretions and areas affected by them.
Perennial: a plant that lives for more than two years.
Petiole: the stalk of a leaf.
Pharmacology: medical science of drugs that deals with their actions, properties and characteristics.
Pharmacopoeia: an official publication of drugs in common use, in a given country.
Physiological: describes the natural biological processes of a living organism.
Phytohormones: plant substances that mimic the action of human hormones.
Phytotherapy: the treatment of disease by plants; herbal medicine.
Pinnate: a leaf composed of more than three leaflets arranged in two rows along a common stalk.
Pomade: a prepared perfume material obtained by enfleurage.
Poultice: the therapeutic application of a soft moist mass (such as fresh herbs) to the skin.
Prophylactic: preventive of disease or infection.
Psychosomatic: the manifestation of physical symptoms resulting from a mental state.
Pulmonary: pertaining to the lungs.
Purgative: a substance stimulating an evacuation of the bowels.
Pyelitis: inflammation of the kidney.

Raceme: an inflorescence, usually conical in outline, in which the lowest flowers open first.
Receptacle: the upper part of the stem from which the floral parts arise.
Rectification: the process of redistillation applied to essential oils to rid them of certain constituents.
Refrigerant: cooling – reduces fever.
Regulator: an agent that helps balance and regulate the functions of the body.
Relaxant: soothing, causing relaxation, relieving strain or tension.
Renal: pertaining to the kidney.
Resin: a natural or prepared product, either solid or semi-solid in nature. Natural resins are exudations from trees, such as mastic; prepared resins are oleoresins from which essential oil has been removed.
Resinoid: a perfumery material prepared from natural resinous matter, such as balsams, gum resins, etc., by extraction with a hydrocarbon type of solvent.
Resolvent: an agent that disperses swelling, or effects absorption of a new growth.
Restorative: an agent that helps strengthen and revive the body systems.
Revulsive: relieves pain by means of the diversion of blood or disease from one part of the body to another.
Rhinitis: inflammation of nasal mucous membrane.
Rhizome: a root-like underground stem.
Rosette: leaves that are closely arranged in a spiral.
Rubefacient: a substance that causes redness of the skin.

Sclerosis: hardening of tissue due to inflammation.
Scrofula: an outdated name for tuberculosis.
Seborrhea: increased secretion of sebum.
Sedative: an agent that reduces functional activity; calming.
Sessile: without a stalk.
Sialogogue: an agent that stimulates the secretion of saliva.
Soporific: a substance that induces sleep.
Spike: an inflorescence in which the sessile flowers are arranged in a raceme.
Splenic: relating to the spleen, the largest endocrine gland.
Splenitis: inflammation of the spleen.
Stimulant: an agent that quickens the physiological functions of the body.
Stomachic: digestive aid and tonic; improving appetite.
Styptic: an astringent agent that stops or reduces external bleeding.
Sudorific: an agent that causes sweating.
Synergy: agents working together harmoniously.
Tannin: a substance that has an astringent action, and helps seal the tissue.
Thrombosis: formation of a thrombus or blood clot.
Thrush: an infection of the mouth or vaginal region caused by a fungus (candida).
Tincture: a herbal remedy, or perfumery material prepared in an alcohol base.
Tonic: strengthens and enlivens the whole or specific parts of the body.
Tracheitis: inflammation of the windpipe.
Trifoliate: a plant having three distinct leaflets.
Tuber: a swollen part of an underground stem of one year's duration, capable of new growth.

Umbel: umbrella-like; a flower where the petioles all arise from the top of the stem.
Uterine: pertaining to the uterus.

Vasoconstrictor: an agent that causes narrowing of the blood vessels.
Vasodilator: an agent that dilates the blood vessels.
Vermifuge: expels intestinal worms.
Vesicant: causing blistering to the skin; a counterirritant.
Vesicle: a small blister or sac containing fluid.
Volatile: unstable, evaporates easily, as in "volatile oil"; see essential oil.
Vulnerary: an agent that helps heal wounds and sores by external application.

Further Reading

Aqua Oleum, *The Essential Oil Catalogue*, Aqua Oleum, 1994

Arber, A. *Herbals, Their Origin and Evolution*, Cambridge University Press, 1912

Arctander, S., *Perfume and Flavor Materials of Natural Origin*, published by the author, Elizabeth, New Jersey, 1960

Baerheim, S.A. & Scheffer, J.J.C., *Essential Oils and Aromatic Plants*, Dr. W. Junk Publications, 1989

de Bairacli, Levy, J., *The Illustrated Herbal Handbook*, Faber & Faber, 1982

Beckett, S., *Herbs to Soothe Your Nerves*, Thorsons, 1977

Beresford-Cooke, C., *Massage for Healing and Relaxation*, Arlington, 1986

Bianchini, F. & Corbetta. F., *Health Plants of the World – Atlas of Medicinal Plants*, Newsweek Books, New York, 1977

Boulos, C. & Danin, A., *Medicinal Plants of North Africa*, Reference Publications, 1983

British Herbal Pharmacopoeia, British Herbal Medicine Association, 1983

Buchman, D.D., *Feed Your Face*, Duckworth, 1973, 1980

— *Herbal Medicine*, Rider, 1984

Carrington, H., *Perfumes, Their Sensual Lure and Charm*, Haldeman-Julius Publications, 1947

Ceres, *Herbs for Healthy Hair*, Thorsons, 1977.

Chiej, R., *The Macdonald Encyclopedia of Medicinal Plants*, Arnoldo Mondadori Editore, Milan, 1984

Conway, D., *The Magic of Herbs*, Mayflower, 1973

Coon, N., *The Dictionary of Useful Plants*, Rodale, Emmaus, Pa., 1974

Cribb, A.B. & J.W., *Useful Wild Plants in Australia*, Fontana/Collins, 1982

Culpeper, N., *Culpeper's Complete Herbal*, W. Foulsham & Co. Ltd, 1952

Dastur, J.F., *Useful Plants of India and Pakistan*, D.B. Taraporevala Sons & Co. Ltd, India, 1985

Davies, W.C., *New Zealand Native Plant Studies*, A.H. & A.W. Reed, Wellington, 1961

Davis, P., *Subtle Aromatherapy*, C.W. Daniel, 1991

— *Aromatherapy An A–Z*, C.W. Daniel, 1988

Day, I., *Perfumery with Herbs*, Darton, Longman & Todd, Ltd, 1979

Dodd, G.H. & Van Toller, S., *Perfumery: The Psychology and Biology of Fragrance I*, Chapman & Hall, 1990

— *Perfumery: The Psychology and Biology of Fragrance II*, Elsevier Science, 1992

Douglas, J.S., *Making Your Own Cosmetics*, Pelham Books, 1979

Downing, G., *The Massage Book*, Penguin, 1974

Fay, I., *Perfumery with Herbs*, Darton, Longman and Todd, Ltd, 1979

Fischer-Rizzi, S., *Complete Aromatherapy Handbook*, Sterling 1990

Franchomme, P. *Phytoguide*, International Phytomedical Foundation, La Courtête, France, 1985

– and Penoël, D., *L'Aromathérapie Exactement*, Roger Jollois, Limoges, 1990

Gardner, J., *Healing Yourself During Pregnancy*, The Crossing Press, California, 1987

Gattefossé, R., *Gattefossé's Aromatherapy*, C.W. Daniel, 1993

Genders, R., *Natural Beauty*, Webb & Bower, 1986

Grieve, M., *A Modern Herbal*, Penguin, 1982

Griggs, B., *The Home Herbal*, Pan, 1983

Groom, N., *The Perfume Handbook*, Chapman & Hall, 1992

Guenther, E., *The Essential Oils*, Van Nostrand, New York, 1948

Hall, R., Klemme, D. & Nienhaus, J., *The H & R Book: Guide to Fragrance Ingredients*, Johnson Publishing, 1985

Hepper, C., *Herbal Cosmetics*, Thorsons, 1987

Heriteatu, J., *Potpourris and other Fragrant Delights*, Penguin, 1975

Hoffman, D., *The Complete Illustrated Holistic Herbal*, Element Books, 1996

Huxley, A., *Natural Beauty With Herbs*, Darton, Longman and Todd, Ltd, 1977

Jessee, J.E., *Perfume Album*, Robert E. Krieger, 1974

Jellinek, P., *The Practice of Modern Perfumery*, Leonard Hill, 1959

Kahn, I., *The Development of Spiritual Healing*, Sufi Publishing Co., 1974

Lassak, E.V., & McCarthy, T., *Australian Medicinal Plants*, Methuen, Australia, 1983

Launert, E., *Edible and Medicinal Plants of Britain and Northern Europe*, Hamlyn, 1981

Lautie, R. & Passebecq, A., *Aromatherapy; the Use of Plant Essences in Healing*, Thorsons, 1982

Lavabre, M., *Aromatherapy Workbook*, Healing Arts Press, Vermont, 1990

Lawrence, B.M., *Essential Oils*, Allured Publishing Co., Wheaton, USA, 1978

Lawless, J., *The Illustrated Encyclopedia of Essential Oils*, Element Books, 1995

— *Home Aromatherapy*, Kyle Cathie, 1993

— *Aromatherapy and the Mind*, Thorsons, 1994

— *Lavender Oil*, Thorsons, 1994

— *Tea Tree Oil*, Thorsons, 1994

— *Rose Oil*, Thorsons, 1995

— *Rosemary Oil*, Thorsons, 1996

Le Gue, A., *Scent: The Mysterious Power of Smell*, Chatto & Windus, 1993

Leung, A.Y., *Encyclopedia of Common Natural Ingredients*, John Wiley, New York, 1980

Lewis, R. *Natural Data Base UK: Aromatherapy*, Vols I-V (1993-1997), Chessington, Surrey

Lis-Balchin, Dr. M., *Aromascience*, Amberwood, 1995

Little, K., *Kitty Little's Book of Herbal Beauty*, Penguin, 1980

Maury, M., *Marguerite Maury's Guide to Aromatherapy*, C.W. Daniel, 1989

Mabey, R., *The Complete New Herbal*, Elm Tree Books, 1988

Maxwell-Hudson, C., *Aromatherapy Massage Book*, Dorling Kindersley, 1994

McIntyre, A., *Herbs for Pregnancy and Childbirth*, Sheldon Press, 1988

Metcalfe, J., *Herbs and Aromatherapy*, Webb & Bower, 1989

Meunier, C., *Lavandes et Lavandins*, Charle-Yves Chaudoreille, Edisud, Aix-en-Provence, France, 1985

Mills, S.Y., *The A–Z of Modern Herbalism*, Thorsons, 1989

Mitchell, S., *The Complete Illustrated Guide to Massage*, Element Books, 1997

Morris, E.T., *Fragrance, The Story of Perfume from Cleopatra to Chanel*, Charles Scribner & Sons, New York

Muller, P.M. & Lamparsky, D., *Perfumes, Art, Science, Technology*, Elsevier Applied Science, 1991

Naves, Y.R. & Mazuyer, G., *Natural Perfume Materials*, Reinhold Publishing, New York, 1947

Page, M., *The Observers Book of Herbs*, Frederick Warne, 1980

Parvati, J. Hygieia, *A Woman's Herbal*, Wildwood House, 1979

Poucher, W.A., *Perfumes, Cosmetics and Soaps Vol. II*, Chapman and Hall, 1932

Price, S., *Practical Aromatherapy*, Thorsons, 1983

Rapgay, L., *Tibetan Therapeutic Massage*, published by the author, India, 1985

Roudnitska, E., *The Art of Perfumery*, Cabris, France

Ryman, D., *The Aromatherapy Handbook*, Century, 1984

Sellar, Wanda, *The Directory of Essential Oils*, C.W. Daniel, 1992

Stead, C., *The Power of Holistic Aromatherapy*, Javelin Books, 1986

Stobart, T., *Herbs, Spices and Flavourings*, Penguin, 1979

Stoddart, D.M., *The Scented Ape*, Cambridge University Press, 1990

Le Strange, R., *A History of Herbal Plants*, Angus and Robertson, 1977

Suskind, P., *Perfume, the Story of a Murderer*, Hamish Hamilton, London, 1986

Temple, A.A., *Flowers and Trees of Palestine*, SPCK, Macmillan, 1978

Thomson, W.A.R., *Healing Plants – A Modern Herbal*, Macmillan, 1978

Tisserand, R., *Aromatherapy for Women*, Thorsons, 1985

Tisserand, R., *The Essential Oil Safety Data Manual*, The Association of Tisserand Aromatherapists, 1985

Tisserand, R., *The Art of Aromatherapy*, C.W. Daniel, 1985

Valnet, J., *The Practice of Aromatherapy*, C.W. Daniel (English translation), 1982

Weiss, R.F., *Herbal Medicine*, Arcanum, 1988

Whitmont, E.C., *Psyche and Substance*, North Atlantic Books, 1980

Williams, D., *Lecture Notes on Essential Oils*, Eve Taylor Ltd, 1989

Worwood, V.A., *The Fragrant Pharmacy*, Macmillan, 1990

Wren, R.C., *Potters New Cyclopaedia of Botanical Drugs and Preparations*, C.W. Daniel, 1988

Yearbook of Pharmacy and Transactions of the British Pharmaceutical Conference, The Pharmaceutical Press, Bloomsbury, London, 1907

Wright, R., *The Science of Smell*, Allen & Unwin, 1964

Younger, D., *Household Gods*, E.W. Allen, 1898

Useful Addresses

A wide selection of top quality essential oils, base oils, aromatherapy books, and other aromatic products is available from Aqua Oleum UK. International Mail Order (including Australia); professional and export lists are also offered on request. Safety information, quality control, and up-to-date product data are outlined in "The Essential Oil Catalogue" supplied free with price list.

Aqua Oleum
Unit 3
Lower Wharf
Wallbridge
Stroud
Gloucestershire GL5 3JA, UK
Tel: (01453) 753555
Fax: (01453) 752179

Aqua Oleum products are also available from:

CANADA & USA
Nature Trading Limited
Box 263
1857 West 4th Avenue
Vancouver
B.C. V63 1M4, Canada

DENMARK
URTEKRAM A/S
Duft Atelieret
Peder Hvitfeldts Straede 13
1173 Kibenhavn 13

NORWAY
TERAPI CONSULTAS
Frysjaveien 27
0883 Oslo

FINLAND
LUONNONRUOKKATUKKU ADUKI KY
Kirvesmelhankatu 10
00810 Helsinki, Finland

IRELAND
WHOLEFOODS WHOLESALE
Unit 2D
Kylemore Industrial Estate
Dublin 10
Republic of Ireland

SOAP OPERA LTD
Unit 3
Enterprise Centre
Stafford Street
Nenagh
Co. Tipperary
Republic of Ireland

JAPAN
MARUNAKE K.K.
1-12-4 Ginza Chuo-ku
Tokyo, Japan

HONG KONG
7 Old Bailey Street
Central
Hong Kong

TAIWAN
Grace and Pearl Corporation
6 Lane 97
Tung An Street
Tapei 100

Information regarding qualified aromatherapists and training programs can be obtained from:

USA
THE AMERICAN ALLIANCE OF AROMATHERAPY
PO Box 750428
Petaluma
CA 94975, US
Tel: (707) 778 6762

UK
THE INTERNATIONAL FEDERATION OF AROMATHERAPISTS
Stamford House
2/4 Chiswick High Road
London W4 1TH, UK
Tel: (0181) 742 2605

AROMATHERAPY ORGANISATIONS COUNCIL
3 Latymer Close
Braybrooke
Market Harborough
Leicestershire LE16 8LN
Tel: (1858) 434242

INTERNATIONAL THERAPY EXAMINATION COUNCIL
James House
Oakelbrook Mill
Newent
Gloucestershire GL18 1HD
Tel: 01531 821875

AUSTRALIA
THE INTERNATIONAL FEDERATION OF AROMATHERAPISTS
1/390 Burwood Road
Hawthorne
Melbourne
Victoria 3122, Australia
Tel: (613) 819 2502
Fax: (613) 819 2399

Information regarding qualified medical herbalists and training programs can be obtained from:

USA
AMERICAN BOTANICAL COUNCIL AND HERB RESEARCH FOUNDATION
PO Box 201660
Austin,
Texas 78720
USA

CALIFORNIA SCHOOL OF HERBAL STUDIES
9309 HWY 116
Forestville
CA 95436
USA

UK
THE SCHOOL OF HERBAL MEDICINE/ PHYTOTHERAPY
Bucksteep Manor
Bodle Street Green
Hailsham
East Sussex BN27 4RJ, UK
Tel: (01323) 833 812/4

THE NATIONAL INSTITUTE OF MEDICAL HERBALISTS
56 Longbrook Street
Exeter
Devon EX4 6AH, UK
Tel: (01392) 426022

AUSTRALIA
NATIONAL HERBALISTS ASSOCIATION OF AUSTRALIA
Suite 305
3 Smail Street
Broadway
New South Wales 2007, Australia
Tel: (02) 211 6437
Fax: (02) 211 6452

General information on holistic forms of treatment can be obtained from:

USA
AMERICAN HOLISTIC MEDICAL ASSOCIATION
Suite 201
4101 Lake Boone Trail
Raleigh
NC 27607, USA
Tel: (919) 787 5146
Fax: (919) 787 4916

CANADA
CANADIAN HOLISTIC MEDICAL ASSOCIATION
700 Bay Street
PO Box 101
Suite 604
Toronto
Ontario M5G 1Z6, Canada

UK
BRITISH HOLISTIC MEDICAL ASSOCIATION
Trust House
Royal Shrewsbury Hospital South
Shrewsbury
Shropshire SY3 8XF, UK
Tel: (01743) 261155
Fax: (01743) 353637

AUSTRALIA
AUSTRALIAN NATURAL THERAPISTS ASSOCIATION
PO Box 308
Melrose Park
South Australia 5039
Tel: 8297 9533
Fax: 8297 0003

Index

REFERENCES

1 Davis, P., *Aromatherapy An A–Z*, p. 173
2 Cited in J. Lawless, *Aromatherapy and the Mind*, p. 114
3 Maury, M., *Marguerite Maury's Guide to Aromatherapy*, p. 51
4 Anderson, Extract from files of Museum of Applied Arts and Sciences, Sydney 1974, cited in C. W. Olsen, *Australian Tea Tree Oil*, p. 25
5 Weintraub, P., cited in "Sentimental Journeys," *Omni*, p. 52
6 Stoddard, M., *The Scented Ape*, pp. 135–141
7 Ehrlichman, H. and Bastone, L., "The use of odour in the study of emotion," in G. H. Dodds and S. Van Toller, *Perfumery: the Psychology and Biology of Fragrance*, pp. 143, 156
8 Schwartz, G., cited in "Sentimental Journeys," *Omni*, p. 116
8 Cited in H. Carrington, *Perfumes, Their Sensual Lure and Charm*, p. 4
10 Maury, *op. cit.*, p. 82
11 *Ibid.*, p. 95–6
12 Maxwell-Hudson, C., *Aromatherapy Massage Book*, p. 7
13 Tisserand, R., "Success with Stress," *International Journal of Aromatherapy*, Vol. 4, No. 2, 1992, p. 14
14 Coxon, Ann, cited in *Aromatherapy Quarterly*, No. 31, p. 9
15 Rovesti, cited in R. Tisserand, *The Art of Aromatherapy*, p. 98
16 Tisserand, R., *Safety Data Manual*, p. 36
17 Valnet, J., *The Practice of Aromatherapy*, p. 48
18 Blackwell, R., *Health Independent*, 30 January 1996
19 Smith, *ibid.*
20 Lis-Balchin, M., *Aromascience: The Chemistry and Bioactivity of Essential Oils*, p. 26
21 Gattefossé, R. M., *Gattefossé's Aromatherapy*, p. 70